THE GOLFEI

to

East Anglia

By
David Hamilton

Published by:

Travel Publishing Ltd
7a Apollo House, Calleva Park
Aldermaston, Berks, RG7 8TN
Tel: 0118 981 7777 Fax: 0118 982 0077

ISBN 1-902-00758-1

First Published: 2001

Golfers Guides

East Anglia	Ireland
West Country	Wales

Hidden Places Regional Titles

Cambs & Lincolnshire	Chilterns
Cornwall	Derbyshire
Devon	Dorset, Hants & Isle of Wight
East Anglia	Gloucestershire & Wiltshire
Heart of England	Hereford, Worcs & Shropshire
Highlands & Islands	Kent
Lake District & Cumbria	Lancashire & Cheshire
Lincolnshire	Northumberland & Durham
Somerset	Sussex
Thames Valley	Yorkshire

Hidden Places National Titles

England	Ireland
Scotland	Wales

Printing by: Scotprint, Haddington
Maps by: © Maps in Minutes ™ (2000)
Editor: David Hamilton
Cover Design: Lines & Words, Aldermaston

Photographs:

Front Cover: Costessey Golf Club, Norfolk; Crosskeys Riverside Hotel, Norfolk; Cawthorpe Hall, Lincolnshire; The Lifeboat Inn, Norfolk

Rear Cover: Suffolk Golf and Country Club, Suffolk

Foreword

With nearly 2000 golf clubs, England offers the travelling golfer a wide choice of courses on which to play the Royal & Ancient game. England of course is blessed with a wonderful variety of inland and coastal scenery which is mirrored in the golf courses themselves. This is particularly true of the 113 golf clubs covered by *The Golfers Guide to East Anglia* where the courses range from the impressive links of the Royal West Norfolk to the heathland gems of Aldeburgh, Thorpeness and Woodbridge .

There are an increasing number of golfers from this country and overseas who are very happy to play away from their home courses to experience the many different types of terrain (and weather!) available in this country. In fact in the U.K. each year well over 3 million trips, involving varying lengths of overnight stay, are made to play at least one game of golf. Golf and travel therefore are inextricably linked and this was a prime driving force behind the creation of the *Golfers Guide* series that will eventually cover the whole of the U.K. and Ireland and which was launched with the publication of the much acclaimed *Golfers Guide to Ireland* last year.

The Golfers Guide to East Anglia is very much a comprehensive guide to playing 18-hole golf in Norfolk, Suffolk, Essex, Cambridgeshire and South Lincolnshire but it also offers the golfer an insight into the wonderful scenery and many places of interest in these counties. And importantly it provides the golfing visitor with details of nearly 200 places to stay, eat and drink all of which have been linked to the nearest golf courses. It is therefore the ideal guide for planning every aspect of a golfing trip to East Anglia.

We are indebted to David Hamilton (a very experienced golf journalist and currently press officer for the English Golf Union as well as permanent correspondent for the PGA European Challenge Tour) for his knowledgeable introductions to golf in each county of East Anglia (including recommended golf course itineraries for those golfers who wish to experience a variety of golfing terrains) and for his interesting personal reviews of over 50 golf courses in the counties covered by the guide. We hope that his references to the scenery and many places of interest will encourage the golfing visitor to spend some time exploring the landscape beyond the 18 holes – definitely worth the time! We would also like to thank all the golf clubs who provided information and photographs for their courses.

We hope you enjoy reading and using *The Golfers Guide to East Anglia*. We are always interested to receive readers' comments on the contents of the book, on the golf courses covered (or not covered) and of course on the places to stay, eat and drink. This will help us refine and improve the future editions. Enjoy your golf!

Travel Publishing

Map of East Anglia

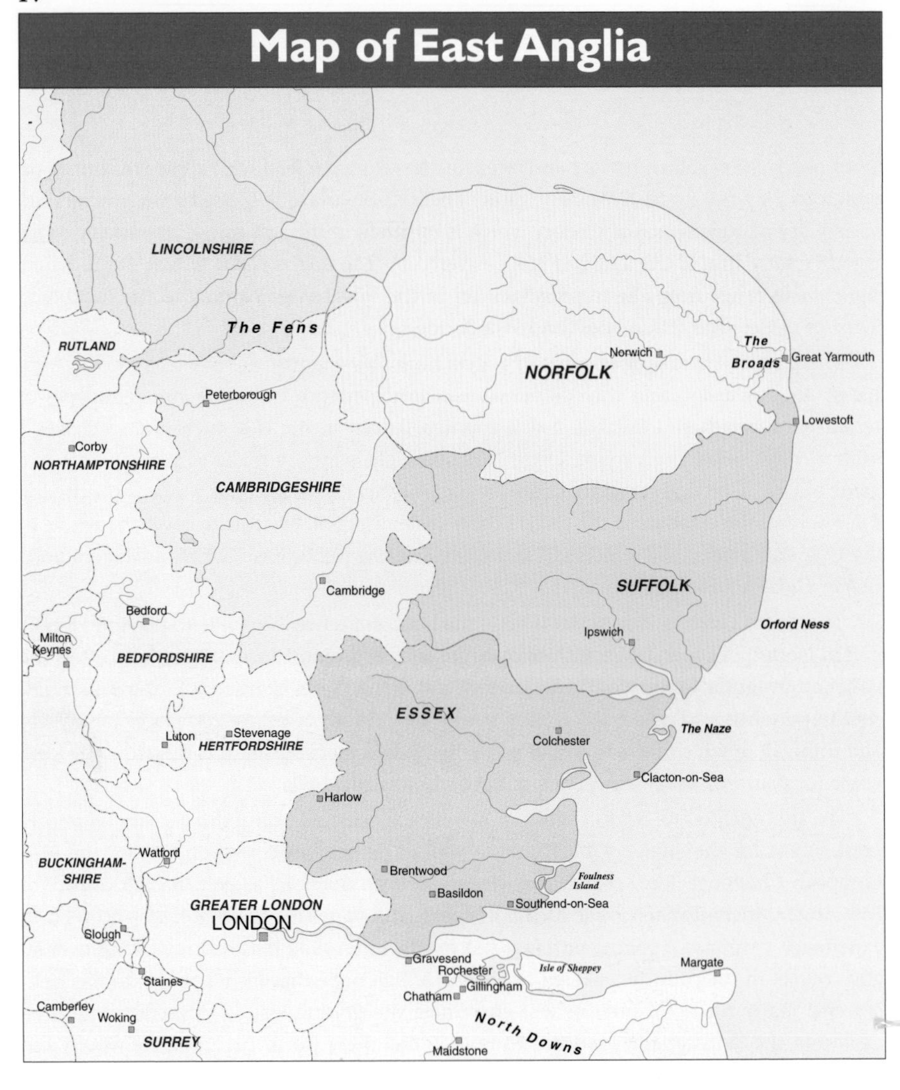

Contents

How to Use

The Golfers Guide to East Anglia has been specifically designed as an easy-to-use guide so there is no need for complicated instructions. However the reader may find the following guidelines helpful in planning the perfect golfing holiday.

Choosing where to play golf in East Anglia

The golfing information for each county may be found as "chapters" in Section I of the guide. Use the *Contents Page* to find the county of your choice. Each "chapter" contains a review of golf in the county, useful information for players on each golf club and detailed reviews of selected courses. Use this information to decide where to play. Whether you are individuals or a society we do recommend that you contact the Golf Club in advance to avoid disappointment. The telephone number, fax number and e-mail address (where available) may be found under each golf club listing.

Golfing Itineraries

If you wish to experience the varied terrains (links, parkland or heathland) on offer in East Anglia without travelling long distances during your golfing holiday you should refer to the list of recommended golfing itineraries prepared by David Hamilton. This can be found on the next page.

Choosing where to stay, eat and drink

When you have decided on the golf courses you wish to play simply refer to the list of places to stay, eat and drink found after each golf course. Use the *reference number* beside each listed entry to find more information (including a photograph) on the places of your choice in Section II of the guide. The telephone number, fax number and email address (where available) is listed for each place should you wish to make a booking

International Calling

Please note that callers form outside the United Kingdom should first dial the country code (00 44) followed by the number shown in the guide with the leading zero dropped.

Local Currency

All prices quoted in the guide are in *Pounds Sterling.*

Golfing Itineraries

For those golfers who want to enjoy a variety of golfing experiences in East Anglia (links, parkland, heathland for example) during their visit without travelling the length and breadth of Norfolk, Suffolk, Essex, Cambridgeshire and South Lincolnshire David Hamilton recommends you select a group from the following combination of courses:

NORFOLK

Royal Norwich, Eaton, Dunston Hall, Wensum Valley
Hunstanton, Royal West Norfolk, Royal Cromer, Sheringham
King's Lynn, Middleton Hall, Fakenham, Ely City
Barnham Broom, Richmond Park, The Norfolk, Costessey Park, Weston Park
Gt Yarmouth & Caister, Bungay & Waveney Valley, Caldecott Hall, Gorleston

SUFFOLK

Felixstowe Ferry, Waldringfield Heath, Ipswich (Purdis Heath), Rushmere
Aldeburgh, Thorpeness, Woodbridge, Ufford Park, Fynn Valley
Bury St Edmunds, The Suffolk, Hindlesham Hall, Brett Vale
Royal Worlington, Haverhill, Links (Newmarket), Saffron Walden

ESSEX

Bentley, Weald Park, Warley Park, Thorndon Park, Hartswood
Basildon, Orsett, St Clere's Hall, Top Meadow, Langdon Hills
The Burstead, Stock Brook Manor, Crondon Park, Chelmsford, Channels
The Warren, Three Rivers, Burnham on Crouch, Forrester Park, Five Lakes
Thorpe Hall, Boyce Hill, Hanover, Rochford Hundred
Braintree, Benton Hall, Gosfield Lakes, Colne Valley, The Essex
Colchester, Clacton, Frinton, Stoke by Nayland
Toot Hill, Canons Brook, North Weald, Epping, Nazeing

CAMBRIDGESHIRE

Cambridge Meridian, Bourn, Royston, Heydon Grange
Cambridge, Girton, Cambridge Moat House, Gog Magog
Abbotsley, St Neots, Brampton Park, Ramsey, Lakeside Lodge
Elton Furze, Orton Meadows, Peterborough Milton, Thorpe Wood

LINCOLNSHIRE

Burghley Park, Gedney Hill, Spalding, Sutton Bridge, Toft Hotel

We do hope you enjoy playing at these golf clubs but please do not hesitate to send us your own recommendations on the ideal combination of courses to play. We look forward to hearing from you!

INTRODUCTION

In the overall scheme of things, East Anglia and its constituent counties may be considered a golfing backwater. You won't find it featuring significantly on any of the leading professional circuits, men's or women's, although it still stages top amateur tournaments, it is not a golfing Mecca on the lines of the Lancashire Coast, Ayrshire, or Fife, nor has it produced a Who's Who of the game's leading figures. Nevertheless, this most easterly part of Britain has much to offer, more than a few gems to stand alongside more familiar destinations, and a variety of challenges to test the most accomplished player.

East Anglia is perceived as a quiet, soft region given over to farming and fishing. These still predominate despite their current woes, yet that is only part of the picture. Tourism plays a major role in the area for there is much to see and enjoy. Quiet and soft it certainly is. There are few major road arteries so getting around is not about speed but taking your time and taking everything in. The softness comes with the rolling countryside, as there are no mountain ranges or major hills to capture the eye. Neither is it as flat and dreary as many outside the region would have you believe as each county possesses low, challenging hills, which help give their area that extra perspective. All those qualities arguably play their part in golf for East Anglia possesses links, heathland and parkland courses of quality and variety to satisfy the most avid of fairway explorers.

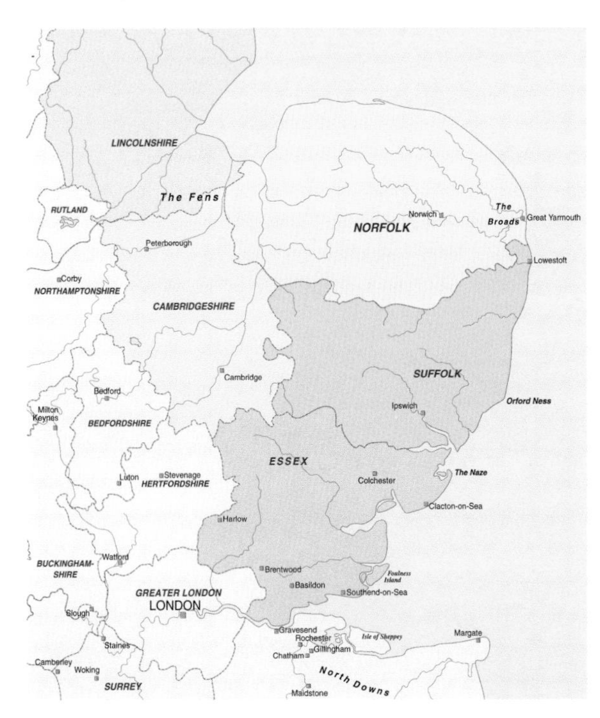

Contents - East Anglia

NORFOLK

Norfolk, as the name implies, is the most northerly county of the region and enjoys a lengthy coastline stretching from The Wash eastwards then curving south to Great Yarmouth and the River Yare. Any visit to Norfolk is usually eventful. There is much to see and enjoy whatever your taste and much could be water associated. Several resorts cater for seaside holidays, Hunstanton, Cromer, Sheringham, Great Yarmouth, while the famous Broads have much to offer in the way of yachting, sailing and fishing. So much of Norfolk's history is associated with the sea and it can claim to be the birthplace of perhaps the greatest sailor this county has produced. Horatio Nelson was born at Burnham Thorpe in 1758 and in the Church of All Saints you will find a lectern and a crucifix carved from the timbers of his flagship, HMS Victory.

Blakeney Harbour

Medieval churches, historic buildings, famous houses, museums, and Roman remains are all there in abundance along with the more recent attractions such as theme parks and preserved railways. All can be found within the county while a visit to the city of Norwich is a must.

If your taste is wildlife, either at sea or on land, that can also be satisfied. The North Norfolk coast is a Mecca for bird watching with many species either being resident or dropping in on their way to so far flung destination. Perhaps the best way to explore off the beaten track is to take the Coastal Footpath which stretches for 36 miles from Holme next the Sea to Cromer, while you can also take a boat to see the seals that populate the sandbanks off this particular part of the coastline. Then, at the end of your trip, what better than to feast on the shellfish that the area is famous for.

Cuisine is another facet of Norfolk life to explore. While many villages appear to be sleepy with little or no population, a little exploring will unearth a wealth of dining oases where you will find many old recipes and dishes associated with the area.

Norfolk is a county where you should wander and delve. All may not be apparent at first sight but you will be surprised what is around the next corner.

Although it possesses just 33 golf clubs there is an infinite variety in this relatively small number. Furthermore, Norfolk boasts the highest ratio of Royal clubs than any other English county with three – Royal Cromer, Royal Norwich, and Royal West Norfolk – reflecting the region's close association with the Monarchy and the royal family's traditional country retreat of Sandringham at its midst.

Cley Windmill

Historically, other parts of the country don't have a monopoly when it comes to long-established clubs. Seven Norfolk clubs have already celebrated their centenary and two more will reach three figures within five years.

Sandringham House

To mark these milestones, an annual competition, the ***Centenary Clubs Cup***, was created in 1989 among those club that have reached their 'ton'. The first event was played at Fakenham and currently the clubs involved are **Fakenham**, **Gt Yarmouth & Caister**, **Royal Cromer**, **Hunstanton**, **Sheringham**, **Royal West Norfolk**, and **Royal Norwich**. The venue rotates between the clubs until another reaches its centenary when it plays host. In 2001 Mundesley will swell the entry to eight.

So golf has been around the region as long, and sometimes longer, than in many other areas. In fact, a glance at Norfolk's golfing history shows that there were fewer golfing holes in the county in 1981 than there were 70 years earlier.

Back in 1908 you could play 252 holes across the county but by the early Eighties that figure had been reduced to 234. Not that there is less interest in the sport in the east but some six or seven clubs had fallen by the wayside for one reason or another. Among those departed bore such names as Attleborough, Mid Norfolk Golf Club, Blickling Golf Club, Loddon and Hales Golf Club, and Wells-Next-the-Sea Golf Club. Fortunately, over the past two decades, Norfolk, like most counties in Britain, responded to the R&A's request for more courses and now the number of holes has reached 495.

Norwich Cathedral

The Norfolk County Golf Union was formed in January 1908 with 10 affiliated clubs when the entrance fee ranged from 10 shillings, or 50p in today's money, to five guineas. Membership numbers also varied but reflected the centres of population such as 400 at Hunstanton to 55 at Fakenham and 40 at Wymondham. Today the figures are somewhat bigger but the trend is the same.

There is a certain longevity with the County Union itself, which has had only four secretaries in 92 years. Frank Janion, then the Secretary at Sheringham, served from the start until 1915, then Henry Craske, returning from military service in France, took

Castle Acre

up the reins in 1921 and was in office for 41 years before handing over to Wilfred Cullington in April 1983. The present incumbent, Roger Trower, has served for the past 17 years

Perhaps the greatest name in Norfolk golf has been Arthur Perowne, who was an England international for 10 years from 1947, three times a Walker Cup player, and a member of the 1958 GB&I Eisenhower Trophy team. All this at a comparatively tender age. He won the England Boys Under-18 Championship for the Carris Trophy in 1946, the same year he was capped for England Boys, then was called up for the senior squad the following year when just 17.

He also had the distinction of playing for his country before being called up for Norfolk. Domestically, he dominated Norfolk golf, winning the county championship 11 times, 10 in a row from 1951. The English Amateur Strokeplay Championship (Brabazon Trophy) also came into his possession in 1958 at Royal Birkdale when he won by three shots. Arthur still lives near Norwich but doesn't play any more.

Blickling Hall

Another character of Norfolk golf was the late Alan 'Tiger' Poulton, for many years the professional at Great Yarmouth. After playing a 36-hole match, he would delight in laying a wager that he would beat allcomers playing the first hole at the club in the dark. Invariably he would secure a par over the 327-yard hole, which crosses the racecourse, and pocket the money.

© MAPS IN MINUTES ™ (2000)

Barnham Broom

Barnham Broom Hotel, Honingham Road, Barnham Broom, Norwich NR9 4DD

Tel: 01603 759393 Fax: 01603 758224

Once described as 'The Jewel in the Crown' of golf hotels, Barnham Broom is set in 250 acres just 10 miles south west of Norwich just off the A11 and A47 trunk routes in the tranquil River Yare valley and possesses a host of facilities waiting to be discovered.

The hotel is situated alongside its two 18-hole golf courses. The 6,603-yard, par 72, **Valley Course**, designed by Frank Pennink, one of Europe's most prominent and respected golf course architects, opened in 1976 and has mature trees and water features providing a challenge to the more experienced golfer. The 6,495-yard, par 71 **Hill Course** is the work of Donald Steel based on a Pennink design. This opened in 1989, has wider fairways and offers fine views of the surrounding countryside with the main challenges coming from the constant breezes and the many bunkers guarding the greens.

Facilities at Barnham Broom include 52 refurbished en-suite bedrooms including: superior, four-poster bedrooms and suites, leisure centre with indoor swimming pool, spa, sauna, steam room, gymnasium, hair salon, tennis and squash courts, and, of course, the two golf courses.

In its early days, Barnham Boom hosted two European Challenge Tour events and it continues to be chosen as the venue for many corporate and golfing occasions. The Peter Ballingall Golf School has a team of experienced PGA professionals who are on hand to ensure the smooth running of corporate golf events while it also provides tuition clinics, residential and overseas golf schools, individual lessons and the Peter Ballingall Junior Golf Academy. The hotel, besides being an ideal base from which to explore the area, also has four conference suites accommodating 200 delegates.

Sec/Manager: Robin Brocks

Professional: Peter Ballingall

Directions: 8 miles west of Norwich. From Norwich take B1108 (west). After 7 miles turn right to Barnham Broom and then take Horningham Road. The entrance is on the right hand side.

Date Founded: 1977

Visitors: Welcome: Subject to availability: Contact Club in advance

Societies: Welcome: Contact Club in advance

Facilities: Putting Green, Chipping Green, Club Hire, Trolley Hire, Buggy Hire, Bar, Restaurant, Driving Range, Caddy Service, Practice Ground

Valley Course

Type of Course: Parkland

No of Holes: 18

Length: 6483 yds (5984 mtrs)

Par: 72

SSS: 71

Green Fees: Weekdays: £25.00 Weekends/ Bank Holidays: Contact Club for Details

Hill Course

Type of Course: Parkland

No of Holes: 18 holes

Length: 6495 yds (5995 mtrs)

Par: 71

SSS: 71

Green Fees: Weekdays: £20.00 Weekends/ Bank Holidays: Contact Club for Details

Accommodation, Food and Drink

Reference numbers below refer to detailed information provided in section 2

Accommodation

The George Hotel, Swaffham Road, East Dereham, Norfolk NR19 2AZ

Tel: 01362 696801 Fax: 01362 695711

Eight en-suite bedrooms, including two suites, in a handsome listed building just off the town centre. Bar and restaurant. Large car park.

Phoenix Hotel, Dereham, Norfolk NR19 1DL

Tel: 01362 692276 Fax: 01362 691752

Twenty-two en-suite bedrooms in a smartly refurbished hotel with a popular seven-days-a-week restaurant.

The Victoria Inn, Deopham, Wymondham, Norfolk NR18 9DX

Tel: 01953 850783

Real ales, hot and cold food, traditional Sunday lunches and Bed & Breakfast accommodation in a fine country inn. 309

Barnham Broom, Norwich, Norfolk NR9 4DD

Tel: 01603 759393 Fax: 01603 758224

A luxurious hotel with golf club, leisure centre and conference centre in a tranquil valley setting 10 miles west of Norwich. 301

Food and Drink

The Kings Head, Hethersett, Norfolk NR9 3DD

Tel: 01603 810206

16th-century public house in a pretty village south of Norwich. Good home-cooked food, real ales. Lovely garden. 341

The George Hotel, Swaffham Road, East Dereham, Norfolk NR19 2AZ

Tel: 01362 696801 Fax: 01362 695711

Eight en-suite bedrooms, including two suites, in a handsome listed building just off the town centre. Bar and restaurant. Large car park.

Phoenix Hotel, Dereham, Norfolk NR19 1DL

Tel: 01362 692276 Fax: 01362 691752

Twenty-two en-suite bedrooms in a smartly refurbished hotel with a popular seven-days-a-week restaurant.

The Victoria Inn, Hockering, Nr Norwich, Norfolk NR20 3HL

Tel: 01603 880507

A 1930s village pub with a cosy eating area and a beer garden. Home-cooked food; good beers and wines. 333

The Victoria Inn, Deopham, Wymondham, Norfolk NR18 9DX

Tel: 01953 850783

Real ales, hot and cold food, traditional Sunday lunches and Bed & Breakfast accommodation in a fine country inn. 309

The Cock, Barford, Norwich, Norfolk NR9 4AS

Tel: 01603 757646

A 200-year-old country inn eight miles west of Norwich that's gaining a great reputation for its superb food. 306

Barnham Broom, Norwich, Norfolk NR9 4DD

Tel: 01603 759393 Fax: 01603 758224

A luxurious hotel with golf club, leisure centre and conference centre in a tranquil valley setting 10 miles west of Norwich. 301

Bawburgh

Glen Lodge, Marlingford Road, Bowburgh, Norwich, Norfolk, NR9 3LU

Tel: 01603 740404 Fax: 01603 740403

Sec/Manager: John Barnard

Professional: Chris Potter

Directions: 5 miles west of Norwich. From Norwich take the A1074 (West). After 4 miles turn left (Bawburgh) and the entrance is at T Junction after one mile.

Date Founded: 1979

Type of Course: Parkland

No of Holes: 18

Length: 6231 yds (5751mtrs)

Par: 70

SSS: 70

Green Fees: Weekdays: £20.00 Weekends/ Bank Holidays: £25.00

Visitors:	Welcome: Contact club in advance
Societies:	Welcome: Contact club in advance
Facilities:	Putting Green, Chipping Green, Driving Range, Club Hire, Trolley Hire, Buggy Hire, Caddy Service, Bar, Restaurant, Private Rooms

Accommodation, Food and Drink

Reference numbers below refer to detailed information provided in section 2

Accommodation

The Victoria Inn, Deopham, Wymondham, Norfolk NR18 9DX

Tel: 01953 850783

Real ales, hot and cold food, traditional Sunday lunches and Bed & Breakfast accommodation in a fine country inn. 309

The Woolpack Inn, Norwich, Norfolk NR1 3JD

Tel: 01603 611139 Fax: 01603 616993

A 300-year-old free house close to the city centre, serving excellent ales and home-cooked food. Also Bed & Breakfast accommodation. 304

Barnham Broom, Norwich, Norfolk NR9 4DD

Tel: 01603 759393 Fax: 01603 758224

A luxurious hotel with golf club, leisure centre and conference centre in a tranquil valley setting 10 miles west of Norwich. 301

Wensum Valley Hotel, Taverham, Norwich, Norfolk NR8 6HP

Tel: 01603 261012 Fax: 01603 261664

Hotel, golf and country club set in 240 acres of lovely countryside. 39 en-suite bedrooms, restaurant, golf courses, leisure club, fishing. 307

Food and Drink

The Kings Head, Hethersett, Norfolk NR9 3DD

Tel: 01603 810206

16th-century public house in a pretty village south of Norwich. Good home-cooked food, real ales. Lovely garden. 341

The Black Horse, Norwich, Norfolk NR2 3DE

Tel: 01603 624682 Fax: 01603 617893

An 18th century inn five minutes from the city centre, serving snacks and full menus, real ales and wines. Garden. 332

The Victoria Inn, Deopham, Wymondham, Norfolk NR18 9DX

Tel: 01953 850783

Real ales, hot and cold food, traditional Sunday lunches and Bed & Breakfast accommodation in a fine country inn. 309

The Woolpack Inn, Norwich, Norfolk NR1 3JD

Tel: 01603 611139 Fax: 01603 616993

A 300-year-old free house close to the city centre, serving excellent ales and home-cooked food. Also Bed & Breakfast accommodation. 304

The Cock, Barford, Norwich, Norfolk NR9 4AS

Tel: 01603 757646

A 200-year-old country inn eight miles west of Norwich that's gaining a great reputation for its superb food. 306

Rose Valley Tavern, Norwich, Norfolk NR2 2PE

Tel: 01603 626068

Bags of atmosphere in a cheerful pub five minutes from the city centre. Good-value menu of snacks and full meals. 311

Barnham Broom, Norwich, Norfolk NR9 4DD

Tel: 01603 759393 Fax: 01603 758224

A luxurious hotel with golf club, leisure centre and conference centre in a tranquil valley setting 10 miles west of Norwich. 301

Wensum Valley Hotel, Taverham, Norwich, Norfolk NR8 6HP

Tel: 01603 261012 Fax: 01603 261664

Hotel, golf and country club set in 240 acres of lovely countryside. 39 en-suite bedrooms, restaurant, golf courses, leisure club, fishing. 307

Caldecott Hall

Caldecott Hall, Beccles Road, Fritton, Norfolk NR31 9EY

Tel: 01493 488488 Fax: 01493 488561

Sec/Manager:	Roger Beales
Professional:	Syer Schulver

Directions:	4 miles south west of Great Yarmouth. Take the A143 (South West). After 5 miles, just past Fritton, the entrance is on the right hand side.
Date Founded:	1992
Visitors:	Welcome: Contact Club by phone in advance
Societies:	Welcome: Contact club in advance
Facilities:	Putting Green, Chipping Green, Trolley Hire, Buggy Hire, Bar, Restaurant, Driving Range, Hotel

18 Hole Course

Type of Course:	Parkland
No of Holes:	18
Length:	6329 yds (5842 mtrs)
Par:	72
SSS:	70
Green Fees:	Weekdays: £20.00 Weekends/ Bank Holidays: £25.00

9 Hole Course

Type of Course:	Parkland
No of Holes:	9
Length:	1353 yds (1248 mtrs)
Par:	3
SSS:	27
Green Fees:	Weekdays: £6.00 Weekends/ Bank Holidays: £9.00

Accommodation, Food and Drink

Reference numbers below refer to detailed information provided in section 2

Accommodation

The Victoria Inn, Deopham, Wymondham, Norfolk NR18 9DX

Tel: 01953 850783

Real ales, hot and cold food, traditional Sunday lunches and Bed & Breakfast accommodation in a fine country inn. 309

Barnham Broom, Norwich, Norfolk NR9 4DD

Tel: 01603 759393 Fax: 01603 758224

A luxurious hotel with golf club, leisure centre and conference centre in a tranquil valley setting 10 miles west of Norwich. 301

The Swan Motel, Lodden Road, Gillingham, Beccles, Suffolk NR34 0LD

Tel: 01502 712055 Fax: 01502 711786

14 spick-and-span self-contained apartments in a friendly free house motel with a convivial bar and day-long restaurant. Live music Sunday.

The Kings Head Hotel, New Market, Beccles, Suffolk NR34 9HA

Tel: 01502 712147 Fax: 01502 715386

12 en-suite bedrooms in a comfortable town-centre hotel. Busy bars, beer garden, restaurant with steakhouse menu.

Food and Drink

The Kings Head, Hethersett, Norfolk NR9 3DD

Tel: 01603 810206

16th-century public house in a pretty village south of Norwich. Good home-cooked food, real ales. Lovely garden. 341

The White Horse, Chedgrave, Norwich, Norfolk NR14 6ND

Tel/Fax: 01508 520250

19th century pub with a fine reputation for its home-cooked food (steaks a speciality) and for its real ales. 323

The Nags Head, East Harling, Norfolk NR16 2AD

Tel: 01953 718140

Village pub in traditional style, serving an extensive range of splendid home-cooked food. On the B1111 south of Attleborough. 317

The Victoria Inn, Deopham, Wymondham, Norfolk NR18 9DX

Tel: 01953 850783

Real ales, hot and cold food, traditional Sunday lunches and Bed & Breakfast accommodation in a fine country inn. 309

Barnham Broom, Norwich, Norfolk NR9 4DD

Tel: 01603 759393 Fax: 01603 758224

A luxurious hotel with golf club, leisure centre and conference centre in a tranquil valley setting 10 miles west of Norwich. 301

The Swan Motel, Lodden Road, Gillingham, Beccles, Suffolk NR34 0LD

Tel: 01502 712055 Fax: 01502 711786

14 spick-and-span self-contained apartments in a friendly free house motel with a convivial bar and day-long restaurant. Live music Sunday.

The Kings Head Hotel, New Market, Beccles, Suffolk NR34 9HA

Tel: 01502 712147 Fax: 01502 715386

12 en-suite bedrooms in a comfortable town-centre hotel. Busy bars, beer garden, restaurant with steakhouse menu.

Costessey Park

Costessey Park, Old Costessey, Norwich, Norfolk NR8 5AL

Tel: 01603 746333 Fax: 01603 746185

Sec/Manager:	Steve Beckham
Professional:	Andrew Young
Directions:	5 miles west of Norwich. From Norwich take A1074 (West) after 4 miles turn right to Costessey. Turn left along West End and the entrance is on the left hand side
Date Founded:	1985
Type of Course:	Parkland
No of Holes:	18
Length:	5900 yds (5446 mtrs)
Par:	71
SSS:	69
Green Fees:	Weekdays: £20.00 per round, £28.00 per day; Weekends/ Bank Holidays: £25.00 per round, £36.00 per day

Visitors:	Welcome: Contact club in advance
Societies:	Welcome: Contact club in advance
Facilities:	Putting Green, Trolley Hire, Buggy Hire, Bar, Restaurant, Club Hire

Accommodation, Food and Drink

Reference numbers below refer to detailed information provided in section 2

Accommodation

The Blue Boar, Sprowston, Norfolk NR7 8RL

Tel: 01603 426802

Comfortable overnight accommodation and fine food in a pub of style and character. 325

The George Hotel, Swaffham Road, East Dereham, Norfolk NR19 2AZ

Tel: 01362 696801 Fax: 01362 695711

Eight en-suite bedrooms, including two suites, in a handsome listed building just off the town centre. Bar and restaurant. Large car park.

Wensum Country Hotel, Great Witchingham, Norwich, Norfolk NR9 5QP

Tel: 01603 872288

A haven of comfort and fine food in the heart of the Norfolk countryside. 36 well-appointed bedrooms; extensive leisure facilities. 312

The Woolpack Inn, Norwich, Norfolk NR1 3JD

Tel: 01603 611139 Fax: 01603 616993

A 300-year-old free house close to the city centre, serving excellent ales and home-cooked food. Also Bed & Breakfast accommodation. 304

The Georgian House Hotel, Norwich, Norfolk NR2 2RB

Tel: 01603 615655 Fax: 01603 765689

Twenty-seven well-appointed en-suite bedrooms in a family-run hotel within easy reach of the city centre. Restaurant, bar, lounge. 310

Wensum Valley Hotel, Taverham, Norwich, Norfolk NR8 6HP

Tel: 01603 261012 Fax: 01603 261664
Hotel, golf and country club set in 240 acres of lovely countryside. 39 en-suite bedrooms, restaurant, golf courses, leisure club, fishing. 307

Food and Drink

The Blue Boar, Sprowston, Norfolk NR7 8RL
Tel: 01603 426802
Comfortable overnight accommodation and fine food in a pub of style and character. 325

The George Hotel, Swaffham Road, East Dereham, Norfolk NR19 2AZ
Tel: 01362 696801 Fax: 01362 695711
Eight en-suite bedrooms, including two suites, in a handsome listed building just off the town centre. Bar and restaurant. Large car park.

The Black Horse, Norwich, Norfolk NR2 3DE
Tel: 01603 624682 Fax: 01603 617893
An 18th century inn five minutes from the city centre, serving snacks and full menus, real ales and wines. Garden. 332

Wensum Country Hotel, Great Witchingham, Norwich, Norfolk NR9 5QP
Tel: 01603 872288
A haven of comfort and fine food in the heart of the Norfolk countryside. 36 well-appointed bedrooms; extensive leisure facilities. 312

The Woolpack Inn, Norwich, Norfolk NR1 3JD
Tel: 01603 611139 Fax: 01603 616993
A 300-year-old free house close to the city centre, serving excellent ales and home-cooked food. Also Bed & Breakfast accommodation. 304

The Cock, Barford, Norwich, Norfolk NR9 4AS
Tel: 01603 757646
A 200-year-old country inn eight miles west of Norwich that's gaining a great reputation for its superb food. 306

Rose Valley Tavern, Norwich, Norfolk NR2 2PE
Tel: 01603 626068
Bags of atmosphere in a cheerful pub five minutes from the city centre. Good-value menu of snacks and full meals. 311

The Georgian House Hotel, Norwich, Norfolk NR2 2RB
Tel: 01603 615655 Fax: 01603 765689
Twenty-seven well-appointed en-suite bedrooms in a family-run hotel within easy reach of the city centre. Restaurant, bar, lounge. 310

The Pickwick, Norwich, Norfolk NR2 3AD
Tel: 01603 628155
A Georgian pub-restaurant three minutes from the city centre. Snack and à la carte menus, Sunday roasts. Good wines. 302

Wensum Valley Hotel, Taverham, Norwich, Norfolk NR8 6HP
Tel: 01603 261012 Fax: 01603 261664
Hotel, golf and country club set in 240 acres of lovely countryside. 39 en-suite bedrooms, restaurant, golf courses, leisure club, fishing. 307

Dunston Hall

Ipswich Road, Dunston, Norwich, Norfolk NR14 8PQ

Tel: 01508 470178 Fax: 01508 471499

Sec/Manager:	Peter Briggs
Professional:	Peter Briggs
Directions:	4 miles south of Norwich. From Norwich take the A140 (South) and after 4 miles the entrance is on the left hand side
Date Founded:	1995
Type of Course:	Parkland
No of Holes:	18
Length:	6319 yds (5832 mtrs)
Par:	71
SSS:	70 (men) 61 (ladies)
Green Fees:	Weekdays: £25.00 Weekends/ Bank Holidays: £30.00
Visitors:	Welcome: Contact club in advance
Societies:	Welcome: Contact club in advance
Facilities:	Putting Green, Trolley Hire, Buggy Hire, Bar, Restaurant, Club Hire, Chipping Green, Driving Range, Private Rooms, Hotel, Gym, Pool, Sauna

Accommodation, Food and Drink

Reference numbers below refer to detailed information provided in section 2

Accommodation

Hill House Guest House, Hillside Road, Thorpe St Andrew, Norfolk NR7 0QS
Tel: 01603 432165
Three en-suite bedrooms in an Edwardian house overlooking the River Yare. Bed & Breakfast. 2 miles east of Norwich.

The Woolpack Inn, Norwich, Norfolk NR1 3JD
Tel: 01603 611139 Fax: 01603 616993
A 300-year-old free house close to the city centre, serving excellent ales and home-cooked food.

Also Bed & Breakfast accommodation. 304

The Georgian House Hotel, Norwich, Norfolk NR2 2RB

Tel: 01603 615655 Fax: 01603 765689

Twenty-seven well-appointed en-suite bedrooms in a family-run hotel within easy reach of the city centre. Restaurant, bar, lounge. 310

Barnham Broom, Norwich, Norfolk NR9 4DD

Tel: 01603 759393 Fax: 01603 758224

A luxurious hotel with golf club, leisure centre and conference centre in a tranquil valley setting 10 miles west of Norwich. 301

Food and Drink

The Kings Head, Hethersett, Norfolk NR9 3DD

Tel: 01603 810206

16th-century public house in a pretty village south of Norwich. Good home-cooked food, real ales. Lovely garden. 341

The Branford Arms, Sprowston, Norwich, Norfolk NR3 4QD

Tel: 01603 427488

A 100-year-old pub of great character, serving generous helpings of good-value home-cooked food. Available Wed-Fri evenings, all day Sat and Sun lunch. 343

The White Horse, Chedgrave, Norwich, Norfolk NR14 6ND

Tel/Fax: 01508 520250

19th century pub with a fine reputation for its home-cooked food (steaks a speciality) and for its real ales. 323

The Woolpack Inn, Norwich, Norfolk NR1 3JD

Tel: 01603 611139 Fax: 01603 616993

A 300-year-old free house close to the city centre, serving excellent ales and home-cooked food. Also Bed & Breakfast accommodation. 304

Rose Valley Tavern, Norwich, Norfolk NR2 2PE

Tel: 01603 626068

Bags of atmosphere in a cheerful pub five minutes from the city centre. Good-value menu of snacks and full meals. 311

The Georgian House Hotel, Norwich, Norfolk NR2 2RB

Tel: 01603 615655 Fax: 01603 765689

Twenty-seven well-appointed en-suite bedrooms in a family-run hotel within easy reach of the city centre. Restaurant, bar, lounge. 310

Barnham Broom, Norwich, Norfolk NR9 4DD

Tel: 01603 759393 Fax: 01603 758224

A luxurious hotel with golf club, leisure centre and conference centre in a tranquil valley setting 10 miles west of Norwich. 301

Eaton

Newmarket Road, Norwich, Norfolk NR4 6SF

Tel/Fax: 01603 451686

Despite being situated just a mile or so from the centre of Norwich, Eaton is quiet, pretty, and mature with greens that have been described by professional agronomists as among the best in the region – "a veritable golfing oasis within the city".

The club was founded in 1910, which makes it among the oldest in Norfolk. The course designed by J H Taylor offers a challenging test to golfers of all standards.

Eaton prides itself on being an extremely open and friendly club, free of the cliques that are so often associated with old establishments. It draws its 800 members from all walks of life and membership is entirely free of discrimination to anyone on interview and acceptance by the membership committee.

In May 1997, after years of negotiation, the club secured its future by purchasing the freehold of the course. The financial backing for this came in the form of a mortgage, gifts and loans from members, and the proceeds of the fighting fund, which had been built up over the years from annual surpluses. Members also donated the refund of their VAT contributions. Never the less, that still left a shortfall so it was agreed that it should be met by everyone purchasing a £400 Loan Bond as a prerequisite of membership.

In order to protect members from financial liability, the club converted itself into a company limited by guarantee, but it continues as a members' club, democratically run by an elected Board of Directors responsible to the membership.

Eaton does not intend to rest upon its present success. Plans are in being for further improvements to the course and the clubhouse facilities. The social aspect of the club is very much part of its ethos. New members are encouraged to participate in all manner of activities to assist their integration into the club and to enhance their enjoyment of an establishment that is not just a place to play golf but to socialise, make new friends and enjoy oneself.

Sec/Manager: Mrs Bovill

Professional: Mark Allen

Directions: 2 miles south west of Norwich. From Norwich city centre go to the junction of A140 and A11 at Eaton. Take the Newmarket road and after half a mile turn left onto Sunningdale.

Date Founded: 1910
Type of Course: Parkland
No of Holes: 18
Length: 6114 yds (5643 mtrs)
Par: 70
SSS: 70
Green Fees: Weekdays: £30.00 Weekends/ Bank Holidays: £40.00
Visitors: Welcome: Contact club in advance
Societies: Welcome: Contact club in advance
Facilities: Trolley Hire, Bar, Restaurant, Club Hire

Accommodation, Food and Drink

Reference numbers below refer to detailed information provided in section 2

Accommodation

Hill House Guest House, Hillside Road, Thorpe St Andrew, Norfolk NR7 0QS

Tel: 01603 432165

Three en-suite bedrooms in an Edwardian house overlooking the River Yare. Bed & Breakfast. 2 miles east of Norwich.

The Woolpack Inn, Norwich, Norfolk NR1 3JD

Tel: 01603 611139 Fax: 01603 616993

A 300-year-old free house close to the city centre, serving excellent ales and home-cooked food. Also Bed & Breakfast accommodation. 304

The Georgian House Hotel, Norwich, Norfolk NR2 2RB

Tel: 01603 615655 Fax: 01603 765689

Twenty-seven well-appointed en-suite bedrooms in a family-run hotel within easy reach of the city centre. Restaurant, bar, lounge. 310

Barnham Broom, Norwich, Norfolk NR9 4DD

Tel: 01603 759393 Fax: 01603 758224

A luxurious hotel with golf club, leisure centre and conference centre in a tranquil valley setting 10 miles west of Norwich. 301

Food and Drink

The Kings Head, Hethersett, Norfolk NR9 3DD

Tel: 01603 810206

16th-century public house in a pretty village south of Norwich. Good home-cooked food, real ales. Lovely garden. 341

The Black Horse, Norwich, Norfolk NR2 3DE

Tel: 01603 624682 Fax: 01603 617893

An 18th century inn five minutes from the city centre, serving snacks and full menus, real ales and wines. Garden. 332

The Woolpack Inn, Norwich, Norfolk NR1 3JD

Tel: 01603 611139 Fax: 01603 616993

A 300-year-old free house close to the city centre, serving excellent ales and home-cooked food. Also Bed & Breakfast accommodation. 304

Rose Valley Tavern, Norwich, Norfolk NR2 2PE

Tel: 01603 626068

Bags of atmosphere in a cheerful pub five minutes from the city centre. Good-value menu of snacks and full meals. 311

The Georgian House Hotel, Norwich, Norfolk NR2 2RB

Tel: 01603 615655 Fax: 01603 765689

Twenty-seven well-appointed en-suite bedrooms in a family-run hotel within easy reach of the city centre. Restaurant, bar, lounge. 310

Barnham Broom, Norwich, Norfolk NR9 4DD

Tel: 01603 759393 Fax: 01603 758224

A luxurious hotel with golf club, leisure centre and conference centre in a tranquil valley setting 10 miles west of Norwich. 301

Gorleston

Warren Road, Gorleston, Gt Yarmouth, Norfolk NR31 6JT

Tel/Fax: 01493 661911

Sec/Manager: Mr Longbottom
Professional: Nick Brown
Directions: 3 miles south of Great Yarmouth. From Great Yarmouth take A12 (south) through Gorleston-on-Sea and turn left onto Links Road. Entrance is on the right hand side
Date Founded: 1906

Type of Course:	Clifftop
No of Holes:	18
Length:	6391 yds (5899 mtrs)
Par:	71
SSS:	71
Green Fees:	Weekdays: £22.00; Weekends/ Bank Holidays: £26.00
Visitors:	Welcome: Contact Club in advance
Societies:	Welcome: Contact Club in writing
Facilities:	Putting Green, Chipping Green, Club Hire, Trolley Hire, Bar, Restaurant

Accommodation, Food and Drink

Reference numbers below refer to detailed information provided in section 2

Accommodation

Kingsley House Hotel, Great Yarmouth, Norfolk NR30 2PP

Tel/Fax: 01493 850948

Seven en-suite bedrooms in a family run hotel handy for the town centre and the seafront. B&B plus evening meal option. 328

The Marsham Arms, Hevingham, Norfolk NR10 5NP

Tel: 01603 754268 Fax: 01603 754839

Characterful family-run country inn with eight spacious en-suite bedrooms and comfortable rooms for bar and restaurant dining. 331

Marine Lodge, Great Yarmouth, Norfolk NR30 1DY

Tel: 01493 331120 Fax: 01493 332040

Bright, up-to-date Bed & Breakfast accommodation in 39 well-appointed rooms 50 yards from the seafront. 321

The Swan Motel, Lodden Road, Gillingham, Beccles, Suffolk NR34 0LD

Tel: 01502 712055 Fax: 01502 711786

14 spick-and-span self-contained apartments in a friendly free house motel with a convivial bar and day-long restaurant. Live music Sunday.

Pakefield Caravan Park, Arbor Lane, Pakefield, Lowestoft, Suffolk NR33 7BQ

Tel: 01502 561136 Fax: 01502 539264

Comfortable, well-equipped modern caravan holiday homes for hire in a clifftop location a short drive south of Lowestoft. Open April-October.

Homelea Guest House, 33 Marine Parade, Lowestoft, Suffolk NR3 3QN

Tel: 01502 511640

Guest house with five double rooms, located on the promenade 50 yards from the sea. Evening meals by arrangement.

The Kings Head Hotel, New Market, Beccles, Suffolk NR34 9HA

Tel: 01502 712147 Fax: 01502 715386

12 en-suite bedrooms in a comfortable town-centre hotel. Busy bars, beer garden, restaurant with steakhouse menu.

Food and Drink

The White Horse, Chedgrave, Norwich, Norfolk NR14 6ND

Tel/Fax: 01508 520250

19th century pub with a fine reputation for its home-cooked food (steaks a speciality) and for its real ales. 323

The Swan Motel, Lodden Road, Gillingham, Beccles, Suffolk NR34 0LD

Tel: 01502 712055 Fax: 01502 711786

14 spick-and-span self-contained apartments in a friendly free house motel with a convivial bar and day-long restaurant. Live music Sunday.

The Kings Head Hotel, New Market, Beccles, Suffolk NR34 9HA

Tel: 01502 712147 Fax: 01502 715386

12 en-suite bedrooms in a comfortable town-centre hotel. Busy bars, beer garden, restaurant with steakhouse menu.

Great Yarmouth & Caister

Beach House, Caister-on-Sea, Gt Yarmouth, Norfolk NR30 5TD

Tel: 01493 728699

Great Yarmouth is famous for many things, as a holiday resort, for bloaters, and as a gateway to the Broads. What is not so well known is that the club was the birthplace of the term 'bogey'. In 1890 a member at Coventry conceived the idea of playing a match under handicap against the number of shots a scratch golfer would take playing perfect golf. This was known as the ground score. This idea was suggested at Yarmouth's autumn meeting and, after being approved by members, was introduced on a match play basis throughout the winter. At the same time a music hall song "Hush! Here comes the Bogey man" was popular. During a competition, one prominent member said to another: "This player of yours is a regular Bogey man". This was seized on and the score became known at Yarmouth and elsewhere as the Bogey score. Bogey competitions are still played at many clubs although in general the term bogey has come to mean one over par. As the name suggests, the club was the amalgamation, in 1913, of the Great Yarmouth and Caister clubs, which occupied adjacent sites in the latter years of the 19th Century. Development 'pushed' the two towns together and eventually brought a link up. The current course is also a meeting of minds, some holes coming from both clubs.

The Great Yarmouth Golf Club, the oldest in Norfolk, was founded in 1882 by Dr Thomas Browne RN who, on moving to The Royal Naval Hospital in Yarmouth, observed that the North Denes was a suitable place for golf. His first attempt to form a club proved a non-starter for after calling a meeting, nobody turned up. Undaunted, Dr Browne declared himself Hon. Secretary, Treasurer, Committee and Captain, but eventually membership grew and matches were arranged against Royal Blackheath, Felixstowe and Cambridge University.

The Club was fortunate, in those early years, in being adopted by members of Royal Blackheath who provided captains, officers, members and trophies. The Club still plays the Blackheath Medal and Royal Blackheath has the Great Yarmouth Cup. In 1883 the first prize meeting was held and later that year the first East Anglian inter club match, Felixstowe v Yarmouth. The match was repeated 100 years later, in 1983, and again – with players dressed in 19th century costume - in June 2000 to celebrate the millennium.

The course is a fine example of traditional links and famous for the quality and stability of the greens. It was laid out in its present form in 1920 when the Racecourse moved from the South Denes at Yarmouth to the North Denes. The Racecourse forms part of the golf course acting as rough on some holes and the outer rails as an out of bounds demarcation on others. In fact, the 1st has an unusual drive that cuts across the turn of the racecourse, as does the approach to the green.

Sec/Manager:	M J Harvey
Professional:	James Hill
Directions:	2 miles north of Great Yarmouth. From Great Yarmouth take the A149 (north) along Lawn Avenue. Entrance is on the left hand side on the outskirts of the town
Date Founded:	1882
Type of Course:	Links
No of Holes:	18
Length:	6330 yds (5843 mtrs)
Par:	70
SSS:	70
Green Fees:	Weekdays: Summer £30.00 Winter £18.00; Weekends/ Bank Holidays: Summer £35.00 Winter £18.00
Visitors:	Welcome: Contact Club in advance
Societies:	Welcome: Contact Club in advance
Facilities:	Putting Green, Chipping Green, Trolley Hire, Bar, Restaurant, Practice Ground

Accommodation, Food and Drink

Reference numbers below refer to detailed information provided in section 2

Accommodation

Kingsley House Hotel, Great Yarmouth, Norfolk NR30 2PP

Tel/Fax: 01493 850948

Seven en-suite bedrooms in a family run hotel handy for the town centre and the seafront. B&B plus evening meal option. 328

The Marsham Arms, Hevingham, Norfolk NR10 5NP

Tel: 01603 754268 Fax: 01603 754839

Characterful family-run country inn with eight spacious en-suite bedrooms and comfortable rooms for bar and restaurant dining. 331

Marine Lodge, Great Yarmouth, Norfolk NR30 1DY

Tel: 01493 331120 Fax: 01493 332040

Bright, up-to-date Bed & Breakfast accommodation in 39 well-appointed rooms 50 yards from the seafront. 321

The Norfolk Mead Hotel, Coltishall, Norfolk NR12 7DN

Tel: 01603 737531 Fax: 01603 737521

An impressive Georgian manor house with characterful en-suite bedrooms and a lovely setting in grounds running down to the River Bure. 314

The Old Rectory Hotel, Crostwick, Norwich, Norfolk NR12 7BG

Tel: 01603 738513 Fax: 01603 738712

18th century country rectory with a modern bedroom block and lovely gardens. Thirteen well-appointed en-suite rooms; two restaurants. 320

Golden Beach Holiday Centre, Sea Palling, Norfolk NR12 0AL

Tel: 01692 598269

Luxury holiday caravans in a well-run centre nestling beneath a bank of dunes just back from the sea. Full on-site facilities. 303

Hill House Guest House, Hillside Road, Thorpe St Andrew, Norfolk NR7 0QS

Tel: 01603 432165

Three en-suite bedrooms in an Edwardian house overlooking the River Yare. Bed & Breakfast. Two miles east of Norwich.

Food and Drink

The Red Lion Inn, Coltishall, Norfolk NR12 7DW

Tel: 01603 737402

300-year-old pub with cosy beamed bars, special real ales and an all-day menu of home-cooked food. 329

The Norfolk Mead Hotel, Coltishall, Norfolk NR12 7DN

Tel: 01603 737531 Fax: 01603 737521

An impressive Georgian manor house with characterful en-suite bedrooms and a lovely setting in grounds running down to the River Bure. 314

The Old Rectory Hotel, Crostwick, Norwich, Norfolk NR12 7BG

Tel: 01603 738513 Fax: 01603 738712

18th century country rectory with a modern bedroom block and lovely gardens. Thirteen well-appointed en-suite rooms; two restaurants. 320

Pebbles Country Inn, Happisburgh, Norfolk NR12 0RD

Tel: 01622 651183

Home-cooked English fare keeps visitors happy in a village pub on the B1159 coast road. Local accommodation available. 327

The White Horse, Chedgrave, Norwich, Norfolk NR14 6ND

Tel/Fax: 01508 520250

19th century pub with a fine reputation for its home-cooked food (steaks a speciality) and for its real ales. 323

Hunstanton

Golf Course Road, Old Hunstanton, Norfolk PE36 6JQ

Tel: 01485 532811 Fax: 01485 532319

Arguably one of the most under-rated courses in Britain but not by those who know it and welcome every visit. If quality is beholden to championship-staging then Hunstanton is up there with the best. Donald Steel, gifted golf writer and course designer, believes Hunstanton has a special place in British golf because it is the only championship course on more than 400 miles of East Coast between Sandwich and Muirfield. Sir Peter Allen in his book, Famous Fairways, nominated Hunstanton as the best course between the Tweed and the Thames.

The club was formed in 1891, roughly 30 years after Hunstanton was established as a new seaside town. The course lies between the shoreline, with its huge beach, and the River Hun. A range of shaggy sandhills divides it into two parts, flatter, low-lying holes on the inland side with more classic links through the dunes. As with every links course, the wind can often prove a defining feature here. But the layout offers plenty of variety while the greens are a delight to putt on. The current course bears little resemblance to the original concept, which took shape in a wilderness of marram grass, rushes and rabbit burrows. Those early nine holes were soon altered to become more acceptable and the rabbit population thinned. But the club didn't become firmly established until 1894 with the formation of the Hunstanton Golf Club Company, which acquired the lease of the ground, erected a new clubhouse and further improved the course. This brought an expansion to 18 holes in 1896, the extra nine holes costing £25.

Despite its proximity to Sandringham and close association to the Royal Family, Hunstanton has never become 'Royal' which is something of a mystery. The Duke of York, who later became King George V, was the club's patron, his two sons, the Duke of York and Duke of Kent, were honorary playing members, while the former, when he acceded as King George VI, became patron. But while West Norfolk, Cromer and Norwich were permitted to add Royal to their name, Hunstanton never took the step of seeking it. John Hughes was the club's first professional and stayed for 28 years. He created the Sandringham course, taught the game to the Royal Family, and played with four future kings, a record that few pros could match. His successor, James Sherlock, was a more accomplished player in terms of competition success and played in the Great Britain v America match that preceded the setting up of the Ryder Cup.

Many famous players have visited Hunstanton over the years, from Harry Vardon and James Braid to Bobby Locke and Dai Rees. Although Hunstanton hosted the Schweppes Championship in 1967, in modern times only major amateur events such as the English Championship and the Brabazon Trophy have graced its attractive links.

Sec/Manager: Mr Whybrow
Professional: James Dodds
Directions: 2 miles north east of Hunstanton. From Hunstanton take the A149 (north). On the sharp bend turn left to Le Strange Arms Hotel and take the Golf Course Road. Entrance is on the left hand side
Date Founded: 1891
Type of Course: Links
No of Holes: 18
Length: 6735 yds (6216 mtrs)
Par: 72
SSS: 72
Green Fees: Weekdays: 55.00; Weekends/ Bank Holidays: 65.00
Visitors: Welcome: Contact Club in advance
Societies: Welcome: Contact Club in advance
Facilities: Putting Green, Chipping Green, Trolley Hire, Bar, Restaurant, Practice Ground, Club Hire, Buggy Hire

Accommodation, Food and Drink

Reference numbers below refer to detailed information provided in section 2

Accommodation

The White House, Dersingham, King's Lynn, Norfolk PE31 6HQ

Tel: 01485 541895 Fax: 01485 544880

A handsome detached period house with six en-suite letting bedrooms. Excellent breakfasts. Large car park. No smoking. 334

Knights Hill Hotel, South Wootton, King's Lynn, Norfolk PE30 3HQ

Tel: 01553 675566 Fax: 01553 675568

A complex of 61 spacious, well-equipped bedrooms and apartments, restaurant, pub, health and leisure club, conference centre and 11 acres of grounds. 338

The Feathers Hotel, Dersingham, Norfolk PE31 6LN

Tel/Fax: 01485 540207

A family-run hotel that was once a coaching inn. Four traditionally appointed bedrooms, home-cooked food, landscaped gardens. 340

Marine Hotel, Hunstanton, Norfolk PE36 5EH

Tel: 01485 533310

Friendly family-run hotel handy for golf and shops, with most of the eight bedrooms enjoying sea views. Food served all day in the bar. 342

Le Strange Arms Hotel, Old Hunstanton, Norfolk PE36 6JJ

Tel: 01485 534411 Fax: 01485 534724

A handsome, well-appointed Best Western hotel, with 36 en-suite bedrooms, fine restaurant and its own pub. The gardens run down to the beach. 344

The Wash and Tope Hotel, Hunstanton, Norfolk PE36 5AJ

Tel: 01485 532250

A small family-run hotel facing the sea, with ten guest bedrooms, most en-suite. Restaurant open for breakfast, lunch and dinner; two bars. 346

The Lifeboat Inn, Thornham, Nr Hunstanton, Norfolk PE36 6LT

Tel: 01485 512236

A really lovely old inn with 13 excellent en-suite bedrooms affording views across the harbour to the sea. Bar and restaurant menus. 313

Food and Drink

Knights Hill Hotel, South Wootton, King's Lynn, Norfolk PE30 3HQ

Tel: 01553 675566 Fax: 01553 675568

A complex of 61 spacious, well-equipped bedrooms and apartments, restaurant, pub, health and leisure club, conference centre and 11 acres of grounds. 338

The Feathers Hotel, Dersingham, Norfolk PE31 6LN

Tel/Fax: 01485 540207

A family-run hotel that was once a coaching inn. Four traditionally appointed bedrooms, home-cooked food, landscaped gardens. 340

Marine Hotel, Hunstanton, Norfolk PE36 5EH

Tel: 01485 533310

Friendly family-run hotel handy for golf and shops, with most of the eight bedrooms enjoying sea views. Food served all day in the bar. 342

Le Strange Arms Hotel, Old Hunstanton, Norfolk PE36 6JJ

Tel: 01485 534411 Fax: 01485 534724

A handsome, well-appointed Best Western hotel, with 36 en-suite bedrooms, fine restaurant and its own pub. The gardens run down to the beach. 344

The Wash and Tope Hotel, Hunstanton, Norfolk PE36 5AJ

Tel: 01485 532250

A small family-run hotel facing the sea, with ten guest bedrooms, most en-suite. Restaurant open for breakfast, lunch and dinner; two bars. 346

The Jolly Sailors, Brancaster Staithe, Norfolk PE31 8BJ

Tel: 01485 210314

Delightful family-run 18th-century free house on the North Norfolk coast. All-day snack menu and main menu. Local seafood. 345

The Lifeboat Inn, Thornham, Nr Hunstanton, Norfolk PE36 6LT

Tel: 01485 512236

A really lovely old inn with 13 excellent en-suite bedrooms affording views across the harbour to the sea. Bar and restaurant menus. 313

King's Lynn

Castle Rising, King's Lynn, Norfolk PE31 6BD

Tel: 01553 631656 Fax: 01553 631036

King's Lynn's present location at Castle Rising is not where it first saw the light of day. The club was founded in 1923 and the original course at Leziate was among the many created by James Braid. The five-time Open champion laid out nine holes, which eventually became 18, over a heathland site near the town. Unfortunately, the club only owned the freehold to land on which six holes were situated. The other 12 were on a site belonging to British Industrial Sand beneath which lay high quality silicon sand used in glassmaking. When this became one of the last deposits in the United Kingdom the company wanted to extract it and negotiations began to find an alternative site for King's Lynn golfers.

This led to the construction of the present site at Castle Rising, some four miles north east of the town, while the old course was transformed into a quarry. This is now worked out and has become a boating lake while the old clubhouse has been transformed into a restaurant. Meanwhile, at Castle Rising, a new course was laid out by Peter Alliss and Dave Thomas, the combination behind such layouts as The Belfry,

Blairgowrie, and Hill Valley. The new layout lies on well-drained, relatively flat sandy soil, heavily wooded with silver birch and pine and quite demanding. Every fairway is tree-lined and being comparatively narrow places a high demand on straight shot making. There are a number of dog-legs but very little water apart from a couple of dykes which cross parts of the site. The course, which measures 6,609 yards, has a good scattering of bunkers and arguably the par-four eighth hole is the toughest. It measures only 386 yards from the white tees but has a very narrow fairway, If you are not accurate with your tee shot you could find the out of bounds left while the approach mustn't be too strong with out of bounds also behind the green.

Sec/Manager:	Mr Higgins
Professional:	Mr Reynolds
Directions:	2 miles north east of Kings Lynn. From Kings Lynn take the A148 (north). At the junction with the A1078 turn along Lynn Road. Entrance is, after one mile, on the right hand side.
Date Founded:	1923
Type of Course:	Forest
No of Holes:	18
Length:	6609 yds (6100 mtrs)
Par:	72
SSS:	73
Green Fees:	Weekdays: £40.00 (Dec-Feb inclusive £25.00); Weekends/ Bank Holidays: £50.00
Visitors:	Welcome: Contact club in advance (unable to play on Tuesday or at weekends)
Societies:	Welcome: Contact club in advance (unable to play Monday & Tuesdays)
Facilities:	Putting Green, Chipping Green, Practice Ground, Trolley Hire, Bar, Restaurant

Accommodation, Food and Drink

Reference numbers below refer to detailed information provided in section 2

Accommodation

The White House, Dersingham, King's Lynn, Norfolk PE31 6HQ

Tel: 01485 541895 Fax: 01485 544880

A handsome detached period house with six en-suite letting bedrooms. Excellent breakfasts. Large car park. No smoking. 334

Congham Hall, Grimston, King's Lynn, Norfolk PE32 1AH

Tel: 01485 600250 Fax: 01485 601191

One of the county's top hotels, an elegant Georgian manor set in 30 lovely acres. Seventeen exclusive bedrooms; superb restaurant. 337

Knights Hill Hotel, South Wootton, King's Lynn, Norfolk PE30 3HQ

Tel: 01553 675566 Fax: 01553 675568

A complex of 61 spacious, well-equipped bedrooms and apartments, restaurant, pub, health and leisure club, conference centre and 11 acres of grounds. 338

The Feathers Hotel, Dersingham, Norfolk PE31 6LN

Tel/Fax: 01485 540207

A family-run hotel that was once a coaching inn. Four traditionally appointed bedrooms, home-cooked food, landscaped gardens. 340

Marine Hotel, Hunstanton, Norfolk PE36 5EH

Tel: 01485 533310

Friendly family-run hotel handy for golf and shops, with most of the eight bedrooms enjoying sea views. Food served all day in the bar. 342

Le Strange Arms Hotel, Old Hunstanton, Norfolk PE36 6JJ

Tel: 01485 534411 Fax: 01485 534724

A handsome, well-appointed Best Western hotel, with 36 en-suite bedrooms, fine restaurant and its own pub. The gardens run down to the beach. 344

The Wash and Tope Hotel, Hunstanton, Norfolk PE36 5AJ

Tel: 01485 532250

A small family-run hotel facing the sea, with ten guest bedrooms, most en-suite. Restaurant open for breakfast, lunch and dinner; two bars. 346

King Harolds Head, Bumbles Green, Nazeing Common, Waltham Abbey, Essex EN9 2RY

Tel: 01992 893110 Fax: 01992 893412

A charming old free house on the Waltham Abbey-Harlow road. Friendly ambience, good company, exceptional food. 503

Food and Drink

Congham Hall, Grimston, King's Lynn, Norfolk PE32 1AH

Tel: 01485 600250 Fax: 01485 601191

One of the county's top hotels, an elegant Georgian manor set in 30 lovely acres. Seventeen exclusive bedrooms; superb restaurant. 337

Knights Hill Hotel, South Wootton, King's Lynn, Norfolk PE30 3HQ

Tel: 01553 675566 Fax: 01553 675568

A complex of 61 spacious, well-equipped bedrooms and apartments, restaurant, pub, health and leisure club, conference centre and 11 acres of grounds. 338

The Feathers Hotel, Dersingham, Norfolk PE31 6LN

Tel/Fax: 01485 540207

A family-run hotel that was once a coaching inn. Four traditionally appointed bedrooms, home-cooked food, landscaped gardens. 340

Marine Hotel, Hunstanton, Norfolk PE36 5EH

Tel: 01485 533310

Friendly family-run hotel handy for golf and shops, with most of the eight bedrooms enjoying sea views. Food served all day in the bar. 342

Le Strange Arms Hotel, Old Hunstanton, Norfolk PE36 6JJ

Tel: 01485 534411 Fax: 01485 534724

A handsome, well-appointed Best Western hotel, with 36 en-suite rooms, a fine restaurant and its own pub. The gardens run down to the beach. 344

The Gate Inn, Middleton, King's Lynn, Norfolk PE32 1RW

Tel: 01553 840518

A traditional country pub with loads of natural charm and cheer. Meals served in bar or restaurant. Beer garden. Pool table. 347

The Wash and Tope Hotel, Hunstanton, Norfolk PE36 5AJ

Tel: 01485 532250

A small family-run hotel facing the sea, with ten guest bedrooms, most en-suite. Restaurant open for breakfast, lunch and dinner; two bars. 346

The Lifeboat Inn, Thornham, Nr Hunstanton, Norfolk PE36 6LT

Tel: 01485 512236

A really lovely old inn with 13 excellent en-suite bedrooms affording views across the harbour to the sea. Bar and restaurant menus. 313

King Harolds Head, Bumbles Green, Nazeing Common, Waltham Abbey, Essex EN9 2RY

Tel: 01992 893110 Fax: 01992 893412

A charming old free house on the Waltham Abbey-Harlow road. Friendly ambience, good company, exceptional food. 503

Middleton Hall

Hall Orchards, Middleton, Kings Lynn, Norfolk PE32 1RH

Tel/Fax: 01553 841800

Sec/Manager: Jim Holland

Professional: Steve White

Directions: 3 miles south east of Kings Lynn. From Kings Lynn take the A47 (Norwich). After 2 miles turn left in Middleton by the church. Entrance is 200 yds on the left hand side.

Date Founded: 1990

Type of Course: Parkland

No of Holes: 18

Length: 6007 yds (5544 mtrs)

Par: 71

SSS: 67

Green Fees: Weekdays: £25.00; Weekends/ Bank Holidays: £30.00

Visitors: Welcome: Contact club in advance by phone

Societies: Welcome: Contact club in advance by phone - unable to play Monday,Tuesday & Wednesday

Facilities: Putting Green, Chipping Green, Practice Ground, Trolley Hire, Bar, Restaurant, Driving Range, Buggy Hire

Accommodation, Food and Drink

Reference numbers below refer to detailed information provided in section 2

Accommodation

Congham Hall, Grimston, King's Lynn, Norfolk PE32 1AH

Tel: 01485 600250 Fax: 01485 601191

One of the county's top hotels, an elegant Georgian manor set in 30 lovely acres. Seventeen exclusive bedrooms; superb restaurant. 337

The Feathers Hotel, Dersingham, Norfolk PE31 6LN

Tel/Fax: 01485 540207

A family-run hotel that was once a coaching inn.

Four traditionally appointed bedrooms, home-cooked food, landscaped gardens. 340

Crosskeys Riverside Hotel, Hilgay, Downham Market, Norfolk PE38 0LD

Tel/Fax: 01366 387777

A small country hotel in a 17th-century building in grounds beside the River Wissey. Four en-suite bedrooms. Breakfast, cream teas. 348

Rose & Crown, Hilgay, Downham Market, Norfolk PE38 0LJ

Tel: 01366 385414

A traditional village pub offering real ales, snacks and meals, entertainments and a choice of accommodation. 339

King Harolds Head, Bumbles Green, Nazeing Common, Waltham Abbey, Essex EN9 2RY

Tel: 01992 893110 Fax: 01992 893412

A charming old free house on the Waltham Abbey-Harlow road. Friendly ambience, good company, exceptional food. 503

Food and Drink

Congham Hall, Grimston, King's Lynn, Norfolk PE32 1AH

Tel: 01485 600250 Fax: 01485 601191

One of the county's top hotels, an elegant Georgian manor set in 30 lovely acres. Seventeen exclusive bedrooms; superb restaurant. 337

The Gate Inn, Middleton, King's Lynn, Norfolk PE32 1RW

Tel: 01553 840518

A traditional country pub with loads of natural charm and cheer. Meals served in bar or restaurant. Beer garden. Pool table. 347

Rose & Crown, Hilgay, Downham Market, Norfolk PE38 0LJ

Tel: 01366 385414

A traditional village pub offering real ales, snacks and meals, entertainments and a choice of accommodation. 339

King Harolds Head, Bumbles Green, Nazeing Common, Waltham Abbey, Essex EN9 2RY

Tel: 01992 893110 Fax: 01992 893412

A charming old free house on the Waltham Abbey-Harlow road. Friendly ambience, good company, exceptional food. 503

Lydney House Hotel, Swaffham, Norfolk PE37 7QS

Tel: 01760 723355 Fax: 01760 721410

Nine comfortable en-suite bedrooms in a Georgian hotel near the centre of Swaffham. Bar and restaurant menus. Garden. 305

Norfolk G&CC

Hingham Road, Reymerston, Norwich, Norfolk NR9 4QQ

Tel: 01362 850297 Fax: 01362 850614

When this site, which was originally Church Farm, was bought early in 1988 as a 200-acre working farm by Robert Bunn Ltd, a family run business, it was soon destined for greater things. The landscape with its valley contours, ponds, ditches, mature trees and hedging lent itself ideally as a golf course.

During construction in the early 1990s more than adequate drainage was installed along with a sprinkler system to all greens that would allow for the contrary nature of the Norfolk weather. All fairways were stone buried before seeding took place while over 4,000 trees were planted as part of the forestry programme to ensure the continuation of indigenous species. When finished the course was allowed to mature for two years before it opened for play in June 1993 as Reymerston Golf Club. The name was changed to The Norfolk Golf and Country Club when entrepreneur Eddy Shah gained control a few years ago.

As the sister course to The Suffolk, it is part of Messenger Leisure Ltd and is regarded as one of the finest new courses in East Anglia. It has been

the intention to ensure that the golf course and clubhouse at Reymerston should offer the finest facilities in the most agreeable setting but that it should not be at the expense of the local flora and fauna but in a way that will encourage both to enhance the rural setting through sympathetic planning, careful management and regeneration. The 6,603-yard, par 72, layout winds its way through gently undulating Norfolk countryside on mature parkland, with plenty of natural hazards to challenge the ability of all golfers whatever their ability. A key feature is the substantial greens, built to USGA specifications, with the ninth being in the region of 1,000 square yards. Beware the bunkers are also large in size. There is also a nine-hole pitch and putt course plus an outdoor driving range, golf academy, restaurant and extensive golf shop.

Other sports are also catered for with trout fishing and clay pigeon shooting, both offering tuition.

Sec/Manager: Mervin Amo
Professional: Tony Varney
Directions: 13 miles west of Norwich. From Norwich take the A11 to Wymondham. Turn right on the B1135 (East Dereham). 1 mile after Kimberley turn left on the B road towards Reymerston. Entrance is after 2 miles on the right hand side
Date Founded: 1993
Visitors: Welcome: Contact club in advance
Societies: Welcome: Contact in advance
Facilities: Putting Green, Club Hire, Trolley Hire, Buggy Hire, Bar, Restaurant, Driving Range, Leisure Complex

18 Hole Course

Type of Course: Parkland
No of Holes: 18
Length: 6609 yds (6100 mtrs)
Par: 72
SSS: 72
Green Fees: Weekdays: £20.00; Weekends/ Bank Holidays: £25.00

Par 3 Pitch & Putt Course

Type of Course: Parkland
No of Holes: 9
Length: unmeasured
Par: 27
Green Fees: Weekdays: £3.00; Weekends/ Bank Holidays: £3.00

Accommodation, Food and Drink

Reference numbers below refer to detailed information provided in section 2

Accommodation

The Crown Hotel, Watton, Norfolk IP25 6AB
Tel: 01953 882375 Fax: 01953 884120
Good food and comfortable overenight accommodation in a handsome old coaching inn on the main street. 335

The Longham White Horse, Longham, Dereham, Norfolk NR19 2RD
Tel: 01362 687464
Spick-and-span accommodation and good-value eating in a popular village pub with a pleasant garden. 330

Scarningdale Country Guest House, Scarning, East Dereham, Norfolk NR19 2QN
Tel: 01362 687269 Fax: 01362 687378
Delightful secluded country house with three en-suite bedrooms and five self-catering cottages. Indoor pool. Lovely gardens. www.scarningdale.co.uk

The George Hotel, Swaffham Road, East Dereham, Norfolk NR19 2AZ
Tel: 01362 696801 Fax: 01362 695711
Eight en-suite bedrooms, including two suites, in a handsome listed building just off the town centre. Bar and restaurant. Large car park.

Phoenix Hotel, Dereham, Norfolk NR19 1DL
Tel: 01362 692276 Fax: 01362 691752
Twenty-two en-suite bedrooms in a smartly refurbished hotel with a popular seven-days-a-week restaurant.

The Victoria Inn, Deopham, Wymondham, Norfolk NR18 9DX
Tel: 01953 850783
Real ales, hot and cold food, traditional Sunday lunches and Bed & Breakfast accommodation in a fine country inn. 309

Barnham Broom, Norwich, Norfolk NR9 4DD
Tel: 01603 759393 Fax: 01603 758224
A luxurious hotel with golf club, leisure centre and conference centre in a tranquil valley setting 10 miles west of Norwich. 301

Food and Drink

The Kings Head, Hethersett, Norfolk NR9 3DD

Tel: 01603 810206

16th-century public house in a pretty village south of Norwich. Good home-cooked food, real ales. Lovely garden. 341

The Crown Hotel, Watton, Norfolk IP25 6AB

Tel: 01953 882375 Fax: 01953 884120

Good food and comfortable overenight accommodation in a handsome old coaching inn on the main street. 335

The Longham White Horse, Longham, Dereham, Norfolk NR19 2RD

Tel: 01362 687464

Spick-and-span accommodation and good-value eating in a popular village pub with a pleasant garden. 330

The George Hotel, Swaffham Road, East Dereham, Norfolk NR19 2AZ

Tel: 01362 696801 Fax: 01362 695711

Eight en-suite bedrooms, including two suites, in a handsome listed building just off the town centre. Bar and restaurant. Large car park.

Phoenix Hotel, Dereham, Norfolk NR19 1DL

Tel: 01362 692276 Fax: 01362 691752

Twenty-two en-suite bedrooms in a smartly refurbished hotel with a popular seven-days-a-week restaurant.

The Victoria Inn, Hockering, Nr Norwich, Norfolk NR20 3HL

Tel: 01603 880507

A 1930s village pub with a cosy eating area and a beer garden. Home-cooked food; good beers and wines. 333

The Victoria Inn, Deopham, Wymondham, Norfolk NR18 9DX

Tel: 01953 850783

Real ales, hot and cold food, traditional Sunday lunches and Bed & Breakfast accommodation in a fine country inn. 309

The Cock, Barford, Norwich, Norfolk NR9 4AS

Tel: 01603 757646

A 200-year-old country inn eight miles west of Norwich that's gaining a great reputation for its superb food. 306

Barnham Broom, Norwich, Norfolk NR9 4DD

Tel: 01603 759393 Fax: 01603 758224

A luxurious hotel with golf club, leisure centre and conference centre in a tranquil valley setting 10 miles west of Norwich. 301

Richmond Park

Saham Road, Watton, Norfolk IP25 6EA

Tel: 01953 881803 Fax: 01953 881817

Sec/Manager: Alan Helmsley

Professional: Alan Helmsley

Directions: 20 miles west of Norwich. From Norwich take the A11 to Attleborough and turn right onto the B1077 to Watton. Take a right onto the B1108. After a quarter of a mile turn right into Saham Road and the entrance is 200 yds on the left hand side.

Date Founded: 1990

Type of Course: Parkland

No of Holes: 18

Length: 6289 yds (5805 mtrs)

Par: 71

SSS: 70

Green Fees: Weekdays: £18.00; Weekends/ Bank Holidays: £24.00

Visitors: Welcome: Contact club by phone in advance (unable to play prior to 10.30 at weekends)

Societies: Welcome: Contact club by phone in advance (unable to play at weekends)

Facilities: Putting Green, Chipping Green, Driving Range, Trolley Hire, Buggy Hire, Bar, Restaurant

Accommodation, Food and Drink

Reference numbers below refer to detailed information provided in section 2

Accommodation

The Crown Hotel, Watton, Norfolk IP25 6AB

Tel: 01953 882375 Fax: 01953 884120

Good food and comfortable overenight accommodation in a handsome old coaching inn on the main street. 335

The Longham White Horse, Longham, Dereham, Norfolk NR19 2RD

Tel: 01362 687464

Spick-and-span accommodation and good-value eating in a popular village pub with a pleasant garden. 330

Scarningdale Country Guest House, Scarning, East Dereham, Norfolk NR19 2QN

Tel: 01362 687269 Fax: 01362 687378

Delightful secluded country house with three en-suite bedrooms and five self-catering cottages. Indoor pool. Lovely gardens. www.scarningdale.co.uk

The George Hotel, Swaffham Road, East Dereham, Norfolk NR19 2AZ

Tel: 01362 696801 Fax: 01362 695711

Eight en-suite bedrooms, including two suites, in a handsome listed building just off the town centre. Bar and restaurant. Large car park.

Phoenix Hotel, Dereham, Norfolk NR19 1DL

Tel: 01362 692276 Fax: 01362 691752

Twenty-two en-suite bedrooms in a smartly refurbished hotel with a popular seven-days-a-week restaurant.

The Victoria Inn, Deopham, Wymondham, Norfolk NR18 9DX

Tel: 01953 850783

Real ales, hot and cold food, traditional Sunday lunches and Bed & Breakfast accommodation in a fine country inn. 309

Lydney House Hotel, Swaffham, Norfolk PE37 7QS

Tel: 01760 723355 Fax: 01760 721410

Nine comfortable en-suite bedrooms in a Georgian hotel near the centre of Swaffham. Bar and restaurant menus. Garden. 305

Food and Drink

The Crown Hotel, Watton, Norfolk IP25 6AB

Tel: 01953 882375 Fax: 01953 884120

Good food and comfortable overenight accommodation in a handsome old coaching inn on the main street. 335

The Longham White Horse, Longham, Dereham, Norfolk NR19 2RD

Tel: 01362 687464

Spick-and-span accommodation and good-value eating in a popular village pub with a pleasant garden. 330

The George Hotel, Swaffham Road, East Dereham, Norfolk NR19 2AZ

Tel: 01362 696801 Fax: 01362 695711

Eight en-suite bedrooms, including two suites, in a handsome listed building just off the town centre. Bar and restaurant. Large car park.

Phoenix Hotel, Dereham, Norfolk NR19 1DL

Tel: 01362 692276 Fax: 01362 691752

Twenty-two en-suite bedrooms in a smartly refurbished hotel with a popular seven-days-a-week restaurant.

The Nags Head, East Harling, Norfolk NR16 2AD

Tel: 01953 718140

Village pub in traditional style, serving an extensive range of splendid home-cooked food. On the B1111 south of Attleborough. 317

The Victoria Inn, Deopham, Wymondham, Norfolk NR18 9DX

Tel: 01953 850783

Real ales, hot and cold food, traditional Sunday lunches and Bed & Breakfast accommodation in a fine country inn. 309

Lydney House Hotel, Swaffham, Norfolk PE37 7QS

Tel: 01760 723355 Fax: 01760 721410

Nine comfortable en-suite bedrooms in a Georgian hotel near the centre of Swaffham. Bar and restaurant menus. Garden. 305

Royal Cromer

145 Overstrand Road, Cromer, Norfolk NR27 0JH

Tel: 01263 512884 Fax: 01263 512430

The late lamented Percy 'Laddie' Lucas, a fighter pilot hero of the Second World War, renowned golfer and writer, is firmly linked with Royal Cromer. His father was secretary for 10 years around the turn of the 20th century, as well as captain, while in 1943 Laddie commanded the Spitfire wing at Coltishall, the RAF station some 15 miles away. In his foreword to the club's Centenary Book he writes: "I would often fly my aeroplane low over the course just to be satisfied that the holes I remembered from the halcyon days were still there. The thought of being able, one day, to play them again in peace was a spur to victory. And then there was that blessed sight

of the Cromer cliffs, with the course nestling above them, as we returned across 120 miles of swirling North Sea. The relief was akin to getting a four at the 18th to win the monthly medal."

There is still a link with the RAF, its personnel forming an active and valued section of the club. Royal Cromer celebrated its centenary in 1988, being the second oldest club in Norfolk, and owes its beginnings, like many others, to a Scot. Henry Broadhurst, an MP of the day, holidayed in Cromer and was struck by the land behind the cliffs; sandy hills covered with bracken and gorse, with grassy valleys would be ideal for golf. He approached the owner, Lord Suffield, a friend and often host to the Prince of Wales, who agreed to rent an area including Happy Valley, a dell below the lighthouse. The Prince consented to become the club's patron on Christmas Day 1887, which meant the club was Royal before it was a golf club.

The first clubhouse was an old butcher's shop, dismantled and re-erected in 1890. Several notable figures played at Cromer in the early years, royal princes and princesses as well as Prime Ministers Herbert Asquith and Arthur Balfour. There were also writers such as James Barrie, Alfred, Lord Tennyson and Bernard Darwin. The present course, remodelled just before the First World War and altered again in 1979, owes much to Harry Colt and J H Taylor. As with much of the East Anglian coastline, erosion is a constant concern and in 1962 a great cliff fall carried away part of the 17th fairway. No changes were possible until the mid-Seventies when the club was able to purchase more land, allowing new holes to be built and the cliff-edge holes, including the 17th, to be abandoned. Like Turnberry's famous Ailsa Course in Scotland, Royal Cromer also possesses a lighthouse hole, their's being the 14th.

Sec/Manager:	Ray Fields
Professional:	Lee Paterson
Directions:	1½ miles south east of Cromer. From Cromer take the B1159 towards Mundesley. The entrance is on the left hand side on Overstrand Road on the outskirts of Cromer.
Date Founded:	1886
Type of Course:	Clifftop
No of Holes:	18
Length:	6508 yds (6007 mtrs)
Par:	72
SSS:	72
Green Fees:	Weekdays: 1st April-31st October inclusive £37.00, 1st November-31st March inclusive £27.00; Weekends/ Bank Holidays: 1st April-31st October inclusive £42.00, 1st November -31st March inclusive £32.00; Half price at twilight
Visitors:	Welcome: Contact club by phone in advance
Societies:	Welcome: Contact club by phone in advance
Facilities:	Putting Green, Chipping Green, Driving Range, Trolley Hire, Buggy Hire, Bar, Restaurant

Accommodation, Food and Drink

Reference numbers below refer to detailed information provided in section 2

Accommodation

The Bay Leaf Guest House, Sheringham, Norfolk NR26 8QY

Tel: 01263 823779

A charming Victorian licensed guest house handy for the seafront and local amenities. Seven twin or double bedrooms, all en-suite, with tv. 308

Virginia Court Hotel, Cromer, Norfolk NR27 0AN

Tel: 01263 512398

Twenty-three delightful, spacious en-suite bedrooms in a late-Victorian hotel two minutes from the town centre and the sea. 324

Birch House, 34 Cabbell Road, Cromer, Norfolk NR27 9HX

Tel: 01263 512521

Eight comfortably furnished bedrooms - non-smoking, most en-suite - in a Victorian house a short walk from the sea. Optional evening meal.

Rosedale Farm Guesthouse, Holt Road, Weybourne, Norfolk NR25 7TS

Tel: 01263 588788

En-suite bedrooms, breakfast and evening meals in a flint-and-brick farmhouse with a walled garden and heated swimming pool.

The John H. Stracey, Briston, Melton Constable, Norfolk NR24 2JA

Tel: 01263 860891

Great food and real ales bring the crowds to a grand old hostelry on the edge of the village. B&B also available. 319

The Shannocks Hotel & Restaurant, Sheringham, Norfolk NR26 8JP

Tel: 01263 820368

12 en-suite bedrooms in a modernised Victorian seafront hotel. Restaurant with à la carte menu and carvery. 326

Highfields Guest House, Sheringham, Norfolk NR26 8LN

Tel: 01263 825524

Eight en-suite bedrooms in a comfortable, spotless guesthouse in sight of Sheringham Golf Course. No smoking. Dinner by arrangement. 315

Parsons Pleasure, Church Street, Northrepps, Cromer, Norfolk NR27 0LG

Tel/Fax: 01263 579691

Tranquil village setting for a delightful country inn offering fine food and eight en-suite letting bedrooms, including three luxury suites.

The Norfolk Mead Hotel, Coltishall, Norfolk NR12 7DN

Tel: 01603 737531 Fax: 01603 737521

An impressive Georgian manor house with characterful en-suite bedrooms and a lovely setting in grounds running down to the River Bure. 314

The Dales Country House Hotel, Upper Sheringham, Norfolk NR26 8TJ

Tel: 01263 824555

A handsome listed building in a lovely parkland setting provides spacious accommodation in 18 superb bedrooms. Fine restaurant. 322

Overcliff Lodge, Cromer Road, Mundesley, Norfolk NR11 8DB

Tel/Fax: 01263 720016

Four delightful en-suite bedrooms in a smart white house on the coast road down from Cromer. Excellent home cooking.

Ostend Place Chalet Park, Ostend Place, Walcott, Norfolk NR12 0NJ

Tel: 01692 650462

The park comprises three self-catering flats in the house; eight chalets on the seafront; and a bungalow sleeping six.

Golden Beach Holiday Centre, Sea Palling, Norfolk NR12 0AL

Tel: 01692 598269

Luxury holiday caravans in a well-run centre nestling beneath a bank of dunes just back from the sea. Full on-site facilities. 303

Food and Drink

Virginia Court Hotel, Cromer, Norfolk NR27 0AN

Tel: 01263 512398

Twenty-three delightful, spacious en-suite bedrooms in a late-Victorian hotel two minutes from the town centre and the sea. 324

The John H. Stracey, Briston, Melton Constable, Norfolk NR24 2JA

Tel: 01263 860891

Great food and real ales bring the crowds to a grand old hostelry on the edge of the village. B&B also available. 319

The Shannocks Hotel & Restaurant, Sheringham, Norfolk NR26 8JP

Tel: 01263 820368

12 en-suite bedrooms in a modernised Victorian seafront hotel. Restaurant with à la carte menu and carvery. 326

Parsons Pleasure, Church Street, Northrepps, Cromer, Norfolk NR27 0LG

Tel/Fax: 01263 579691

Tranquil village setting for a delightful country inn offering fine food and eight en-suite letting bedrooms, including three luxury suites.

The Red Lion Inn, Coltishall, Norfolk NR12 7DW

Tel: 01603 737402

300-year-old pub with cosy beamed bars, special real ales and an all-day menu of home-cooked food. 329

The Norfolk Mead Hotel, Coltishall, Norfolk NR12 7DN

Tel: 01603 737531 Fax: 01603 737521

An impressive Georgian manor house with characterful en-suite bedrooms and a lovely setting in grounds running down to the River Bure. 314

The Dales Country House Hotel, Upper Sheringham, Norfolk NR26 8TJ

Tel: 01263 824555

A handsome listed building in a lovely parkland setting provides spacious accommodation in 18 superb bedrooms. Fine restaurant. 322

Pebbles Country Inn, Happisburgh, Norfolk NR12 0RD

Tel: 01622 651183

Home-cooked English fare keeps visitors happy in a village pub on the B1159 coast road. Local accommodation available. 327

Royal Norwich

Drayton High Road, Hellesdon, Norwich, Norfolk NR6 5AH

Tel: 01603 429928 Fax: 01603 417945

Royal Norwich is one of hundreds of courses fashioned by the hand of James Braid. But the five-time Open champion can't have worked on many in the middle of a city. The course, set in mature, undulating parkland, straddles the Drayton Road at Hellesdon on its original site just two miles from the city centre. Braid's redesigned course, essentially what is played today, opened in 1924 but the original layout was the work of John Deuchar, a Scot who worked for the Norwich Union Life Assurance Company. He hailed from North Berwick and the first nine holes were opened on 30 November 1893, just 22 days after the Club was formed. The official opening came on 1 February 1894 by which time 18 holes were in existence measuring 4,925 yards.

At that time it was felt that Royal patronage should be sought, following those of Royal Cromer and Royal West Norfolk. It came just a day after the formation when the Duke of York, later to become King George V, agreed to the request and to this day the white rose of York features on the Club's emblem. Braid, together with J H Taylor and Harry Vardon, the other members of the Great Triumvirate, played at Royal Norwich on various occasions, heading a list of visitors down the years that reads like a Who's Who of golf. The great American Walter Hagen dropped in to play in 1933, while in more recent times, the Club hosted the Martini Tournament in 1971, won by future Ryder Cup captain Bernard Gallacher.

The highlight of that occasion came when John Hudson holed-in-one on successive holes, the 12th

(195 yds) and 13th (311 yds). The Club has also staged the Girls' Home Internationals in 1972 and the Ladies British Open Amateur Stroke Play Championship in 1981.

Sec/Manager:	John Meggy
Professional:	Dean Futter
Directions:	2 miles north west of Norwich. From Norwich centre take the A1067 (Fakenham) . After crossing the A140 the entrance is on the left hand side.
Date Founded:	1893
Type of Course:	Parkland
No of Holes:	18
Length:	6506 yds (6005 mtrs)
Par:	72
SSS:	72
Green Fees:	Weekdays: £30.00; Weekends/ Bank Holidays: £36.00
Visitors:	Welcome: Contact Club in advance, due to limited availability.
Societies:	Welcome: Contact club in writing in advance.
Facilities:	Putting Green, Chipping Green, Trolley Hire, Buggy Hire, Bar, Restaurant, Private Rooms

Accommodation, Food and Drink

Reference numbers below refer to detailed information provided in section 2

Accommodation

The Ship Hotel, Gorleston-on-Sea, Norfolk NR31 6DJ

Tel/Fax: 01493 662746

A few yards from the seafront, The Ship is a

family run hotel with eight cosy en-suite bedrooms. B&B & dinner. 336

Parsons Pleasure, Church Street, Northrepps, Cromer, Norfolk NR27 0LG

Tel/Fax: 01263 579691

Tranquil village setting for a delightful country inn offering fine food and eight en-suite letting bedrooms, including three luxury suites.

The Blue Boar, Sprowston, Norfolk NR7 8RL

Tel: 01603 426802

Comfortable overnight accommodation and fine food in a pub of style and character. 325

The Norfolk Mead Hotel, Coltishall, Norfolk NR12 7DN

Tel: 01603 737531 Fax: 01603 737521

An impressive Georgian manor house with characterful en-suite bedrooms and a lovely setting in grounds running down to the River Bure. 314

Buxton Mill Hotel, Buxton, Norfolk NR10 5JF

Tel: 01603 278194 Fax: 01603 279332

A mill on the River Bure has been converted to a fine hotel with 14 en-suite bedrooms, a candlelit restaurant and a bar. 316

The Old Rectory Hotel, Crostwick, Norwich, Norfolk NR12 7BG

Tel: 01603 738513 Fax: 01603 738712

18th century country rectory with a modern bedroom block and lovely gardens. Thirteen well-appointed en-suite bedrooms; two restaurants. 320

Overcliff Lodge, Cromer Road, Mundesley, Norfolk NR11 8DB

Tel/Fax: 01263 720016

Four delightful en-suite bedrooms in a smart white house on the coast road down from Cromer. Excellent home cooking.

Ostend Place Chalet Park, Ostend Place, Walcott, Norfolk NR12 0NJ

Tel: 01692 650462

The park comprises three self-catering flats in the house; eight chalets on the seafront; and a bungalow sleeping six.

Hill House Guest House, Hillside Road, Thorpe St Andrew, Norfolk NR7 0QS

Tel: 01603 432165

Three en-suite bedrooms in an Edwardian house overlooking the River Yare. Bed & Breakfast. 2 miles east of Norwich.

Wensum Country Hotel, Great Witchingham, Norwich, Norfolk NR9 5QP

Tel: 01603 872288

A haven of comfort and fine food in the heart of the Norfolk countryside. 36 well-appointed bedrooms; extensive leisure facilities. 312

The Georgian House Hotel, Norwich, Norfolk NR2 2RB

Tel: 01603 615655 Fax: 01603 765689

Twenty-seven well-appointed en-suite bedrooms in a family-run hotel within easy reach of the city centre. Restaurant, bar, lounge. 310

Wensum Valley Hotel, Taverham, Norwich, Norfolk NR8 6HP

Tel: 01603 261012 Fax: 01603 261664

Hotel, golf and country club set in 240 acres of lovely countryside. 39 en-suite bedrooms, restaurant, golf courses, leisure club, fishing. 307

Food and Drink

The Ship Hotel, Gorleston-on-Sea, Norfolk NR31 6DJ

Tel/Fax: 01493 662746

A few yards from the seafront, The Ship is a family run hotel with eight cosy en-suite bedrooms. B&B & dinner. 336

Parsons Pleasure, Church Street, Northrepps, Cromer, Norfolk NR27 0LG

Tel/Fax: 01263 579691

Tranquil village setting for a delightful country inn offering fine food and eight en-suite letting bedrooms, including three luxury suites.

The Blue Boar, Sprowston, Norfolk NR7 8RL

Tel: 01603 426802

Comfortable overnight accommodation and fine food in a pub of style and character. 325

The Branford Arms, Sprowston, Norwich, Norfolk NR3 4QD

Tel: 01603 427488

A 100-year-old pub of great character, serving generous helpings of good-value home-cooked food. Available Wed-Fri evenings, all day Sat and Sun lunch. 343

The Norfolk Mead Hotel, Coltishall, Norfolk NR12 7DN

Tel: 01603 737531 Fax: 01603 737521

An impressive Georgian manor house with characterful en-suite bedrooms and a lovely setting in grounds running down to the River Bure. 314

Buxton Mill Hotel, Buxton, Norfolk NR10 5JF

Tel: 01603 278194 Fax: 01603 279332

A mill on the River Bure has been converted to a fine hotel with 14 en-suite bedrooms, a candlelit restaurant and a bar. 316

The Old Rectory Hotel, Crostwick, Norwich, Norfolk NR12 7BG

Tel: 01603 738513 Fax: 01603 738712

18th century country rectory with a modern

bedroom block and lovely gardens. Thirteen well-appointed en-suite rooms; two restaurants. 320

The Black Horse, Norwich, Norfolk NR2 3DE

Tel: 01603 624682 Fax: 01603 617893

An 18th century inn five minutes from the city centre, serving snacks and full menus, real ales and wines. Garden. 332

Wensum Country Hotel, Great Witchingham, Norwich, Norfolk NR9 5QP

Tel: 01603 872288

A haven of comfort and fine food in the heart of the Norfolk countryside. 36 well-appointed bedrooms; extensive leisure facilities. 312

The Georgian House Hotel, Norwich, Norfolk NR2 2RB

Tel: 01603 615655 Fax: 01603 765689

Twenty-seven well-appointed en-suite bedrooms in a family-run hotel within easy reach of the city centre. Restaurant, bar, lounge. 310

The Pickwick, Norwich, Norfolk NR2 3AD

Tel: 01603 628155

A Georgian pub-restaurant three minutes from the city centre. Snack and à la carte menus, Sunday roasts. Good wines. 302

Wensum Valley Hotel, Taverham, Norwich, Norfolk NR8 6HP

Tel: 01603 261012 Fax: 01603 261664

Hotel, golf and country club set in 240 acres of lovely countryside. 39 en-suite bedrooms, restaurant, golf courses, leisure club, fishing. 307

Royal West Norfolk

Brancaster, King's Lynn, Norfolk PE31 8AX
Tel: 01485 210223 Fax: 01485 210087

A visit to Royal West Norfolk or Brancaster as it is more familiarly known, is not to be missed. It is an experience, which cannot be repeated anywhere in the world, a trip back in time to what many would describe as true golf. Brancaster is remote, perched as it is on the exposed upper lip of East Anglia. But its remoteness is part of its appeal as is its cosy and welcoming clubhouse

that clings to the beach just above the breaking waves of the North Sea. And that is the defining feature of golf here.

The sea, backed by the occasional winter storm, has been doing its best to wipe Brancaster off the map for as long as most of us can remember. So far, it has defied the elements although the fight is ongoing. An assessment of how the course and the sea live in such close proximity is to arrive at the time of a high tide and find the access road under several foot of water. Then it means parking in the nearby lane and walking the half-mile or so along the nearby dyke to the shelter of the clubhouse.

The tide is a constant feature at Brancaster, which is why the times are posted on a board beside the front door of the clubhouse. Once inside there are few formalities. The atmosphere is relaxed, often with a log fire, a clubroom that has felt the studded shoes of golfers for 108 years, and a locker room that is spartan to say the least. You will also find an impressive list of past captains posted on wooden boards that read like Debrett's Peerage. Being close to Sandringham, it names four members of the Royal Family, earls, viscounts, knights, military men, professors, doctors, even journalists.

Royal West Norfolk dates back to 1892 and the course has changed little since apart from when the sea stole two holes in 1939 and 1940. It is still out-and-back between the sea and the vast saltmarsh with several shared fairways, following the red flags going out and the yellows coming in, usually to the cries of many varieties of sea birds. There are red tin tee boxes on every tee, something every club possessed in former days. These contain sand to build a tee as well as water to wash your ball, while there is also a brush for cleaning your spikes. It is another side aspect that marks Royal West Norfolk apart from most other clubs.

Sec/Manager: Major Carrington-Smith
Professional: Simon Rayner
Directions: 8 miles east of Hunstanton.

	From Hunstanton take the A149 (Cromer). After seven miles turn left in Brancaster onto London Street. The entrance is after about one mile.
Date Founded:	1891
Type of Course:	Links
No of Holes:	18
Length:	6371 yds (5880 mtrs)
Par:	71
SSS:	71
Green Fees:	Weekdays: £60.00; Weekends/ Bank Holidays: £70.00
Visitors:	Welcome: Contact Club in advance. Unable to play at various times in summer months.
Societies:	Welcome: Contact club in advance. Unable to play prior to 10 a.m. at weekends.
Facilities:	Putting Green, Chipping Green, Club Hire, Trolley Hire, Bar, Restaurant

Accommodation, Food and Drink

Reference numbers below refer to detailed information provided in section 2

Accommodation

The White House, Dersingham, King's Lynn, Norfolk PE31 6HQ

Tel: 01485 541895 Fax: 01485 544880

A handsome detached period house with six en-suite letting bedrooms. Excellent breakfasts. Large car park. No smoking. 334

Marine Hotel, Hunstanton, Norfolk PE36 5EH

Tel: 01485 533310

Friendly family-run hotel handy for golf and shops, with most of the eight bedrooms enjoying sea views. Food served all day in the bar. 342

Le Strange Arms Hotel, Old Hunstanton, Norfolk PE36 6JJ

Tel: 01485 534411 Fax: 01485 534724

A handsome, well-appointed Best Western hotel, with 36 en-suite bedrooms, fine restaurant and its own pub. The gardens run down to the beach. 344

The Wash and Tope Hotel, Hunstanton, Norfolk PE36 5AJ

Tel: 01485 532250

A small family-run hotel facing the sea, with ten guest bedrooms, most en-suite. Restaurant open for breakfast, lunch and dinner; two bars. 346

The Bay Leaf Guest House, Sheringham, Norfolk NR26 8QY

Tel: 01263 823779

A charming Victorian licensed guest house handy for the seafront and local amenities. Seven twin or double bedrooms, all en-suite, with tv. 308

Rosedale Farm Guesthouse, Holt Road, Weybourne, Norfolk NR25 7TS

Tel: 01263 588788

En-suite bedrooms, breakfast and evening meals in a flint-and-brick farmhouse with a walled garden and heated swimming pool.

The John H. Stracey, Briston, Melton Constable, Norfolk NR24 2JA

Tel: 01263 860891

Great food and real ales bring the crowds to a grand old hostelry on the edge of the village. B&B also available. 319

Highfields Guest House, Sheringham, Norfolk NR26 8LN

Tel: 01263 825524

Eight en-suite bedrooms in a comfortable, spotless guesthouse in sight of Sheringham Golf Course. No smoking. Dinner by arrangement. 315

The Lifeboat Inn, Thornham, Nr Hunstanton, Norfolk PE36 6LT

Tel: 01485 512236

A really lovely old inn with 13 excellent en-suite bedrooms affording views across the harbour to the sea. Bar and restaurant menus. 313

Food and Drink

Marine Hotel, Hunstanton, Norfolk PE36 5EH

Tel: 01485 533310

Friendly family-run hotel handy for golf and shops, with most of the eight bedrooms enjoying sea views. Food served all day in the bar. 342

Le Strange Arms Hotel, Old Hunstanton, Norfolk PE36 6JJ

Tel: 01485 534411 Fax: 01485 534724

A handsome, well-appointed Best Western hotel, with 36 en-suite bedrooms, fine restaurant and its own pub. The gardens run down to the beach. 344

The Wash and Tope Hotel, Hunstanton, Norfolk PE36 5AJ

Tel: 01485 532250

A small family-run hotel facing the sea, with ten guest bedrooms, most en-suite. Restaurant open for breakfast, lunch and dinner; two bars. 346

The Jolly Sailors, Brancaster Staithe, Norfolk PE31 8BJ

Tel: 01485 210314

Delightful family-run 18th-century free house on the North Norfolk coast. All-day snack menu and main menu. Local seafood. 345

The John H. Stracey, Briston, Melton Constable, Norfolk NR24 2JA

Tel: 01263 860891

Great food and real ales bring the crowds to a grand old hostelry on the edge of the village. B&B also available. 319

The Lifeboat Inn, Thornham, Nr Hunstanton, Norfolk PE36 6LT

Tel: 01485 512236

A really lovely old inn with 13 excellent en-suite bedrooms affording views across the harbour to the sea. Bar and restaurant menus. 313

Sheringham

Weybourne Road, Sheringham, Norfolk NR26 8HG

Tel: 01263 822038 Fax: 01263 825189

Just to walk out on the Sheringham fairways on a fine day and to gaze out over the North Sea is a pleasure in itself. Perched as it is along the clifftops, Sheringham's situation is often the envy of golfers visiting from more mundane layouts and while it is always at the mercy of what might blow in from an icy Scandinavia or the Russian Steppes, it rarely loses its appeal. There are splendid views in both directions over wide sandy beaches while inland a line of shallow hills forms a perfect backdrop. When Sheringham Golf Club first saw the light of day in 1891, it owed much to the initiative of Henry Broadhurst, the local MP, and Tom Dunn. Broadhurst wanted to introduce "the march of civilisation" into what was a remote region and after obtaining the consent of the Upcher family of Sheringham Hall, who owned the clifftop site, it was Dunn, the professional at the now defunct Tooting Bec club, who laid out nine holes.

Like other East Anglian clubs, Sheringham's history is punctuated with famous names that have been members. Venture into its clubhouse just prior to the First World War and you might have found Lord Jellicoe of Jutland fame, the explorer Sir Ernest Shackleton, and Captain Robert Scott of the Antarctic taking tea together. The club can also boast Stanley Christopherson, later to be Deputy Chairman of the Midland Bank, who played in the inaugural England v Australia Test Match at Lord's in 1884. He also captained the first England international hockey side against Ireland at Richmond in 1895.

The course, which is virtually an out-and-back layout, is bounded by the cliffs and the sea on one side and the railway on the other. The last four holes run alongside what began as the Great Northern and Midland Joint Railway, became the London and North Eastern, and is now the preserved North Norfolk Railway. In the old days trains were more frequent as they brought holidaymakers to the town and on one occasion led to a famous story which has become part of the fabric of the game.

In 1920 the club hosted the English Ladies Close Championship, the culmination of which was a final between Joyce Wethered and defending champion Cecil Leitch, two of the greatest women golfers of the day. The climax of a monumental battle came in the afternoon on the 17th green, which was situated alongside the railway. The story goes that just as Miss Wethered was about to sink the winning putt, a train roared by. Asked if that had affected her, she is reputed to have replied: "What train?" She had the ability to drop into a cocoon of concentration when required which no doubt led to her retaining the title over the next four years. But whether she uttered those words is conjecture.

Sec/Manager: Chris Davis

Professional: Mike Jubb

Directions: 5 miles west of Cromer. From Cromer take the A149 (Sheringham). Travel a quarter of a mile beyond Sheringham and the entrance is on the right hand side.

Date Founded: 1891

Type of Course: Clifftop

No of Holes: 18

Length: 6495 yds (5995 mtrs)

Par: 70

SSS:	71
Green Fees:	Weekdays: £40.00; Weekends/ Bank Holidays: £45.00
Visitors:	Welcome: Contact Club in advance. Unable to play before 9.30 a.m.
Societies:	Welcome: Contact Club by phone in advance.
Facilities:	Putting Green, Chipping Green, Trolley Hire, Bar, Restaurant, Private Rooms

Accommodation, Food and Drink

Reference numbers below refer to detailed information provided in section 2

Accommodation

The Bay Leaf Guest House, Sheringham, Norfolk NR26 8QY

Tel: 01263 823779

A charming Victorian licensed guest house handy for the seafront and local amenities. Seven twin or double bedrooms, all en-suite, with tv. 308

Virginia Court Hotel, Cromer, Norfolk NR27 0AN

Tel: 01263 512398

Twenty-three delightful, spacious en-suite bedrooms in a late-Victorian hotel two minutes from the town centre and the sea. 324

Birch House, 34 Cabbell Road, Cromer, Norfolk NR27 9HX

Tel: 01263 512521

Eight comfortably furnished bedrooms - non-smoking, most en-suite - in a Victorian house a short walk from the sea. Optional evening meal.

Rosedale Farm Guesthouse, Holt Road, Weybourne, Norfolk NR25 7TS

Tel: 01263 588788

En-suite bedrooms, breakfast and evening meals in a flint-and-brick farmhouse with a walled garden and heated swimming pool.

The John H. Stracey, Briston, Melton Constable, Norfolk NR24 2JA

Tel: 01263 860891

Great food and real ales bring the crowds to a grand old hostelry on the edge of the village. B&B also available. 319

The Shannocks Hotel & Restaurant, Sheringham, Norfolk NR26 8JP

Tel: 01263 820368

12 en-suite bedrooms in a modernised Victorian seafront hotel. Restaurant with à la carte menu and carvery. 326

Highfields Guest House, Sheringham, Norfolk NR26 8LN

Tel: 01263 825524

Eight en-suite bedrooms in a comfortable, spotless guesthouse in sight of Sheringham Golf Course. No smoking. Dinner by arrangement. 315

Parsons Pleasure, Church Street, Northrepps, Cromer, Norfolk NR27 0LG

Tel/Fax: 01263 579691

Tranquil village setting for a delightful country inn offering fine food and eight en-suite letting bedrooms, including three luxury suites.

The Dales Country House Hotel, Upper Sheringham, Norfolk NR26 8TJ

Tel: 01263 824555

A handsome listed building in a lovely parkland setting provides spacious accommodation in 18 superb bedrooms. Fine restaurant. 322

Food and Drink

The Jolly Sailors, Brancaster Staithe, Norfolk PE31 8BJ

Tel: 01485 210314

Delightful family-run 18th-century free house on the North Norfolk coast. All-day snack menu and main menu. Local seafood. 345

Virginia Court Hotel, Cromer, Norfolk NR27 0AN

Tel: 01263 512398

Twenty-three delightful, spacious en-suite bedrooms in a late-Victorian hotel two minutes from the town centre and the sea. 324

The John H. Stracey, Briston, Melton Constable, Norfolk NR24 2JA

Tel: 01263 860891

Great food and real ales bring the crowds to a grand old hostelry on the edge of the village. B&B also available. 319

The Shannocks Hotel & Restaurant, Sheringham, Norfolk NR26 8JP

Tel: 01263 820368

12 en-suite bedrooms in a modernised Victorian seafront hotel. Restaurant with à la carte menu and carvery. 326

Parsons Pleasure, Church Street, Northrepps, Cromer, Norfolk NR27 0LG

Tel/Fax: 01263 579691

Tranquil village setting for a delightful country inn offering fine food and eight en-suite letting bedrooms, including three luxury suites.

The Dales Country House Hotel, Upper Sheringham, Norfolk NR26 8TJ

Tel: 01263 824555

A handsome listed building in a lovely parkland setting provides spacious accommodation in 18 superb bedrooms. Fine restaurant. 322

Sprowston Park

Wroxham Road, Sprowston, Norwich,
Norfolk NR7 8RP

Tel: 01603 254290 Fax: 01603 788884

Sec/Manager: Jason O'Malley

Professional: Guy Ireson

Directions: 2 miles north east of Norwich. From Norwich City centre take the A1151 (Sprowston). On the outskirts of Sprowston the entrance is on the right hand side on the Wroxham Road.

Date Founded: 1986

Type of Course: Parkland

No of Holes: 18

Length: 5763 yds (5319 mtrs)

Par: 70

SSS: 68

Green Fees: Weekdays: £21.00; Weekends/ Bank Holidays: £27.00

Visitors: Welcome: Contact Club in advance by phone

Societies: Welcome: Contact Club in advance

Facilities: Putting Green, Chipping Green, Driving Range, Club Hire, Trolley Hire, Buggy Hire, Bar, Restaurant

Accommodation, Food and Drink

Reference numbers below refer to detailed information provided in section 2

Accommodation

The Blue Boar, Sprowston, Norfolk NR7 8RL

Tel: 01603 426802

Comfortable overnight accommodation and fine food in a pub of style and character. 325

The Norfolk Mead Hotel, Coltishall, Norfolk NR12 7DN

Tel: 01603 737531 Fax: 01603 737521

An impressive Georgian manor house with characterful en-suite bedrooms and a lovely setting in grounds running down to the River Bure. 314

Buxton Mill Hotel, Buxton, Norfolk NR10 5JF

Tel: 01603 278194 Fax: 01603 279332

A mill on the River Bure has been converted to a fine hotel with 14 en-suite bedrooms, a candlelit restaurant and a bar. 316

The Old Rectory Hotel, Crostwick, Norwich, Norfolk NR12 7BG

Tel: 01603 738513 Fax: 01603 738712

18th century country rectory with a modern bedroom block and lovely gardens. Thirteen well-appointed en-suite rooms; two restaurants. 320

Overcliff Lodge, Cromer Road, Mundesley, Norfolk NR11 8DB

Tel/Fax: 01263 720016

Four delightful en-suite bedrooms in a smart white house on the coast road down from Cromer. Excellent home cooking.

Ostend Place Chalet Park, Ostend Place, Walcott, Norfolk NR12 0NJ

Tel: 01692 650462

The park comprises three self-catering flats in the house; eight chalets on the seafront; and a bungalow sleeping six.

Golden Beach Holiday Centre, Sea Palling, Norfolk NR12 0AL

Tel: 01692 598269

Luxury holiday caravans in a well-run centre nestling beneath a bank of dunes just back from the sea. Full on-site facilities. 303

Hill House Guest House, Hillside Road, Thorpe St Andrew, Norfolk NR7 0QS

Tel: 01603 432165

Three en-suite bedrooms in an Edwardian house overlooking the River Yare. Bed & Breakfast. 2 miles east of Norwich.

Food and Drink

The Blue Boar, Sprowston, Norfolk NR7 8RL
Tel: 01603 426802
Comfortable overnight accommodation and fine food in a pub of style and character. 325

The Branford Arms, Sprowston, Norwich, Norfolk NR3 4QD
Tel: 01603 427488
A 100-year-old pub of great character, serving generous helpings of good-value home-cooked food. Available Wed-Fri evenings, all day Sat and Sun lunch. 343

The Red Lion Inn, Coltishall, Norfolk NR12 7DW
Tel: 01603 737402
300-year-old pub with cosy beamed bars, special real ales and an all-day menu of home-cooked food. 329

The Norfolk Mead Hotel, Coltishall, Norfolk NR12 7DN
Tel: 01603 737531 Fax: 01603 737521
An impressive Georgian manor house with characterful en-suite bedrooms and a lovely setting in grounds running down to the River Bure. 314

Buxton Mill Hotel, Buxton, Norfolk NR10 5JF
Tel: 01603 278194 Fax: 01603 279332
A mill on the River Bure has been converted to a fine hotel with 14 en-suite bedrooms, a candlelit restaurant and a bar. 316

The Old Rectory Hotel, Crostwick, Norwich, Norfolk NR12 7BG
Tel: 01603 738513 Fax: 01603 738712
18th century country rectory with a modern bedroom block and lovely gardens. Thirteen well-appointed en-suite rooms; two restaurants. 320

Pebbles Country Inn, Happisburgh, Norfolk NR12 0RD
Tel: 01622 651183
Home-cooked English fare keeps visitors happy in a village pub on the B1159 coast road. Local accommodation available. 327

Swaffham

Cley Road, Swaffham, Norfolk PE37 8AE

Tel: 01760 721621 Fax: 01760 721611

Sec/Manager:	Robin Parry
Professional:	Peter Field
Directions:	1 mile south west of Swaffham. From Swaffham centre take the B road signed Cockley Cley. The entrance is on the right hand side three quarters of a mile from the outskirts.
Date Founded:	1922
Type of Course:	Heathland
No of Holes:	9 (18 from summer 2001)
Length:	6252 yds (5771 mtrs)
Par:	72
SSS:	70
Green Fees:	Weekdays: £20.00
Visitors:	Welcome: Contact Club in advance unable to play at weekends.
Societies:	Welcome: Contact Club in advance.
Facilities:	Putting Green, Driving Range, Bar, Restaurant, Practice Area

Accommodation, Food and Drink

Reference numbers below refer to detailed information provided in section 2

Accommodation

Congham Hall, Grimston, King's Lynn, Norfolk PE32 1AH
Tel: 01485 600250 Fax: 01485 601191
One of the county's top hotels, an elegant Georgian manor set in 30 lovely acres. Seventeen exclusive bedrooms; superb restaurant. 337

The Crown Hotel, Watton, Norfolk IP25 6AB

Tel: 01953 882375 Fax: 01953 884120

Good food and comfortable overenight accommodation in a handsome old coaching inn on the main street. 335

The Longham White Horse, Longham, Dereham, Norfolk NR19 2RD

Tel: 01362 687464

Spick-and-span accommodation and good-value eating in a popular village pub with a pleasant garden. 330

Scarningdale Country Guest House, Scarning, East Dereham, Norfolk NR19 2QN

Tel: 01362 687269 Fax: 01362 687378

Delightful secluded country house with three en-suite bedrooms and five self-catering cottages. Indoor pool. Lovely gardens. www.scarningdale.co.uk

Phoenix Hotel, Dereham, Norfolk NR19 1DL

Tel: 01362 692276 Fax: 01362 691752

Twenty-two en-suite bedrooms in a smartly refurbished hotel with a popular seven-days-a-week restaurant.

Lydney House Hotel, Swaffham, Norfolk PE37 7QS

Tel: 01760 723355 Fax: 01760 721410

Nine comfortable en-suite bedrooms in a Georgian hotel near the centre of Swaffham. Bar and restaurant menus. Garden. 305

Food and Drink

Congham Hall, Grimston, King's Lynn, Norfolk PE32 1AH

Tel: 01485 600250 Fax: 01485 601191

One of the county's top hotels, an elegant Georgian manor set in 30 lovely acres. Seventeen exclusive bedrooms; superb restaurant. 337

The Gate Inn, Middleton, King's Lynn, Norfolk PE32 1RW

Tel: 01553 840518

A traditional country pub with loads of natural charm and cheer. Meals served in bar or restaurant. Beer garden. Pool table. 347

The Crown Hotel, Watton, Norfolk IP25 6AB

Tel: 01953 882375 Fax: 01953 884120

Good food and comfortable overenight accommodation in a handsome old coaching inn on the main street. 335

The Longham White Horse, Longham, Dereham, Norfolk NR19 2RD

Tel: 01362 687464

Spick-and-span accommodation and good-value eating in a popular village pub with a pleasant garden. 330

Phoenix Hotel, Dereham, Norfolk NR19 1DL

Tel: 01362 692276 Fax: 01362 691752

Twenty-two en-suite bedrooms in a smartly refurbished hotel with a popular seven-days-a-week restaurant.

Lydney House Hotel, Swaffham, Norfolk PE37 7QS

Tel: 01760 723355 Fax: 01760 721410

Nine comfortable en-suite bedrooms in a Georgian hotel near the centre of Swaffham. Bar and restaurant menus. Garden. 305

Thetford

Brandon Road, Thetford, Norfolk IP24 3NE

Tel: 01842 752258

Sec/Manager:	Sally Redpass
Professional:	Gary Kitley
Directions:	2 miles west of Thetford on the Thetford outskirts From the junction of the A11 and the A134 take the B1107 Brandon Road. The entrance is about 100 yards on the left hand side.
Date Founded:	1912
Type of Course:	Brackland
No of Holes:	18
Length:	6849 yds (6322 mtrs)
Par:	72
SSS:	73

Green Fees: Weekdays: £33.00
Visitors: Welcome: Contact Club in advance unable to play at weekends
Societies: Welcome: Contact Club in advance by telephone.
Facilities: Putting Green, Chipping Green, Practice Ground, Trolley Hire, Bar, Restaurant

Accommodation, Food and Drink

Reference numbers below refer to detailed information provided in section 2

Accommodation

The Crown Hotel, Watton, Norfolk IP25 6AB

Tel: 01953 882375 Fax: 01953 884120

Good food and comfortable overenight accommodation in a handsome old coaching inn on the main street. 335

The Priory Hotel, Bury St Edmunds, Suffolk IP32 6EH

Tel: 01284 766181 Fax: 01284 767604

Period charm and elegance in a comfortable 39-bedroom hotel with modern amenities and a fine à la carte restaurant. 402

Wagner Cottage, The Street, Walsham-le-Willows, Bury St Edmunds, Suffolk IP33 3AA

Tel: 01359 259380

Three delightful bedrooms in a Grade ll listed building with a walled garden opposite the village church. Bed & Breakfast.

The Old Bull, The Street, Barton Mills, Bury St Edmunds, Suffolk IP27 6AE

Tel: 01638 713230

Twenty double bedrooms in an extended old inn by the A11 north of Newmarket and west of Bury.

Food and Drink

The Crown Hotel, Watton, Norfolk IP25 6AB

Tel: 01953 882375 Fax: 01953 884120

Good food and comfortable overenight accommodation in a handsome old coaching inn on the main street. 335

The Nags Head, East Harling, Norfolk NR16 2AD

Tel: 01953 718140

Village pub in traditional style, serving an extensive range of splendid home-cooked food. On the B1111 south of Attleborough. 317

The Priory Hotel, Bury St Edmunds, Suffolk IP32 6EH

Tel: 01284 766181 Fax: 01284 767604

Period charm and elegance in a comfortable 39-bedroom hotel with modern amenities and a fine à la carte restaurant. 402

The Cock, The Street, Stanton, Bury St Edmunds, Suffolk IP31 2BP

Tel: 01359 250230

Cheerful pub with beams and open fires, pool, darts, monthly quiz. Restaurant and bar menus - steaks a speciality. No food Mon evening.

The Old Bull, The Street, Barton Mills, Bury St Edmunds, Suffolk IP27 6AE

Tel: 01638 713230

Twenty double bedrooms in an extended old inn by the A11 north of Newmarket and west of Bury.

The Bell Inn, Bury Road, Kennett, Nr Newmarket, Suffolk CB8 7PP

Tel: 01638 750286

Exposed beams and cheerful open fires in an atmospheric old coaching inn at the village crossroads. 60-cover restaurant.

Wensum Valley

Beech Avenue, Taverham, Norwich, Norfolk NR8 6HP

Tel: 01603 261012 Fax: 01603 261664

Just five miles north west of the historic city of Norwich at Taverham lies Wensum Valley Hotel, Golf and Country Club set in 240 acres of beautiful Norfolk countryside. Although comparatively new – it was established in 1990 - Wensum Valley shows a remarkable maturity and offers first class golf on two courses, the 18-hole Valley Course and the nine-hole **Wensum**, both constructed on free-draining soil making them all year round layouts.

The Valley, which measures 6,172 yards with a par of 71, has the testing 12th hole, a par four

of 420 yards, played from an elevated tee some 60 feet above the fairway which requires a good tee shot to clear the well placed avenue of oak trees. The nine-hole **Wensum Course** boasts two par fives – the first and the ninth - each requiring accuracy and distance from the tee and is constructed on the same free draining soil as the Valley. The nine can be played twice to a par of 70 while guests are also invited to play the club's other nine-hole circuit in the nearby village of Mattishall, just six miles away.

The Wensum Valley club also boasts a covered floodlit driving range for those wanting to improve their swing, while a practice green and bunkers provide an ideal opportunity to warm up before a round. The hotel, which adjoins the clubhouse, has 39 en suite bedrooms, many with spectacular views over the valley and the golf course. All bedrooms have full facilities, while there are A La Carte and table d'hôte menus plus a daily specials board provided by a team of first class chefs.

If your taste doesn't stretch to golf, then you can sample the leisure club with its indoor swimming pool, spa, sauna and steam room as well as a fully equipped gymnasium. Fishing is also available on a mile and a half of the River Wensum, which borders the golf course, as well as splendid walks in the nearby Ringland Hills and the Wensum Valley itself.

Sec/Manager:	Martin Collins
Professional:	Peter Whittle
Directions:	7 miles north west of Norwich. From Norwich take the A1067 (Taverham). From Ringland Road on the western outskirts the entrance is on the left hand side .
Date Founded:	1993
Visitors:	Welcome: Apart from Sunday mornings
Societies:	Welcome: Contact in advance
Facilities:	Putting Green, Chipping Green, Club Hire, Trolley Hire, Buggy Hire, Bar, Restaurant, Driving Range

The Valley

Type of Course:	Parkland
No of Holes:	18
Length:	6172 yds (5697 mtrs)
Par:	71
SSS:	69
Green Fees:	Weekdays: £18.00; Weekends/ Bank Holidays: £18.00

Wensum

Type of Course:	Parkland
No of Holes:	9
Length:	5812 yds (5364 mtrs)
Par:	70
SSS:	69
Green Fees:	Weekdays: £18.00; Weekends/ Bank Holidays: £18.00

Accommodation, Food and Drink

Reference numbers below refer to detailed information provided in section 2

Accommodation

The Ship Hotel, Gorleston-on-Sea, Norfolk NR31 6DJ

Tel/Fax: 01493 662746

A few yards from the seafront, The Ship is a family run hotel with eight cosy en-suite bedrooms. B&B & dinner. 336

Buxton Mill Hotel, Buxton, Norfolk NR10 5JF

Tel: 01603 278194 Fax: 01603 279332

A mill on the River Bure has been converted to a fine hotel with 14 en-suite bedrooms, a candlelit restaurant and a bar. 316

The Old Rectory Hotel, Crostwick, Norwich, Norfolk NR12 7BG

Tel: 01603 738513 Fax: 01603 738712

18th century country rectory with a modern bedroom block and lovely gardens. Thirteen well-appointed en-suite rooms; two restaurants. 320

The Dales Country House Hotel, Upper Sheringham, Norfolk NR26 8TJ

Tel: 01263 824555

A handsome listed building in a lovely parkland setting provides spacious accommodation in 18 superb bedrooms. Fine restaurant. 322

Wensum Country Hotel, Great Witchingham, Norwich, Norfolk NR9 5QP

Tel: 01603 872288

A haven of comfort and fine food in the heart of the Norfolk countryside. 36 well-appointed bedrooms; extensive leisure facilities. 312

Wensum Valley Hotel, Taverham, Norwich, Norfolk NR8 6HP

Tel: 01603 261012 Fax: 01603 261664

Hotel, golf and country club set in 240 acres of lovely countryside. 39 en-suite bedrooms, restaurant, golf courses, leisure club, fishing. 307

Food and Drink

The Ship Hotel, Gorleston-on-Sea, Norfolk NR31 6DJ

Tel/Fax: 01493 662746

A few yards from the seafront, The Ship is a family run hotel with eight cosy en-suite bedrooms. B&B & dinner. 336

Buxton Mill Hotel, Buxton, Norfolk NR10 5JF

Tel: 01603 278194 Fax: 01603 279332

A mill on the River Bure has been converted to a fine hotel with 14 en-suite bedrooms, a candlelit restaurant and a bar. 316

The Old Rectory Hotel, Crostwick, Norwich, Norfolk NR12 7BG

Tel: 01603 738513 Fax: 01603 738712

18th century country rectory with a modern bedroom block and lovely gardens. Thirteen well-appointed en-suite rooms; two restaurants. 320

The Dales Country House Hotel, Upper Sheringham, Norfolk NR26 8TJ

Tel: 01263 824555

A handsome listed building in a lovely parkland setting provides spacious accommodation in 18 superb bedrooms. Fine restaurant. 322

The Victoria Inn, Hockering, Nr Norwich, Norfolk NR20 3HL

Tel: 01603 880507

A 1930s village pub with a cosy eating area and a beer garden. Home-cooked food; good beers and wines. 333

Wensum Country Hotel, Great Witchingham, Norwich, Norfolk NR9 5QP

Tel: 01603 872288

A haven of comfort and fine food in the heart of the Norfolk countryside. 36 well-appointed bedrooms; extensive leisure facilities. 312

The Pickwick, Norwich, Norfolk NR2 3AD

Tel: 01603 628155

A Georgian pub-restaurant three minutes from the city centre. Snack and à la carte menus, Sunday roasts. Good wines. 302

Wensum Valley Hotel, Taverham, Norwich, Norfolk NR8 6HP

Tel: 01603 261012 Fax: 01603 261664

Hotel, golf and country club set in 240 acres of lovely countryside. 39 en-suite bedrooms, restaurant, golf courses, leisure club, fishing. 307

Weston Park

Weston Longville, Norwich, Norfolk NR9 5JW

Tel: 01603 872363 Fax: 01603 873040

Sec/Manager: Richard Wright

Professional: Michael Few

Directions: 9 miles north west of Norwich. From Norwich take

the A1067 (Lenwade). Turn left before village and after three quarters of a mile turn left into Moreton Lane. The entrance is on the left hand side.

Date Founded:	1993
Type of Course:	Parkland
No of Holes:	18
Length:	6609 yds (6100mtrs)
Par:	72
SSS:	72
Green Fees:	Weekdays: £28.00; Weekends/ Bank Holidays: £33.00
Visitors:	Welcome: Contact Club by phone in advance
Societies:	Welcome: Contact Club by phone in advance
Facilities:	Putting Green, Chipping Green, Practice Ground, Trolley Hire, Buggy Hire, Bar, Restaurant

Accommodation, Food and Drink

Reference numbers below refer to detailed information provided in section 2

Accommodation

Virginia Court Hotel, Cromer, Norfolk NR27 0AN

Tel: 01263 512398

Twenty-three delightful, spacious en-suite bedrooms in a late-Victorian hotel two minutes from the town centre and the sea. 324

Birch House, 34 Cabbell Road, Cromer, Norfolk NR27 9HX

Tel: 01263 512521

Eight comfortably furnished bedrooms - non-smoking, most en-suite - in a Victorian house a short walk from the sea. Optional evening meal.

The Shannocks Hotel & Restaurant, Sheringham, Norfolk NR26 8JP

Tel: 01263 820368

12 en-suite bedrooms in a modernised Victorian seafront hotel. Restaurant with à la carte menu and carvery. 326

The Ship Hotel, Gorleston-on-Sea, Norfolk NR31 6DJ

Tel/Fax: 01493 662746

A few yards from the seafront, The Ship is a family run hotel with eight cosy en-suite bedrooms. B&B & dinner. 336

Wensum Country Hotel, Great Witchingham, Norwich, Norfolk NR9 5QP

Tel: 01603 872288

A haven of comfort and fine food in the heart of the Norfolk countryside. 36 well-appointed bedrooms; extensive leisure facilities. 312

Wensum Valley Hotel, Taverham, Norwich, Norfolk NR8 6HP

Tel: 01603 261012 Fax: 01603 261664

Hotel, golf and country club set in 240 acres of lovely countryside. 39 en-suite bedrooms, restaurant, golf courses, leisure club, fishing. 307

Food and Drink

Virginia Court Hotel, Cromer, Norfolk NR27 0AN

Tel: 01263 512398

Twenty-three delightful, spacious en-suite bedrooms in a late-Victorian hotel two minutes from the town centre and the sea. 324

The Shannocks Hotel & Restaurant, Sheringham, Norfolk NR26 8JP

Tel: 01263 820368

12 en-suite bedrooms in a modernised Victorian seafront hotel. Restaurant with à la carte menu and carvery. 326

The Ship Hotel, Gorleston-on-Sea, Norfolk NR31 6DJ

Tel/Fax: 01493 662746

A few yards from the seafront, The Ship is a family run hotel with eight cosy en-suite bedrooms. B&B & dinner. 336

The Victoria Inn, Hockering, Nr Norwich, Norfolk NR20 3HL

Tel: 01603 880507

A 1930s village pub with a cosy eating area and a beer garden. Home-cooked food; good beers and wines. 333

Wensum Country Hotel, Great Witchingham, Norwich, Norfolk NR9 5QP

Tel: 01603 872288

A haven of comfort and fine food in the heart of the Norfolk countryside. 36 well-appointed bedrooms; extensive leisure facilities. 312

Wensum Valley Hotel, Taverham, Norwich, Norfolk NR8 6HP

Tel: 01603 261012 Fax: 01603 261664

Hotel, golf and country club set in 240 acres of lovely countryside. 39 en-suite bedrooms,

SUFFOLK

A recent survey held among 3,000 Suffolk residents revealed that the county's most appealing feature was its peaceful and quiet nature. Many other facets were considered but virtually half the population felt that the tranquillity of life was the redeeming factor. That would seem an apt description of Suffolk and the reason why many of those living in the county swapped the hustle and bustle of London for the calmer waters of the East Coast.

Artist, Flatford Mill

It was that tranquillity that inspired artists such as John Constable, Thomas Gainsborough and more recently Sir Alfred Munnings to produce most of their masterpieces. Indeed, the southern part of Suffolk and northern Essex around the River Stour is known as Constable country. He was born at East Bergholt, which is a major tourist attraction as are the sites along the river, especially Flatford Mill, where much of his work was created.

Gainsborough was born in Sudbury and gained a reputation as a portrait painter in Ipswich before moving further afield, while Mendham in the north of the county was where Munnings entered the world in 1878 becoming one of the great sporting painters. He was to become President of the Royal Academy just after the last war but exited that august body in somewhat controversial terms after some abrasive comments about modern art.

It doesn't stop with that talented trio. Suffolk has a long association with the arts through such writers as Rider Haggard and Rupert Brooke, while the composer Benjamin Britten lived here and with Peter Pears established the Aldeburgh music festival in the town and at the nearby Snape Maltings. So Suffolk has much going for it whatever your interest.

The west of the county may not be quite so quiet especially around Newmarket, the headquarters of horse racing in Britain. On race days it is a buzz of activity and none more so than when the two classics, the 1,000 and 2,000 Guineas, are run. The town is also home to the Jockey Club, while among the many stables dotted around the area you can watch many of the finest thoroughbreds in the world being put through their paces every day over the gallops. The National Stud is also situated next to the racecourse, south west of the town, and is worth a visit along with the National Horseracing Museum, Tattersalls, where thoroughbred

House in the Clouds, Thorpeness

Heveningham Hall

sales are held, and the British Racing School where jockeys are taught their skills.

Not far away is Bury St Edmunds, named after St Edmund, England's patron saint until being replaced by St George. St Edmund, born in Nuremburg in 841, became the last king of East Anglia. He was a devout Christian who refused to deny his faith and was subsequently beheaded by the Danes. The story goes that although his body was recovered, his head went missing for 40 days until discovered being protected between the paws of a wolf. To commemorate the deed, the town's crest, and that of the golf club, depicts a wolf protecting a man's head. While in the town you may care to refresh yourself at The Nutshell, claimed to be the smallest pub in Britain.

The central part of Suffolk is also steeped in history and possesses many interesting places to visit. Many of the villages in this area have changed little down the years with architecture ranging from Tudor-style country houses to ancient timber-framed buildings. Stowmarket is the largest town in the area and as the name suggests was an old market and industrial town, as is the nearby Needham Market. Stowmarket stands on the River Gipping, which was a thoroughfare for trade in past centuries. These days the avid traveller can explore the Gipping Valley River Walk all the way to Ipswich. The town also houses the Museum of East Anglian Life where you can check the history of the area and visit several historic buildings that have been moved from other parts of the county.

This area is also noted for its splendid windmills and water mills. In former days, no picture of Suffolk would have been complete without an example of these wonderful structures and although their numbers have dwindled in recent times, there are still around 20 of each in full working order.

Beach, Aldeburgh

Suffolk has a number of castles and one of the finest is at Framlingham, which sits on a hill, overlooking the town. Built in the 12th Century, it was the home of the Dukes of Norfolk until they left for Sussex in 1635. Splendid views over the town and countryside are available from the battlements and from the 13 towers, nine of which are accessible.

As with Norfolk, the coastal region of Suffolk is a holiday playground in the summer. From Lowestoft, England's most easterly town, to Felixstowe, there are a number of popular and welcoming resorts such as Southwold, Aldeburgh, Thorpeness, Orford and Woodbridge, all of, which offer good sailing, particularly on the Rivers Blyth and Deben, while the area is one of the most rewarding for bird-watchers. The Minsmere Bird Sanctuary near the village of Westleton, offers a perfect habitat and over 100 species nest there, including the rare Avocet. The Suffolk Coastal Path runs along the foreshore but much erosion has and is still taking place in this area. Thorpeness was created as a holiday village in the early part of the 20th Century by architect, barrister and playwright Glencairn Stuart Ogilvie as a place for relaxation and healthy family fun. He built mock-Tudor houses, cottages around the centrepiece, a shallow boating and pleasure lake called the Meare plus his ultimate folly, the House in the Clouds, a dwelling perched on top of an 85ft water tower as a form of disguise and which offers somewhere unique to stay. The village of Dunwich is testament to this. Once the capital of East Anglia, it was a thriving community back in the 13th Century, a large port and the centre of shipbuilding. There were also many monasteries and churches but the relentless power of the sea slowly silted the harbour and now, some 700 years later, virtually everything lies beneath the waves. The story of the town can be studied at the Dunwich Museum while locals say that if you hear the tolling of a submerged church bell a storm is threatening.

The Maltings, Snape

Kersey Ford

In golfing terms, the county has much to offer. There are a number of superb coastal courses which, perhaps not possessing the fame or reputation of those elsewhere in Britain are nonetheless gems in their own right. **Aldeburgh**, **Thorpeness**, **Felixstowe Ferry** and **Woodbridge** have a certain Scottish feel about them, as do the Ipswich layouts of **Purdis Heath** and **Rushmere**. Then there are the more inland attractions of **Stowmarket**, **Bury St Edmunds** and **Stoke by Nayland** to whet the appetite in a different sort of way but all without exception hold a challenge that is a joy to meet even if it is not mastered.

The Suffolk Golfing Union was formed in June 1924 when representatives from nine clubs met in Ipswich, and within a month officers had been elected, rules and regulations drawn up, and competitions outlined. By the end of 2000, 10 clubs had celebrated their centenaries, while the county's oldest club is Felixstowe Ferry, formed in 1880, followed by Aldeburgh and Southwold four years later.

There haven't been too many top golfers coming out of Suffolk but that by no means detracts from the county's fairway appeal or its hospitality. Indeed, there are many places to play and stay while the cuisine with its locally caught fish and homemade delicacies should not be missed.

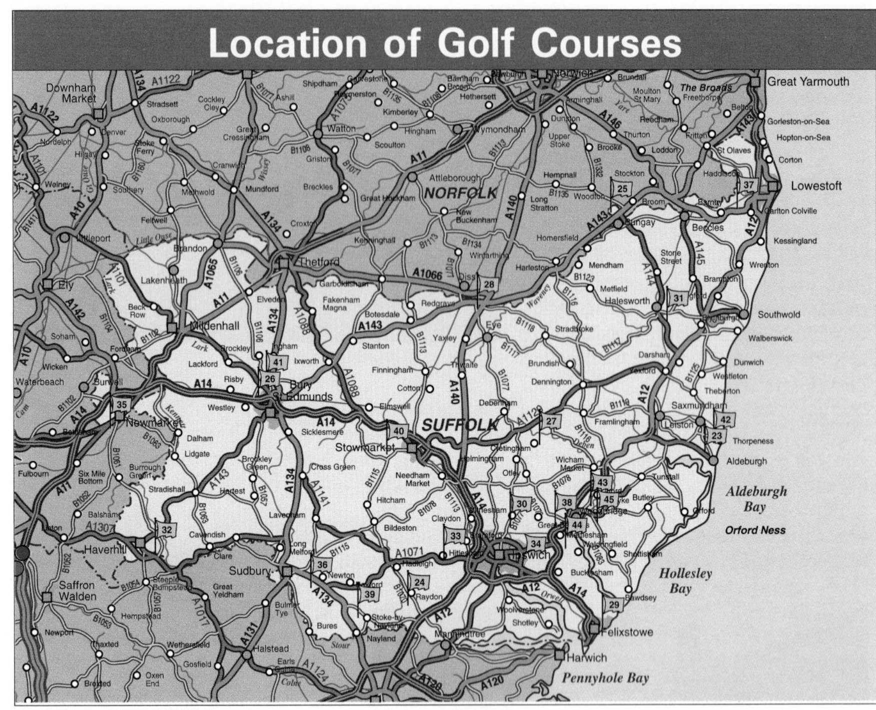
Location of Golf Courses
Downham Market
A1122
Stradsett
Oxborough
Cockley Cley
Shipdham
Barnham Broom
Hethersett
Norwich
Brundall
Moulton St Mary
The Broads
Freethorpe
Great Yarmouth
Gorleston-on-Sea
Hopton-on-Sea
Corton
Lowestoft
Denver
Nordelph
Hilgay
Stoke Ferry
Great Cressingham
Watton
Kimberley
Hingham
Wymondham
Scoulton
Arminghall
Upper Stoke
Dunston
Brooke
Thurton
Loddon
Reedham
St Olaves
Welney
Southery
Methwold
Mundford
Cranwich
Griston
Breckles
Great Hockham
Attleborough
NORFOLK
A11
Hempnall
Stockton
Long Stratton
Broome
Bungay
Beccles
Carlton Colville
Kessingland
Feltwell
Littleport
Brandon
Croxton
Kenninghall
New Buckenham
Homersfield
Stone Street
Wrentham
Ely
Lakenheath
Thetford
A1066
Diss
Harleston
Mendham
Metfield
Halesworth
Southwold
Walberswick
Beck Row
Mildenhall
Elveden
Fakenham Magna
Botesdale
Redgrave
Eye
Stradbroke
Soham
Wicken
Waterbeach
Burwell
Fordham
Lackford
Risby
Brockley
Ingham
Ixworth
Stanton
Yaxley
Thwaite
Brundish
Darsham
Dunwich
Westleton
Theberton
A14
Bury St Edmunds
Finningham
Cotton
Dennington
Saxmundham
Leiston
Thorpeness
Aldeburgh
Newmarket
Westley
Elmswell
SUFFOLK
Framlingham
Dalham
Lidgate
Sicklesmere
Stowmarket
Cretingham
Helmingham
Otley
Wickham Market
Tunstall
Fulbourn
Six Mile Bottom
Burrough Green
Brockley Green
Cross Green
Needham Market
Stradishall
Hartest
Hitcham
Aldeburgh Bay
Orford Ness
Balsham
Lavenham
Bildeston
Claydon
Haverhill
Cavendish
Clare
Long Melford
A1071
Hadleigh
Ipswich
Butley
Orford
Shottisham
Bucklesham
Sudbury
Newton
Raydon
Hollesley Bay
Saffron Walden
Steeple Bumpstead
Great Yeldham
Bulmer Tye
Stoke-by-Nayland
Nayland
Bures
Shotley
Felixstowe
Newport
Thaxted
Hempstead
Wethersfield
Gosfield
Halstead
Manningtree
Harwich
Pennyhole Bay
Oxen End
Earls Colne
Bardfield

Aldeburgh

Saxmundham Road, Aldeburgh, Suffolk IP15 5PE

Tel: 01728 452890 Fax: 01728 452937

Any course that can claim an Open champion as its designer has a certain pedigree. One that has designs on two is special. But a club that has been crafted by three Open champions has to be up there with the best, which accurately describes Aldeburgh. Horace Hutchinson, twice Amateur champion before the turn of the 20th Century, wrote: "Among all the British golf links, it would be hard to find half a dozen that can compare with this course, whether judged by its proximity to the sea, salubrious air, lovely scenery, or (most important of all) by the natural advantages of turf and ground, which form an ideal spot for the pursuit of the Royal and Ancient game under the most enjoyable conditions." Those words were penned three years after the Aldeburgh club was formed in 1884 but they could have been written yesterday.

Occupying a magnificent heathland site, it is a gem that could easily be transferred to the heart of Scotland and not look out of place. The first Open champion to play a part in Aldeburgh's history was Willie Fernie, then of Felixstowe, who with John Thomson from Wimbledon, was invited to design the first course on heathland rented by J G Skelton Anderson, a Scot and husband of Elizabeth Garrett Anderson, the country's first woman doctor. In true Scottish style, all the holes were named, not numbered, the whole course measured 4,719 yards, and Fernie's brother Tom became the first professional. However, when the one of the joint landlords died in 1905, the other was not interested in golf so moves were made to acquire a new site.

The benefactor was Thomas Vernon Wentworth, Lord of the Manor, who came to the rescue. Cue the second and third Open champions, J H Taylor and Willie Park Junior, who joined forces to design the layout, which is much as it is today. At first glance, Aldeburgh appears somewhat easy until you actually step on to the tee. Then you realise it is anything but. This is particularly evident on the second nine where accuracy is essential as you seek to avoid the brilliant yellow gorse while staying on the rolling fairways, many of which have a links appearance. And the short holes are not an easy touch, even the 127-yard fourth, which has a huge sleepered bunker. When the redesign opened in 1908, it measured 6,105 yards. Today that has been extended to 6,333 and still provides a stern test, as does the bunkerless nine hole River Course that offers a contrast to the main battleground.

Sec/Manager: I M Simpson

Professional: Keith Preston

Directions: 1 mile north west of Aldeburgh. From Aldeburgh centre take the A1094 (Saxmundham). The entrance is on the right hand side 200 yards after Linden Road.

Date Founded: 1880

Visitors: Welcome: Contact Club in advance by telephone.

Societies: Welcome: Contact In advance in writing.

Facilities: Putting Green, Chipping Green, Club Hire, Trolley Hire, Bar, Restaurant

Aldeburgh

Type of Course: Maritime Heathland

No of Holes: 18

Length: 6323 yds (5836 mtrs)

Par: 68

SSS: 71

Green Fees: Weekdays: £45.00; Weekends/ Bank Holidays: £60.00

River Course

Type of Course: Parkland

No of Holes: 9

Length: 2114 yds (1951 mtrs)

Par: 32

SSS: 61

Green Fees: Weekdays: £12.00; Weekends/ Bank Holidays: £15.00

Accommodation, Food and Drink

Reference numbers below refer to detailed information provided in section 2

Accommodation

Ocean House, 25 Crag Path, Aldeburgh, Suffolk IP15 5BS

Tel: 01728 452094

Characterful Bed & Breakfast accommodation in a Victorian house just a stone's throw from the beach. Excellent breakfasts. No smoking.

The Railway Inn, Leiston Road, Aldeburgh, Suffolk IP15 5PP

Tel: 01728 453864

Food and accommodation in a long-established

pub on a roundabout at the top of the town. Darts, big-screen tv. 413

The Mill Inn, Market Cross Place, Aldeburgh, Suffolk IP15 5BJ

Tel: 01728 452563

16th century pub on the seafront, with 4 letting bedrooms, two bars and a good choice of home-cooked food.

Wentworth Hotel, Aldeburgh, Suffolk IP15 5BD

Tel: 01728 452312 Fax: 01728 454343

Owned by the same family for 80 years, the Wentworth offers comfort, elegance and style in its 38 rooms. Good food. Seafront location. 408

Thorpeness Hotel & Golf Club, Thorpeness, Suffolk IP16 4NH

Tel: 01728 452176 Fax: 01728 453868

In the unique holiday village of Thorpeness, a fine hotel with 30 en-suite bedrooms and an adjacent golf course and Country Club. 414

The Beeches Guest House, 117 High Street, Leiston, Suffolk IP16 4BX

Tel: 01728 832541

A delightful high street guest house with a friendly welcome, five comfortable letting bedrooms and good breakfasts.

The Brudenell Hotel, Aldeburgh, Suffolk IP15 5BU

Tel: 01728 452071 Fax: 01728 454082

A stunning location right on the seafront for the town's top hotel, with 47 spacious bedrooms and a well-regarded restaurant. 417

The Crown and Castle, Orford, Nr Woodbridge, Suffolk IP12 2LJ

Tel: 01394 450205 Fax: 01394 450176

Atmosphere and character aplenty in a handsome old inn by the imposing castle. 18 stylish en-suite bedrooms; super food. 418

The Kings Head Inn, Orford, Suffolk IP12 2LW

Tel: 01394 450271

Authentic 13th century inn with period charm and up-to-date comfort. Three en-suite bedrooms. Snacks and full meals. 411

Food and Drink

The Railway Inn, Leiston Road, Aldeburgh, Suffolk IP15 5PP

Tel: 01728 453864

Food and accommodation in a long-established pub on a roundabout at the top of the town. Darts, big-screen tv. 413

The Mill Inn, Market Cross Place, Aldeburgh, Suffolk IP15 5BJ

Tel: 01728 452563

16th century pub on the seafront, with 4 letting bedrooms, two bars and a good choice of home-cooked food.

Wentworth Hotel, Aldeburgh, Suffolk IP15 5BD

Tel: 01728 452312 Fax: 01728 454343

Owned by the same family for 80 years, the Wentworth offers comfort, elegance and style in its 38 rooms. Good food. Seafront location. 408

The Lighthouse, Aldeburgh, Suffolk IP15 5AU

Tel/Fax: 01728 453377

One of the top restaurants in East Anglia, with a constantly changing menu of mouthwatering dishes using the pick of the catch and the best local suppliers. Book. 404

Thorpeness Hotel & Golf Club, Thorpeness, Suffolk IP16 4NH

Tel: 01728 452176 Fax: 01728 453868

In the unique holiday village of Thorpeness, a fine hotel with 30 en-suite bedrooms and an adjacent golf course and Country Club. 414

The Lion Inn, The Street, Theberton, Nr Leiston, Suffolk IP16 4RU

Tel: 01728 830185

Pretty village public house open every lunchtime and evening. Excellent home-cooked meals. Easily reached from the A12.

The Brudenell Hotel, Aldeburgh, Suffolk IP15 5BU

Tel: 01728 452071 Fax: 01728 454082

A stunning location right on the seafront for the town's top hotel, with 47 spacious bedrooms and a well-regarded restaurant. 417

The Bell Inn, Marlsford, Nr Woodbridge, Suffolk IP13 0AY

Tel: 01728 746242

Fish dishes are the speciality at this charming old thatched country inn on the A12. Log fires, beams, collection of wartime memorabilia. 419

The Castle Inn, Church Street, Framlingham, Suffolk IP13 9BT

Tel: 01728 724801

Home cooking of traditional and more modern dishes in a 16th century inn on the edge of the castle grounds. Soon to expand.

The Crown and Castle, Orford, Nr Woodbridge, Suffolk IP12 2LJ

Tel: 01394 450205 Fax: 01394 450176

Atmosphere and character aplenty in a handsome old inn by the imposing castle. 18 stylish en-suite bedrooms; super food. 418

The Kings Head Inn, Orford, Suffolk IP12 2LW

Tel: 01394 450271

Authentic 13th century inn with period charm and up-to-date comfort. Three en-suite bedrooms. Snacks and full meals. 411

Brett Vale

Noakes Road, Raydon, Ipswich, Suffolk IP7 5LR

Tel: 01473 310718 Fax: 01473 312270

Sec/Manager:	John Reid
Professional:	Robert Taylor
Directions:	9 miles south west of Ipswich. From Ipswich take the A12 (Colchester) and after 5 miles turn right onto the B1070 (Raydon). Turn left in Raydon and the eEntrance is on the right hand side
Date Founded:	1991
Type of Course:	Parkland
No of Holes:	18
Length:	5797 yds (5351 mtrs)
Par:	70
SSS:	69
Green Fees:	Weekdays: £20.00; Weekends/ Bank Holidays: £25.00
Visitors:	Welcome: Contact club in advance
Societies:	Welcome: Contact club in advance
Facilities:	Putting Green, Chipping Green, Driving Range, Club Hire, Trolley Hire, Buggy Hire, Caddy Service, Bar, Restaurant

Accommodation, Food and Drink

Reference numbers below refer to detailed information provided in section 2

Accommodation

The Golden Key, 438 Woodbridge Road, Ipswich, Suffolk IP4 4EN

Tel: 01473 723916

Home cooking and real ales served in a pub a mile east of the town centre Patio garden.

The Golf Hotel, Ipswich, Suffolk IP4 5TR

Tel: 01473 727450

A 100-year-old pub in Elizabethan style, serving an impressive range of snacks and full meals throughout the day. Also eight bedrooms. 407

The Woolpack, Ipswich, Suffolk IP4 2SH

Tel: 01473 253059

A fine old brick-built pub only moments from Ipswich centre but with a 'country' feel. Extensive menu served seven days a week. 406

Stoke by Nayland Club Hotel, Leavenheath, Colchester, Essex CO6 4PZ

Tel: 01206 262836 Fax: 01206 263356

A spacious modern country hotel in 300 acres of rolling countryside. 30 fine bedrooms, restaurant, golf courses, health & fitness centre. 508

Maison Talbooth, Dedham, Essex CO7 6HN

Tel: 01206 322367 Fax: 01206 322752

Ten top-notch en-suite bedrooms in a Victorian country house with superb views. Meals are served in the restaurant Le Talbooth, a short walk away. 504

Food and Drink

Stoke by Nayland Club Hotel, Leavenheath, Colchester, Essex CO6 4PZ

Tel: 01206 262836 Fax: 01206 263356

A spacious modern country hotel in 300 acres of rolling countryside. 30 fine bedrooms, restaurant, golf courses, health & fitness centre. 508

Maison Talbooth, Dedham, Essex CO7 6HN

Tel: 01206 322367 Fax: 01206 322752

Ten top-notch en-suite bedrooms in a Victorian country house with superb views. Meals are served in the restaurant Le Talbooth, a short walk away. 504

The Rose Inn, Thorington Street, Stoke-by-Nayland, Colchester, Essex CO6 4SN

Tel/Fax: 01206 337243

Pub with 50-cover restaurant, large car park and extensive gardens. Outstanding food, particularly seafood, with lots of daily specials. Closed Monday.

The Red Lion, High Street, Bildeston, Ipswich, Suffolk IP7 7EX

Tel: 01449 740476

A charming village pub, deep red outside, deep red with black beams in the bar areas. Food served throughout. Beer garden.

Bungay & Waveney Valley

Outney Common, Bungay, Suffolk NR35 1DS

Tel: 01986 892337 Fax: 01986 892222

As with many other East Anglian clubs, Bungay and Waveney Valley was graced with a 'name' in its early days who was to become famous. In this case it was the Henry Rider Haggard, writer of adventure stories such as *King Solomon's Mines*, *She*, and *Alan Quartermain*. All these were penned in the years prior to his joining the golf club three weeks after its foundation in January 1889. His

later work earned him a knighthood in 1912 for his services to agriculture, while he also served on the club committee, became a Vice-President, and in 1915 the club's President.

Outney Common at Bungay, granted to the town by an early Duke of Norfolk, was a traditional venue for local sport. A form of football was held there while a crowd of 15,000 attended a prize fight in 1817. The annual Bungay races took place there in the 18th and 19th centuries and were held under National Hunt Rules from 1883 to 1956. So it was a natural progression for golf to be played over the Common. Waveney Valley Golf Club was born and a nine-hole course was laid out. It must have been tough to play because after one round Rider Haggard 'earnestly requested' that more of the gorse should be cut. "Have just been obliged to give up playing owing to the loss of all the balls and that with two boys ahead," he wrote.

Rider Haggard became a member of the first Green Committee in 1891 and improvements were forthcoming. In 1901, James Braid, then of Romford, was invited to advise on the layout, which was extended to 18 holes. Two years later, Bob Jacobs, an assistant at Brancaster, was appointed professional and stayed for three years before moving to Bedford. He married there and had a son, Maurice, now known as John Jacobs, the celebrated golf teacher and writer.

In April 1907 the club changed its name to its present title so that visitors could locate it. That would have proved unnecessary if the club had gone out of business in March 1940. Fortunately the sale of National Savings Certificates and a special appeal brought in £86 to solve the financial crisis. It has always occupied the site just outside the town, where the course sits in a horseshoe-shaped loop formed by the River Waveney with plenty of gorse and a mixture of pine and birch trees. Set in only 84 acres of well-drained land, it is a very comfortable course to walk and rarely suffers from excessive water. The greens are quite small and well-protected, and the challenge is therefore in accuracy rather than length. In early spring the course is at its best, with the abundance of gorse in flower and some lovely views over the surrounding marshes. There is a variety of wildlife to distract you from your game, and skylarks can often be heard singing overhead.

Sec/Manager:	Mr Long
Professional:	Nigel Whyte
Directions:	1 mile north west of Bungay. From Bungay take the A144 (North) and turn left onto A143 (Diss). The entrance is on the right hand side.
Date Founded:	1889
Type of Course:	Heathland
No of Holes:	18
Length:	6044 yds (5579 mtrs)
Par:	69
SSS:	69
Green Fees:	Weekdays: £22.00 per round £28.00 per day
Visitors:	Welcome: Contact club in advance Unable to play at weekends
Societies:	Welcome: Contact club in advance in writing
Facilities:	Putting Green, Chipping Green, Trolley Hire, Buggy Hire, Bar, Restaurant, Practice Ground

Accommodation, Food and Drink

Reference numbers below refer to detailed information provided in section 2

Accommodation

Woodlands Farm, The Street, Brundish, Nr Framlingham, Suffolk IP13 8BP

Tel: 01379 384444

Three en-suite bedrooms in a rural farmhouse. Good breakfast using local produce. e-mail: woodlandsfarm@hotmail.com

Tannington Hall, Tannington, Nr Framlingham, Suffolk IP13 7NH

Tel: 01728 628226

Four en-suite bedrooms in a fine country house set in extensive gardens. B&B, dinner by arrangement. Carriage rides.

The Swan Motel, Lodden Road, Gillingham, Beccles, Suffolk NR34 0LD

Tel: 01502 712055 Fax: 01502 711786

14 spick-and-span self-contained apartments in a friendly free house motel with a convivial bar and day-long restaurant. Live music Sunday.

Homelea Guest House, 33 Marine Parade, Lowestoft, Suffolk NR3 3QN

Tel: 01502 511640

Guest house with five double rooms, located on the promenade 50 yards from the sea. Evening meals by arrangement.

The Kings Head Hotel, New Market, Beccles, Suffolk NR34 9HA

Tel: 01502 712147 Fax: 01502 715386

12 en-suite bedrooms in a comfortable town-centre hotel. Busy bars, beer garden, restaurant with steakhouse menu.

Food and Drink

The White Horse, Chedgrave, Norwich, Norfolk NR14 6ND

Tel: 01508 520250

19th century pub with a fine reputation for its home-cooked food (steaks a speciality) and for its real ales. 323

The Swan Motel, Lodden Road, Gillingham, Beccles, Suffolk NR34 0LD

Tel: 01502 712055 Fax: 01502 711786

14 spick-and-span self-contained apartments in a friendly free house motel with a convivial bar and day-long restaurant. Live music Sunday.

The Kings Head Hotel, New Market, Beccles, Suffolk NR34 9HA

Tel: 01502 712147 Fax: 01502 715386

12 en-suite bedrooms in a comfortable town-centre hotel. Busy bars, beer garden, restaurant with steakhouse menu.

Bury St Edmunds

Tut Hill, Bury St Edmunds, Suffolk IP28 6LG

Tel: 01284 755979 Fax: 01284 763288

Most well established golf clubs, particularly those formed over 100 years ago or in the early part of the 20th Century, owe their creation to a benefactor and Bury St Edmunds is no exception. It was Colonel Walter Guinness, the town's MP from 1907 to 1932, who took it on himself to purchase a suitable piece of land for £1,700 in 1922 and donate it to the town. The Colonel's gift proved the catalyst after many abortive efforts to establish a Bury club over the previous 25 years.

A golf club had been formed in 1895 at Flempton and bore the name Flempton and Bury St Edmunds Golf Club. But being some five miles from Bury it wasn't regarded as the town club. The Colonel's land, part of the Sexton's Hall estate, just on the western fringe of the town, proved ideal and saw the birth of a long-standing and flourishing club. That couldn't be said of

Colonel Guinness, later to become Lord Moyne, a move that coined the catchphrase 'Moyne's a Guinness'. He served successive post-First World War Governments as Under-Secretary of State for War, Financial Secretary to the Treasury, Minister for Agriculture and Fisheries and later the Leader of the House of Lords. Unfortunately he met a tragic end when he was assassinated in Cairo in 1944.

Without the Colonel's grand gesture the current club might never have seen the light of day. Owning its own land has enabled Bury to plot its own destiny. Back in 1922, Open champions James Braid and Ted Ray were approached over planning and it was Ray who finally presented a design for a fee of £25, the course being opened by Lady Evelyn Guinness in October 1924. The layout remained virtually the same until the late Sixties when the town's development as well as the construction of a by-pass encroached on the course and necessitated the purchase of extra land. Six holes were replaced thanks to the work of Frank Pennink, adding around 500 yards to its length. A renumbering also took place along with the building of a new clubhouse. Apart from a few minor changes this is the shape of today's course over undulating land which presents an attractive test to every standard of player.

Sec/Manager:	John Sayer
Professional:	Mark Jillings
Directions:	1 mile west of Bury St Edmunds. From Bury St Edmunds take the A144 (north) and turn left onto the A143 (Diss). The entrance is on the right hand side.
Date Founded:	1924
Visitors:	Welcome: Contact Club in Advance
Societies:	Welcome: Contact Club in advance by phone. Handicap certificate preferred.
Facilities:	Putting Green, Bar, Restaurant, Chipping Green, Trolley Hire, Practice Area, Club Hire

18 Hole Course

Type of Course:	Parkland
No of Holes:	18
Length:	6669 yds (6156 mtrs)
Par:	72
SSS:	72
Green Fees:	Weekdays: £25.00; Weekends/ Bank Holidays: not available

9 Hole Course

Type of Course:	Parkland
No of Holes:	9
Length:	2217 yds (2046 mtrs)
Par:	31
SSS:	31
Green Fees:	Weekdays: £12.00; Weekends/ Bank Holidays: £15.00

Accommodation, Food and Drink

Reference numbers below refer to detailed information provided in section 2

Accommodation

The Plough Inn, Hundon, Sudbury, Suffolk CO10 8DT

Tel: 01440 786789 Fax: 01440 786710

Eight well-appointed bedrooms and a good restaurant in a traditional country inn with views over the Stour Valley. 401

The Priory Hotel, Bury St Edmunds, Suffolk IP32 6EH

Tel: 01284 766181 Fax: 01284 767604

Period charm and elegance in a comfortable 39-bedroom hotel with modern amenities and a fine à la carte restaurant. 402

Marquis Cornwallis, The Street, Chedburgh, Bury St Edmunds, Suffolk IP29 4UH

Tel: 01284 850246

Village pub serving food lunchtime and evening (not Sun eve or Mon). Real ales. Beer garden. One letting bedroom.

Wagner Cottage, The Street, Walsham-le-Willows, Bury St Edmunds, Suffolk IP33 3AA

Tel: 01359 259380

Three delightful bedrooms in a Grade ll listed building with a walled garden opposite the village church. Bed & Breakfast.

Red House Farm, Haughley, Stowmarket, Suffolk IP14 3QP

Tel: 01449 673323 Fax: 01449 675413

Four B&B bedrooms in a large red-painted cottage on a farm estate close to the A14. Guest sitting room; dining room. 410

The Rutland Arms Hotel, Newmarket, Suffolk CB8 8NB

Tel: 01638 664251 Fax: 01638 666298

Forty-six well-equipped modern bedrooms in a handsome hotel built round a cobbled courtyard. Bar meals and full restaurant menu. 405

Food and Drink

The Plough Inn, Hundon, Sudbury, Suffolk CO10 8DT

Tel: 01440 786789 Fax: 01440 786710

Eight well-appointed bedrooms and a good restaurant in a traditional country inn with views over the Stour Valley. 401

The Priory Hotel, Bury St Edmunds, Suffolk IP32 6EH

Tel: 01284 766181 Fax: 01284 767604

Period charm and elegance in a comfortable 39-bedroom hotel with modern amenities and a fine à la carte restaurant. 402

Marquis Cornwallis, The Street, Chedburgh, Bury St Edmunds, Suffolk IP29 4UH

Tel: 01284 850246

Village pub serving food lunchtime and evening (not Sun eve or Mon). Real ales. Beer garden. One letting bedroom.

The Cock, The Street, Stanton, Bury St Edmunds, Suffolk IP31 2BP

Tel: 01359 250230

Cheerful pub with beams and open fires, pool, darts, monthly quiz. Restaurant and bar menus - steaks a speciality. No food Mon evening.

The Bell Inn, Bury Road, Kennett, Nr Newmarket, Suffolk CB8 7PP

Tel: 01638 750286

Exposed beams and cheerful open fires in an atmospheric old coaching inn at the village crossroads. 60-cover restaurant.

The Rutland Arms Hotel, Newmarket, Suffolk CB8 8NB

Tel: 01638 664251 Fax: 01638 666298

Forty-six well-equipped modern bedrooms in a handsome hotel built round a cobbled courtyard. Bar meals and full restaurant menu. 405

Cretingham

Grove Farm, Cretingham, Woodbridge, Suffolk IP13 7BA

Tel: 01728 685275 Fax: 01728 685037

Sec/Manager:	Kate Jackson
Professional:	Neil Jackson
Directions:	11 miles east of Stowmarket. From Stowmarket take the A1120 (East Soham). Turn right onto the B road to Cretingham. The entrance is on the left hand side 2 miles from Earl Soham.
Date Founded:	1981
Type of Course:	Parkland
No of Holes:	18
Length:	6500 yds (6000 mtrs)
Par:	72
SSS:	Not available at time of going to print
Green Fees:	Not available at time of going to print
Visitors:	Welcome: Contact Club in advance
Societies:	Welcome: Contact Club in advance
Facilities:	Putting Green, Chipping Green, Trolley Hire, Buggy Hire, Bar, Restaurant, Club Hire, Driving Range

Accommodation, Food and Drink

Reference numbers below refer to detailed information provided in section 2

Accommodation

Woodlands Farm, The Street, Brundish, Nr Framlingham, Suffolk IP13 8BP

Tel: 01379 384444

Three en-suite bedrooms in a rural farmhouse. Good breakfast using local produce. e-mail: woodlandsfarm@hotmail.com

Tannington Hall, Tannington, Nr Framlingham, Suffolk IP13 7NH

Tel: 01728 628226

Four en-suite bedrooms in a fine country house set in extensive gardens. B&B, dinner by arrangement. Carriage rides.

The Three Tuns Coaching Inn, Pettistree, Woodbridge, Suffolk IP13 0HW

Tel: 01728 747979 Fax: 01728 746244

150-year-old coaching inn en-suite bedrooms, real ales and excellent home-cooked food. 416

The Ramsholt Arms, Woodbridge, Suffolk IP12 3AB

Tel: 01394 411229 Fax: 01394 411818

A riverside free house in a scenic, out-of-the-way location overlooking the estuary. Lunches and dinners. Three letting bedrooms. 415

Food and Drink

The Bell Inn, Marlsford, Nr Woodbridge, Suffolk IP13 0AY

Tel: 01728 746242

Fish dishes are the speciality at this charming old thatched country inn on the A12. Log fires, beams, collection of wartime memorabilia. 419

The Castle Inn, Church Street, Framlingham, Suffolk IP13 9BT

Tel: 01728 724801

Home cooking of traditional and more modern dishes in a 16th century inn on the edge of the castle grounds. Soon to expand.

Clio's Restaurant, High Street, Debenham, Suffolk IP14 6QH

Tel: 01728 862062

Restaurant-cum-coffee shop in a 15th century house. Excellent home cooked lunches & Saturday evening meals; other evenings by arrangement.

The Dog Inn, The Green, Grundisburgh, Woodbridge, Suffolk IP13 6TA

Tel: 01473 735267

16th century pub in a pretty village 3 miles from Woodbridge. Food served lunch and dinner Mon-Sat & Sunday lunch.

The Three Tuns Coaching Inn, Pettistree, Woodbridge, Suffolk IP13 0HW

Tel: 01728 747979 Fax: 01728 746244

150-year-old coaching inn en-suite bedrooms, real ales and excellent home-cooked food. 416

The Ramsholt Arms, Woodbridge, Suffolk IP12 3AB

Tel: 01394 411229 Fax: 01394 411818

A riverside free house in a scenic, out-of-the-way location overlooking the estuary. Lunches and dinners. Three letting bedrooms. 415

Diss

Stuston Common, Diss, Suffolk IP22 4AA
Tel: 01379 641025

Sec/Manager: Mr Lesley McRow
Professional: Mr Nigel Taylor
Directions: 2 miles south east of Diss. From the east side of Diss take the B1077 towards Stuston. the entrance is on the east side of the village.
Date Founded: 1903
Type of Course: Heathland
No of Holes: 18
Length: 6262 yds (5780 mtrs)
Par: 70
SSS: 70
Green Fees: Weekdays: £30.00 per day, £25.00 per round; Weekends/ Bank Holidays: £30.00 perday, £25.00 per round.
Visitors: Welcome : Contact Club in advance. Weekend play with a member only.
Societies: Welcome: Contact Club in advance.

Facilities: Putting Green, Chipping Green, Driving Range, Club Hire, Trolley Hire, Buggy Hire, Caddy Service, Bar, Restaurant, Private Rooms

Accommodation, Food and Drink

Reference numbers below refer to detailed information provided in section 2

Accommodation

Woodlands Farm, The Street, Brundish, Nr Framlingham, Suffolk IP13 8BP

Tel: 01379 384444

Three en-suite bedrooms in a rural farmhouse. Good breakfast using local produce. e-mail: woodlandsfarm@hotmail.com

Tannington Hall, Tannington, Nr Framlingham, Suffolk IP13 7NH

Tel: 01728 628226

Four en-suite bedrooms in a fine country house set in extensive gardens. B&B, dinner by arrangement. Carriage rides.

Wagner Cottage, The Street, Walsham-le-Willows, Bury St Edmunds, Suffolk IP33 3AA

Tel: 01359 259380

Three delightful bedrooms in a Grade ll listed building with a walled garden opposite the village church. Bed & Breakfast.

Red House Farm, Haughley, Stowmarket, Suffolk IP14 3QP

Tel: 01449 673323 Fax: 01449 675413

Four B&B bedrooms in a large red-painted cottage on a farm estate close to the A14. Guest sitting room; dining room. 410

Food and Drink

The Nags Head, East Harling, Norfolk NR16 2AD

Tel: 01953 718140

Village pub in traditional style, serving an extensive range of splendid home-cooked food. On the B1111 south of Attleborough. 317

Clio's Restaurant, High Street, Debenham, Suffolk IP14 6QH

Tel: 01728 862062

Restaurant-cum-coffee shop in a 15th century house. Excellent home cooked lunches & Saturday evening meals; other evenings by arrangement.

The Cock, The Street, Stanton, Bury St Edmunds, Suffolk IP31 2BP

Tel: 01359 250230

Cheerful pub with beams and open fires, pool, darts, monthly quiz. Restaurant and bar menus - steaks a speciality. No food Mon evening.

Felixstowe Ferry

Ferry Road, Felixstowe, Suffolk IP11 2RY

Tel: 01394 286834 Fax: 01394 273679

Founded in 1880 not only makes Felixstowe Ferry the oldest club in Suffolk but one of the oldest in England. In fact, it was the fifth to be formed after Blackheath, Westward Ho! The London Scottish at Wimbledon, and Hoylake, which leaves it with a special role within the fabric of English golf. Bernard Darwin wrote in his 1910 book *Golf Courses of the British Isles*: "Of the many good courses in East Anglia I have the tenderest and most sentimental association with Felixstowe, because it was there, in 1884, that I began to play golf." And consider this: "Give me my tools, my golf clubs and leisure, and I would ask for nothing more. My ideal in life is to read a lot, write a little, play plenty of golf, and have nothing to worry about." That was penned by the Right Honourable Arthur Balfour, Conservative MP and Prime Minister from 1902 to 1905, who was club captain in 1889, five years after holding similar office with the R&A.

Golf was played near the town before 1880 by members from Blackheath and particularly those from the London Scottish serving on the Harwich Harbour guardship HMS Penelope. Lord Elcho MP, President of London Scottish, was a frequent visitor to the area and he felt that land at East End was suitable for golf. Consequently, in the spring of 1880, accompanied by Tom Dunn, then the Wimbledon professional, they visited Deben side and laid out a nine-hole course. Members of Wimbledon were persuaded to play there and consequently when the club was formed that autumn many of the founder members were London based.

The first course comprised 18 holes but as membership increased so did the congestion as well as the danger, so this was cut to 15 with three holes being played twice. However, there was a further reduction to 11 and then to nine, which it remained until the First World War. One of the two Martello Towers on the course became the first clubhouse until more suitable accommodation was available. During the 1914-18 conflict the course was taken over by the military and used as a rifle range, after which James Braid reconstructed the course and added nine more holes. Something more drastic occurred during the Second World War when, because Felixstowe was in the forefront of a possible invasion, pill boxes, barbed wire and gun emplacements were installed.

In 1947, the course was remodelled by Henry Cotton and the opening was marked by an exhibition match between Cotton and the club pro Reg Knight against Cecil Denny from Thorpe Hall and Max Faulkner, who was to become Open champion four years later. Frequent flooding from the sea has been a constant problem for the club. Extra land has been purchased and new holes built, including the construction of a nine-hole layout, the Kingsfleet, and a practice area, so that today Felixstowe Ferry has plenty to offer. Perhaps the club's most successful golfer on a world stage has been Julie Hall, the winner of many titles, a Curtis Cup player and a recent secretary of the Ladies Golf Union.

Sec/Manager: Nigel Fosker

Professional: Ian McFerson

Directions: 11 miles south east of Ipswich. Take the A14 (Felixstowe) from the centre of Ipswich. At the roundabout take the A154, leading to the A1021 and follow signs to Old Felixstowe, via High Road, Cliff Road and Ferry Road.

Date Founded: 1880

Visitors: Welcome: Weekdays only on Martello anyday on Kingsfleet

Societies: Welcome: Contact Club in advance

Facilities: Putting Green, Chipping Green, Club Hire, Trolley Hire, Buggy Hire, Bar, Restaurant

Martello

Type of Course: Seaside

No of Holes: 18

Length: 6285 yds (5801 mtrs)

Par: 72

SSS: 70

Green Fees: Weekdays: £30.00; Weekends/ Bank Holidays: Guests & Members only

Kingsfleet

Type of Course: Seaside

No of Holes: 9

Length: 2986 yds (2756 mtrs)

Par: 35

SSS: 35

Green Fees: Weekdays: £10.00; Weekends/ Bank Holidays: £10.00

Accommodation, Food and Drink

Reference numbers below refer to detailed information provided in section 2

Accommodation

The Castle Inn, Church Street, Framlingham, Suffolk IP13 9BT

Tel: 01728 724801

Home cooking of traditional and more modern dishes in a 16th century inn on the edge of the castle grounds. Soon to expand.

The Kings Head Inn, Orford, Suffolk IP12 2LW

Tel: 01394 450271

Authentic 13th century inn with period charm and up-to-date comfort. Three en-suite bedrooms. Snacks and full meals. 411

The Ramsholt Arms, Woodbridge, Suffolk IP12 3AB

Tel: 01394 411229 Fax: 01394 411818

A riverside free house in a scenic, out-of-the-way location overlooking the estuary. Lunches and dinners. Three letting bedrooms. 415

The Ferry Boat Inn, Felixstowe, Suffolk IP11 9RZ

Tel: 01394 284203

Fine old seaside inn next to the 4th tee at Felixstowe Golf Club. Well-prepared bar food, including children's dishes. Three letting bedrooms. 409

Food and Drink

The White Lion, Lower Ufford, Woodbridge, Suffolk IP13 6DW

Tel: 01394 460770

A friendly welcome, traditional surroundings and super home-cooked food in a country pub dating back to the 14th century. 412

The Castle Inn, Church Street, Framlingham, Suffolk IP13 9BT

Tel: 01728 724801

Home cooking of traditional and more modern dishes in a 16th century inn on the edge of the castle grounds. Soon to expand.

The Kings Head Inn, Orford, Suffolk IP12 2LW

Tel: 01394 450271

Authentic 13th century inn with period charm and up-to-date comfort. Three en-suite bedrooms. Snacks and full meals. 411

The Ramsholt Arms, Woodbridge, Suffolk IP12 3AB

Tel: 01394 411229 Fax: 01394 411818

A riverside free house in a scenic, out-of-the-way location overlooking the estuary. Lunches and dinners. Three letting bedrooms. 415

The Ferry Boat Inn, Felixstowe, Suffolk IP11 9RZ

Tel: 01394 284203

Fine old seaside inn next to the 4th tee at Felixstowe Golf Club. Well-prepared bar food, including children's dishes. Three letting bedrooms. 409

Fynn Valley

Witnesham, Ipswich, Suffolk IP6 9JA

Tel: 01473 785267 Fax: 01473 785632

Sec/Manager: A R Tyrrell

Professional: Kelvin Vince

Directions: 3 miles north of Ipswich. From Ipswich City centre takes the B1077 (Westerfield). The entrance is on the right hand side 1 mile beyond Westerfield.

Date Founded: 1990

Visitors: Welcome: Apart from Sunday mornings

Societies: Welcome: Contact Club in advance

Facilities:	Putting Green, Chipping Green, Club Hire, Trolley Hire, Buggy Hire, Bar, Restaurant, Driving Range

18 Hole Course

Type of Course:	Parkland
No of Holes:	18
Length:	6373 yds (5882 mtrs)
Par:	70
SSS:	70
Green Fees:	Weekdays: £20.00; Weekends/ Bank Holidays: £30.00

9 Hole Course

Type of Course:	Parkland
No of Holes:	9
Length:	1010 yds (932 mtrs)
Par:	27
SSS:	27
Green Fees:	Weekdays: £3.50; Weekends/ Bank Holidays: £3.50

Accommodation, Food and Drink

Reference numbers below refer to detailed information provided in section 2

Accommodation

The Golf Hotel, Ipswich, Suffolk IP4 5TR

Tel: 01473 727450

A 100-year-old pub in Elizabethan style, serving an impressive range of snacks and full meals throughout the day. Also eight letting rooms. 407

The Three Tuns Coaching Inn, Pettistree, Woodbridge, Suffolk IP13 0HW

Tel: 01728 747979 Fax: 01728 746244

150-year-old coaching inn en-suite bedrooms, real ales and excellent home-cooked food. 416

The Ramsholt Arms, Woodbridge, Suffolk IP12 3AB

Tel: 01394 411229 Fax: 01394 411818

A riverside free house in a scenic, out-of-the-way location overlooking the estuary. Lunches and dinners. Three letting bedrooms. 415

Food and drink

The Dog Inn, The Green, Grundisburgh, Woodbridge, Suffolk IP13 6TA

Tel: 01473 735267

16th century pub in a pretty village 3 miles from Woodbridge. Food served lunch and dinner Mon-Sat & Sunday lunch.

The Golden Key, 438 Woodbridge Road, Ipswich, Suffolk IP4 4EN

Tel: 01473 723916

Home cooking and real ales served in a pub a mile east of the town centre Patio garden.

The Golf Hotel, Ipswich, Suffolk IP4 5TR

Tel: 01473 727450

A 100-year-old pub in Elizabethan style, serving an impressive range of snacks and full meals throughout the day. Also eight letting rooms. 407

The Woolpack, Ipswich, Suffolk IP4 2SH

Tel: 01473 253059

A fine old brick-built pub only moments from Ipswich centre but with a 'country' feel. Extensive menu served seven days a week. 406

The Three Tuns Coaching Inn, Pettistree, Woodbridge, Suffolk IP13 0HW

Tel: 01728 747979 Fax: 01728 746244

150-year-old coaching inn en-suite bedrooms, real ales and excellent home-cooked food. 416

Kings Head Inn, Woodbridge, Suffolk IP12 4LX

Tel: 01394 387750

Some of the best pub food in Suffolk is served this ancient hostelry in the town centre. A warm, friendly place with bags of atmosphere. 403

The Ramsholt Arms, Woodbridge, Suffolk IP12 3AB

Tel: 01394 411229 Fax: 01394 411818

A riverside free house in a scenic, out-of-the-way location overlooking the estuary. Lunches and dinners. Three letting bedrooms. 415

Halesworth

Bramfield Road, Halesworth, Suffolk IP19 9XA

Tel: 01986 875567 Fax: 01986 874565

Sec/Manager:	Paula Stimpson
Professional:	Simon Harrison
Directions:	8 miles north of Saxmundham. Take the A12 (Lowestoft) and after 5 miles turn left onto the A144 (Halesworth). The entrance is on the right hand side one mile before Halesworth.
Date Founded:	1991
Visitors:	Welcome: Contact Club in Advance

Societies:	Welcome: Contact Club in advance
Facilities:	Putting Green, Club Hire, Trolley Hire, Bar, Restaurant, Driving Range, Chipping Green, Buggy Hire

Blythe

Type of Course:	Parkland
No of Holes:	18
Length:	6178 yds (5702 mtrs)
Par:	72
SSS:	72
Green Fees:	Weekdays: £15.00; Weekends/ Bank Holidays: £15.00

Valley

Type of Course:	Parkland
No of Holes:	9
Length:	5146 yds (4750 mtrs)
Par:	33
SSS:	33
Green Fees:	Weekdays: £7.50; Weekends/ Bank Holidays: £7.50

Accommodation, Food and Drink

Reference numbers below refer to detailed information provided in section 2

Accommodation

The Beeches Guest House, 117 High Street, Leiston, Suffolk IP16 4BX

Tel: 01728 832541

A delightful high street guest house with a friendly welcome, five comfortable letting bedrooms and good breakfasts.

Woodlands Farm, The Street, Brundish, Nr Framlingham, Suffolk IP13 8BP

Tel: 01379 384444

Three en-suite bedrooms in a rural farmhouse. Good breakfast using local produce. e-mail: woodlandsfarm@hotmail.com

Tannington Hall, Tannington, Nr Framlingham, Suffolk IP13 7NH

Tel: 01728 628226

Four en-suite bedrooms in a fine country house set in extensive gardens. B&B, dinner by arrangement. Carriage rides.

The Swan Motel, Lodden Road, Gillingham, Beccles, Suffolk NR34 0LD

Tel: 01502 712055 Fax: 01502 711786

14 spick-and-span self-contained apartments in a friendly free house motel with a convivial bar and day-long restaurant. Live music Sunday.

Pakefield Caravan Park, Arbor Lane, Pakefield, Lowestoft, Suffolk NR33 7BQ

Tel: 01502 561136 Fax: 01502 539264

Comfortable, well-equipped modern caravan holiday homes for hire in a clifftop location a short drive south of Lowestoft. Open April-October.

The Kings Head Hotel, New Market, Beccles, Suffolk NR34 9HA

Tel: 01502 712147 Fax: 01502 715386

12 en-suite bedrooms in a comfortable town-centre hotel. Busy bars, beer garden, restaurant with steakhouse menu.

Food and Drink

The Lion Inn, The Street, Theberton, Nr Leiston, Suffolk IP16 4RU

Tel: 01728 830185

Pretty village public house open every lunchtime and evening. Excellent home-cooked meals. Easily reached from the A12.

The Bell Inn, Marlsford, Nr Woodbridge, Suffolk IP13 0AY

Tel: 01728 746242

Fish dishes are the speciality at this charming old thatched country inn on the A12. Log fires, beams, collection of wartime memorabilia. 419

The Castle Inn, Church Street, Framlingham, Suffolk IP13 9BT

Tel: 01728 724801

Home cooking of traditional and more modern dishes in a 16th century inn on the edge of the castle grounds. Soon to expand.

The Swan Motel, Lodden Road, Gillingham, Beccles, Suffolk NR34 0LD

Tel: 01502 712055 Fax: 01502 711786

14 spick-and-span self-contained apartments in a friendly free house motel with a convivial bar and day-long restaurant. Live music Sunday.

The Kings Head Hotel, New Market, Beccles, Suffolk NR34 9HA

Tel: 01502 712147 Fax: 01502 715386

12 en-suite bedrooms in a comfortable town-centre hotel. Busy bars, beer garden, restaurant with steakhouse menu.

Haverhill

Coupals Road, Haverhill, Suffolk CB9 7UW

Tel/Fax: 01440 761951

In historical terms, Haverhill is one of the new boys on the block, having been formed in 1974. But it may be able to claim a first in that it received an early Lottery grant to help build its new clubhouse, opened in 1995. Other monies came from a favourably constructed loan and a £100 levy on every member. Togetherness is very much a byword with the Haverhill membership as it was back in 1982 when the local council decided Haverhill wasn't a viable proposition and allowed the club to assume control with assets of around £3,000 plus some clapped-out greenkeeping equipment.

The club had a tough beginning. Its birth arose from work by a mixed group including one or two members of the local council and immigrants from Greater London. The land was originally a water meadow, which ran gently down to the

River Stow, a tributary of the Stour, forming the boundary between Suffolk and Essex. Ironically, although most of the course lies in Essex, the club is affiliated to the Suffolk Golf Union and plays in its competitions. There was only room for nine holes and early construction work involved considerable quantities of earth being packed into the areas adjoining the river to prevent annual flooding. Charles Lawrie, twice a Walker Cup captain, was the designer and his holes, which opened in 1975, remain virtually unchanged.

Following the members' take over, a combination of a growing population and heavy use of the nine hole course, persuaded the members that expansion was essential and after considerable negotiations with St Edmundsbury Borough Council, sufficient land was acquired for a further nine holes. This led to the aforementioned Lottery grant. The club would have liked Lawrie to complete the 18 but by then he had passed away, so Philip Pilgrim was commissioned to work with the new land. His design basically runs along both sides of a deep ravine but only one hole actually crosses it.

The club has a strong junior section, which bodes well for the future while the membership includes former world table tennis champion Johnny Leach and Dr Robert Fleming, a son of Dr Alexander Fleming, who discovered penicillin.

Sec/Manager: Jill Edwards
Professional: Simon Mayfield
Directions: Half a mile south east of Haverhill. From the A1017 Chalkstone Road junction take Chalkstone Road. After 200 yds turn right into Coupar Road. The entrance is on the right hand side after half a mile.
Date Founded: 1970
Type of Course: Parkland
No of Holes: 18
Length: 5898 yds (5444 mtrs)
Par: 70
SSS: 69
Green Fees: Weekdays: £20.00; Weekends/ Bank Holidays: £25.00
Visitors: Welcome: Contact Club in advance
Societies: Welcome: Contact Club in advance
Facilities: Putting Green, Practice Ground, Club Hire, Trolley Hire, Bar, Restaurant

Accommodation, Food and Drink

Reference numbers below refer to detailed information provided in section 2

Accommodation

The Plough Inn, Hundon, Sudbury, Suffolk CO10 8DT
Tel: 01440 786789 Fax: 01440 786710
Eight well-appointed bedrooms and a good restaurant in a traditional country inn with views over the Stour Valley. 401

Marquis Cornwallis, The Street, Chedburgh, Bury St Edmunds, Suffolk IP29 4UH
Tel: 01284 850246
Village pub serving food lunchtime and evening (not Sun eve or Mon). Real ales. Beer garden. One letting bedroom.

Juniper Bed & Breakfast, Church Lane, Cheveley, Suffolk CB8 9DJ
Tel: 01638 731244
Next to the church in rural Cheveley, Juniper is a new house offering top-notch Bed & Breakfast accommodation in three beautifully appointed bedrooms.

Food and Drink

The Sugar Loaves, 175 Swan Street, Sible Hedingham, Nr Halstead, Essex CO9 3PX
Tel: 01787 462720
A long-hours pub with two bars and a separate eating area, where pizzas and dishes with chips are favourites - served till 7pm daily.

The Pheasant, Audley End, Gestingthorpe, Nr Halstead, Essex CO9 3AX
Tel: 01787 461196
A small, cosy village pub, off the beaten track but well worth seeking out for some of the best food in the area. 509

The Plough Inn, Hundon, Sudbury, Suffolk CO10 8DT
Tel: 01440 786789 Fax: 01440 786710
Eight well-appointed bedrooms and a good restaurant in a traditional country inn with views over the Stour Valley. 401

Marquis Cornwallis, The Street, Chedburgh, Bury St Edmunds, Suffolk IP29 4UH
Tel: 01284 850246
Village pub serving food lunchtime and evening (not Sun eve or Mon). Real ales. Beer garden. One letting bedroom.

The Chestnut Tree, West Wratting, Cambridgeshire CB1 5LU
Tel: 01223 290384
A well-kept redbrick village pub on the B1052, serving a fine selection of first-class food, with Sunday lunch a highlight. 620

Hintlesham Hall

Hintlesham, Ipswich, Suffolk IP8 3NS
Tel: 01473 652761 Fax: 01473 652750

Hintlesham Hall Golf Club is a self-contained private club, which also serves Hintlesham Hall Hotel, situated four miles west of Ipswich. In the same ownership, the two share the beautiful 175-acre estate.

HHGC is now widely recognised as having one of the finest golf courses in East Anglia. Designed by Hawtree, it blends perfectly into the undulating parkland of rural Suffolk offering a remarkably peaceful environment. With its beautifully manicured fairways, the course measures 6,602 yards and features superbly contoured all-weather greens, interesting water hazards and a host of strategically placed bunkers.

The extensive practice facilities include a driving range, chipping area, a practice bunker and putting green. For those golfers requiring lessons, qualified PGA staff are available to offer tuition at all levels.

The award-winning clubhouse beautifully complements the elegance of the course. Its location with views over greens, tees and ancient woodland offers peace and tranquillity. Inside are light and airy changing rooms looking on to an inner courtyard and attractive dining and bar areas. Saunas, steam room and a spa bath encourage members to unwind before enjoying a snack or meal in the restaurant or on the verandah.

Hintlesham Hall has a colourful history dating back to the 15th Century. It has had many owners but in the 18th Century, when it belonged to Richard Lloyd, the Solicitor General, Thomas Gainsborough visited to paint portraits of his children. During the Second World War it served as a Red Cross Hospital, while in 1972 famous chef, Robert Carrier, bought the property, restored it and ran it as a flourishing restaurant and cookery school.

Throughout much of the life of the Hall, the Lord of the Manor of Hintlesham has been in residence. The current owner, David Allan, acquired the title in 1995 thus reuniting the Lordship with its traditional seat.

Sec/Manager: Ian Procktor

Professional: Alistair Spink

Directions: 5 miles west of Ipswich. From the A12/A14 junction take the A1071 (Hadleigh) and pass through Hintlesham. The entrance is on the right hand side.

Date Founded: 1991

Type of Course: Parkland

No of Holes: 18

Length: 6638 yds (6127 mtrs)

Par: 72

SSS: 72

Green Fees: Weekdays: £30.00; Weekends/ Bank Holidays: £38.00

Visitors: Welcome: Contact Club in advance.

Societies: Welcome: Contact Club in advance by telephone.

Facilities: Putting Green, Chipping Green, Driving Range, Club Hire, Trolley Hire, Buggy Hire, Bar, Restaurant

Accommodation, Food and Drink

Reference numbers below refer to detailed information provided in section 2

Accommodation

Tannington Hall, Tannington, Nr Framlingham, Suffolk IP13 7NH

Tel: 01728 628226

Four en-suite bedrooms in a fine country house set in extensive gardens. B&B, dinner by arrangement. Carriage rides.

The Golf Hotel, Ipswich, Suffolk IP4 5TR

Tel: 01473 727450

A 100-year-old pub in Elizabethan style, serving an impressive range of snacks and full meals throughout the day. Also eight letting rooms. 407

Maison Talbooth, Dedham, Essex CO7 6HN

Tel: 01206 322367 Fax: 01206 322752

Ten top-notch en-suite bedrooms in a Victorian country house with superb views. Meals are served in the restaurant Le Talbooth, a short walk away. 504

Food and Drink

Tannington Hall, Tannington, Nr Framlingham, Suffolk IP13 7NH

Tel: 01728 628226

Four en-suite bedrooms in a fine country house set in extensive gardens. B&B, dinner by arrangement. Carriage rides.

The Golden Key, 438 Woodbridge Road, Ipswich, Suffolk IP4 4EN

Tel: 01473 723916

Home cooking and real ales served in a pub a mile east of the town centre Patio garden.

The Golf Hotel, Ipswich, Suffolk IP4 5TR

Tel: 01473 727450

A 100-year-old pub in Elizabethan style, serving an impressive range of snacks and full meals throughout the day. Also eight letting rooms. 407

The Woolpack, Ipswich, Suffolk IP4 2SH

Tel: 01473 253059

A fine old brick-built pub only moments from Ipswich centre but with a 'country' feel. Extensive menu served seven days a week. 406

Maison Talbooth, Dedham, Essex CO7 6HN

Tel: 01206 322367 Fax: 01206 322752

Ten top-notch en-suite bedrooms in a Victorian country house with superb views. Meals are served in the restaurant Le Talbooth, a short walk away. 504

The Rose Inn, Thorington Street, Stoke-by-Nayland, Colchester, Essex CO6 4SN

Tel/Fax: 01206 337243

Pub with 50-cover restaurant, large car park and extensive gardens. Outstanding food, particularly seafood, with lots of daily specials. Closed Monday.

The Red Lion, High Street, Bildeston, Ipswich, Suffolk IP7 7EX

Tel: 01449 740476

A charming village pub, deep red outside, deep red with black beams in the bar areas. Food served throughout. Beer garden.

Ipswich (Purdis Heath)

Purdis Heath, Bucklesham Road, Ipswich, Suffolk IP3 8UQ

Tel: 01473 727474 Fax; 01473 715236

The founding of Ipswich Golf Club is indelibly linked with its neighbour Rushmere in that the original club was founded in 1895 and played on leased commoners' land at Rushmere Heath. It wasn't until 1927 that the club moved to 217 acres of freehold land known as Black Heath, part of Broke Hall Estate, acquired in 1926 following consultation with James Braid who was commissioned to design the 18-hole course.

Renamed Purdis Heath, possibly to avoid confusion with the famous Blackheath Golf Club, course construction under the direction of Messrs Hawtree and Taylor resulted in an informal opening on 15 October 1927. The official opening, on 16 June 1928, was marked by an exhibition match involving famous professionals, Abe Mitchell, James Braid, J.H. Taylor and Henry Cotton. Like many other clubs, Ipswich owes much to the businessmen of the time. In its case particularly James Edward Ransome, father of the first petrol-driven lawnmower and agricultural tractor, a name still revered in golf maintenance circles today, and H Munro Cautley, a leading local architect, who was the driving force behind the present course and clubhouse.

The course compares favourably with the finest heathland courses in England and is substantially as it was at birth - a testament to James Braid's design. Measuring 6,435 yards from the back tees, par 71, it is a delight to play and full of surprises. None more so than the par-four fourth, where the approach is blind to a green that lies in a 'canyon' some 20 feet below the level of the fairway. A few major changes, include the addition of the practice ground beside the

17th hole, extensive landscaping of the fourth together with opening up of the water here and at the 15th, took place in the 1980s. In 1929, Captain Cautley generously bought 11 additional acres of land adjoining Bucklesham Road. This eventually enabled the club to construct a nine-hole course, which was initially intended as a training ground for juniors and beginners but has become popular since being opened to the public on a pay and play basis. Course architect Hawtree was consulted as to the layout, but the nine holes were rapidly constructed by the club's own staff. While in 1927 the main course was built with spades and 20 men, a bulldozer and half a dozen men created the new course. Henry Cotton again played an exhibition match to mark the official opening on 15 June 1968 and remarked on the difficulty of the course for beginners.

Sec/Manager: Neil Ellice

Professional: Stephen Whymark

Directions: 2 miles south east of Ipswich. From the roundabout at the junction of the A1156/A1189 (northern ring road) take the B road towards Bucklesham. The entrance is on the left hand side after one mile.

Date Founded: 1927

Visitors: Welcome: Contact Club in Advance

Societies: Welcome: Contact Club in Advance

Facilities: Putting Green, Bar, Restaurant

18 Hole Course

Type of Course: Heathland

No of Holes: 18

Length: 6435 yds

Par: 71

SSS: 71

Green Fees: Weekdays: £40.00 per day, £25.00 per round; Weekends/ Bank Holidays: £43.00 per day, £30.00 per round

9 Hole Course

Type of Course: Heathland

No of Holes: 9

Length: 1930 yds (1648 mtrs)

Par: 31

SSS: 59 (Ladies) 61 (Gents)

Green Fees: Weekdays: £10.00; Weekends/ Bank Holidays: £12.50

Accommodation, Food and Drink

Reference numbers below refer to detailed information provided in section 2

Accommodation

The Golf Hotel, Ipswich, Suffolk IP4 5TR

Tel: 01473 727450

A 100-year-old pub in Elizabethan style, serving an impressive range of snacks and full meals throughout the day. Also eight letting rooms. 407

Maison Talbooth, Dedham, Essex CO7 6HN

Tel: 01206 322367 Fax: 01206 322752

Ten top-notch en-suite bedrooms in a Victorian country house with superb views. Meals are served in the restaurant Le Talbooth, a short walk away. 504

The Ramsholt Arms, Woodbridge, Suffolk IP12 3AB

Tel: 01394 411229 Fax: 01394 411818

A riverside free house in a scenic, out-of-the-way location overlooking the estuary. Lunches and dinners. Three letting bedrooms. 415

The Ferry Boat Inn, Felixstowe, Suffolk IP11 9RZ

Tel: 01394 284203

Fine old seaside inn next to the 4th tee at Felixstowe Golf Club. Well-prepared bar food, including children's dishes. Three letting bedrooms. 409

Food and Drink

The Dog Inn, The Green, Grundisburgh, Woodbridge, Suffolk IP13 6TA

Tel: 01473 735267

16th century pub in a pretty village 3 miles from Woodbridge. Food served lunch and dinner Mon-Sat & Sunday lunch.

The Golden Key, 438 Woodbridge Road, Ipswich, Suffolk IP4 4EN

Tel: 01473 723916

Home cooking and real ales served in a pub a mile east of the town centre Patio garden.

The Golf Hotel, Ipswich, Suffolk IP4 5TR

Tel: 01473 727450

A 100-year-old pub in Elizabethan style, serving an impressive range of snacks and full meals throughout the day. Also eight letting rooms. 407

The Woolpack, Ipswich, Suffolk IP4 2SH

Tel: 01473 253059

A fine old brick-built pub only moments from Ipswich centre but with a 'country' feel. Extensive menu served seven days a week. 406

Maison Talbooth, Dedham, Essex CO7 6HN

Tel: 01206 322367 Fax: 01206 322752

Ten top-notch en-suite bedrooms in a Victorian country house with superb views. Meals are served in the restaurant Le Talbooth, a short walk away. 504

The Ramsholt Arms, Woodbridge, Suffolk IP12 3AB

Tel: 01394 411229 Fax: 01394 411818

A riverside free house in a scenic, out-of-the-way location overlooking the estuary. Lunches and dinners. Three letting bedrooms. 415

The Ferry Boat Inn, Felixstowe, Suffolk IP11 9RZ

Tel: 01394 284203

Fine old seaside inn next to the 4th tee at Felixstowe Golf Club. Well-prepared bar food, including children's dishes. Three letting bedrooms. 409

Links (Newmarket)

Cambridge Road, Newmarket,
Suffolk CB8 0TG

Tel: 01638 663000 Fax: 01638 661476

Sec/Manager:	Margaret MacGregor
Professional:	John Sharkey
Directions:	2½ miles south west of Newmarket. From the south west outskirts of Newmarket take the A1304 (Newmarket Race Course) Entrance on left hand side after one mile.
Date Founded:	1902
Type of Course:	Parkland
No of Holes:	18
Length:	6366 yds (5876 mtrs)
Par:	72
SSS:	70
Green Fees:	Weekdays: £32.00; Weekends/ Bank Holidays: £36.00
Visitors:	Welcome: Contact Club in advance by telephone. Unable to play Sunday mornings.
Societies:	Welcome: Contact Club in advance by writing. Unable to play Monday, Friday, Saturday and Sunday
Facilities:	Practice Ground, Club Hire, Trolley Hire, Bar, Restaurant

Accommodation, Food and Drink

Reference numbers below refer to detailed information provided in section 2

Accommodation

Marquis Cornwallis, The Street, Chedburgh, Bury St Edmunds, Suffolk IP29 4UH

Tel: 01284 850246

Village pub serving food lunchtime and evening (not Sun eve or Mon). Real ales. Beer garden. One letting bedroom.

Juniper Bed & Breakfast, Church Lane, Cheveley, Suffolk CB8 9DJ

Tel: 01638 731244

Next to the church in rural Cheveley, Juniper is a new house offering top-notch Bed & Breakfast accommodation in three beautifully appointed bedrooms.

The Old Bull, The Street, Barton Mills, Bury St Edmunds, Suffolk IP27 6AE

Tel: 01638 713230

Twenty double bedrooms in an extended old inn by the A11 north of Newmarket and west of Bury.

The Rutland Arms Hotel, Newmarket, Suffolk CB8 8NB

Tel: 01638 664251 Fax: 01638 666298

Forty-six well-equipped modern bedrooms in a handsome hotel built round a cobbled courtyard. Bar meals and full restaurant menu. 405

The White Hart, Fulbourn, Cambridgeshire CB1 5BZ

Tel: 01223 880264

A mid-Victorian pub of character, with garden and patio. Seven bedrooms, all en-suite; fully licensed restaurant, carvery Friday evening and Sunday lunch. 611

Food and Drink

Marquis Cornwallis, The Street, Chedburgh, Bury St Edmunds, Suffolk IP29 4UH

Tel: 01284 850246

Village pub serving food lunchtime and evening (not Sun eve or Mon). Real ales. Beer garden. One letting bedroom.

The Old Bull, The Street, Barton Mills, Bury St Edmunds, Suffolk IP27 6AE

Tel: 01638 713230

Twenty double bedrooms in an extended old inn by the A11 north of Newmarket and west of Bury.

The Bell Inn, Bury Road, Kennett, Nr Newmarket, Suffolk CB8 7PP

Tel: 01638 750286

Exposed beams and cheerful open fires in an atmospheric old coaching inn at the village crossroads. 60-cover restaurant.

The Rutland Arms Hotel, Newmarket, Suffolk CB8 8NB

Tel: 01638 664251 Fax: 01638 666298

Forty-six well-equipped modern bedrooms in a handsome hotel built round a cobbled courtyard. Bar meals and full restaurant menu. 405

The White Hart, Fulbourn, Cambridgeshire CB1 5BZ

Tel: 01223 880264

A mid-Victorian pub of character, with garden and patio. Seven bedrooms, all en-suite; fully licensed restaurant, carvery Friday evening and Sunday lunch. 611

The Rose & Crown, Teversham, Cambridgeshire CB1 5AF

Tel: 01223 292245

A handsome 100-year-old pub in a pretty village just off the A1303. Excellent-value home-cooked food, from bar snacks to full meals. 623

The Chestnut Tree, West Wratting, Cambridgeshire CB1 5LU

Tel: 01223 290384

A well-kept redbrick village pub on the B1052, serving a fine selection of first-class food, with Sunday lunch a highlight. 620

Newton Green

Newton Green, Sudbury, Suffolk CO10 0QN

Tel: 01787 377501 Fax: 01787 377549

Sec/Manager:	Ken Mazdon
Professional:	Tim Cooper
Directions:	2 miles south east of Sudbury. From Sudbury take the A134 (Hadleigh). The entrance is on the right hand side after one mile at Newton.
Date Founded:	1907
Type of Course:	Grassland
No of Holes:	18
Length:	5947 yds (5489 mtrs)
Par:	69
SSS:	68
Green Fees:	Weekdays: £17.50; Weekends/ Bank Holidays: £25.00
Visitors:	Welcome: Contact Club in advance
Societies:	Welcome: Contact Club in advance
Facilities:	Putting Green, Club Hire,Trolley Hire, Bar, Restaurant

Accommodation, Food and Drink

Reference numbers below refer to detailed information provided in section 2

Accommodation

Stoke by Nayland Club Hotel, Leavenheath, Colchester, Essex CO6 4PZ

Tel: 01206 262836 Fax: 01206 263356

A spacious modern country hotel in 300 acres of rolling countryside. 30 fine bedrooms, restaurant, golf courses, health & fitness centre. 508

The Plough Inn, Hundon, Sudbury, Suffolk CO10 8DT

Tel: 01440 786789 Fax: 01440 786710

Eight well-appointed bedrooms and a good restaurant in a traditional country inn with views over the Stour Valley. 401

Marquis Cornwallis, The Street, Chedburgh, Bury St Edmunds, Suffolk IP29 4UH

Tel: 01284 850246

Village pub serving food lunchtime and evening (not Sun eve or Mon). Real ales. Beer garden. One letting bedroom.

Food and Drink

The Pheasant, Audley End, Gestingthorpe, Nr Halstead, Essex CO9 3AX

Tel: 01787 461196

A small, cosy village pub, off the beaten track but well worth seeking out for some of the best food in the area. 509

Stoke by Nayland Club Hotel, Leavenheath, Colchester, Essex CO6 4PZ

Tel: 01206 262836 Fax: 01206 263356

A spacious modern country hotel in 300 acres of rolling countryside. 30 fine bedrooms, restaurant, golf courses, health & fitness centre. 508

The Plough Inn, Hundon, Sudbury, Suffolk CO10 8DT

Tel: 01440 786789 Fax: 01440 786710

Eight well-appointed bedrooms and a good restaurant in a traditional country inn with views over the Stour Valley. 401

Marquis Cornwallis, The Street, Chedburgh, Bury St Edmunds, Suffolk IP29 4UH

Tel: 01284 850246

Village pub serving food lunchtime and evening (not Sun eve or Mon). Real ales. Beer garden. One letting bedroom.

The Rose Inn, Thorington Street, Stoke-by-Nayland, Colchester, Essex CO6 4SN

Tel/Fax: 01206 337243

Pub with 50-cover restaurant, large car park and extensive gardens. Outstanding food, particularly seafood, with lots of daily specials. Closed Monday.

The Red Lion, High Street, Bildeston, Ipswich, Suffolk IP7 7EX

Tel: 01449 740476

A charming village pub, deep red outside, deep red with black beams in the bar areas. Food served throughout. Beer garden.

Rookery Park

Carlton Colville, Lowestoft, Suffolk NR33 8HJ

Tel/Fax: 01502 560380

Sec/Manager: David Kelly

Professional: Martin Ellsworthy

Directions: 2 miles south west of Lowestoft. From Lowestoft take the A146 (Beccles). Go past B1384 to Carlton Colville and the entrance is on the right hand side after ¼ mile.

Date Founded: 1975

18 Hole Course

Type of Course: Parkland

No of Holes: 18

Length: 6714 yds (6197 mtrs)

Par: 72

SSS: 72

Green Fees: Weekdays: £30.00; Weekends/ Bank Holidays: £35.00

Par 3 Course

Type of Course: Parkland

No of Holes: 9

Length: 1010 yds (932 mtrs)

Par: 72

SSS: 72

Green Fees: Weekdays: £5.00; Weekends/ Bank Holidays: £5.00

Visitors: Welcome: Contact Club in Advance. Unable to play on Tuesday mornings.

Societies: Welcome: Contact Club in advance by writing.

Facilities: Putting Green, Club Hire, Trolley Hire, Bar, Restaurant, Practice Area

Accommodation, Food and Drink

Reference numbers below refer to detailed information provided in section 2

Accommodation

Kingsley House Hotel, Great Yarmouth, Norfolk NR30 2PP

Tel/Fax: 01493 850948

Seven en-suite bedrooms in a family run hotel handy for the town centre and the seafront. B&B plus evening meal option. 328

The Marsham Arms, Hevingham, Norfolk NR10 5NP

Tel: 01603 754268 Fax: 01603 754839

Characterful family-run country inn with eight spacious en-suite bedrooms and comfortable rooms for bar and restaurant dining. 331

Marine Lodge, Great Yarmouth, Norfolk NR30 1DY

Tel: 01493 331120 Fax: 01493 332040

Bright, up-to-date Bed & Breakfast accommodation in 39 well-appointed rooms 50 yards from the seafront. 321

The Swan Motel, Lodden Road, Gillingham, Beccles, Suffolk NR34 0LD

Tel: 01502 712055 Fax: 01502 711786

14 spick-and-span self-contained apartments in a friendly free house motel with a convivial bar and day-long restaurant. Live music Sunday.

Pakefield Caravan Park, Arbor Lane, Pakefield, Lowestoft, Suffolk NR33 7BQ

Tel: 01502 561136 Fax: 01502 539264

Comfortable, well-equipped modern caravan holiday homes for hire in a clifftop location a short drive south of Lowestoft. Open April-October.

Homelea Guest House, 33 Marine Parade, Lowestoft, Suffolk NR3 3QN

Tel: 01502 511640

Guest house with five double rooms, located on the promenade 50 yards from the sea. Evening meals by arrangement.

The Kings Head Hotel, New Market, Beccles, Suffolk NR34 9HA

Tel: 01502 712147 Fax: 01502 715386

12 en-suite bedrooms in a comfortable town-centre hotel. Busy bars, beer garden, restaurant with steakhouse menu.

Food and Drink

The White Horse, Chedgrave, Norwich, Norfolk NR14 6ND

Tel: 01508 520250

19th century pub with a fine reputation for its home-cooked food (steaks a speciality) and for its real ales. 323

The Lion Inn, The Street, Theberton, Nr Leiston, Suffolk IP16 4RU

Tel: 01728 830185

Pretty village public house open every lunchtime and evening. Excellent home-cooked meals. Easily reached from the A12.

The Swan Motel, Lodden Road, Gillingham, Beccles, Suffolk NR34 0LD

Tel: 01502 712055 Fax: 01502 711786

14 spick-and-span self-contained apartments in a friendly free house motel with a convivial bar and day-long restaurant. Live music Sunday.

The Kings Head Hotel, New Market, Beccles, Suffolk NR34 9HA

Tel: 01502 712147 Fax: 01502 715386

12 en-suite bedrooms in a comfortable town-centre hotel. Busy bars, beer garden, restaurant with steakhouse menu.

Rushmere

Rushmere Heath, Ipswich, Suffolk IP4 5QQ

Tel: 01473 727109 Fax: 01473 273852

Golf has been played on Rushmere Heath on the north east outskirts of Ipswich since the late 1880s, then a few years later it became the home of the Ipswich Golf Club. The first course opened on 1 June 1895 and there is a record that the colonel of the local artillery was asked to induce his men to refrain from riding over putting greens.

The Ipswich club flourished, thanks to the good offices of powerful local businessmen, while golf on Rushmere Heath gained a glowing reputation. A report in the *East Anglian Daily Times* of 1914 says: "The pure air and joyful surroundings of the heath have a certain effect of dispelling any feelings of brain fatigue or depression. The breezy plateau upon which the links are situated is indeed a fresh and truly delightful spot, and most welcome to the man who seeks to forget his work and daily duties for some two hours." No such talk of slow play in those days on a course measuring over 5,000 yards although the sentiments of the writer is equally adept for today at Rushmere.

However, the present club was born in 1927, when a majority of Ipswich members elected to move to nearby private land at Purdis Heath. A successful public appeal was launched, while donations from founder members enabled Rushmere Golf Club to be formed. The heath is a fine, natural golf course. Most holes are bordered by gorse and there are many fine old oak trees providing not only natural habitat for birds and other wildlife but demanding care from many of the tees.

The course now measures 6,262 yards, par 70, and enjoys the space and hole-by-hole separation afforded by the expanse of the heath. The nature of the course demands accuracy and good course management skills and this probably explains the constant high number of players with handicaps of five or better at Rushmere. Over 400 acres of Rushmere Heath is registered common land, administered by a committee and, in addition to the 15 holes rented from the commoners, the club privately owns 17 acres which constitute the third, fourth and fifth holes.

The clubhouse was formerly a junior school, purchased in 1928 and which has been extended over the years into a specious and welcoming venue enjoyed by members and visitors together. Rushmere has also earned a reputation for being a fiercely competitive members club with a strong playing presence in all its sections. There is no doubt that this is a fine test of golf, which is underlined by the fact that Rushmere plays host to many top competitions and charity events while societies regard it as a true golfing challenge.

Sec/Manager:	A.N.Harris
Professional:	Nick McNeil
Directions:	2 miles east of Ipswich. From Ipswich centre take the A1071 (Kesgrave). Continue on the A124, Woodbridge road and after a ¼ mile turn right onto Glenavon road followed by Melbourne Road. The entrance is on the right hand side.
Date Founded:	1897
Type of Course:	Parkland
No of Holes:	18
Length:	6282 yds (5798 mtrs)
Par:	70
SSS:	70
Green Fees:	Weekdays: £25.00; Weekends/ Bank Holidays: £25.00
Visitors:	Welcome: Contact Club in advance by telephone.
Societies:	Welcome: Contact Club in advance, unable to play at weekends and on Wednesday mornings.
Facilities:	Putting Green, Club Hire, Trolley Hire, Bar, Restaurant, Chipping Green

Accommodation, Food and Drink

Reference numbers below refer to detailed information provided in section 2

Accommodation

The Golf Hotel, Ipswich, Suffolk IP4 5TR

Tel: 01473 727450

A 100-year-old pub in Elizabethan style, serving an impressive range of snacks and full meals throughout the day. Also eight letting rooms. 407

The Three Tuns Coaching Inn, Pettistree, Woodbridge, Suffolk IP13 0HW

Tel: 01728 747979 Fax: 01728 746244

150-year-old coaching inn en-suite bedrooms, real ales and excellent home-cooked food. 416

The Ramsholt Arms, Woodbridge, Suffolk IP12 3AB

Tel: 01394 411229 Fax: 01394 411818

A riverside free house in a scenic, out-of-the-way location overlooking the estuary. Lunches and dinners. Three letting bedrooms. 415

Food and Drink

The Dog Inn, The Green, Grundisburgh, Woodbridge, Suffolk IP13 6TA

Tel: 01473 735267

16th century pub in a pretty village 3 miles from Woodbridge. Food served lunch and dinner Mon-Sat & Sunday lunch.

The Golden Key, 438 Woodbridge Road, Ipswich, Suffolk IP4 4EN

Tel: 01473 723916

Home cooking and real ales served in a pub a mile east of the town centre Patio garden.

The Golf Hotel, Ipswich, Suffolk IP4 5TR

Tel: 01473 727450

A 100-year-old pub in Elizabethan style, serving an impressive range of snacks and full meals throughout the day. Also eight letting rooms. 407

The Woolpack, Ipswich, Suffolk IP4 2SH

Tel: 01473 253059

A fine old brick-built pub only moments from Ipswich centre but with a 'country' feel. Extensive menu served seven days a week. 406

The Three Tuns Coaching Inn, Pettistree, Woodbridge, Suffolk IP13 0HW

Tel: 01728 747979 Fax: 01728 746244

150-year-old coaching inn en-suite bedrooms, real ales and excellent home-cooked food. 416

The Ramsholt Arms, Woodbridge, Suffolk IP12 3AB

Tel: 01394 411229 Fax: 01394 411818

A riverside free house in a scenic, out-of-the-way location overlooking the estuary. Lunches and dinners. Three letting bedrooms. 415

Stoke-by-Nayland

Keepers Lane, Leavenheath, Colchester, Suffolk CO6 4PZ

Tel: 01206 262836 Fax: 01206 263356

It could be said that Stoke by Nayland was the apple of its creators' eye. After all, the fruit was at the forefront of the lives of Bill and Devora Peake who developed the club in the early 1970s. The Peake family has been farming in Suffolk for 60 years. From a small 120-acre apple farm, their entrepreneurial skills have developed a thriving and diverse group of companies, which have grown to include golf, leisure, and conferencing plus fruit growing and processing on 900 acres of land.

In 1996, in recognition of her lifetime's work, Devora Peake was awarded the MBE for services to the Fruit and Fruit Juice Industries and she was made a fellow of the Royal Agricultural Society. The club comprises two 18-holes courses built on 300 acres of arable farmland in undulating Constable Country on the edge of the picturesque Dedham Vale, now designated as an area of outstanding natural beauty.

The par-72 **Gainsborough**, opened in 1972, measures 6,498 yards and a feature of the design is the subtle use of the undulating terrain. The 10th, being the signature hole, requires a drive and second shot over a lake, when played from the medal tees, and has been voted one of the most outstanding holes in East Anglia. **The Constable**, built in 1979, enhanced the club's reputation and is considered by many to be the premier course. Measuring 6,544 yards, par-72, the course is noted for its water hazards, which come into play on six holes. As with the Gainsborough, the final hole presents a formidable drive over one of the four lakes to a plateau green with the clubhouse beyond.

With conservation always a priority, the Peakes planted large areas of woodland with 30,000 trees surrounding the fairways and lakes. In 1999 the club underwent a major redevelopment and was extended to include a 500-seater Conference Centre, a Health and Fitness Club, and a luxury hotel. Consequently, the club has been selected to host a Ladies European Tour event in 2001. The Peake family business was spotlighted by Sir John Harvey-Jones in his BBC Documentary Series *Troubleshooter* in 1990, 1992 and 2000, and he formally opened the new Conference Centre in his last programme. He advised the family about their various enterprises including Copella Apple Juice, and the golf club. Bill Peake died in 1979 and Devora in 1999, but their children, who have been working in the family business for a number of years, are now running the Group and its subsidiaries.

Sec/Manager: Peter Barfield

Professional: Kevin Lovelock

Directions: 8 miles north of Colchester. From Colchester centre take the A134 (Sudbury). After 7 miles turn right at Leavenheath onto the B1068 (Stoke By Nayland). After a further mile turn right into Keepers Lane and the entrance is on the left hand side.

Date Founded: 1972

Visitors: Welcome: Subject to availability, Contact Club in advance

Societies: Welcome: Contact Club in advance

Facilities: Putting Green, Trolley Hire, Buggy Hire, Bar, Restaurant, Practice Area, Chipping Green, Driving Range, Hotel, Leisure Centre

Gainsborough

Type of Course: Parkland

No of Holes: 18

Length: 6498 yds (5998 mtrs)

Par: 72

SSS: 71

Green Fees: Weekdays: Winter £18.00, Summer £25.00; Weekends/ Bank Holidays: Winter £25.00, Summer £35.00

Constable

Type of Course: Parkland

No of Holes:	18 holes
Length:	6544 yds (6040 mtrs)
Par:	72
SSS:	71
Green Fees:	Weekdays: Winter £18.00, Summer £25.00; Weekends/ Bank Holidays: Winter £25.00, Summer £35.00

Accommodation, Food and Drink

Reference numbers below refer to detailed information provided in section 2

Accommodation

Stoke by Nayland Club Hotel, Leavenheath, Colchester, Essex CO6 4PZ

Tel: 01206 262836 Fax: 01206 263356

A spacious modern country hotel in 300 acres of rolling countryside. 30 fine bedrooms, restaurant, golf courses, health & fitness centre. 508

Maison Talbooth, Dedham, Essex CO7 6HN

Tel: 01206 322367 Fax: 01206 322752

Ten top-notch en-suite bedrooms in a Victorian country house with superb views. Meals are served in the restaurant Le Talbooth, a short walk away. 504

Athelston House, 201 Maldon Road, Colchester, Essex CO3 3BQ

Tel: 01206 548652 e-mail: mackman@mcmail.com

Excellent B&B with friendly and helpful owners. There are 3 bedrooms furnished to a high standard of comfort. The dining room is spacious and there is a pretty garden. No smoking.

The Five Bells, 7 Mill Lane, Colne Engaine, Colchester, Essex CO6 2HY

Tel: 01787 224166

A 500 year old inn in a quiet and secluded location, boasting an extremely handsome interior yet retaining its old world charm. An extensive menu of freshly prepared food is on offer as are 3 comfortable guest bedrooms. A spot perfect for exploring the area.

Food and Drink

The Pheasant, Audley End, Gestingthorpe, Nr Halstead, Essex CO9 3AX

Tel: 01787 461196

A small, cosy village pub, off the beaten track but well worth seeking out for some of the best food in the area. 509

Stoke by Nayland Club Hotel, Leavenheath, Colchester, Essex CO6 4PZ

Tel: 01206 262836 Fax: 01206 263356

A spacious modern country hotel in 300 acres of rolling countryside. 30 fine bedrooms, restaurant, golf courses, health & fitness centre. 508

Maison Talbooth, Dedham, Essex CO7 6HN

Tel: 01206 322367 Fax: 01206 322752

Ten top-notch en-suite bedrooms in a Victorian country house with superb views. Meals are served in the restaurant Le Talbooth, a short walk away. 504

The Rose Inn, Thorington Street, Stoke-by-Nayland, Colchester, Essex CO6 4SN

Tel/Fax: 01206 337243

Pub with 50-cover restaurant, large car park and extensive gardens. Outstanding food, particularly seafood, with lots of daily specials. Closed Monday.

The Red Lion, High Street, Bildeston, Ipswich, Suffolk IP7 7EX

Tel: 01449 740476

A charming village pub, deep red outside, deep red with black beams in the bar areas. Food served throughout. Beer garden.

The Three Horseshoes, Church Road, Fordham, Colchester, Essex CO6 3NJ

Tel: 01206 240195

A beautiful whitewashed 16th century inn retaining many original features. It has gained a high regard for its delicious, home-cooked dishes, its great choice of drinks including real ales and for its homely atmosphere.

The Five Bells, 7 Mill Lane, Colne Engaine, Colchester, Essex CO6 2HY

Tel: 01787 224166

A 500 year old inn in a quiet and secluded location, boasting an extremely handsome interior yet retaining its old world charm. An extensive menu of freshly prepared food is on offer as are 3 comfortable guest bedrooms. A spot perfect for exploring the area.

Stowmarket

Lower Road, Onehouse, Stowmarket, Suffolk IP14 3DA

Tel: 01449 736473

Many years ago a husband and wife were scouring Suffolk for a golf club that would serve their needs on retirement. The criteria were quite simple for the couple that originally hailed from Scotland: the course should be pretty and challenging and the club friendly.

After several weeks of hunting, the husband was delighted when he called his wife to say: "I've found it." It turned out to be Stowmarket, a parkland course as pretty and challenging as you'll find anywhere and where you are assured of a warm welcome. And don't be put off by the fact that a rat runs through the course. On this occasion it turns out to be the River Rat, which adds that extra challenge to the 2nd and 3rd holes. The undulating Suffolk hills of the back nine provide some of the most scenic views that you will find anywhere in the county. Although Stowmarket is comparatively young by golfing standards having been formed in 1962, it is a mature course, with a wide variety of trees that provide a wonderful spectrum of colour throughout the changing seasons. It lies just over two miles from the centre of the town, at Onehouse, far enough away from the busy A14 not to inflict the constant drone of traffic, but close enough to offer easy access.

The course is set among trees with an array of wildlife that makes one feel part of nature. In fact, if you miss a short putt on the 8th, the crows will join in with the mirth of your partners! At 6,107 yards, Stowmarket has a par of 69 that is rarely beaten, even by the most accomplished of players. It is challenging enough for the English Golf Union to designate it as a "Centre of Excellence" for use on a regular basis to develop and train the county's best Junior Golfers, while in the autumn of 2000 it played host to the annual contest between England's Under-16 boys and Under-18 girls.

Sec/Manager: Roger West

Professional: Duncan Burl

Directions: 2 miles west of Stowmarket. From Stowmarket centre take the B1115 (Great Finborough). After¾ mile turn right into Lower Road. The entrance is 1½ miles on the right hand side.

Date Founded: 1962

Type of Course: Parkland

No of Holes: 18

Length: 6107 yds (5637 mtrs)

Par: 69

SSS: 69

Green Fees: Weekdays: £25.00 per round, £31.00 per day; Weekends/ Bank Holidays: £31.00 per round, £43.00 per day

Visitors: Welcome: Contact Club in advance by telephone, unable to play on Wednesday mornings prior to 9.15 am.

Societies: Welcome: Contact Club in advance by telephone

Facilities: Putting Green, Trolley Hire, Bar, Restaurant, Buggy Hire, Club Hire

Accommodation, Food and Drink

Reference numbers below refer to detailed information provided in section 2

Accommodation

The Golf Hotel, Ipswich, Suffolk IP4 5TR

Tel: 01473 727450

A 100-year-old pub in Elizabethan style, serving an impressive range of snacks and full meals throughout the day. Also eight letting rooms. 407

The Priory Hotel, Bury St Edmunds, Suffolk IP32 6EH

Tel: 01284 766181 Fax: 01284 767604

Period charm and elegance in a comfortable 39-bedroom hotel with modern amenities and a fine à la carte restaurant. 402

Wagner Cottage, The Street, Walsham-le-Willows, Bury St Edmunds, Suffolk IP33 3AA

Tel: 01359 259380

Three delightful bedrooms in a Grade ll listed building with a walled garden opposite the village church. Bed & Breakfast.

Red House Farm, Haughley, Stowmarket, Suffolk IP14 3QP

Tel: 01449 673323 Fax: 01449 675413

Four B&B bedrooms in a large red-painted cottage on a farm estate close to the A14. Guest sitting room; dining room. 410

Food and Drink

Clio's Restaurant, High Street, Debenham, Suffolk IP14 6QH

Tel: 01728 862062

Restaurant-cum-coffee shop in a 15th century house. Excellent home cooked lunches & Saturday evening meals; other evenings by arrangement.

The Golf Hotel, Ipswich, Suffolk IP4 5TR

Tel: 01473 727450

A 100-year-old pub in Elizabethan style, serving an impressive range of snacks and full meals throughout the day. Also eight letting rooms. 407

The Priory Hotel, Bury St Edmunds, Suffolk IP32 6EH

Tel: 01284 766181 Fax: 01284 767604

Period charm and elegance in a comfortable 39-bedroom hotel with modern amenities and a fine à la carte restaurant. 402

The Cock, The Street, Stanton, Bury St Edmunds, Suffolk IP31 2BP

Tel: 01359 250230

Cheerful pub with beams and open fires, pool, darts, monthly quiz. Restaurant and bar menus - steaks a speciality. No food Mon evening.

The Red Lion, High Street, Bildeston, Ipswich, Suffolk IP7 7EX

Tel: 01449 740476

A charming village pub, deep red outside, deep red with black beams in the bar areas. Food served throughout. Beer garden.

Suffolk G&CC

St John's Hill Platation, The Street, Fornham All Saints, Bury St Edmunds, Suffolk IP28 6JQ

Tel: 01284 706777 Fax: 10284 706721

A sister club to The Norfolk G&CC, The Suffolk was called Fornham Park until it became part of Messenger Leisure Ltd, headed by entrepreneur Eddy Shah, in 1997. The course dates back to the early Seventies since when it has had several titles and owners. Situated at Fornham St Geneviere, some two miles north west of Bury St Edmunds and just a short drive from Bury St Edmunds Golf Club, the Geneviere course lies in the valley of the River Lark.

It is a classic parkland layout redesigned by course architect Howard Swann with several new tees and greens around the river with various ponds and mature woodland coming into play. This is typical Suffolk countryside but the unwary golfer will pay a heavy price if the many hazards are not considered. You are never far away from the enticing waters of the Lark and on the front nine the short seventh perhaps sums up what is required here. Although the hole measures just 126 yards from the back tee, supreme accuracy is required to a narrow green that lies between the river and a drainage ditch.

There are just as many pitfalls lying in wait on the back nine, the par-4 11th, for instance, requires an arrow-like drive to avoid a stream and an avenue of mature trees that border the left. Pulled shots must also be avoided on the long 15th as the finish presents a test of skill and character. The big-hitters may opt to go for the green in two at 15 but should be wary of an interesting curving water feature some 150 yards from the raised putting surface. Then the long 16th, 474 yards from the back tee, demands two long, accurate shots to reach the green, while a fairway wood or long iron is the only option at the 203-yard 17th. In conclusion, the long, sweeping, dog-leg 18th (479 yards) with yet more water flanking most of the left side and across the approach to the green is all that stands between you and the welcoming 19th.

The well-appointed clubhouse also offers excellent dining and retail services as well as panoramic views over the course. There is also a leisure centre with swimming pool, gymnasium, spa and sauna.

Sec/Manager: Ken Weston

Professional: Stephen Hall

Directions: 1¾ miles north west of Bury St Edmunds. From Bury St Edmunds centre take the B1101 (Fornham All Saints).

	In the village turn right into The Street (B1106). The entrance is on the right hand side
Date Founded:	1974
Type of Course:	Parkland
No of Holes:	18
Length:	6345 yds (5856 mtrs)
Par:	72
SSS:	71
Green Fees:	Weekdays: £25.00; Weekends/ Bank Holidays: £30.00
Visitors:	Welcome: Contact Club by telephone in advance.
Societies:	Welcome: Contact Club by telephone or writing in advance.
Facilities:	Putting Green, Chipping Green, Club Hire, Trolley Hire, Buggy Hire, Bar, Restaurant

Accommodation, Food and Drink

Reference numbers below refer to detailed information provided in section 2

Accommodation

The Priory Hotel, Bury St Edmunds, Suffolk IP32 6EH

Tel: 01284 766181 Fax: 01284 767604

Period charm and elegance in a comfortable 39-bedroom hotel with modern amenities and a fine à la carte restaurant. 402

Wagner Cottage, The Street, Walsham-le-Willows, Bury St Edmunds, Suffolk IP33 3AA

Tel: 01359 259380

Three delightful bedrooms in a Grade ll listed building with a walled garden opposite the village church. Bed & Breakfast.

The Old Bull, The Street, Barton Mills, Bury St Edmunds, Suffolk IP27 6AE

Tel: 01638 713230

Twenty double bedrooms in an extended old inn by the A11 north of Newmarket and west of Bury.

The Rutland Arms Hotel, Newmarket, Suffolk CB8 8NB

Tel: 01638 664251 Fax: 01638 666298

Forty-six well-equipped modern bedrooms in a handsome hotel built round a cobbled courtyard. Bar meals and full restaurant menu. 405

Food and Drink

The Priory Hotel, Bury St Edmunds, Suffolk IP32 6EH

Tel: 01284 766181 Fax: 01284 767604

Period charm and elegance in a comfortable 39-bedroom hotel with modern amenities and a fine à la carte restaurant. 402

The Old Bull, The Street, Barton Mills, Bury St Edmunds, Suffolk IP27 6AE

Tel: 01638 713230

Twenty double bedrooms in an extended old inn by the A11 north of Newmarket and west of Bury.

The Bell Inn, Bury Road, Kennett, Nr Newmarket, Suffolk CB8 7PP

Tel: 01638 750286

Exposed beams and cheerful open fires in an atmospheric old coaching inn at the village crossroads. 60-cover restaurant.

The Rutland Arms Hotel, Newmarket, Suffolk CB8 8NB

Tel: 01638 664251 Fax: 01638 666298

Forty-six well-equipped modern bedrooms in a handsome hotel built round a cobbled courtyard. Bar meals and full restaurant menu. 405

Thorpeness Golf Club and Hotel

Lakeside Avenue, Thorpeness, Leiston, Suffolk IP16 4NH

Tel: 01728 452176 Fax: 01728 453868

Yet another of the legendary James Braid's heathland creations laid out in 1922 just a couple of miles north along the Heritage Coast from Aldeburgh and which is very much the same today. The quality of his design is as evident now as it was then and it continues to offer endless variety and extraordinary challenges to golfers of all levels. It has often been favourable compared to Sunningdale and Woodhall Spa which is high praise indeed.

It is built on similar terrain as those two prestigious golfing venues, while just a few minor changes have been made at Thorpeness to aid the flow of play. To play Thorpeness on a glorious summer day is an experience not to be missed especially if the gorse is providing a stunning background of yellow. The Aldeburgh branchline railway, which left the main line at Saxmundham, used to bisect the course. Its closure, under the axe wielded by the infamous Dr Beeching, has deprived the area as well as the course of a slice of bygone country life, but a road still cuts the course in two.

Braid's handiwork has provided a tough selection of par fours, seven of which are over 400 yards, but only one par five, allied to a quartet of short holes that all require sound shot-making. The short seventh is perhaps the pick and has been modified in that a pond, which puts that extra bit of fear into the tee-shot, has replaced the marsh. As you progress from the seventh green across the road to the eighth tee, you pass the site of the old Thorpeness Station and dream of what a picturesque scene it must have been with the little train steaming away. The course then takes you through avenues of gorse and heather and eventually back to the road, across which is the 18th hole where the drive is towards the unique House in the Clouds, the curious dwelling perched on top of an 85ft water tower which is a landmark for miles around.

The clubhouse has an attractive oak panelled bar serving a wide selection of beverages, while adjoining this is the patio lounge where morning coffee and snack lunches are served. Here, there is also a small spike bar that overlooks the terrace. The Hotel on site offers traditional hospitality throughout the year, while guests are also welcome to enjoy the tennis courts and bar at the nearby Country Club or to hire a boat on the Meare.

Sec/Manager: John Montague

Professional: Frank Hill

Directions: 2 miles north of Aldeburgh. From Aldeburgh centre take Thorpe Road north along the coast. At Thorpeness turn left onto the B1353 and after 200 yds turn left into Lakeside Avenue. The entrance is about a quarter of a mile along this road.

Date Founded: 1920

Type of Course: Heathland

No of Holes: 18

Length: 6370 yds (5880 mtrs)

Par: 69

SSS: 70

Green Fees: Weekdays: £32.50; Weekends/Bank Holidays: £37.50

Visitors: Welcome: Contact Club in advance by telephone.

Societies: Welcome: Contact Club in advance by writing, subject to availability.

Facilities: Putting Green, Trolley Hire, Bar, Restaurant, Buggy Hire, Club Hire, Chipping Green, Practice Ground, Hotel

Accommodation, Food and Drink

Reference numbers below refer to detailed information provided in section 2

Accommodation

Ocean House, 25 Crag Path, Aldeburgh, Suffolk IP15 5BS

Tel: 01728 452094

Characterful Bed & Breakfast accommodation in a Victorian house just a stone's throw from the beach. Excellent breakfasts. No smoking.

The Railway Inn, Leiston Road, Aldeburgh, Suffolk IP15 5PP

Tel: 01728 453864

Food and accommodation in a long-established pub on a roundabout at the top of the town. Darts, big-screen tv. 413

The Mill Inn, Market Cross Place, Aldeburgh, Suffolk IP15 5BJ

Tel: 01728 452563

16th century pub on the seafront, with 4 letting bedrooms, two bars and a good choice of home-cooked food.

Wentworth Hotel, Aldeburgh, Suffolk IP15 5BD

Tel: 01728 452312 Fax: 01728 454343

Owned by the same family for 80 years, the Wentworth offers comfort, elegance and style in its 38 rooms. Good food. Seafront location. 408

Thorpeness Hotel & Golf Club, Thorpeness, Suffolk IP16 4NH

Tel: 01728 452176 Fax: 01728 453868

In the unique holiday village of Thorpeness, a fine hotel with 30 en-suite bedrooms and an adjacent golf course and Country Club. 414

The Beeches Guest House, 117 High Street, Leiston, Suffolk IP16 4BX

Tel: 01728 832541

A delightful high street guest house with a friendly welcome, five comfortable letting bedrooms and good breakfasts.

The Brudenell Hotel, Aldeburgh, Suffolk IP15 5BU

Tel: 01728 452071 Fax: 01728 454082

A stunning location right on the seafront for the town's top hotel, with 47 spacious bedrooms and a well-regarded restaurant. 417

The Kings Head Inn, Orford, Suffolk IP12 2LW

Tel: 01394 450271

Authentic 13th century inn with period charm and up-to-date comfort. Three en-suite bedrooms. Snacks and full meals. 411

Food and Drink

The Railway Inn, Leiston Road, Aldeburgh, Suffolk IP15 5PP

Tel: 01728 453864

Food and accommodation in a long-established pub on a roundabout at the top of the town. Darts, big-screen tv. 413

The Mill Inn, Market Cross Place, Aldeburgh, Suffolk IP15 5BJ

Tel: 01728 452563

16th century pub on the seafront, with 4 letting bedrooms, two bars and a good choice of home-cooked food.

Wentworth Hotel, Aldeburgh, Suffolk IP15 5BD

Tel: 01728 452312 Fax: 01728 454343

Owned by the same family for 80 years, the Wentworth offers comfort, elegance and style in its 38 rooms. Good food. Seafront location. 408

The Lighthouse, Aldeburgh, Suffolk IP15 5AU

Tel/Fax: 01728 453377

One of the top restaurants in East Anglia, with a constantly changing menu of mouthwatering dishes using the pick of the catch and the best local suppliers. Book. 404

Thorpeness Hotel & Golf Club, Thorpeness, Suffolk IP16 4NH

Tel: 01728 452176 Fax: 01728 453868

In the unique holiday village of Thorpeness, a fine hotel with 30 en-suite bedrooms and an adjacent golf course and Country Club. 414

The Lion Inn, The Street, Theberton, Nr Leiston, Suffolk IP16 4RU

Tel: 01728 830185

Pretty village public house open every lunchtime and evening. Excellent home-cooked meals. Easily reached from the A12.

The Brudenell Hotel, Aldeburgh, Suffolk IP15 5BU

Tel: 01728 452071 Fax: 01728 454082

A stunning location right on the seafront for the town's top hotel, with 47 spacious bedrooms and a well-regarded restaurant. 417

The Bell Inn, Marlsford, Nr Woodbridge, Suffolk IP13 0AY

Tel: 01728 746242

Fish dishes are the speciality at this charming old thatched country inn on the A12. Log fires, beams, collection of wartime memorabilia. 419

The Castle Inn, Church Street, Framlingham, Suffolk IP13 9BT

Tel: 01728 724801

Home cooking of traditional and more modern dishes in a 16th century inn on the edge of the castle grounds. Soon to expand.

The Kings Head Inn, Orford, Suffolk IP12 2LW

Tel: 01394 450271

Authentic 13th century inn with period charm and up-to-date comfort. Three en-suite bedrooms. Snacks and full meals. 411

Ufford Park Hotel

Yarmouth Road, Ufford, Woodbridge, Suffolk IP12 1QW

Tel: 01394 382836 Fax: 01394 383582

Sec/Manager:	Bob Tidy
Professional:	Stuart Robertson
Directions:	1¾ miles north east of Woodbridge. From Woodbridge centre take the B1438 (Ufford). The entrance is on the right hand side.
Date Founded:	1991

Type of Course:	Parkland
No of Holes:	18
Length:	6400 yds (5944 mtrs)
Par:	71
SSS:	71
Green Fees:	Weekdays: £25.00; Weekends/ Bank Holidays: £30.00
Visitors:	Welcome: Contact Club in advance
Societies:	Welcome: Contact Club in advance
Facilities:	Putting Green, Trolley Hire, Bar, Restaurant, Buggy Hire, Club Hire, Chipping Green, Practice Ground

Accommodation, Food and Drink

Reference numbers below refer to detailed information provided in section 2

Accommodation

The Railway Inn, Leiston Road, Aldeburgh, Suffolk IP15 5PP

Tel: 01728 453864

Food and accommodation in a long-established pub on a roundabout at the top of the town. Darts, big-screen tv. 413

Wentworth Hotel, Aldeburgh, Suffolk IP15 5BD

Tel: 01728 452312 Fax: 01728 454343

Owned by the same family for 80 years, the Wentworth offers comfort, elegance and style in its 38 rooms. Good food. Seafront location. 408

Thorpeness Hotel & Golf Club, Thorpeness, Suffolk IP16 4NH

Tel: 01728 452176 Fax: 01728 453868

In the unique holiday village of Thorpeness, a fine hotel with 30 en-suite bedrooms and an adjacent golf course and Country Club. 414

The Brudenell Hotel, Aldeburgh, Suffolk IP15 5BU

Tel: 01728 452071 Fax: 01728 454082

A stunning location right on the seafront for the town's top hotel, with 47 spacious bedrooms and a well-regarded restaurant. 417

The Three Tuns Coaching Inn, Pettistree, Woodbridge, Suffolk IP13 0HW

Tel: 01728 747979 Fax: 01728 746244

150-year-old coaching inn en-suite bedrooms, real ales and excellent home-cooked food. 416

The Ramsholt Arms, Woodbridge, Suffolk IP12 3AB

Tel: 01394 411229 Fax: 01394 411818

A riverside free house in a scenic, out-of-the-way location overlooking the estuary. Lunches and dinners. Three letting bedrooms. 415

Food and Drink

The Railway Inn, Leiston Road, Aldeburgh, Suffolk IP15 5PP

Tel: 01728 453864

Food and accommodation in a long-established pub on a roundabout at the top of the town. Darts, big-screen tv. 413

Wentworth Hotel, Aldeburgh, Suffolk IP15 5BD

Tel: 01728 452312 Fax: 01728 454343

Owned by the same family for 80 years, the Wentworth offers comfort, elegance and style in its 38 rooms. Good food. Seafront location. 408

The Lighthouse, Aldeburgh, Suffolk IP15 5AU

Tel/Fax: 01728 453377

One of the top restaurants in East Anglia, with a constantly changing menu of mouthwatering dishes using the pick of the catch and the best local suppliers. Book. 404

Thorpeness Hotel & Golf Club, Thorpeness, Suffolk IP16 4NH

Tel: 01728 452176 Fax: 01728 453868

In the unique holiday village of Thorpeness, a fine hotel with 30 en-suite bedrooms and an adjacent golf course and Country Club. 414

The Brudenell Hotel, Aldeburgh, Suffolk IP15 5BU

Tel: 01728 452071 Fax: 01728 454082

A stunning location right on the seafront for the town's top hotel, with 47 spacious bedrooms and a well-regarded restaurant. 417

The White Lion, Lower Ufford, Woodbridge, Suffolk IP13 6DW

Tel: 01394 460770

A friendly welcome, traditional surroundings and super home-cooked food in a country pub dating back to the 14th century. 412

The Three Tuns Coaching Inn, Pettistree, Woodbridge, Suffolk IP13 0HW

Tel: 01728 747979 Fax: 01728 746244

150-year-old coaching inn en-suite bedrooms, real ales and excellent home-cooked food. 416

Kings Head Inn, Woodbridge, Suffolk IP12 4LX

Tel: 01394 387750

Some of the best pub food in Suffolk is served this ancient hostelry in the town centre. A warm, friendly place with bags of atmosphere. 403

The Ramsholt Arms, Woodbridge, Suffolk IP12 3AB

Tel: 01394 411229 Fax: 01394 411818

A riverside free house in a scenic, out-of-the-way location overlooking the estuary. Lunches and dinners. Three letting bedrooms. 415

Waldringfield Heath

Newbourne Road, Waldringfield, Woodbridge, Suffolk IP12 4PT

Tel: 01473 736768 Fax: 01473 736793

Nestling in beautiful countryside just a few miles east of Ipswich lies Waldringfield Heath, one of a number of Suffolk clubs created over the past two decades. It is the brainchild of Arthur Clarke, a local businessman, who decided to build a nine-hole course on arable farmland in 1981.

His company's designer, Philip Pilgrim, who was also responsible for other Suffolk courses at Ufford Park, Newton Green and Haverhill, laid out nine holes with 18 tees which opened in April 1983. Four years later more land was acquired to develop the course to 18 holes and the expanded design was opened by former England and Ipswich soccer boss Bobby Robson, who is still an honorary member. Unfortunately, the 1987 Hurricane which hit south east England destroyed 60 mature trees, especially a large avenue of pines, so a programme of replanting took place with over 12,000 saplings including maple, ash, oak, rowan, birch and poplars being installed along with a number of ponds.

At the time when the new nine was under construction, a member, extending his home, offered the club a considerable amount of topsoil which was gladly accepted when it was found to contain the seeds of gorse and bracken. On top of the sandy soil, these have boosted the natural heathland aspect of the course while the new trees have matured so that Waldringfield Heath is now a thriving and superbly challenging layout. As secretary Les McWade puts it: "A new golf course is always developing. Many changes have occurred over the years and the course has been renumbered several times."

One thing is paramount at Waldringfield, you must be a straight driver, while club professional Robin Mann, one of the most successful players in East Anglia, places the emphasis on course management. The par 70 circuit has several memorable holes, notably the 352-yard fifth with its heavily bunkered three-tier green, the 185-yard ninth, where water encircles the entire right boundary of the green, and the index one 16th. This plays every one of its 464 yards, is invariably into the prevailing wind, and where your shots have to be threaded between the left-hand gorse and out of bounds to the right.

The magnificent new clubhouse, built in 1999, offers every facility while the soccer connection is maintained with the Bobby Robson Bar along with a signed portrait of Ipswich's other famous son, Sir Alf Ramsey. There is also the Carl Giles Bar, named in memory of the late *Daily Express* cartoonist, who was a frequent visitor to the club.

Sec/Manager: Les Macwade

Professional: Robert Wann

Directions: 6 miles east of Ipswich. From Ipswich centre take the A124 (Marhesham Heath). Turn right onto the A12 (Felixstowe). After 1½ miles, at roundabout, turn left into Newbourne road and entrance is on the left hand side.

Date Founded: 1983

Type of Course: Heathland

No of Holes: 18

Length: 6079 yds (5611mtrs)

Par: 70

SSS: 69

Green Fees: Weekdays: £19.00; Weekends/ Bank Holidays: £22.00

Visitors: Welcome: Contact Club in advance.

Societies: Welcome: Contact Club in advance.

Facilities: Putting Green, Trolley Hire, Bar, Restaurant, Buggy Hire, Club Hire, Practice Ground

Accommodation, Food and Drink

Reference numbers below refer to detailed information provided in section 2

Accommodation

The Crown and Castle, Orford, Nr Woodbridge, Suffolk IP12 2LJ

Tel: 01394 450205 Fax: 01394 450176

Atmosphere and character aplenty in a handsome old inn by the imposing castle. 18 stylish en-suite bedrooms; super food. 418

The Golf Hotel, Ipswich, Suffolk IP4 5TR

Tel: 01473 727450

A 100-year-old pub in Elizabethan style, serving an impressive range of snacks and full meals throughout the day. Also eight letting rooms. 407

The Ramsholt Arms, Woodbridge, Suffolk IP12 3AB

Tel: 01394 411229 Fax: 01394 411818

A riverside free house in a scenic, out-of-the-way location overlooking the estuary. Lunches and dinners. Three letting bedrooms. 415

The Ferry Boat Inn, Felixstowe, Suffolk IP11 9RZ

Tel: 01394 284203

Fine old seaside inn next to the 4th tee at Felixstowe Golf Club. Well-prepared bar food, including children's dishes. Three letting bedrooms. 409

Food and Drink

The White Lion, Lower Ufford, Woodbridge, Suffolk IP13 6DW

Tel: 01394 460770

A friendly welcome, traditional surroundings and super home-cooked food in a country pub dating back to the 14th century. 412

The Crown and Castle, Orford, Nr Woodbridge, Suffolk IP12 2LJ

Tel: 01394 450205 Fax: 01394 450176

Atmosphere and character aplenty in a handsome old inn by the imposing castle. 18 stylish en-suite bedrooms; super food. 418

The Golf Hotel, Ipswich, Suffolk IP4 5TR

Tel: 01473 727450

A 100-year-old pub in Elizabethan style, serving an impressive range of snacks and full meals throughout the day. Also eight letting rooms. 407

Kings Head Inn, Woodbridge, Suffolk IP12 4LX

Tel: 01394 387750

Some of the best pub food in Suffolk is served this ancient hostelry in the town centre. A warm, friendly place with bags of atmosphere. 403

The Ramsholt Arms, Woodbridge, Suffolk IP12 3AB

Tel: 01394 411229 Fax: 01394 411818

A riverside free house in a scenic, out-of-the-way location overlooking the estuary. Lunches and dinners. Three letting bedrooms. 415

The Ferry Boat Inn, Felixstowe, Suffolk IP11 9RZ

Tel: 01394 284203

Fine old seaside inn next to the 4th tee at Felixstowe Golf Club. Well-prepared bar food, including children's dishes. Three letting bedrooms. 409

Woodbridge

Bromswell Heath, Woodbridge, Suffolk, P12 2PF

Tel: 01394 383212 Fax: 01394 382392

Another of Suffolk's heathland gems forming a thrilling quartet along with Purdis Heath, Aldeburgh and Thorpeness. Situated near the banks of the River Deben, the club lies a couple of miles outside Woodbridge on the road to Orford.

The club celebrated its centenary in 1993, having, like many other clubs, owed its birth to a benefactor. In Woodbridge's case it was Major J E W Howey, an all-round sportsman yet one who had never played golf and who held the game in great contempt. However, he was 'converted' on his annual visit to the South of France when he was induced to play golf and found it: 'A damned good game'. The bug had bitten and he duly laid out six holes in front of his house. He was convinced there was a site in the area for a first class course and at his own expense the Major brought professional Davie Grant from Scotland to spy out the land. They explored around, eventually settling on the present heathland site at Bromeswell and the farmer, Alfred Smith, agreed to rent the land. He asked £15 per annum, the Major offered £10, and as negotiations dragged on, the Major grew impatient. In the end he took the shooting on the farm for three years on the proviso that the golf would be free.

So Woodbridge was up and running and the good Major played an ever-active role in its development until his death in 1924. The official opening took place just a week prior to Christmas 1893 following swift progress on building the course. The original nine holes soon became 18, while a timber and iron clubhouse was constructed and lasted until replaced by the present

building in 1969. James Braid, who along with Harry Vardon and J H Taylor played Woodbridge before the First World War, returned several times to advise on course changes. The course then measured 6,088 yards but during the war two holes became unplayable because they were on the site of an army camp and had to be replaced in 1919. During World War II scaffolding and wrecked cars were strewn over the flatter parts of the course as a deterrent to gliders and parachutists in the event of an invasion. But the quality of the course, something Woodbridge always prides itself on, still applies today.

Considering the flat nature of the surrounding terrain, the course is surprisingly undulating and always a challenge. You would be hard pressed to find a poor hole and while it may only be a par 70, its biggest defence lies in its variety of par fours, which account for two-thirds of the layout. And adding variety there is the nine-hole Forest Course, which dates from 1968.

Sec/Manager: Tony Theunissen
Professional: Adrian Hubert
Directions: 1½ miles east of Woodbridge. From the north side of town, take the A1153 (Rendlesham). Turn left into Orford road and the entrance is on the right hand side.
Date Founded: 1903
Visitors: Welcome: Contact Club in advance. Weekends not available.
Societies: Welcome: Contact Club in advance
Facilities: Putting Green, Bar, Restaurant, Chipping Green, Trolley Hire, Practice Area

Main

Type of Course: Heathland
No of Holes: 18
Length: 6299 yds (5814mtrs)
Par: 70
SSS: 70
Green Fees: Weekdays: £33.00; Weekends/ Bank Holidays: not available

Forest

Type of Course: Heathland
No of Holes: 9
Length: 3191 yds (2945mtrs)
Par: 35
SSS: 35
Green Fees: Weekdays: £16.00; Weekends/ Bank Holidays: £16.00

Accommodation, Food and Drink

Reference numbers below refer to detailed information provided in section 2

Accommodation

Ocean House, 25 Crag Path, Aldeburgh, Suffolk IP15 5BS
Tel: 01728 452094
Characterful Bed & Breakfast accommodation in a Victorian house just a stone's throw from the beach. Excellent breakfasts. No smoking.

The Mill Inn, Market Cross Place, Aldeburgh, Suffolk IP15 5BJ
Tel: 01728 452563
16th century pub on the seafront, with 4 letting bedrooms, two bars and a good choice of home-cooked food.

The Crown and Castle, Orford, Nr Woodbridge, Suffolk IP12 2LJ
Tel: 01394 450205 Fax: 01394 450176
Atmosphere and character aplenty in a handsome old inn by the imposing castle. 18 stylish en-suite bedrooms; super food. 418

The Three Tuns Coaching Inn, Pettistree, Woodbridge, Suffolk IP13 0HW
Tel: 01728 747979 Fax: 01728 746244
150-year-old coaching inn en-suite bedrooms, real ales and excellent home-cooked food. 416

The Kings Head Inn, Orford, Suffolk IP12 2LW
Tel: 01394 450271
Authentic 13th century inn with period charm and up-to-date comfort. Three en-suite bedrooms. Snacks and full meals. 411

The Ramsholt Arms, Woodbridge, Suffolk IP12 3AB
Tel: 01394 411229 Fax: 01394 411818
A riverside free house in a scenic, out-of-the-way location overlooking the estuary. Lunches and dinners. Three letting bedrooms. 415

Food and Drink

The Mill Inn, Market Cross Place, Aldeburgh, Suffolk IP15 5BJ
Tel: 01728 452563
16th century pub on the seafront, with 4 letting bedrooms, two bars and a good choice of home-cooked food.

The White Lion, Lower Ufford, Woodbridge, Suffolk IP13 6DW

Tel: 01394 460770

A friendly welcome, traditional surroundings and super home-cooked food in a country pub dating back to the 14th century. 412

The Crown and Castle, Orford, Nr Woodbridge, Suffolk IP12 2LJ

Tel: 01394 450205 Fax: 01394 450176

Atmosphere and character aplenty in a handsome old inn by the imposing castle. 18 stylish en-suite bedrooms; super food. 418

The Three Tuns Coaching Inn, Pettistree, Woodbridge, Suffolk IP13 0HW

Tel: 01728 747979 Fax: 01728 746244

150-year-old coaching inn en-suite bedrooms, real ales and excellent home-cooked food. 416

Kings Head Inn, Woodbridge, Suffolk IP12 4LX

Tel: 01394 387750

Some of the best pub food in Suffolk is served this ancient hostelry in the town centre. A warm, friendly place with bags of atmosphere. 403

The Kings Head Inn, Orford, Suffolk IP12 2LW

Tel: 01394 450271

Authentic 13th century inn with period charm and up-to-date comfort. Three en-suite bedrooms. Snacks and full meals. 411

The Ramsholt Arms, Woodbridge, Suffolk IP12 3AB

Tel: 01394 411229 Fax: 01394 411818

A riverside free house in a scenic, out-of-the-way location overlooking the estuary. Lunches and dinners. Three letting bedrooms. 415

ESSEX

Like the Irish, the populous of Essex has been the butt of comedians in recent times. Essex man has become a symbol of the seedier side of business and living, while Essex girl is far removed from the low morals figure characterised in certain tabloid newspapers. It is a label that is hard to detach yet Essex has much going for it and contrary to popular belief it is not the ultra flat landscape that many writers suggest. Its immediate proximity to London and its commerce means Essex is largely a commuter county while the capital's unending expansion into the Home Counties has gobbled up much of the original Essex into what is now Greater London. That now extends to the M25 motorway, which is where most people feels Essex now starts. That being so, some important parts of ancient Essex such as the remnants of Epping Forest, the ancient hunting ground of the Saxons and Normans, are now enclosed by the London Orbital Motorway.

Epping Forest

To many, Essex is depicted by three different faces dependant in which part of the county you happen to be. There is the Thames-side corridor stretching past the resort of Southend, formerly marshland but now generally industrialised; the coastal belt sweeping up to the Suffolk border, areas claimed from the sea, now packed with hidden creeks and remote islands; and the rest which is part rural, part suburban but always under threat of development as London pushes its tentacles ever outwards. Although industrial complexes have swallowed up much of the north bank of the Thames, there are still considerable pockets of marshes offering habitat for wildlife.

Saffron Walden Parish Church

The Borough of Thurrock has a rich history dating back to the Romans and beyond and also played an important role in the defence of the capital. Henry VIII had Block Houses built at Tilbury and these became Coalhouse Fort and Tilbury Fort. It was also at Tilbury that Queen Elizabeth I delivered her famous address to her troops prior to taking on the Spanish Armada. Tilbury itself was until recent times an important dock area, while nearby Grays featured shipbuilding in past ages. Just a few miles down the A13 lies the New Town of Basildon, while at the end of the trunk road is Southend-on-Sea, once the number one holiday destination for London's workers. It still boasts the longest pleasure pier in the

Thames Barges at Maldon

world, stretching 1.3 miles into the Thames Estuary. In days past, holiday-makers would board one of the many paddle steamers in central London and disembark at the end of the pier and use the electric railway to reach the many attractions in the town. These days, Southend is less of a holiday destination but it still sees many visitors especially to places like the Sealife Centre. Just a few miles away in the Thames Estuary lies Canvey Island, which suffered in the 1953 East Coast floods yet still holds a fatal fascination to all who visit, while nearby Leigh-on-Sea is the centre for cockle fishing.

Moving north up the coast brings a more rural and mystifying part of the county. Here you find the picturesque towns of Burnham on Crouch and Mersey Island as well as the seaside resorts of Clacton, Frinton and Walton and the ports of Maldon and Harwich. In past days, this area was a haven for smugglers and it is easy to see why with the many remote creeks and inlets. Burnham, along with Maldon, is an historical maritime town with its colourful quayside houses and cottages of ex-seafaring folk where you can still buy fresh fish when the boats come in. This is a popular yachting centre as is the whole area between the Crouch and the Orwell where often you can't seem to put a cigarette paper between the many bobbing masts. Clacton and Walton, like Southend, cater for the holidaymaker with their piers and amusement, while Frinton is noted as being secluded and unspoilt. The ancient town of Maldon, which celebrated its 900th anniversary a few years ago, at the mouth of the River Blackwater, was an important port in past times when Thames Barges were moored in profusion. These days you can still see one or two of these sturdy vessels as you relax with a refreshing beer on the quayside. A few miles away is the large village of Tiptree, home of the famous Wilkins jam factory, in the centre of a fruit-growing region, while Colchester, Britain's oldest recorded town, has over 2,000 years of history.

Established before Christ, it was a prime target for a Roman invasion, which occurred during the 1st century. Then known as Camulodunum, it was the capital of Roman Britain until AD 60 when Queen Boudica took revenge on the Romans by burning the town to the ground and massacred the occupants. In the Dark Ages the Danes were frequent raiders but by 1085 the Normans had built a castle which still occupies a prominent site. It is well worth a visit as is its museum, which provides an insight into what life was like in those times. Colchester also has a Dutch Quarter, the home of Dutch Prodestants, who arrived in the 16th century after fleeing Spanish rule in their homeland. These days, Colchester is a bustling town with a theatre, a thriving zoo and it plays host in

Gardens, Clacton-on-Sea

the autumn to the annual oyster Feast, the oysters being cultivated in the lower reaches of the River Colne. Nearby is the port of Wivenhoe, and to the north east lies Harwich and Parkeston Quay, landfall for ferries from Holland and Scandinavia as well as cruise liners. Above Colchester, the Stour Valley provides tranquil, rolling countryside around Dedham and West Bergholt, while to the west you find Chappel, home of the East Anglian Railway Museum, Coggeshall, centre of the antiques trade, and Braintree, where Samuel Courtauld established a silk mill in 1816. A former mill has been faithfully restored and is now the Working Silk Museum.

The north part of Essex is particularly historical. All the towns are packed with fascinating architecture narrow streets and quaint shops where you can wile away hours just browsing. Halstead, which means healthy place, was another weaving centre, while Saffron Walden derives its name from the Saffron crocus, which was grown in the area to make dyes. Just outside the town lies the Jacobean mansion, Audley End House, the Braybrooke family home where Capability Brown landscaped the gardens and Robert Adam designed some of the outbuildings. Nearby Thaxted was originally a Saxon settlement and its magnificent Guildhall, standing in the middle of the town, dates back to 1390. This blends in superbly with the many timber-framed houses and was once a meeting place for cutlers. However, on the demise of the industry it became a school and is now where the Parish council meets. The village of Finchingfield with its thatched cottages and duck pond at its centre, is a familiar picture postcard of Essex, while further east lies Great Dunmow, home of the ancient flitch ceremony. This goes back to the 12th century, is still enacted and refers to a flitch or side of bacon which is awarded to any married couple 'who have not had a brawl in their home nor wished to be unmarried for the last 12 months and a day'.

Ramsey Mill

Of the four East Anglian counties, Essex has been the most productive as far as top golfers are concerned. Michael Bonallack, arguably the greatest amateur England has produced with five Amateur Championships and nine Walker Cup appearances among many others, spent most of his playing days at Thorpe Hall near Southend, while Geoff Godwin from Thorndon Park was a Walker Cup player in 1979 and '81. Current members of the European Tour include Mark Davis from Brentwood, Harlow-based Daren Lee, and Robert Coles from Hornchurch, while on the amateur front Essex were boys county champions in 1997 and have twice reached the men's final. The Essex County Amateur Golf Union was inaugurated at a meeting at Romford Golf Club in February 1924 attended by 16 of the 23 clubs existing at that time. Bowers Gifford and Monkhams, two of the clubs present, no longer exist and Mersea Island, Naze, Nazeing, Lee Wick, Lee-over-Sands, Walthamstow, Highams Park, Bury, Little Warley and Creeksea have either become defunct or changed their names.

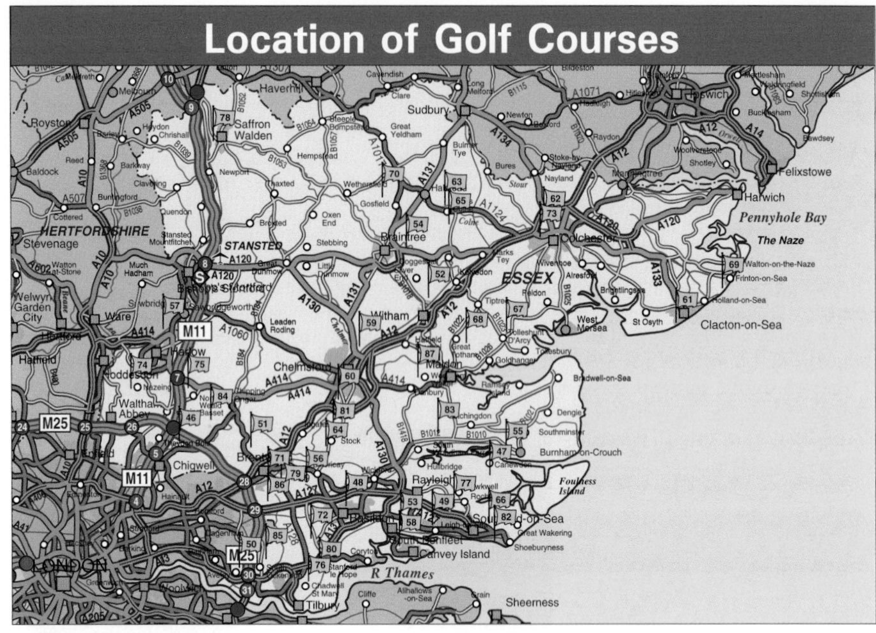

© MAPS IN MINUTES ™ (2000)

Abridge

Epping Lane, Stapleford Tawney,
Essex RM4 1ST

Tel: 01708 688396 Fax: 01708 688550

Sec/Manager:	Miss Payne
Professional:	Stewart Layton
Directions:	2 miles east of Theydon Bois. From Theydon Bois take the B172 (Abridge) and before the village turn left onto Epping Lane (Stapleford Tawney).
Date Founded:	1964
Type of Course:	Parkland
No of Holes:	18
Length:	6686 yds (6171 mtrs)
Par:	72
SSS:	72
Green Fees:	Weekdays: £30.00; Weekends/ Bank Holidays: £40.00
Visitors:	Welcome: Contact Club in advance. Unable to play weekend mornings.
Societies:	Welcome: Contact Club in advance by writing.
Facilities:	Putting Green, Chipping Green, Driving Range, Club Hire, Trolley Hire, Buggy Hire, Bar, Restaurant, Private Rooms, Swimming Pool. Snooker Room

Accommodation, Food and Drink

Reference numbers below refer to detailed information provided in section 2

Food and Drink

King Harolds Head, Bumbles Green, Nazeing Common, Waltham Abbey, Essex EN9 2RY

Tel: 01992 893110 Fax: 01992 893412

A charming old free house on the Waltham Abbey-Harlow road. Friendly ambience, good company, exceptional food. 503

The Queens Head, Fyfield, Essex CM5 0RY

Tel: 01277 899118

A 500-year-old pub near the church in the centre of the little village of Fyfield. Exceptional food has earned wide acclaim. 507

The Horseshoes, Horseshoe Hill, Upshire, Waltham Abbey, Essex EN9 3SN

Tel/Fax: 01992 712745

A grown-ups pub in the countryside just outside Waltham Abbey. Real ales, lunches, darts, quizzes, karaoke.

The New Inn, Waltham Abbey, Essex EN9 1EJ

Tel: 01992 712939

Sociable town centre pub with a good line in food (excellent meat dishes) and 10 letting bedrooms. Live music at the weekend. 510

The Alma Arms, Horsemanside, Navestock, Brentwood, Essex CM14 5ST

Tel: 01277 372629 Fax: 01277 375440

Delicious food and outstanding real ales and wines in an 18th century pub of character by Navestock Common.

Ballards Gore G&CC

Gore Road, Canewdon, Rochford,
Essex SS4 2DA

Tel: 01702 258917 Fax: 01702 258571

Sec/Manager:	David Caton
Professional:	Richard Emery
Directions:	5 miles north of Southend.

	From Southend centre take the A127 for one mile to Priory Park, then the B road to Rochford. Follow signs to Great Stambridge and the entrance is at the first T Junction.
Date Founded:	1980
Type of Course:	Parkland
No of Holes:	18
Length:	6874 yds (6345 mtrs)
Par:	73
SSS:	73
Green Fees:	Weekdays: £20.00; Weekends/ Bank Holidays: £20.00
Visitors:	Welcome: Contact Club by telephone in advance. Unable to play Saturday and Sunday mornings.
Societies:	Welcome: By arrangement only
Facilities:	Putting Green, Chipping Green, Practice Ground, Club Hire, Trolley Hire, Buggy Hire, Bar, Restaurant, Private Rooms, Snooker Room

Accommodation, Food and Drink

Reference numbers below refer to detailed information provided in section 2

Accommodation

Hotel Renouf, Bradley Way, Rochford, Essex SS4 1BU

Tel: 01702 549563 Fax: 07102 549563

Modern Town Hotel, offering 23 en-suite rooms. A la Carte restaurant specialising in French cuisine.

Beaches, 192 Eastern Esplanade, Southend -On-Sea, Essex SS1 3AA

Tel: 01702 586124 Fax: 01702 588377

Edwardian house, sea front location. 8 en-suite rooms close to all local facilities.

The Chichester Hotel, Old London Road, Raweth, Wickford, Essex SS11 8UE

Tel: 01268 560555 Fax: 01268 560580

Quiet location, 33 en-suite rooms, and private parking. Superb food in a la carte restaurant, mid-week special menus available. Residents and diners bar.

The Lodge Country Inn, Rettendon Lodge, Hayes Chase Battlesbridge, Wickford, Essex SS11 7QT

Tel: 01245 320060 Fax: 01245 322622

On the outskirts of Wickford, licensed 8 en-suite room hotel, a la carte restaurant. Bar and bar snacks available.

Food and Drink

The Duke of York, Southend Road (A129), South Green, Billericay, Essex CM11 2PR

Tel: 01277 651403

Grand old pub with a restaurant serving freshly prepared food including an exceptional vegetarian choice. Sunday roast, bar snacks, real ales.

The Beehive Tearoom, 12 South Street, Rochford, Essex SS4 1BQ

Tel: 01702 547644

Tiny tearoom in the village centre, serving coffee, tea, hot and cold snacks, fry-ups and roasts - a speciality.

The Last Post, Southend-on-Sea, Essex SS1 1SA

Tel: 01702 431682

A large all-day pub in premises that were once the central Post Office - hence the name. 512

The Ship, Princess Margaret Road, East Tilbury Village, Essex, RM18 8PB

Tel: 01375 843041

Renowned for its excellent ales and food, this comfortable pub is open all day every day. Lunchtime and evening menus are available and the beer garden is safe for children.

Hotel Renouf, Bradley Way, Rochford, Essex SS4 1BU

Tel: 01702 549563 Fax: 07102 549563

Modern Town Hotel, offering 23 en-suite rooms. A la Carte restaurant specialising in French cuisine.

The Chichester Hotel, Old London Road, Raweth, Wickford, Essex SS11 8UE

Tel: 01268 560555 Fax: 01268 560580

Quiet location, 33 en-suite rooms, and private parking. Superb food in a la carte restaurant, mid-week special menus available. Residents and diners bar.

The Lodge Country Inn, Rettendon Lodge, Hayes Chase Battlesbridge, Wickford, Essex SS11 7QT

Tel: 01245 320060 Fax: 01245 322622

On the outskirts of Wickford, licensed 8 en-suite room hotel, a la carte restaurant. Bar and bar snacks available.

Basildon

Clayhill Lane, Sparrow's Hearne, Basildon, Essex SS16 5JP

Tel: 01268 533297 Fax: 01268 533849

Sec/Manager:	A Burch
Professional:	M Oliver
Directions:	1½ miles south of Basildon. From the A13 junction with the A176 take Landon Road and then Nether Mayne Road. The entrance is on the right hand side off the second roundabout ½ mile from A13 via Sparrow's Hearne.
Date Founded:	1967
Type of Course:	Parkland
No of Holes:	18
Length:	6236 yds (5756 mtrs)
Par:	72
SSS:	70
Green Fees:	Weekdays: £9.50; Weekends/ Bank Holidays: £16.00
Visitors:	Welcome: Contact Club in advance.
Societies:	Welcome: Contact club in writing in advance.
Facilities:	Putting Green, Chipping Green, Driving Area, Trolley Hire, Buggy Hire, Bar, Restaurant, Private Rooms

Accommodation, Food and Drink

Reference numbers below refer to detailed information provided in section 2

Accommodation

Hotel Campanile & Restaurant, A127 Southend Arterial Road, Pipps Hill, Basildon, Essex SS14 3AE

Tel: 01268 530810 Fax: 01268 286710

Situated one mile from the town centre, 100 en-suite rooms, full bar facilities with large restaurant serving continental cuisine.

The Quays, New Festival Leisure Park, Cranes Farm Road, Basildon, Essex SS14 3AD

Tel: 01268 290400 Fax: 0870 700 1377

Modern town centre hotel, 64 en-suite rooms, and large restaurant serving traditional English food.

The Chichester Hotel, Old London Road, Raweth, Wickford, Essex SS11 8UE

Tel: 01268 560555 Fax: 01268 560580

Quiet location, 33 en-suite rooms, and private parking. Superb food in a la carte restaurant, mid-week special menus available. Residents and diners bar.

The Lodge Country Inn, Rettendon Lodge, Hayes Chase Battlesbridge, Wickford, Essex SS11 7QT

Tel: 01245 320060 Fax: 01245 322622

On the outskirts of Wickford, licensed 8 en-suite room hotel, a la carte restaurant. Bar and bar snacks available.

Food and Drink

The Duke of York, Southend Road (A129), South Green, Billericay, Essex CM11 2PR

Tel: 01277 651403

Grand old pub with a restaurant serving freshly prepared food including an exceptional vegetarian choice. Sunday roast, bar snacks, real ales.

The Beehive Tearoom, 12 South Street, Rochford, Essex SS4 1BQ

Tel: 01702 547644

Tiny tearoom in the village centre, serving coffee, tea, hot and cold snacks, fry-ups and roasts - a speciality.

The Theobald Arms, Kings Walk, Grays, Essex RM17 6HR

Tel: 01375 372253

A very friendly and popular pub by the dockside in Grays. A variety of home-cooked food is available at lunchtimes accompanied by a wide range of real ales. A beer festival is held each summer.

The Park Tavern, Romford Road, Aveley, South Ockenden, Essex RM15 4PH

Tel: 01708 863798

A family run pub, sporting an interesting collection of celebrity photos. Good food is prepared from the freshest ingredients and served daily 2-5. There's live entertainment on Fridays and Saturdays.

The Ship, Princess Margaret Road, East Tilbury Village, Essex, RM18 8PB

Tel: 01375 843041

Renowned for its excellent ales and food, this comfortable pub is open all day every day. Lunchtime and evening menus are available and the beer garden is safe for children.

Hotel Campanile & Restaurant, A127 Southend Arterial Road, Pipps Hill, Basildon, Essex SS14 3AE

Tel: 01268 530810 Fax: 01268 286710

Situated one mile from the town centre, 100 en-suite rooms, full bar facilities with large restaurant serving continental cuisine.

The Quays, New Festival Leisure Park, Cranes Farm Road, Basildon, Essex SS14 3AD

Tel: 01268 290400 Fax: 0870 700 1377

Modern town centre hotel, 64 en-suite rooms, and large restaurant serving traditional English food.

The Chichester Hotel, Old London Road, Raweth, Wickford, Essex SS11 8UE

Tel: 01268 560555 Fax: 01268 560580

Quiet location, 33 en-suite rooms, and private parking. Superb food in a la carte restaurant, mid-week special menus available. Residents and diners bar.

The Lodge Country Inn, Rettendon Lodge, Hayes Chase Battlesbridge, Wickford, Essex SS11 7QT

Tel: 01245 320060 Fax: 01245 322622

On the outskirts of Wickford, licensed 8 en-suite room hotel, a la carte restaurant. Bar and bar snacks available.

Belfairs

Eastwood Road North, Leigh-on-Sea, Essex SS9 4LR

Tel: 01702 525345

Sec/Manager:	Bob Mace
Professional:	Martin Foreman
Directions:	2½ miles south east of Rayleigh. From the A127, Southend Arterial Road, go 2 miles east of Rayleigh. Take the exit and turn right into Bellhouse Lane then bearing right into Eastwood Road. The entrance is ¾ mile on the right hand side.
Date Founded:	1926
Type of Course:	Parkland
No of Holes:	18
Length:	5800 yds (5353 mtrs)
Par:	68
SSS:	68
Green Fees:	Weekdays: £10.40; Weekends/ Bank Holidays: £15.80
Visitors:	Welcome: Contact Club in advance.
Societies:	Welcome: Contact Club in advance by telephone.
Facilities:	Putting Green, Chipping Green, Practice Field, Club Hire, Trolley Hire

Accommodation, Food and Drink

Reference numbers below refer to detailed information provided in section 2

Accommodation

Hotel Renouf, Bradley Way, Rochford, Essex SS4 1BU

Tel: 01702 549563 Fax: 07102 549563

Modern Town Hotel, offering 23 en-suite rooms. A la Carte restaurant specialising in French cuisine.

Beaches, 192 Eastern Esplanade, Southend -On-Sea, Essex SS1 3AA

Tel: 01702 586124 Fax: 01702 588377

Edwardian house, sea front location. 8 en-suite rooms close to all local facilities.

Ifracombe House Hotel, 9-13 Wilson Road, Southend-on-Sea, Essex SS1 1HG

Tel: 01702 351000

Licensed hotel, 20 en-suite rooms, private parking, evening meals by prior arrangement. Self contained flat available.

The Grand Hotel, The Broadway, Leigh-On-Sea, Essex SS9 1PJ

Tel: 01702 710768

Seafront location, public house with adjoining 16 en-suite room hotel. Private parking, good pub food available.

Food and Drink

The Queens Head, Fyfield, Essex CM5 0RY

Tel: 01277 899118

A 500-year-old pub near the church in the centre of the little village of Fyfield. Exceptional food has earned wide acclaim. 507

The Duke of York, Southend Road (A129), South Green, Billericay, Essex CM11 2PR

Tel: 01277 651403

Grand old pub with a restaurant serving freshly prepared food including an exceptional vegetarian choice. Sunday roast, bar snacks, real ales.

The Beehive Tearoom, 12 South Street, Rochford, Essex SS4 1BQ

Tel: 01702 547644

Tiny tearoom in the village centre, serving coffee, tea, hot and cold snacks, fry-ups and roasts - a speciality.

The Last Post, Southend-on-Sea, Essex SS1 1SA

Tel: 01702 431682

A large all-day pub in premises that were once the central Post Office - hence the name. 512

The Plough, 169 Roman Road, Mountnessing, Brentwood, Essex CM15 0UG

Tel: 01277 352026

A large welcoming pub on the B1002 with brasses and memorabilia adorning the walls inside. The excellent menu changes seasonally and there is a garden equipped for childrens enjoyment.

The Thatchers Arms, Warley Road, Great Warley, Brentwood, Essex CM13 3HU

Tel: 01277 233535
email: JimSarah@supernet.co.uk

A large and handsome pub adjacent to the Warley Place Nature Reserve, makes it an ideal spot for walkers. The panelled interior offers snacks and main meals in the dining room or on the adjoining patio.

The Green Man Pub and Restaurant, Navestock Side, Brentwood, Essex CM14 5SD

Tel: 01277 372231

Previously a hunting lodge, this pristine building has been a pub since 1620. Its menu now offers an exceptional choice of traditional favourites as well as a good selection of ales.

The Ship, Princess Margaret Road, East Tilbury Village, Essex, RM18 8PB

Tel: 01375 843041

Renowned for its excellent ales and food, this comfortable pub is open all day every day. Lunchtime and evening menus are available and the beer garden is safe for children.

Hotel Renouf, Bradley Way, Rochford, Essex SS4 1BU

Tel: 01702 549563 Fax: 07102 549563

Modern Town Hotel, offering 23 en-suite rooms. A la Carte restaurant specialising in French cuisine.

Ifracombe House Hotel, 9-13 Wilson Road, Southend-on-Sea, Essex SS1 1HG

Tel: 01702 351000

Licensed hotel, 20 en-suite rooms, private parking, evening meals by prior arrangement. Self contained flat available.

The Grand Hotel, The Broadway, Leigh-On-Sea, Essex SS9 1PJ

Tel: 01702 710768

Seafront location, public house with adjoining 16 en-suite room hotel. Private parking, good pub food available.

Belhus Park

Belhus Park, South Ockendon, Essex RM15 4QR

Tel/Fax: 01708 854260

Sec/Manager:	John Clerey
Professional:	Gary Lunn
Directions:	1 mile west of South Ockendon. The entrance is ½ mile north west of the M25 junction 30 on the right hand side of the Avery By-Pass (B135).
Date Founded:	1974
Type of Course:	Parkland
No of Holes:	18
Length:	5589 yds (5159 mtrs)
Par:	68
SSS:	67
Green Fees:	Weekdays: £9.50; Weekends/ Bank Holidays: £14.00
Visitors:	Welcome: Contact Club in advance. Tee times require prior booking at weekends.
Societies:	Welcome: Contact Clib in writing in advance.
Facilities:	Putting Green, Driving Range, Club Hire, Trolley Hire, Bar, Restaurant

Accommodation, Food and Drink

Reference numbers below refer to detailed information provided in section 2

Food and Drink

The Duke of York, Southend Road (A129), South Green, Billericay, Essex CM11 2PR

Tel: 01277 651403

Grand old pub with a restaurant serving freshly prepared food including an exceptional vegetarian choice. Sunday roast, bar snacks, real ales.

The Thatchers Arms, Warley Road, Great Warley, Brentwood, Essex CM13 3HU

Tel: 01277 233535 email: JimSarah@supernet.co.uk

A large and handsome pub adjacent to the Warley Place Nature Reserve, makes it an ideal spot for walkers. The panelled interior offers snacks and main meals in the dining room or on the adjoining patio.

The Theobald Arms, Kings Walk, Grays, Essex RM17 6HR

Tel: 01375 372253

A very friendly and popular pub by the dockside in Grays. A variety of home-cooked food is available at lunchtimes accompanied by a wide range of real ales. A beer festival is held each summer.

The Park Tavern, Romford Road, Aveley, South Ockenden, Essex RM15 4PH

Tel: 01708 863798

A family run pub, sporting an interesting collection of celebrity photos. Good food is prepared from the freshest ingredients and served daily 2-5. There's live entertainment on Fridays and Saturdays.

The Ship, Princess Margaret Road, East Tilbury Village, Essex, RM18 8PB

Tel: 01375 843041

Renowned for its excellent ales and food, this comfortable pub is open all day every day. Lunchtime and evening menus are available and the beer garden is safe for children.

Bentley G&CC

Ongar Road, Brentwood, Essex CM15 9SS

Tel: 01277 373179 Fax: 01277 375097

The brainchild of four local businessmen back in the late 1960s, Bentley has overcome drainage problems to become one of the best and toughest courses in Essex. Designed by Alec Swan of Golf Landscapes Ltd., it opened in 1972 on 110 acres of former farmland on the Ongar Road just a few miles north of Brentwood. An exhibition match involving Ryder Cup golfers Brian Huggett, Neil Coles and Bernard Hunt together with the then club's own professional Geoff Robbins marked the opening on 29 April of that year.

The low lying land was often wet in inclement conditions, but judicious work with drainage ditches plus the introduction of several lakes over the past 25 years has brought the early problems under control and left a course that has slowly earned a glowing reputation. The former owners offered the club for sale to the membership but in the end it was bought by farmer John Vivers, who has worked hard to bring the course up to its current high standard.

Water comes into play either from ditches, ponds or lakes on at least 11 holes, while the growth of the trees and hedges over the years has transformed what began as an open landscape into a tight layout where accurate shotmaking is a must. Measuring 6,709 yards from the back tees, the circuit has three par fives in a par 37 front nine but just one in a back nine of 35. The par threes are particularly testing with two of over 200 yards from the tiger tees and the shortest at 145 yards. The short 12th at 164 yards is particularly teasing with a lake to the right of the green, a double ditch at the back and another just short left of the putting surface. Of the par fives, the 9th at 534 yards is bisected by a ditch and has a string of bunkers crossing the fairway just ahead of the green, while two more ditches cross the 487-yard 10th, one just ahead of the green. All in all, if you manage to play to your handicap here you will feel very satisfied.

Sec/Manager:	Mr J Vickers
Professional:	Mr N Garret
Directions:	2 miles north west of Brentwood. From Brentwood centre take the A128 towards Ongar. The entrance is on the right hand side after three miles by Frog Street.(½ mile after service station on left hand side).
Date Founded:	1972
Type of Course:	Parkland
No of Holes:	18
Length:	6700 yds (6184mtrs)
Par:	72
SSS:	72
Green Fees:	Weekdays: £22.00
Visitors:	Welcome: Contact Club in advance. Unable to play at weekends.
Societies:	Welcome: Contact club by phone in advance.
Facilities:	Putting Green, Driving Range, Club Hire, Trolley Hire, Bar, Restaurant

Accommodation, Food and Drink

Reference numbers below refer to detailed information provided in section 2

Food and Drink

The Alma Arms, Horsemanside, Navestock, Brentwood, Essex CM14 5ST

Tel: 01277 372629 Fax: 01277 375440

Delicious food and outstanding real ales and wines in an 18th century pub of character by Navestock Common.

Prince Albert, Blackmore, Brentwood, Essex CM4 0RJ

Tel: 01277 821705

Delightful village pub with a very popular food operation - booking advisable, especially at the weekend. 505

The Plough, 169 Roman Road, Mountnessing, Brentwood, Essex CM15 0UG

Tel: 01277 352026

A large welcoming pub on the B1002 with brasses and memorabilia adorning the walls inside. The excellent menu changes seasonally and there is a garden equipped for childrens enjoyment.

The Green Man Pub and Restaurant, Navestock Side, Brentwood, Essex CM14 5SD

Tel: 01277 372231

Previously a hunting lodge, this pristine building has been a pub since 1620. Its menu now offers an exceptional choice of traditional favourites as well as a good selection of ales.

Benton Hall

Wickham Hill, Witham, Essex CM8 3LH

Tel: 01376 502454 Fax: 01376 521050

Although opened in 1993, Benton Hall already possesses a maturity beyond its tender years. Visible from the A12 trunk road although not accessed directly from it, this attractive course

uses the naturally hilly terrain, river and other water hazards to good effect. The holes to the front of the site and those around the River Blackwater are generally flat but several holes are built on the rising land towards the back and can prove tough. Some of the climbs can take their toll especially on anyone who is not fit or who prefers more level terrain. However, it is a good test of golf for whatever quality of player.

Designers Alan Walker and Charles Cox have made good use of the many mature trees that exist on the site but the primary hazard has to be the abundance of water as well as the wind, which swirls around the upper parts of the layout. After a comparatively calm start, you first tangle with water on the downhill third where a large lake guards the inside of the dog-leg. The fourth is the first major climb to a green perched on a plateau, while the seventh and eight are also up hill and down dale, the latter being guarded by water right of the approach, before you can catch your breath on more level ground around the turn.

It could be argued that the front nine is the easier because it is shorter, but that should not be taken as a comfort zone. The back nine starts with two holes beside the Blackwater but soon drifts back towards the high ground. The short

par-4 13th is particularly interesting with its trio of lakes, followed by the dog-leg 14th, where another lake has to be avoided. But it is the closing three holes that can destroy a good card. The short 16th at 191 yards off the back tee has a green virtually surrounded by the river and if that is safely negotiated then the par-4 17th requires the straightest of drives between the river and drainage ditches. Finally, the long, dog-leg 18th again has the river as a companion along all of its length as well as avenues of trees on both flanks to a green well guarded by three bunkers.

Other facilities include a large, open clubhouse with bar, lakeside terrace and restaurant, pro-shop, all overlooking a large lake that attracts large numbers of birds, a 20-bay driving range and the nine-hole, par-3 Bishops course. Benton Hall has hosted a number of tournaments, the most recent of which was the Clubhaus Seniors Challenge on the PGA European Seniors Tour.

Sec/Manager:	Julie Ruscoe
Professional:	Colin Fairweather
Directions:	1½ miles south of Witham. From Witham centre take the B1018 (Maldon). Turn left 200 yds after going under the A12 into Blue Mills Hill. The entrance is on the right hand side.
Date Founded:	1990
Type of Course:	Parkland
No of Holes:	18
Length:	6495 yds (5995 mtrs)
Par:	72
SSS:	72
Green Fees:	Weekdays: 1st Nov-31st March £14.00, 1st April-31st October £20.00; Weekends/Bank Holidays: 1st Nov-31st March £20.00, 1st April-31st October £25.00
Visitors:	Welcome: Contact Club in advance. Unable to play certain times at weekends.
Societies:	Welcome: Contact Club by telephone in advance.
Facilities:	Putting Green, Practice Ground, Trolley Hire, Buggy Hire, Caddy Service, Bar, Restaurant, Snooker Room

Accommodation, Food and Drink

Reference numbers below refer to detailed information provided in section 2

Accommodation

The Cricketers, Coggeshall, Essex CO6 1NL

Tel: 01376 561533

A convivial country pub in traditional style, good local support and passing trade. Wide choice of food and regularly changing real ales. 501

The Spread Eagle Hotel, Newland Street, Witham, Essex CM8 2BD

Tel: 01376 512131 Fax: 01376 502458

A 13th century former coaching inn, full of character and with a relaxing atmosphere. There are 13 bedrooms, most en-suite and the excellent menu offers a choice of tempting dishes.

The Green Man, Kelvedon Road, Little Braxted, Essex CM8 3LB

Tel: 01621 891659

Originally a farmhouse, this peaceful 500 year old country pub is set in attractive gardens. Winner of the Best Kept Cellar Award 3 years running, it is also mentioned in the Egon Ronay guide for its superb food.

The Chequers, 32 The Street, Wickham Bishops, Essex CM8 3NN

Tel: 01621 891320

Thought to be the oldest pub in Wickham Bishops, it still retains the wattle and daub walls inside. A good selection of food is served in the dining area at lunchtime and evenings.

The Benbridge Hotel, The Square, Heybridge, Maldon, Essex CM9 4LT

Tel: 01621 857666 Fax: 01621 841966

An elegant Georgian hotel with a reputation for quality. There are 14 en-suite rooms and English and Continental cuisine is served in the gracious dining room. An ideal base for outdoor activities.

Food and Drink

The Cricketers, Coggeshall, Essex CO6 1NL

Tel: 01376 561533

A convivial country pub in traditional style, good local support and passing trade. Wide choice of food and regularly changing real ales. 501

Maldon Pie & Eel House, 136 High Street, Maldon, Essex CM9 8LS

Tel: 01621 842859

Traditional pie & eel shop selling what was once the favourite food of London's East End: eels stewed or jellied, double pie 'n' mash.

The Oak, Tiptree, Nr Colchester, Essex CO5 0NF

Tel: 01621 815579

A convivial pub on the outskirts of Tiptree serving all-day snacks and meals. Patio for barbecue and music. 506

The Spread Eagle Hotel, Newland Street, Witham, Essex CM8 2BD

Tel: 01376 512131 Fax: 01376 502458

A 13th century former coaching inn, full of character and with a relaxing atmosphere. There are 13 bedrooms, most en-suite and the excellent menu offers a choice of tempting dishes.

The Green Man, Kelvedon Road, Little Braxted, Essex CM8 3LB

Tel: 01621 891659

Originally a farmhouse, this peaceful 500 year old country pub is set in attractive gardens. Winner of the Best Kept Cellar Award 3 years running, it is also mentioned in the Egon Ronay guide for its superb food.

The Chequers, 32 The Street, Wickham Bishops, Essex CM8 3NN

Tel: 01621 891320

Thought to be the oldest pub in Wickham Bishops, it still retains the wattle and daub walls inside. A good selection of food is served in the dining area at lunchtime and evenings.

The Benbridge Hotel, The Square, Heybridge, Maldon, Essex CM9 4LT

Tel: 01621 857666 Fax: 01621 841966

An elegant Georgian hotel with a reputation for quality. There are 14 en-suite rooms and English and Continental cuisine is served in the gracious dining room. An ideal base for outdoor activities.

The Old Ship, Lock Hill, Heybridge Basin, Maldon, Essex CM9 4RX

Tel: 01621 854150

Situated on the lock-side with beautiful views across the water, this old pub has an excellent a la carte menu and range of ales which can be enjoyed in the dining room or perhaps outside at one of the picnic tables.

Boyce Hill

Vicarage Hill, Benfleet, Essex SS7 1PD

Tel: 01268 793625 Fax: 01268 750497

Anyone who is convinced that Essex is a flat county should visit Boyce Hill. The course situated six miles west of Southend can only be described as a hilly, parkland layout where you will get plenty of practise with downhill, uphill and sidehill lies. It is not the course to play unless you are used to climbs, yet it is still a delight to tackle although it places the emphasis on shotmaking.

Tucked away on a hillside like an oasis in a residential area at Benfeet, overlooking the Thames marshes with Canvey Island beyond, Boyce Hill had its foundations in Leigh Park Golf Club that existed a few miles away around the First World War. Its members, dissatisfied with the conditions available and the fact that the estate within which the club existed was to be compulsorily purchased by Southend Council, began to seek an alternative site. In 1921, they were encouraged to look at Boyce Hill Farm and within months a group of members from Leigh Park had formed a company 'Boyce Hill Golf and Country Club Ltd' with the intention of renting the land for conversion into a golf course.

The first meeting of the new club took place in August 1922 at Leigh on Sea when it was agreed that the Leigh Park Club would not be purchased and that the 119-acre Boyce Hill Farm would be leased for 99 years at a rental of £200 per annum with an option to purchase within 21 years for £2,900. By the end of 1922 a nine-hole course had been laid out to a design by Joe Steel, professional at nearby Rochford Hundred Golf Club, with another nine on the way. When completed the 18-hole layout measured 5,355 yards with a bogey of 71. However, in 1925 James Braid carried out a redesign, which is very much how the course is today. To mark the opening of the new layout that September, Braid played exhibition matches against J H Taylor, Percy Alliss, and Ernie Barker, the club's professional.

World War II saw the course used as a training area for light tanks, while the old clubhouse and the course received several direct hits from bombs. In 1948 the club almost disappeared when, because of the financial position, it was suggested that Boyce Hill be sold for housing development. Thankfully it wasn't and in 1956 the present clubhouse was opened after aid from the War Damage Commission. In more recent times, Dutch Elm Disease plus the 1987 hurricane took their toll so over 3,000 trees have been planted to ensure the course is as appealing as ever. All the holes at Boyce Hill bear names, many of which derive from the early years, but the 12th, the only par-five in the par 68 circuit, has recently been renamed from 'Dog Leg' to 'Braid's Corner', redressing an omission in recognising the great man's connection with the club.

Today, local knowledge gives a distinct advantage in playing Boyce Hill although a certain young Spaniard found no problems back in 1976. When Brian Barnes withdrew late from a pro-am, his team of club members was disappointed. That was until the Scot's place was taken by a dashing 20-year-old called Seve Ballesteros, who went on to take the top prize.

Sec/Manager: Peter Keeble
Professional: Graham Barroughs
Directions: ½ mile south east of South Benfleet. From the A127 at Rayleigh Junction, turn south on the A129 at B.P. Westwood service station. Take the B1014 (Benfleet Road) and after one mile turn right onto Vicarage Hill. The entrance is on the left hand side after 300 yds.
Date Founded: 1922
Type of Course: Parkland
No of Holes: 18
Length: 5983 yds (5522 mtrs)
Par: 68
SSS: 68
Green Fees: Weekdays: £25.00
Visitors: Welcome: Contact Club in adavance by telephone. Unable to play at weekends.
Societies: Welcome: Contact Club in advance. Welcome on Thursday only.
Facilities: Putting Green, Chipping Green, Club Hire, Trolley Hire, Bar, Restaurant, Indoor Net

Accommodation, Food and Drink

Reference numbers below refer to detailed information provided in section 2

Accommodation

The Quays, New Festival Leisure Park, Cranes Farm Road, Basildon, Essex SS14 3AD

Tel: 01268 290400 Fax: 0870 700 1377

Modern town centre hotel, 64 en-suite rooms, and large restaurant serving traditional English food.

The Chichester Hotel, Old London Road, Raweth, Wickford, Essex SS11 8UE

Tel: 01268 560555 Fax: 01268 560580

Quiet location, 33 en-suite rooms, and private parking. Superb food in a la carte restaurant, mid-week special menus available. Residents and diners bar.

The Lodge Country Inn, Rettendon Lodge, Hayes Chase Battlesbridge, Wickford, Essex SS11 7QT

Tel: 01245 320060 Fax: 01245 322622

On the outskirts of Wickford, licensed 8 en-suite room hotel, a la carte restaurant. Bar and bar snacks available.

The Grand Hotel, The Broadway, Leigh-On-Sea, Essex SS9 1PJ

Tel: 01702 710768

Seafront location, public house with adjoining 16 en-suite room hotel. Private parking, good pub food available.

Food and Drink

The Duke of York, Southend Road (A129), South Green, Billericay, Essex CM11 2PR

Tel: 01277 651403

Grand old pub with a restaurant serving freshly prepared food including an exceptional vegetarian choice. Sunday roast, bar snacks, real ales.

The Beehive Tearoom, 12 South Street, Rochford, Essex SS4 1BQ

Tel: 01702 547644

Tiny tearoom in the village centre, serving coffee, tea, hot and cold snacks, fry-ups and roasts - a speciality.

The Last Post, Southend-on-Sea, Essex SS1 1SA

Tel: 01702 431682

A large all-day pub in premises that were once the central Post Office - hence the name. 512

The Theobald Arms, Kings Walk, Grays, Essex RM17 6HR

Tel: 01375 372253

A very friendly and popular pub by the dockside in Grays. A variety of home-cooked food is available at lunchtimes accompanied by a wide range of real ales. A beer festival is held each summer.

The Ship, Princess Margaret Road, East Tilbury Village, Essex, RM18 8PB

Tel: 01375 843041

Renowned for its excellent ales and food, this comfortable pub is open all day every day. Lunchtime and evening menus are available and the beer garden is safe for children.

The Quays, New Festival Leisure Park, Cranes Farm Road, Basildon, Essex SS14 3AD

Tel: 01268 290400 Fax: 0870 700 1377

Modern town centre hotel, 64 en-suite rooms, and large restaurant serving traditional English food.

The Chichester Hotel, Old London Road, Raweth, Wickford, Essex SS11 8UE

Tel: 01268 560555 Fax: 01268 560580

Quiet location, 33 en-suite rooms, and private parking. Superb food in a la carte restaurant, mid-week special menus available. Residents and diners bar.

The Lodge Country Inn, Rettendon Lodge, Hayes Chase Battlesbridge, Wickford, Essex SS11 7QT

Tel: 01245 320060 Fax: 01245 322622

On the outskirts of Wickford, licensed 8 en-suite room hotel, a la carte restaurant. Bar and bar snacks available.

The Grand Hotel, The Broadway, Leigh-On-Sea, Essex SS9 1PJ

Tel: 01702 710768

Seafront location, public house with adjoining 16 en-suite room hotel. Private parking, good pub food available.

Braintree

Kings Lane, Stisted, Braintree, Essex CM7 8DA

Tel: 01376 346079 Fax: 01376 348677

Set in the heart of rural Essex, Braintree was among the pioneers of the game in the county. The club is the third oldest club in Essex having been founded in November 1891.

Its current attractive 18-hole, par 70 course is situated in beautiful ancient parkland in the picturesque village of Stisted, just to the east of Braintree, but the club was originally located in the town itself. It started life at Chapel Farm and some founder members played golf just four days after the formation. One wonders what the course was like but on Boxing Day 1891 the first handicap meeting took place when 13 players, men and women, competed. One gentleman went round in 210 strokes, presumably twice round the nine-hole layout, but the winner took 137.

However, the club's early life was a struggle and in 1901 a meeting was called to consider its winding up, there being just 16 men and one lady member. Happily they decided to continue. But the club was not well off financially and on occasions was only kept alive with donations from the members. A meeting to reorganise the club was held in February 1911 at which it was agreed to proceed with the building of a clubhouse and to engage a professional. In November that year extra land became available and the course was extended. However, the committee members were still digging into their pockets.

After World War I, during which the course was given over to grazing cattle as well as for the training of troops, the club faced a battle for survival and in 1920 was given two years notice by its landlord. This saw the club move to Chapel Hill in 1921 and it remained in the town until 1972 when, because of development in the town, it moved to the present site at Stisted.

There is little doubt that this delightful course is now one of the most attractive in Essex, with it's many majestic mature trees and views of the River Blackwater, which meanders alongside some of the later holes. Over the years the course has been cleverly sculptured to fit into the existing mature parkland that was once the Stisted Hall estate. The design and construction work was carried out by Hawtree and Son, and was completed in the spring of 1973. Although the 1987 hurricane devastated parts of the course when 115 trees were lost, there are still many left on this beautiful parkland layout that is a joy to play. The front nine winds it way over gently undulating land and through avenues of trees while the river apart, there are a few water hazards on the back nine to whet the appetite. Although it measures only 6,174 yards (5,904 from the yellow tees) it is no pushover but rewards skilful and accurate golf.

The well-appointed clubhouse has been extended over the winter of 2000/01 while there is a well-stocked shop run efficiently and cheerily by Tony Parcell, the club's professional since its move to Stisted in 1973.

Sec/Manager: David Hart

Professional: Tony Parcell

Directions: 2 miles west of Braintree. From Braintree centre take the A120 Coggleshall Road towards Colchester. Turn left into Kings Lane ¼ mile after crossing the A131Halstead/Chelmsford road . The entrance is on the right hand side after one mile.

Date Founded:	1972
Type of Course:	Parkland
No of Holes:	18
Length:	6174 yds (5699 mtrs)
Par:	70
SSS:	69
Green Fees:	Weekdays: £25.00; Weekends/ Bank Holidays: £42.00
Visitors:	Welcome: Contact Club in advance. Unable to play at weekends and bank holidays. Handicap certificate required on Friday's.
Societies:	Welcome: Contact Club by phone in advance. Unable to play on Moday, Tuesday, Friday and weekends.
Facilities:	Putting Green, Chipping Green, Practice Ground, Trolley Hire, Buggy Hire, Bar, Restaurant

Accommodation, Food and Drink

Reference numbers below refer to detailed information provided in section 2

Accommodation

The Spread Eagle Hotel, Newland Street, Witham, Essex CM8 2BD

Tel: 01376 512131 Fax: 01376 502458

A 13th century former coaching inn, full of character and with a relaxing atmosphere. There are 13 bedrooms, most en-suite and the excellent menu offers a choice of tempting dishes.

The Five Bells, 7 Mill Lane, Colne Engaine, Colchester, Essex CO6 2HY

Tel: 01787 224166

A 500 year old inn in a quiet and secluded location, boasting an extremely handsome interior yet retaining its old world charm. An extensive menu of freshly prepared food is on offer as are 3 comfortable guest bedrooms. A spot perfect for exploring the area.

Brook Farm, Wethersfield, Braintree, Essex CM7 4BX

Tel/Fax: 01371 850284

Amid undulating countryside and set on a working farm, this beautiful listed farmhouse offers accommodation in 3 spacious and tastefully furnished guest bedrooms. Delicious breakfasts are prepared by the host. Evening meals can be easily obtained nearby.

The Bell Inn, Great Dunmow Road, Great Bardfield, Essex CM7 4SA

Tel: 01371 811097

A traditional coaching inn dating back to the 16th century with exposed beams and priests hole, enjoyed by locals and visitors alike. A variety of classic English dishes are served and a choice of comfortable guest rooms are available to anyone wishing to stay.

Food and Drink

The Cricketers, Coggeshall, Essex CO6 1NL

Tel: 01376 561533

A convivial country pub in traditional style. Good local support and passing trade. Wide choice of food and regularly changing real ales. 501

The Sugar Loaves, 175 Swan Street, Sible Hedingham, Nr Halstead, Essex CO9 3PX

Tel: 01787 462720

A long-hours pub with two bars and a separate eating area, where pizzas and dishes with chips are favourites - served till 7pm daily.

The Spread Eagle Hotel, Newland Street, Witham, Essex CM8 2BD

Tel: 01376 512131 Fax: 01376 502458

A 13th century former coaching inn, full of character and with a relaxing atmosphere. There are 13 bedrooms, most en-suite and the excellent menu offers a choice of tempting dishes.

The Five Bells, 7 Mill Lane, Colne Engaine, Colchester, Essex CO6 2HY

Tel: 01787 224166

A 500 year old inn in a quiet and secluded location, boasting an extremely handsome interior yet retaining its old world charm. An extensive menu of freshly prepared food is on offer as are 3 comfortable guest bedrooms. A spot perfect for exploring the area.

The Bell Inn, Great Dunmow Road, Great Bardfield, Essex CM7 4SA

Tel: 01371 811097

A traditional coaching inn dating back to the 16th century with exposed beams and priests hole, enjoyed by locals and visitors alike. A variety of classic English dishes are served and a choice of comfortable guest rooms are available to anyone wishing to stay.

Burnham-on-Crouch

Ferry Road, Creeksea, Burnham-on Crouch, Essex CM0 8PQ

Tel: 01621 782282/785508

Because of its situation overlooking the River Crouch, you wouldn't be surprised to learn that the origins of the golf club are tied up with yachting. In 1923 a small group of men took positive action to form a golf club. Most of those concerned were members of Burnham Yacht Club who had for some time played golf on the fields of nearby Mangapp Manor where a few earth bunkers had been provided to add a little realism.

However, a more suitable site was required and the one selected formed part of the Creeksea Estate. This also provided picturesque views over the Crouch, a major factor in deciding the location and which continues to draw comment today. So a course was laid out and in the following year 20 bunkers were added. Even then, it was the aim of the committee to extend the layout to 18 holes at the 'appropriate time'. That took some time to achieve and in the meantime the club went through some troubled times after World War II. In fact, in March 1956 the members voted to wind up the club and the new owner stripped the course of turf.

However, the golf bug was still biting and in the first half of 1957 the club changed hands again and a great deal of money was spent in putting the course back in order. Now a Proprietary Club, it was renamed The Burnham and Creeksea Golf Club. Still there were upheavals to come and in 1960 the club was disbanded again due to financial problems. But it wouldn't lie down and on 1 July 1961 it officially reopened and has remained so ever since. But there was still that question of extending to 18 holes and that was duly completed and opened on 19 June 1993. At long last the aspirations of those founder members back in the Twenties and the many since had been realised.

Dropping in on this friendly and attractive club won't disappoint you. Some of the views over the Crouch are quite stunning and the course, at first sight quite tame, can prove a tiger especially if the wind blows. It is not long at 6,056 yards, par 70, but you must pay particular attention to club selection if you want a reasonable score. Furthermore, in a county which is regarded as generally flat, Burnham is surprisingly hilly. But at the end of a rewarding round over the Essex countryside there is the sight of the clubhouse and its welcoming first floor bar and lounge which affords magnificent views over the course with the river beyond.

Sec/Manager:	Laurie Posner
Professional:	Mr S Cardy
Directions:	1 mile west of Burnham-On-Crouch. Take the Malden Road (B1010) leading off Church Road and after one mile turn right onto Vicarage Hill. The entrance is on the left hand side after 300 yards.
Date Founded:	1923
Type of Course:	Parkland
No of Holes:	18
Length:	6056 yds (5590 mtrs)
Par:	70
SSS:	69
Green Fees:	Weekdays: £24.00
Visitors:	Welcome: Contact Club in advance. Unable to play at weekends.
Societies:	Welcome: Contact Club by telephone in advance. Unable to play at weekends and Thursday mornings.
Facilities:	Putting Green, Chipping Green, Practice Ground, Trolley Hire, Buggy Hire, Bar, Restaurant

Accommodation, Food and Drink

Reference numbers below refer to detailed information provided in section 2

Accommodation

Anchor Hotel, The Quay, Burnham-On-Crouch, Essex CMO 8AT

Tel: 01621 782117

500-year-old inn, 4 en-suite rooms with small intimate restaurant offering good home cooked food.

Railway Hotel, 12 Station Road, Burnham-On-Crouch, Essex CMO 8BQ

Tel: 01621 786868

Victorian building, good recently refurbished restaurant. Four doubles and 2 single en-suite rooms.

Ye Olde White Harte Hotel, The Quay, Burnham -On -Crouch, Essex. CMO 8AS

Tel: 01621 782106

Quaint hotel, overlooking the quay. Parts of building date to 1700. 19 rooms mostly en-suite, separate bar and restaurant

Food and Drink

Maldon Pie & Eel House, 136 High Street, Maldon, Essex CM9 8LS

Tel: 01621 842859

Traditional pie & eel shop selling what was once the favourite food of London's East End: eels stewed or jellied, double pie 'n' mash.

The Duke of York, Southend Road (A129), South Green, Billericay, Essex CM11 2PR

Tel: 01277 651403

Grand old pub with a restaurant serving freshly prepared food including an exceptional vegetarian choice. Sunday roast, bar snacks, real ales.

Queen Victoria, The Street, Woodham Walter, Maldon, Essex CM9 6RF

Tel: 01245 222176

A lovely 18th century pub situated in a quiet country lane. Snacks and hot meals can be enjoyed in either the comfortable bars or in the small garden, as can a range of real ales.

The Queen's Head Inn, The Hythe, Maldon, Essex CM9 5HN

Tel: 01621 859154 (restaurant)
Tel: 01621 854112 (pub)

An impressive 500 year old building overlooking the Blackwater Estuary, with a nautical feel. Good range of home-cooked food is served in the restaurant and there is a large riverside patio.

The White Horse Inn, Main Road, Mundon, Maldon, Essex CM9 6PB

Tel: 01621 740276

Set in picturesque surroundings, this 400 year old pub with low ceilings, offers a good selection of food and ales. Sunday lunches are a speciality.

Anchor Hotel, The Quay, Burnham-On-Crouch, Essex CMO 8AT

Tel: 01621 782117

500-year-old inn, 4 en-suite rooms with small intimate restaurant offering good home cooked food.

Railway Hotel, 12 Station Road, Burnham-On-Crouch, Essex CMO 8BQ

Tel: 01621 786868

Victorian building, good recently refurbished restaurant. Four doubles and 2 single en-suite rooms.

Ye Olde White Harte Hotel, The Quay, Burnham -On -Crouch, Essex CMO 8AS

Tel: 01621 782106

Quaint hotel, overlooking the quay. Parts of building date to 1700. 19 rooms mostly en-suite, separate bar and restaurant

The Burstead

Tye Common Road, Little Burstead, Billericay, Essex CM12 9ST

Tel: 01277 631171 Fax: 01277 632766

Sec/Manager:	Amanda Hughes
Professional:	Keith Bridges
Directions:	1½ miles south west of Billericay. From Billericay centre take Laindon Road (B1007). Turn right into Laindon Common Road, 200 yards after joining A176 (Basildon). After ¾ mile turn right into Tye Common Road and the entrance is on the right hand side.
Date Founded:	1993
Type of Course:	Parkland
No of Holes:	18
Length:	6727yds (5792 mtrs)
Par:	71
SSS:	70
Green Fees:	Weekdays: £19.00; Weekends/ Bank Holidays: £25.00

Visitors: Welcome: Contact Club in advance. Unable to play mornings at weekends.

Societies: Welcome: Contact Club in advance by telephone.

Facilities: Putting Green, Chipping Green, Trolley Hire, Buggy Hire, Bar, Restaurant, Private Rooms

Accommodation, Food and Drink

Reference numbers below refer to detailed information provided in section 2

Accommodation

Hotel Campanile & Restaurant, A127 Southend Arterial Road, Pipps Hill, Basildon, Essex SS14 3AE

Tel: 01268 530810 Fax: 01268 286710

Situated one mile from the town centre, 100 en-suite rooms, full bar facilities with large restaurant serving continental cuisine.

The Quays, New Festival Leisure Park, Cranes Farm Road, Basildon, Essex SS14 3AD

Tel: 01268 290400 Fax: 0870 700 1377

Modern town centre hotel, 64 en-suite rooms, and large restaurant serving traditional English food.

The Chichester Hotel, Old London Road, Raweth, Wickford, Essex SS11 8UE

Tel: 01268 560555 Fax: 01268 560580

Quiet location, 33 en-suite rooms, and private parking. Superb food in a la carte restaurant, mid-week special menus available. Residents and diners bar.

The Lodge Country Inn, Rettendon Lodge, Hayes Chase Battlesbridge, Wickford, Essex SS11 7QT

Tel: 01245 320060 Fax: 01245 322622

On the outskirts of Wickford, licensed 8 en-suite room hotel, a la carte restaurant. Bar and bar snacks available.

Food and Drink

The Duke of York, Southend Road (A129), South Green, Billericay, Essex CM11 2PR

Tel: 01277 651403

Grand old pub with a restaurant serving freshly prepared food including an exceptional vegetarian choice. Sunday roast, bar snacks, real ales.

Prince Albert, Blackmore, Brentwood, Essex CM4 0RJ

Tel: 01277 821705

Delightful village pub with a very popular food operation - booking advisable, especially at the weekend. 505

The Plough, 169 Roman Road, Mountnessing, Brentwood, Essex CM15 0UG

Tel: 01277 352026

A large welcoming pub on the B1002 with brasses and memorabilia adorning the walls inside. The excellent menu changes seasonally and there is a garden equipped for childrens enjoyment.

The Thatchers Arms, Warley Road, Great Warley, Brentwood, Essex CM13 3HU

Tel: 01277 233535
email: JimSarah@supernet.co.uk

A large and handsome pub adjacent to the Warley Place Nature Reserve, makes it an ideal spot for walkers. The panelled interior offers snacks and main meals in the dining room or on the adjoining patio.

The Park Tavern, Romford Road, Aveley, South Ockenden, Essex RM15 4PH

Tel: 01708 863798

A family run pub, sporting an interesting collection of celebrity photos. Good food is prepared from the freshest ingredients and served daily 2-5. There's live entertainment on Fridays and Saturdays.

Hotel Campanile & Restaurant, A127 Southend Arterial Road, Pipps Hill, Basildon, Essex SS14 3AE

Tel: 01268 530810 Fax: 01268 286710

Situated one mile from the town centre, 100 en-suite rooms, full bar facilities with large restaurant serving continental cuisine.

The Quays, New Festival Leisure Park, Cranes Farm Road, Basildon, Essex SS14 3AD

Tel: 01268 290400 Fax: 0870 700 1377

Modern town centre hotel, 64 en-suite rooms, and large restaurant serving traditional English food.

The Chichester Hotel, Old London Road, Raweth, Wickford, Essex SS11 8UE

Tel: 01268 560555 Fax: 01268 560580

Quiet location, 33 en-suite rooms, and private

parking. Superb food in a la carte restaurant, mid-week special menus available. Residents and diners bar.

The Lodge Country Inn, Rettendon Lodge, Hayes Chase Battlesbridge, Wickford, Essex SS11 7QT

Tel: 01245 320060 Fax: 01245 322622

On the outskirts of Wickford, licensed 8 en-suite room hotel, a la carte restaurant. Bar and bar snacks available.

Canons Brook

Elizabeth Way, Harlow, Essex CM19 5BE

Tel: 01279 421482 Fax: 01279 626393

Henry Cotton's handiwork is written indelibly on this long, tough course situated just outside Harlow New Town. Cotton was commissioned by the Harlow Sports Development Trust back in the early 1960s to provide a course for the fast expanding new town in north Essex that was built to accommodate the overspill from London. The three times Open champion was provided with 112 acres of undulating agricultural land and his aim was to provide a layout with large greens, plenty of bunkers, and no rough. This, he felt, would assist with the speed of play, ensuring few balls would be lost, thereby cutting down on the time spent searching for them.

Over the years the greens have become somewhat smaller, a number of Cotton's many bunkers have been removed, and the rough has been allowed to grow. However, the course is just as difficult as it ever was and plays every inch of its 6,763 yards from the back tees with a par of 73. The first nine holes were available for play in 1964 and the second nine a year later when the official opening took place. On the day, Cotton played an exhibition match with fellow Ryder Cup men Lionel Platts and Peter Townsend along with Michael Bonallack, then the leading amateur of the day and Essex based.

By then the Canons Brook club had been formed from the existing Harlow Golfing Society thanks to the work of Cyril Beaton and Derek Moule, who accumulated 100 signatures for a course in the town, which met with the approval of the Harlow Development Corporation. Both Moule and Beaton have served the club in various leading positions including Captain, Secretary/manager and President and have holes named in their honour, Moule Hill and Beaton Track. Fittingly, there is also Cotton's Cradle.

The club's name comes from the ancient area in which it is situated and from the Canons Brook, which runs through the course, notably across the first hole, ahead of the 17th green, and down the side of and in front of the 18th green. The par-four 3rd at 454 yards is the toughest hole despite not having a single bunker. But it is a slight dog-leg where the approach to a two-tier green has to be threaded between two guarding trees. The short 15th at 201 yards is invariably into the wind and slightly uphill to a green protected by three traps and with a bank at the back to catch the overhit shot. The other signature hole is the 332-yard 17th where the tee is back in an avenue of trees while a ditch crosses the fairway 70 yards from the green and Canons Brook lies just ahead of the putting surface. Bunkers guard each side of the green while there is deep rough off the back. Little wonder this is called "Death or Glory".

Sec/Manager:	Mrs S Langton
Professional:	Mr A McGinn
Directions:	1½ miles north west of Harlow. From the northern outskirts roundabout on the A414 by Harlow Town Park, take Elizabeth Way (A1169) and the entrance is on the right hand side.
Date Founded:	1963
Type of Course:	Parkland
No of Holes:	18
Length:	6750 yds (6230 mtrs)
Par:	72

SSS:	71
Green Fees:	Weekdays: £23.00
Visitors:	Welcome: Contact Club in advance. Unable to play at weekends.
Societies:	Welcome: Contact Club in advance by telephone. Unable to play at weekends, Tuesday and Thursday.
Facilities:	Putting Green, Chipping Green, Club Hire, Trolley Hire, Buggy Hire,Bar, Restaurant, Private Rooms

Accommodation, Food and Drink

Reference numbers below refer to detailed information provided in section 2

Food and Drink

King Harolds Head, Bumbles Green, Nazeing Common, Waltham Abbey, Essex EN9 2RY

Tel: 01992 893110 Fax: 01992 893412

A charming old free house on the Waltham Abbey-Harlow road. Friendly ambience, good company, exceptional food. 503

The Queens Head, Fyfield, Essex CM5 0RY

Tel: 01277 899118

A 500-year-old pub near the church in the centre of the little village of Fyfield. Exceptional food has earned wide acclaim. 507

The Horseshoes, Horseshoe Hill, Upshire, Waltham Abbey, Essex EN9 3SN

Tel/Fax: 01992 712745

A grown-ups pub in the countryside just outside Waltham Abbey. Real ales, lunches, darts, quizzes, karaoke.

The New Inn, Waltham Abbey, Essex EN9 1EJ

Tel: 01992 712939

Sociable town centre pub with a good line in food (excellent meat dishes) and 10 letting bedrooms. Live music at the weekend. 510

The Queens Head, Old Harlow, Essex CM17 0JT

Tel: 01279 427266 Fax: 01279 421272

Good eating and drinking in a popular pub next to the church. There are two bars as well as outside areas. 511

The New Inn, Roydon, Essex CM19 5EE

Tel: 01279 792225 Fax: 01279 793641

Village centre pub with period charm and lovely gardens. Bar snacks and evening meals. 513

The Carpenters Arms, The High Road, Thornwood Common, Epping, Essex CM16 6LS

Tel: 01992 574208

Formerly cottages dating from the late 17th century and standing within the boundaries of Epping Forest, this pub has an extensive choice of ales and food available at lunchtimes.

Castle Point

Somnes Avenue, Canvey Island, Essex SS8 9FG

Tel: 01268 510830 Fax: 01268 511758

Sec/Manager:	Dot Archer
Professional:	Michael Utteridge
Directions:	4½ miles south east of Basildon. From the eastern outskirts at the Bowers Gifford A13 roundabout take Convey Way (A130). At the next roundabout take Somnes Avenue (B1014) and the entrance is on the left hand side.
Date Founded:	1988
Type of Course:	Links
No of Holes:	18
Length:	5888 yds (5435 mtrs)
Par:	71
SSS:	69
Green Fees:	Weekdays: £9.70; Weekends/ Bank Holidays: £13.80
Visitors:	Welcome: Contact Club in advance.
Societies:	Welcome: Contact Club in advance.
Facilities:	Putting Green, Chipping Green, Driving Range, Club Hire, Trolley Hire, Buggy Hire, Caddy Service, Bar, Restaurant, Private Rooms

Accommodation, Food and Drink

Reference numbers below refer to detailed information provided in section 2

Accommodation

Beaches, 192 Eastern Esplanade, Southend -On-Sea, Essex SS1 3AA

Tel: 01702 586124 Fax: 01702 588377

Edwardian house, sea front location. 8 en-suite rooms close to all local facilities.

Hotel Campanile & Restaurant, A127 Southend Arterial Road, Pipps Hill, Basildon, Essex SS14 3AE

Tel: 01268 530810 Fax: 01268 286710

Situated one mile from the town centre, 100 en-suite rooms, full bar facilities with large restaurant serving continental cuisine.

The Quays, New Festival Leisure Park, Cranes Farm Road, Basildon, Essex SS14 3AD

Tel: 01268 290400 Fax: 0870 700 1377

Modern town centre hotel, 64 en-suite rooms, and large restaurant serving traditional English food.

The Grand Hotel, The Broadway, Leigh-On-Sea, Essex SS9 1PJ

Tel: 01702 710768

Seafront location, public house with adjoining 16 en-suite room hotel. Private parking, good pub food available.

Food and Drink

The Duke of York, Southend Road (A129), South Green, Billericay, Essex CM11 2PR

Tel: 01277 651403

Grand old pub with a restaurant serving freshly prepared food including an exceptional vegetarian choice. Sunday roast, bar snacks, real ales.

The Beehive Tearoom, 12 South Street, Rochford, Essex SS4 1BQ

Tel: 01702 547644

Tiny tearoom in the village centre, serving coffee, tea, hot and cold snacks, fry-ups and roasts - a speciality.

The Last Post, Southend-on-Sea, Essex SS1 1SA

Tel: 01702 431682

A large all-day pub in premises that were once the central Post Office - hence the name. 512

The White Hart, Swan Lane, Margaretting Tye, Ingatestone, Essex CM4 9JX

Tel: 01277 840478 Fax: 01277 841178
email: @thewhitehart.uk.com
website: www.thewhitehart.uk.com

An excellent pub dating in parts to the 1600's, with vaulted ceilings and open fires. The mainly traditional menu also caters for children. An ideal base for walking.

The Ship, Princess Margaret Road, East Tilbury Village, Essex, RM18 8PB

Tel: 01375 843041

Renowned for its excellent ales and food, this comfortable pub is open all day every day. Lunchtime and evening menus are available and the beer garden is safe for children.

Hotel Campanile & Restaurant, A127 Southend Arterial Road, Pipps Hill, Basildon, Essex SS14 3AE

Tel: 01268 530810 Fax: 01268 286710

Situated one mile from the town centre, 100 en-suite rooms, full bar facilities with large restaurant serving continental cuisine.

The Quays, New Festival Leisure Park, Cranes Farm Road, Basildon, Essex SS14 3AD

Tel: 01268 290400 Fax: 0870 700 1377

Modern town centre hotel, 64 en-suite rooms, and large restaurant serving traditional English food.

The Grand Hotel, The Broadway, Leigh-On-Sea, Essex SS9 1PJ

Tel: 01702 710768

Seafront location, public house with adjoining 16 en-suite room hotel. Private parking, good pub food available.

Channels

Belsteads Farm Lane, Little Waltham, Chelmsford, Essex CM3 3PT

Tel: 01245 440005 Fax: 01245 442032

Sec/Manager:	Mr Squire
Professional:	Ian Sinclair
Directions:	3 miles north of Chelmsford. From the northern outskirts take Essex Regiment Way (A130). At the roundabout turn right into Belsteads Farm Lane and the entrance is in front after 400 yds.
Date Founded:	1975
Visitors:	Welcome: Contact Club in advance. Unable to play Channels at weekends.
Societies:	Welcome: Contact Club in advance by telephone.
Facilities:	Putting Green, Chipping Green, Club Hire, Trolley Hire,

Buggy Hire, Bar, Restaurant, Driving Range

Channels

Type of Course:	Restored Gravel Pit and Lakes (Unique)
No of Holes:	18
Length:	6402 yds (5909 mtrs)
Par:	71
SSS:	71
Green Fees:	Weekdays: £26.00

Belsteads

Type of Course:	Restored Gravel Pit and Lakes (Unique)
No of Holes:	2x9 holes
Length:	6779 yds (6257 mtrs)
Par:	67
SSS:	63
Green Fees:	Weekdays: £18.00 (18 holes), £12.00 (9 holes); Weekends/ Bank Holidays: £20.00 (18 holes), £14.00 (9 holes)

Accommodation, Food and Drink

Reference numbers below refer to detailed information provided in section 2

Accommodation

The Green Man, Mill End Green, Great Easton, Dunmow, Essex CM6 2DN

Tel/Fax: 01371 870286

A handsome 15th century building with a homely feel. The constantly changing menu of freshly prepared dishes are complemented by good wines and beers. Booking advisable. There is also a self contained 2 bedroom flat available for visitors.

Melford Villas, 191 New London Road, Chelmsford, Essex CM2 OAE

Tel: 01245 357128

A City centre B&B, offering 11 rooms, T.V. and hand basins in each room, evening meals available.

Moor Hall, Newney Green, Chelmsford, Essex CM1 3SE

Tel: 01245 420814 email: moorhall@talk21.com

Rural location, 14th century farmhouse, offering 3 family rooms. Evening meals available on request.

Chelmer Hotel, 2-4 Hamlet Road, Chelmsford, Essex CM2 OEU

Tel: 01245 353360 Fax: 01245 609055

Town house hotel, offering nine rooms evening meal by prior arrangement. Off street parking.

Food and Drink

The Rodney, Little Baddow, Essex CH3 4TQ

Tel: 01245 222385

17th century premises for a comfortable village pub with front patio and sloping gardens. Home-prepared food on a traditional menu. 502

The Wheatsheaf, Malden Road, Hatfield Peveral, Chelmsford, Essex CM3 2JF

Tel: 01245 380330

An attractive and welcoming establishment with low ceilings and open fire. The large beer garden hosts a variety of birds whilst inside there is a good range of home cooked food on offer.

The Green Man, Mill End Green, Great Easton, Dunmow, Essex CM6 2DN

Tel/Fax: 01371 870286

A handsome 15th century building with a homely feel. The constantly changing menu of freshly prepared dishes are complemented by good wines and beers. Booking advisable. There is also a self contained 2 bedroom flat available for visitors.

The Green Dragon, Upper London Road, Young's End, Braintree, Essex CM7 8QN

Tel: 01245 361030 Fax: 01245 362575
e-mail: green.dragon@virgin.net

An air of warmth and hospitality await at this mid 17th century pub. Attractive and comfortable furnishings help to make it the centre of village life. There is an excellent and imaginative menu - sought out by discerning diners.

The Square and Compasses, Fuller Street, Fairstead, Chelmsford, Essex CM3 2BB

Tel: 01245 361477

Hidden along the Essex Way footpath, this large old whitewashed building has been recently renovated and displays an interesting selection of museum quality artifacts. The traditional, hearty food is of high quality and a superb beer garden overlooks the countryside.

Chelmsford

Widford Road, Chelmsford, Essex CM2 9AP

Tel/Fax: 01245 256483

The October 1987 hurricane that cut a swathe through so many clubs in the south and east of England also left its mark on Chelmsford. Over 300 trees were brought down but it was to prove a blessing in disguise. It opened everything up, provided greater air movement and consequently the course became drier. So much so that in the past 14 years the quality has elevated Chelmsford among the best maintained courses in Essex.

The greens are generally immaculate and fast even when you expect them not to be, while the whole course is a pleasure to play. Today's visitors might be surprised to know that the club began life side-by-side with horse racing just a few lusty strikes from its present site. Back in 1893, racing was a familiar sight on Galleywood Common, three miles south of the town, and soon golf was being played alongside on a nine-hole layout by Tom Dunn, who was responsible for several East Anglian courses. The only proviso was no play on race days. As one observer put it: "The course was no Gleneagles or Wentworth, just a great expanse of gorse and heather where more time was spent looking for lost balls than playing." Nevertheless, the club existed at Galleywood until 1910 when it was offered land at Widford, its present home, nearer to the town, and James Braid confirmed the site was suitable for golf.

James MacDonald from Harpenden laid out 18 holes, which opened on 22 June 1911. That course, which was bisected by the London to Ipswich railway line, is not what you see today because various land deals down the years has led to changes culminating in the current compact layout. Additional land in 1924 saw famous golf architect Harry Colt remodel the course and much of his handiwork still exists today although a further land purchase in 1931 enabled much of the present layout to take shape with the four holes on the other side of the railway being sold. In 1993 the club celebrated its centenary when Michael Williams, the much lamented golf correspondent of the *Daily Telegraph*, took over as captain for the second time, having also held office in 1968.

Today's course is laid out across a valley, which comes into play on both nines, and don't be fooled by the overall length of just under 6,000 yards or the par of 68. You won't take it apart because it is well protected and there are still many trees. Although there is only one par five, Chelmsford's test comes with its many par fours, seven of which are 400 yards or more, and its five short holes, two being across that valley. For one, I am always pleased to play here.

Sec/Manager: Mr Winckless

Professional: Mark Welch

Directions: 1½ miles south west of Chelmsford. At the Tesco Junction (A414) on the western outskirts proceed past Tesco and take the immediate right turn into Wood Street, leading into Widford Road. The entrance is after ¼ mile.

Date Founded: 1911

Type of Course: Parkland

No of Holes: 18

Length: 5981 yds (5520 mtrs)

Par: 68

SSS: 69

Green Fees: Weekdays: £35.00

Visitors: Welcome: Contact Club in advance. Unable to play at weekends.

Societies: Welcome: Contact Club in advance by telephone. Unable to play at weekends.

Facilities: Putting Green, Chipping Green, Trolley Hire, Buggy Hire, Bar, Restaurant

Accommodation, Food and Drink

Reference numbers below refer to detailed information provided in section 2

Accommodation

The Green Man, Mill End Green, Great Easton, Dunmow, Essex CM6 2DN

Tel/Fax: 01371 870286

A handsome 15th century building with a homely feel. The constantly changing menu of freshly prepared dishes are complemented by good wines and beers. Booking advisable. There is also a self contained 2 bedroom flat available for visitors.

Melford Villas, 191 New London Road, Chelmsford, Essex CM2 OAE

Tel: 01245 357128

A City centre B&B, offering 11 rooms, T.V. and hand basins in each room, evening meals available.

Moor Hall, Newney Green, Chelmsford, Essex CM1 3SE

Tel: 01245 420814 email: moorhall@talk21.com

Rural location, 14th century farmhouse, offering 3 family rooms. Evening meals available on request.

Chelmer Hotel, 2-4 Hamlet Road, Chelmsford, Essex CM2 OEU

Tel: 01245 353360 Fax: 01245 609055

Town house hotel, offering nine rooms evening meal by prior arrangement. Off street parking.

Food and Drink

The Rodney, Little Baddow, Essex CH3 4TQ

Tel: 01245 222385

17th century premises for a comfortable village pub with front patio and sloping gardens. Home-prepared food on a traditional menu. 502

The Queens Head, Fyfield, Essex CM5 0RY

Tel: 01277 899118

A 500-year-old pub near the church in the centre of the little village of Fyfield. Exceptional food has earned wide acclaim. 507

Prince Albert, Blackmore, Brentwood, Essex CM4 0RJ

Tel: 01277 821705

Delightful village pub with a very popular food operation - booking advisable, especially at the weekend. 505

The White Hart, Swan Lane, Margaretting Tye, Ingatestone, Essex CM4 9JX

Tel: 01277 840478 Fax: 01277 841178 email: @thewhitehart.uk.com website: www.thewhitehart.uk.com

An excellent pub dating in parts to the 1600's, with vaulted ceilings and open fires. The mainly traditional menu also caters for children. An ideal base for walking.

The Green Man, Mill End Green, Great Easton, Dunmow, Essex CM6 2DN

Tel/Fax: 01371 870286

A handsome 15th century building with a homely feel. The constantly changing menu of freshly prepared dishes are complemented by good wines and beers. Booking advisable. There is also a self contained 2 bedroom flat available for visitors.

Clacton-on-Sea

West Road, Clacton-on-Sea, Essex CO15 1AJ

Tel: 01255 424331 Fax: 01255 424602

Sec/Manager:	James Wiggan
Professional:	Stewart Livermore
Directions:	1 mile west of Clacton-On-Sea. From Clacton Pier take West Road, (Jaywicks). The entrance is on the left hand side after Hastings Avenue.
Date Founded:	1892
Type of Course:	Mixture of Links and Parkland.
No of Holes:	18
Length:	6532 yds (6029 mtrs)
Par:	71
SSS:	71
Green Fees:	Weekdays: £20.00 per round, £30.00 per day; Weekends/ Bank Holidays: £25.00 per round, £40.00 per day.
Visitors:	Welcome: Contact Club in advance.
Societies:	Welcome: Contact Club in advance by telephone. Unable to play at weekends.
Facilities:	Putting Green, Chipping Green, Practice Area, Trolley Hire, Buggy Hire,Bar, Restaurant

Accommodation, Food and Drink

Reference numbers below refer to detailed information provided in section 2

Accommodation

Maison Talbooth, Dedham, Essex CO7 6HN

Tel: 01206 322367 Fax: 01206 322752

Ten top-notch en-suite bedrooms in a Victorian country house with superb views. Meals are served in the restaurant Le Talbooth, a short walk away. 504

Athelston House, 201 Maldon Road, Colchester, Essex CO3 3BQ

Tel: 01206 548652 e-mail: mackman@mcmail.com

Excellent B&B with friendly and helpful owners. There are 3 bedrooms furnished to a high standard of comfort. The dining room is spacious and there is a pretty garden. No smoking.

The Blackwater Hotel and Restaurant, 20-22 Church Road, West Mersea, Colchester, Essex CO5 8QH

Tel: 01206 383338 Fax: 01206 384288

A fine hotel with 8 guest rooms all decorated and furnished to a high standard. A superb menu is available in the elegant dining room with an excellent choice of wines to accompany your meal. The lounge, bar and courtyard is open to residents and non residents.

Mill House, High Street, Thorpe-le-Soken, Clacton-on-Sea, Essex CO16 0DY

Tel: 01255 861334

A gracious and impressive Tudor house with Georgian frontage, handsome inside and out. Superb, well appointed B&B accommodation, with first class furnishings, is offered here. No smoking.

Food and Drink

Maison Talbooth, Dedham, Essex CO7 6HN

Tel: 01206 322367 Fax: 01206 322752

Ten top-notch en-suite bedrooms in a Victorian country house with superb views. Meals are served in the restaurant Le Talbooth, a short walk away. 504

The Thatchers Arms, 1 North Street, Tolleshunt D'Arcy, Maldon, Essex CM9 8TF

Tel: 01621 860655 website: www.thethatchersarms.co.uk

A traditional 18th century pub adorned inside with trophies and china. The extensive menu is matched by the range of wines, beers and spirits. There is a large secure beer garden and live music on various evenings.

The Red Lion, 9 South Street, Tolleshunt D'Arcy, Essex CM9 8TR

Tel: 01621 860238 Fax: 01621 858253

This large and impressive building has a convivial atmosphere. A good range of traditional home-cooked food is on offer, including the "Golfers Breakfast" served at 6a.m. every Saturday

The Blackwater Hotel and Restaurant, 20-22 Church Road, West Mersea, Colchester, Essex CO5 8QH

Tel: 01206 383338 Fax: 01206 384288

A fine hotel with 8 guest rooms all decorated and furnished to a high standard. A superb menu is available in the elegant dining room with an excellent choice of wines to accompany your meal. The lounge, bar and courtyard is open to residents and non residents.

Priory Restaurant, 4 Clacton Road, St Osyth, Essex

Tel: 01255 820259

Housed in a magnificent 14th century building, this is a colourful and warm restaurant, tea room and delicatessen. The restaurant specialises in mediterranean cooking , expertly prepared. Check for opening times and booking.

Colchester

Braiswick, Colchester, Essex CO4 5AU

Tel: 01206 853396 Fax: 01206 852698

The club is renowned for possessing one of the best courses in Essex. Situated on the north western outskirts of Colchester, the oldest recorded town in Britain, it lies at Braiswick, less than a mile from Colchester's main line station. Set in gently undulating parkland the course benefits from many varieties of well-established trees, which line every fairway and contribute to the unique nature of each hole.

The Club was founded in 1909 with a private nine-hole course in the grounds of Achnecone House. The course, like so many others in Essex and around the country, was the work of James Braid. At the official opening in July 1910, an exhibition match was played between Braid, his partner in the Great Triumvirate and fellow Open champion, J.H. Taylor, Mr Webb, the professional from nearby Frinton GC, and the Club's first professional Tom Trapp. An additional nine holes were added in 1938, again to a design by Braid and laid out by the club's second professional, Syd Parmenter.

During the First World War the course was ploughed up but due to the poor clay soil and lack of modern fertilisers did not prove very productive. Thus during World War II, the course was given over for training purposes to the Army. Golfers, at the time had to contend with the additional hazard of soldiers jumping out the spinneys with rifles and fixed bayonets in mock combat, while footmarks in bunkers were seldom raked over.

The club currently has over 700 members and takes pride in its friendly and relaxed atmosphere. This is manifest in the fact that over 7,000 visitors play the course each year and the club can cater for golf societies of up to 40 players.

The course, which measures 6,301 yards from the back tees (6,060 from the yellows) par 70, is both comfortable and testing to every facet of golfer and has only two par fives, the sixth and the ninth. After a fairly quiet opening, the par four 3rd borders the busy A12 trunk road which although it cannot be seen, the traffic is audible beyond the trees and bushes. This 408-yard hole with its sloping fairway is the first real test but it is followed by the tricky 325-yard uphill dog-leg 4th to a well-guarded green. The 390-yard 7th is another good hole, while the 10th, which brings you back close to the clubhouse, requires an accurate approach. On the remainder of the back nine, the short 13th at 180 yards is well guarded, while the round reaches its conclusion with two testing par fours, both over 400 yards, the 18th requiring a sound drive to the corner of the dog-leg.

Sec/Manager: Terry Peck

Professional: Mark Angel

Directions: 2 miles north Wwst of Colchester. From the north west outskirts take A134 (Sudbury). After ¼ mile turn left on the B1508 (West Bergholt). The entrance is on the right hand side about¾mile from the roundabout near Colchester Station.

Date Founded: 1906

Type of Course: Parkland

No of Holes: 18

Length: 6347 yds (5858 mtrs)

Par: 70

SSS: 70

Green Fees: Weekdays: £25.00; Weekends/ Bank Holidays: £40.00

Visitors: Welcome: Contact Club in advance. Unable to play on Tuesdays and restricted weekend play.

Societies: Welcome: Contact Club in advance. Unable to play on Tuesday and at weekends.

Facilities: Putting Green, Chipping Green, Driving Range(members only), Trolley Hire, Buggy Hire, Bar, Restaurant, Private Rooms

Accommodation, Food and Drink

Reference numbers below refer to detailed information provided in section 2

Accommodation

Tannington Hall, Tannington, Nr Framlingham, Suffolk IP13 7NH

Tel: 01728 628226

Four en-suite bedrooms in a fine country house set in extensive gardens. B&B, dinner by arrangement. Carriage rides.

Maison Talbooth, Dedham, Essex CO7 6HN

Tel: 01206 322367 Fax: 01206 322752

Ten top-notch en-suite bedrooms in a Victorian country house with superb views. Meals are served in the restaurant Le Talbooth, a short walk away. 504

Athelston House, 201 Maldon Road, Colchester, Essex CO3 3BQ

Tel: 01206 548652 e-mail: mackman@mcmail.com

Excellent B&B with friendly and helpful owners. There are 3 bedrooms furnished to a high standard of comfort. The dining room is spacious and there is a pretty garden. No smoking.

The Five Bells, 7 Mill Lane, Colne Engaine, Colchester, Essex CO6 2HY

Tel: 01787 224166

A 500 year old inn in a quiet and secluded location, boasting an extremely handsome interior yet retaining its old world charm. An extensive menu of freshly prepared food is on offer as are 3 comfortable guest bedrooms. A spot perfect for exploring the area.

Food and Drink

Tannington Hall, Tannington, Nr Framlingham, Suffolk IP13 7NH

Tel: 01728 628226

Four en-suite bedrooms in a fine country house set in extensive gardens. B&B, dinner by arrangement. Carriage rides.

Maison Talbooth, Dedham, Essex CO7 6HN

Tel: 01206 322367 Fax: 01206 322752

Ten top-notch en-suite bedrooms in a Victorian country house with superb views. Meals are served in the restaurant Le Talbooth, a short walk away. 504

The Rose Inn, Thorington Street, Stoke-by-Nayland, Colchester, Essex CO6 4SN

Tel/Fax: 01206 337243

Pub with 50-cover restaurant, large car park and extensive gardens. Outstanding food, particularly seafood, with lots of daily specials. Closed Monday.

The Three Horseshoes, Church Road, Fordham, Colchester, Essex CO6 3NJ

Tel: 01206 240195

A beautiful whitewashed 16th century inn retaining many original features. It has gained a high regard for its delicious, home-cooked dishes, its great choice of drinks including real ales and for its homely atmosphere.

The Five Bells, 7 Mill Lane, Colne Engaine, Colchester, Essex CO6 2HY

Tel: 01787 224166

A 500 year old inn in a quiet and secluded location, boasting an extremely handsome interior yet retaining its old world charm. An extensive menu of freshly prepared food is on offer as are 3 comfortable guest bedrooms. A spot perfect for exploring the area.

Colne Valley

Station Road, Earls Colne, Essex CO6 2LT
Tel: 01787 224233/224343 Fax: 01787 224126

Colne Valley, situated in the delightful village of Earls Colne on the Essex/Suffolk border has enjoyed a short but chequered history. When the original owner and founder went bankrupt it was bought three years ago by professional Paul Curry, a regular on the PGA European Tour until a couple of years ago when he decided to try his luck in America. Paul, who comes from the area, is committed to the future development of the club and is determined to ensure that Colne Valley remains at the forefront of local golf. When not active on the tournament scene, he is a regular visitor to the club and welcomes comments from members and visitors alike.

Designed by Howard Swan in 1989, the course opened two years later in an area of outstanding natural beauty, the mature parkland layout belies its tender years. Swan has incorporated many mature trees in his design, while the River Colne meanders along the length of the course allied to a number of ponds and lakes to give that extra edge to a round of golf. The modern, well equipped and welcoming clubhouse is situated on high ground and affords commanding views over much of the back nine with the River Colne beyond.

Although the course measures 6,303 yards off the back tees and has a par of 70, it is no pushover. There are six short holes, three on each nine, ranging from 145 yards to 210 yards and four par-5s, the longest at 530 yards coming right at the start. Designed in two loops of nine, the clubhouse looks out on a double green, which forms the destination for both the ninth and 18th holes, par-4s that provide testing climbs to the salvation of the welcoming 19th. Perhaps the two holes which stick in the memory are the 143-yard 8th played over water to a narrow green with the river beyond, and the 430-yard dog-leg 14th which runs along the river. Here your drive must avoid two strategically placed ponds to the left and out of bounds to the right.

The club also has a function suite, the Octagon, which can cater for parties of up to 250, and a well-stocked professional's shop.

Sec/Manager:	Veronica Keeble
Professional:	James Taylor
Directions:	2½ miles east of Halstead. From Halstead centre take the A604 towards Earls Colne (Colchester). Take the second turn on the left in Earls Colne (Station Road) and the entrance is on the right hand side
Date Founded:	1991
Type of Course:	Parkland with Lakes.
No of Holes:	18
Length:	6303 yds (5818 mtrs)
Par:	70
SSS:	69
Green Fees:	Weekdays: £18.00; Weekends/ Bank Holidays: £23.00
Visitors:	Welcome: Contact Club in advance. Unable to play certain times at weekends.
Societies:	Welcome: Contact Club by telephone in advance.
Facilities:	Putting Green, Practice Ground, Trolley Hire, Buggy Hire, Caddy Service, Bar, Restaurant, Snooker Room

Accommodation, Food and Drink

Reference numbers below refer to detailed information provided in section 2

Accommodation

Athelston House, 201 Maldon Road, Colchester, Essex CO3 3BQ

Tel: 01206 548652 e-mail: mackman@mcmail.com

Excellent B&B with friendly and helpful owners. There are 3 bedrooms furnished to a high standard of comfort. The dining room is spacious and there is a pretty garden. No smoking.

The Five Bells, 7 Mill Lane, Colne Engaine, Colchester, Essex CO6 2HY

Tel: 01787 224166

A 500 year old inn in a quiet and secluded location, boasting an extremely handsome interior yet retaining its old world charm. An extensive menu of freshly prepared food is on offer as are 3 comfortable guest bedrooms. A spot perfect for exploring the area.

Brook Farm, Wethersfield, Braintree, Essex CM7 4BX

Tel/Fax: 01371 850284

Amid undulating countryside and set on a working farm, this beautiful listed farmhouse offers accommodation in 3 spacious and tastefully furnished guest bedrooms. Delicious breakfasts are prepared by the host. Evening meals can be easily obtained nearby.

Food and Drink

The Cricketers, Coggeshall, Essex CO6 1NL

Tel: 01376 561533

A convivial country pub in traditional style. Good local support and passing trade. Wide choice of food and regularly changing real ales. 501

The Sugar Loaves, 175 Swan Street, Sible Hedingham, Nr Halstead, Essex CO9 3PX

Tel: 01787 462720

A long-hours pub with two bars and a separate eating area, where pizzas and dishes with chips are favourites - served till 7pm daily.

The Pheasant, Audley End, Gestingthorpe, Nr Halstead, Essex CO9 3AX

Tel: 01787 461196

A small, cosy village pub, off the beaten track but well worth seeking out for some of the best food in the area. 509

The Five Bells, 7 Mill Lane, Colne Engaine, Colchester, Essex CO6 2HY

Tel: 01787 224166

A 500 year old inn in a quiet and secluded location, boasting an extremely handsome interior yet retaining its old world charm. An extensive menu of freshly prepared food is on offer as are 3 comfortable guest bedrooms. A spot perfect for exploring the area.

The Three Pigeons, 6 Mount Hill, Halstead, Essex CO9 1AA

Tel: 01787 472336

Classically English pub, recently refurbished and very popular within the locals and visitors. There is a good choice of real ales and a selection of hot and cold bar snacks. Outside is a spacious patio and garden area.

The Green Man, Gosfield, Halstead, Essex CO9 1TP

Tel: 01787 472746

A striking pink washed building built in the 1600's with inglenook fireplace. The menu changes daily serving excellent cuisine using local produce and has won awards for Essex "Pub of the Year". Fine ales are on tap and a lovely beer garden is popular in summer.

Crondon Park

Stock Road, Stock, Essex CM4 9DP

Tel: 01277 841115 Fax: 01277841356

Sec/Manager:	Paul Cranswell
Professional:	Paul Barham
Directions:	4 miles south of Chelmsford. From Chelmsford centre take the B1007 Galleywood (Stock). The entrance is on the right hand side just before Stock.
Date Founded:	1994
Type of Course:	Parkland
No of Holes:	18
Length:	6585 yds (6978 mtrs)
Par:	72
SSS:	71
Green Fees:	Weekdays: £15.00; Weekends/ Bank Holidays: £25.00
Visitors:	Welcome: Contact Club in advance. Unable to play in the morning at weekends.
Societies:	Welcome: Contact Club in advance by telephone. Unable to play at weekends.
Facilities:	Putting Green, Driving Range, Trolley Hire, Buggy Hire, Bar, Restaurant, Private Rooms

Accommodation, Food and Drink

Reference numbers below refer to detailed information provided in section 2

Accommodation

Melford Villas, 191 New London Road, Chelmsford, Essex CM2 OAE

Tel: 01245 357128

A City centre B&B, offering 11 rooms, T.V. and hand basins in each room, evening meals available.

Moor Hall, Newney Green, Chelmsford, Essex CM1 3SE

Tel: 01245 420814 email: moorhall@talk21.com

Rural location, 14th century farmhouse, offering 3 family rooms. Evening meals available on request.

Hotel Campanile & Restaurant, A127 Southend Arterial Road, Pipps Hill, Basildon, Essex SS14 3AE

Tel: 01268 530810 Fax: 01268 286710

Situated one mile from the town centre, 100 en-suite rooms, full bar facilities with large restaurant serving continental cuisine.

Chelmer Hotel, 2-4 Hamlet Road, Chelmsford, Essex CM2 OEU

Tel: 01245 353360 Fax: 01245 609055

Town house hotel, offering nine rooms evening meal by prior arrangement. Off street parking.

The Lodge Country Inn, Rettendon Lodge, Hayes Chase Battlesbridge, Wickford, Essex SS11 7QT

Tel: 01245 320060 Fax: 01245 322622

On the outskirts of Wickford, licensed 8 en-suite room hotel, a la carte restaurant. Bar and bar snacks available.

Food and Drink

The Rodney, Little Baddow, Essex CH3 4TQ

Tel: 01245 222385

17th century premises for a comfortable village pub with front patio and sloping gardens. Home-prepared food on a traditional menu. 502

The Duke of York, Southend Road (A129), South Green, Billericay, Essex CM11 2PR

Tel: 01277 651403

Grand old pub with a restaurant serving freshly prepared food including an exceptional vegetarian choice. Sunday roast, bar snacks, real ales.

Prince Albert, Blackmore, Brentwood, Essex CM4 0RJ

Tel: 01277 821705

Delightful village pub with a very popular food operation - booking advisable, especially at the weekend. 505

The White Hart, Swan Lane, Margaretting Tye, Ingatestone, Essex CM4 9JX

Tel: 01277 840478 Fax: 01277 841178 email: @thewhitehart.uk.com website: www.thewhitehart.uk.com

An excellent pub dating in parts to the 1600's, with vaulted ceilings and open fires. The mainly traditional menu also caters for children. An ideal base for walking.

The Plough, 169 Roman Road, Mountnessing, Brentwood, Essex CM15 0UG

Tel: 01277 352026

A large welcoming pub on the B1002 with brasses and memorabilia adorning the walls inside. The excellent menu changes seasonally and there is a garden equipped for childrens enjoyment.

The Lodge Country Inn, Rettendon Lodge, Hayes Chase Battlesbridge, Wickford, Essex SS11 7QT

Tel: 01245 320060 Fax: 01245 322622

On the outskirts of Wickford, licensed 8 en-suite room hotel, a la carte restaurant. Bar and bar snacks available.

Essex G&CC

Earls Colne, Colchester, Essex CO6 2NS

Tel: 01787 224466 Fax: 01787 224410

The Essex Golf and Country Club at Earls Colne, not to be confused with the Essex Golf Complex at Southend-on-Sea, formed a trilogy with The Norfolk and the Suffolk under the ownership of entrepreneur Eddy Shah. But Shah sold The Essex in late 2000 to the Clubhaus group which also own other Essex clubs; Benton Hall at

Witham, Stapleford Abbots near Brentwood, and Three Rivers in Cold Norton.

Situated in delightful Essex countryside, the site was originally a Second World War air base for the United States Air Force. It remained an aerodrome until local farmer Eric Hobbs developed it as a golf course in the late 1980s when Reg Plumbridge designed the layout. The flying club still exists next door while the course opened in 1990 as Earls Colne Golf Club. But towards the end of 1995 it was bought by Shah who carried out a major development on and off the course.

Extensive leisure facilities including indoor swimming pool, gymnasium, six indoor tennis courts, restaurants, a 20-bay driving range, two professional shops, and a 42-bedroom hotel. The course was also upgraded with several water features and the moving of several mature trees. The new owners, Clubhaus are carrying out a programme of further development, including enlarging the gymnasium. On the golfing side, there are 27 holes, the 18-hole **Country Course** and the nine-hole **Garden** layout.

The Country Course has already won acclaim for its challenging yet fair features. With four par 3's, nine par 4's and five par 5's, 12 lakes and strategically placed bunkering, the course provides a constant choice of shots. The 6,907-yard, par 73 layout sees water on nine of the holes, while the finale to the round is particularly testing with a long par-3 followed by two testing par-4s and a pair of par-5s, 17 and 18. The short Garden Course offers an altogether different challenge. The 2,200-yard, par 34 layout has lakes and tightly guarded greens, while the tricky par 4's and attractive par 3's present an intriguing and popular test for beginners and competent golfers alike. The Essex has a modern clubhouse and a sports brasserie filled with sporting memorabilia from around the world.

Sec/Manager:	David Clark
Professional:	Lee Cocker
Directions:	3 miles south east of Halstead. From Halstead centre take the A604 towards Earls Colne (Colchester). Turn right onto the B1024 (Coggleshall) and the entrance is on the left hand side after 1 mile.
Date Founded:	1990
Visitors:	Welcome: Subject to availability. Contact Club in advance
Societies:	Welcome: Contact Club in advance
Facilities:	Putting Green, Club Hire, Trolley Hire, Buggy Hire, Bar, Restaurant, Driving Range, Private Rooms

Country Course

Type of Course:	Parkland
No of Holes:	18
Length:	6907 yds (6375 mtrs)
Par:	73
SSS:	73
Green Fees:	Weekdays: £25.00; Weekends/ £30.00

Garden Course

Type of Course:	Parkland
No of Holes:	9
Length:	2190 yds (2021 mtrs)
Par:	34
SSS:	34
Green Fees:	Weekdays: £12.00; Weekends/ Bank Holidays: £17.00

Accommodation, Food and Drink

Reference numbers below refer to detailed information provided in section 2

Accommodation

Stoke by Nayland Club Hotel, Leavenheath, Colchester, Essex CO6 4PZ

Tel: 01206 262836 Fax: 01206 263356

A spacious modern country hotel in 300 acres of rolling countryside. 30 fine bedrooms, restaurant, golf courses, health & fitness centre. 508

The Spread Eagle Hotel, Newland Street, Witham, Essex CM8 2BD

Tel: 01376 512131 Fax: 01376 502458

A 13th century former coaching inn, full of character and with a relaxing atmosphere. There are 13 bedrooms, most en-suite and the excellent menu offers a choice of tempting dishes.

Athelston House, 201 Maldon Road, Colchester, Essex CO3 3BQ

Tel: 01206 548652 e-mail: mackman@mcmail.com

Excellent B&B with friendly and helpful owners. There are 3 bedrooms furnished to a high standard of comfort. The dining room is spacious and there is a pretty garden. No smoking.

The Five Bells, 7 Mill Lane, Colne Engaine, Colchester, Essex CO6 2HY

Tel: 01787 224166

A 500 year old inn in a quiet and secluded location, boasting an extremely handsome interior yet retaining its old world charm. An extensive menu of freshly prepared food is on offer as are 3 comfortable guest bedrooms. A spot perfect for exploring the area.

Brook Farm, Wethersfield, Braintree, Essex CM7 4BX

Tel/Fax: 01371 850284

Amid undulating countryside and set on a working farm, this beautiful listed farmhouse offers accommodation in 3 spacious and tastefully furnished guest bedrooms. Delicious breakfasts are prepared by the host. Evening meals can be easily obtained nearby.

Food and Drink

The Cricketers, Coggeshall, Essex CO6 1NL

Tel: 01376 561533

A convivial country pub in traditional style. Good local support and passing trade. Wide choice of food and regularly changing real ales. 501

Maison Talbooth, Dedham, Essex CO7 6HN

Tel: 01206 322367 Fax: 01206 322752

Ten top-notch en-suite bedrooms in a Victorian country house with superb views. Meals are served in the restaurant Le Talbooth, a short walk away. 504

The Three Horseshoes, Church Road, Fordham, Colchester, Essex CO6 3NJ

Tel: 01206 240195

A beautiful whitewashed 16th century inn retaining many original features. It has gained a high regard for its delicious, home-cooked dishes, its great choice of drinks including real ales and for its homely atmosphere.

The Five Bells, 7 Mill Lane, Colne Engaine, Colchester, Essex CO6 2HY

Tel: 01787 224166

A 500 year old inn in a quiet and secluded location, boasting an extremely handsome interior yet retaining its old world charm. An extensive menu of freshly prepared food is on offer as are 3 comfortable guest bedrooms. A spot perfect for exploring the area.

The Three Pigeons, 6 Mount Hill, Halstead, Essex CO9 1AA

Tel: 01787 472336

Classically English pub, recently refurbished and very popular within the locals and visitors. There is a good choice of real ales and a selection of hot and cold bar snacks. Outside is a spacious patio and garden area.

Essex Golf Complex

Garon Park, Eastern Avenue, Southend-on-sea, Essex SS2 4PT

Tel: 01702 601701 Fax: 01702 601033

Sec/Manager: Janice Jamcombe

Professional: Gary Jamcombe

Directions: 1½ miles north east of Southend-On-Sea. From the town centre go north on the A127 and turn right onto the A1159 (Shoeburyness). The entrance is on the left hand side after 1½ miles.

Date Founded: 1994

Visitors: Welcome: Subject to availability, Contact Club in advance

Societies: Welcome: Contact Club in advance

Facilities: Putting Green, Club Hire, Trolley Hire, Buggy Hire, Bar, Restaurant, Driving Range, Private Rooms, Floodlit Driving Range

Essex Golf

Type of Course: Links

No of Holes: 18

Length: 6252 yds (5771 mtrs)

Par: 70

SSS: 68

Green Fees: Weekdays: £15.50; Weekends/ Bank Holidays: £20.00

Par 3 Nine Hole

Type of Course: Links

No of Holes: 9

Length: 948 yds (875 mtrs)

Par: 27

SSS: No standard scratch.

Green Fees: Weekdays: £4.50; Weekends/ Bank Holidays: £5.50

Accommodation, Food and Drink

Reference numbers below refer to detailed information provided in section 2

Accommodation

Hotel Renouf, Bradley Way, Rochford, Essex SS4 1BU

Tel: 01702 549563 Fax: 07102 549563

Modern Town Hotel, offering 23 en-suite rooms. A la Carte restaurant specialising in French cuisine.

Beaches, 192 Eastern Esplanade, Southend -On-Sea, Essex SS1 3AA

Tel: 01702 586124 Fax: 01702 588377

Edwardian house, sea front location. 8 en-suite rooms close to all local facilities.

Ifracombe House Hotel, 9-13 Wilson Road, Southend-on-Sea, Essex SS1 1HG

Tel: 01702 351000

Licensed hotel, 20 en-suite rooms, private parking, evening meals by prior arrangement. Self contained flat available.

The Grand Hotel, The Broadway, Leigh-On-Sea, Essex SS9 1PJ

Tel: 01702 710768

Seafront location, public house with adjoining 16 en-suite room hotel. Private parking, good pub food available.

Food and Drink

The Duke of York, Southend Road (A129), South Green, Billericay, Essex CM11 2PR

Tel: 01277 651403

Grand old pub with a restaurant serving freshly prepared food including an exceptional vegetarian choice. Sunday roast, bar snacks, real ales.

The Beehive Tearoom, 12 South Street, Rochford, Essex SS4 1BQ

Tel: 01702 547644

Tiny tearoom in the village centre, serving coffee, tea, hot and cold snacks, fry-ups and roasts - a speciality.

The Last Post, Southend-on-Sea, Essex SS1 1SA

Tel: 01702 431682

A large all-day pub in premises that were once the central Post Office - hence the name. 512

The Green Man Pub and Restaurant, Navestock Side, Brentwood, Essex CM14 5SD

Tel: 01277 372231

Previously a hunting lodge, this pristine building has been a pub since 1620. Its menu now offers an exceptional choice of traditional favourites as well as a good selection of ales.

The Ship, Princess Margaret Road, East Tilbury Village, Essex, RM18 8PB

Tel: 01375 843041

Renowned for its excellent ales and food, this comfortable pub is open all day every day. Lunchtime and evening menus are available and the beer garden is safe for children.

Hotel Renouf, Bradley Way, Rochford, Essex SS4 1BU

Tel: 01702 549563 Fax: 07102 549563

Modern Town Hotel, offering 23 en-suite rooms. A la Carte restaurant specialising in French cuisine.

Ifracombe House Hotel, 9-13 Wilson Road, Southend-on-Sea, Essex SS1 1HG

Tel: 01702 351000

Licensed hotel, 20 en-suite rooms, private parking, evening meals by prior arrangement. Self contained flat available.

The Grand Hotel, The Broadway, Leigh-On-Sea, Essex SS9 1PJ

Tel: 01702 710768

Seafront location, public house with adjoining 16 en-suite room hotel. Private parking, good pub food available.

Five Lakes Hotel G&CC

Colchester Road, Tolleshunt Knights, Maldon, Essex CM9 8HX

Tel: 01621 868888 Fax: 01621 862349

The Five Lakes complex in the village of Tolleshunt Knights between Maldon and Colchester has had a chequered short history. It was originally a somewhat ordinary 18-hole layout built by a local farmer and opened in 1974 under the name Manifold Golf Club. In the late 1980s

it was bought by Bob Curry, father of tour professional Paul Curry, and renamed Quietwaters. The site included other farmland and in 1989 Neil Coles was commissioned to construct an additional layout along the lines of a stadium course. This took just four months to construct and because the land was generally flat 150,000 cubic metres of soil was removed to construct various lakes and the earth used to construct mounding to give the circuit its character. This course opened in 1991 and was celebrated with the Faldo Challenge involving Nick Faldo, World Motor racing champion Nigel Mansell, Test cricketer Ian Botham, and former Olympic decathlon champion Daley Thompson.

Meanwhile, an extensive hotel, sports hall and other facilities were under construction and in 1992 the PGA European Tour used The Lakes Course for the first time to stage its Pre-Qualifying School. However, that same year the complex went into receivership with the hotel still unfinished.

Although the two courses, the smaller layout having been renamed the Links, remained in use, the complex itself lay dormant until 1994 when hotelier Abraham Bergerano bought it and spent several millions completing the hotel. He increased the number of bedrooms from 58 to 114 and opened for business in 1995 under the name of Five Lakes Hotel Golf and Country Club. Since then the business has flourished, the hotel becoming a favourite venue for important functions and the destination for a string of soccer clubs.

Mr Bergerano, an avid Tottenham fan, installed a pitch for these clubs to prepare for matches in London or East Anglia.

Meanwhile many important golf tournaments have been staged over the Lakes Course besides the annual Tour School Pre-Qualifying. With over 15,000 trees being planted over the years, the courses offer a challenge especially when the wind blows in off the River Blackwater Estuary. As the name suggests, the Lakes has an abundance of water hazards in the form of the five lakes which attract a wealth of bird life. The par 72 **Lakes**, which measures 6,767 yards, is designed in two loops, the culmination of each, the 9th and 18th, require accuracy and length to avoid the water as you return to the hotel. Perhaps the appeal of the Lakes comes with the four short holes, two of which have water close to the green. The putting surfaces are particularly sound and true here and are a feature of the course. Several holes on the smaller **Links** layout have been changed from the old Manifold layout and this now measures 6,188 yards with a par of 71.

Sec/Manager: Mike Taylor

Professional: Gary Carter

Directions: 8 miles north east of Maldon. From Maldon centre take the B1026 towards Tolleshunt D'Arcy. The entrance is on the left hand side one mile after the junction with the B1023.

Date Founded: 1988

Visitors: Welcome: Apart from Sunday mornings

Societies: Welcome: Contact in advance

Facilities: Putting Green, Chipping Green, Club Hire, Trolley Hire, Buggy Hire, Bar, Restaurant, Driving Range

Lakes

Type of Course: Parkland

No of Holes: 18

Length: 6700 yds 6184 mtrs.

Par: 72

SSS: 72

Green Fees: Weekdays: £27.00; Weekends/ Bank Holidays: £35.00

Links

Type of Course: Links

No of Holes: 18

Length: 6100 yds (5630 mtrs)

Par:	71
SSS:	70
Green Fees:	Weekdays: £20.00; Weekends/ Bank Holidays: £28.00

Accommodation, Food and Drink

Reference numbers below refer to detailed information provided in section 2

Accommodation

The Spread Eagle Hotel, Newland Street, Witham, Essex CM8 2BD

Tel: 01376 512131 Fax: 01376 502458

A 13th century former coaching inn, full of character and with a relaxing atmosphere. There are 13 bedrooms, most en-suite and the excellent menu offers a choice of tempting dishes.

The Benbridge Hotel, The Square, Heybridge, Maldon, Essex CM9 4LT

Tel: 01621 857666 Fax: 01621 841966

An elegant Georgian hotel with a reputation for quality. There are 14 en-suite rooms and English and Continental cuisine is served in the gracious dining room. An ideal base for outdoor activities.

The Blackwater Hotel and Restaurant, 20-22 Church Road, West Mersea, Colchester, Essex CO5 8QH

Tel: 01206 383338 Fax: 01206 384288

A fine hotel with 8 guest rooms all decorated and furnished to a high standard. A superb menu is available in the elegant dining room with an excellent choice of wines to accompany your meal. The lounge, bar and courtyard is open to residents and non residents.

Food and Drink

The Cricketers, Coggeshall, Essex CO6 1NL

Tel: 01376 561533

A convivial country pub in traditional style. Good local support and passing trade. Wide choice of food and regularly changing real ales. 501

Maldon Pie & Eel House, 136 High Street, Maldon, Essex CM9 8LS

Tel: 01621 842859

Traditional pie & eel shop selling what was once the favourite food of London's East End: eels stewed or jellied, double pie 'n' mash.

The Oak, Tiptree, Nr Colchester, Essex CO5 0NF

Tel: 01621 815579

A convivial pub on the outskirts of Tiptree serving all-day snacks and meals. Patio for barbecue and music. 506

The Spread Eagle Hotel, Newland Street, Witham, Essex CM8 2BD

Tel: 01376 512131 Fax: 01376 502458

A 13th century former coaching inn, full of character and with a relaxing atmosphere. There are 13 bedrooms, most en-suite and the excellent menu offers a choice of tempting dishes.

The Benbridge Hotel, The Square, Heybridge, Maldon, Essex CM9 4LT

Tel: 01621 857666 Fax: 01621 841966

An elegant Georgian hotel with a reputation for quality. There are 14 en-suite rooms and English and Continental cuisine is served in the gracious dining room. An ideal base for outdoor activities.

The Blackwater Hotel and Restaurant, 20-22 Church Road, West Mersea, Colchester, Essex CO5 8QH

Tel: 01206 383338 Fax: 01206 384288

A fine hotel with 8 guest rooms all decorated and furnished to a high standard. A superb menu is available in the elegant dining room with an excellent choice of wines to accompany your meal. The lounge, bar and courtyard is open to residents and non residents.

Forrester Park

Beckingham Road, Great Totham, Maldon, Essex CM9 8EA

Tel/Fax: 01621 891406

Sec/Manager:	Tim Forrester -Muir
Professional:	Gary Pike
Directions:	3 miles north of Maldon. From the north east outskirts of Maldon take the B1022 (Tiptree). At Great Totham turn right into Beckingham Road and the entrance is on the right hand side.
Date Founded:	1968
Type of Course:	Parkland
No of Holes:	18
Length:	6073 yds (5605 mtrs)
Par:	71
SSS:	71
Green Fees:	Weekdays: £18.00; Weekends/ Bank Holidays: £20.00
Visitors:	Welcome: Contact Club in advance. Unable to play Tuesday, Wednesday, Saturday and Sunday mornings.
Societies:	Welcome: Contact Club in advance.

Facilities: Putting Green, Chipping Green, Practice Ground, Trolley Hire, Buggy Hire, Bar, Restaurant, Private Rooms, Tennis Court

Accommodation, Food and Drink

Reference numbers below refer to detailed information provided in section 2

Accommodation

The Spread Eagle Hotel, Newland Street, Witham, Essex CM8 2BD

Tel: 01376 512131 Fax: 01376 502458

A 13th century former coaching inn, full of character and with a relaxing atmosphere. There are 13 bedrooms, most en-suite and the excellent menu offers a choice of tempting dishes.

The Benbridge Hotel, The Square, Heybridge, Maldon, Essex CM9 4LT

Tel: 01621 857666 Fax: 01621 841966

An elegant Georgian hotel with a reputation for quality. There are 14 en-suite rooms and English and Continental cuisine is served in the gracious dining room. An ideal base for outdoor activities.

Athelston House, 201 Maldon Road, Colchester, Essex CO3 3BQ

Tel: 01206 548652 e-mail: mackman@mcmail.com

Excellent B&B with friendly and helpful owners. There are 3 bedrooms furnished to a high standard of comfort. The dining room is spacious and there is a pretty garden. No smoking.

Food and Drink

Maldon Pie & Eel House, 136 High Street, Maldon, Essex CM9 8LS

Tel: 01621 842859

Traditional pie & eel shop selling what was once the favourite food of London's East End: eels stewed or jellied, double pie 'n' mash.

The Oak, Tiptree, Nr Colchester, Essex CO5 0NF

Tel: 01621 815579

A convivial pub on the outskirts of Tiptree serving all-day snacks and meals. Patio for barbecue and music. 506

The Spread Eagle Hotel, Newland Street, Witham, Essex CM8 2BD

Tel: 01376 512131 Fax: 01376 502458

A 13th century former coaching inn, full of character and with a relaxing atmosphere. There are 13 bedrooms, most en-suite and the excellent menu offers a choice of tempting dishes.

The Chequers, 32 The Street, Wickham Bishops, Essex CM8 3NN

Tel: 01621 891320

Thought to be the oldest pub in Wickham Bishops, it still retains the wattle and daub walls inside. A good selection of food is served in the dining area at lunchtime and evenings.

The Benbridge Hotel, The Square, Heybridge, Maldon, Essex CM9 4LT

Tel: 01621 857666 Fax: 01621 841966

An elegant Georgian hotel with a reputation for quality. There are 14 en-suite rooms and English and Continental cuisine is served in the gracious dining room. An ideal base for outdoor activities.

The Old Ship, Lock Hill, Heybridge Basin, Maldon, Essex CM9 4RX

Tel: 01621 854150

Situated on the lock-side with beautiful views across the water, this old pub has an excellent a la carte menu and range of ales which can be enjoyed in the dining room or perhaps outside at one of the picnic tables.

Frinton

1 The Esplanade, Frinton-on-Sea, Essex CO13 9EP

Tel: 01255 674618

Golf at Frinton is nearly as old as the town itself. The club was founded in 1895 and was situated on a nine-hole course designed by Tom Dunn on land now occupied by housing adjacent to the first fairway. That existed until 1904 when Open champion Willie Park Jnr. designed a new 18-hole course on the present site, an area formerly renowned for hare coursing. On the advice of famous course architect Harry Colt various improvements were made to the original design which left the layout largely as we know it today. However, the coming of the Second World War set back those improvements.

Frinton's position on the Essex coast was thought to be a possible site for an enemy inva-

sion so, with the exception of the first three holes, the remainder of the course was requisitioned by the Army and sown with mines. The resultant damage was considerable and it was not until 1947 that the course began to resume its former shape.

Over the years many famous golfers have played at Frinton, including, in the early part of the 20th century, the Great Triumvirate of Vardon, Braid and Taylor. In 1929, the British and Irish team practised at Frinton prior to their Ryder Cup victory at Moortown. A member of that team was Arthur Havers, the 1923 Open champion. He subsequently returned in 1956 as the club's professional and remained until retiring in 1964.

The club celebrated its centenary in 1995 and moved into the new Millennium on a sound footing. Its future also looks secure as it has a flourishing junior section, which runs into three figures and is an example for other clubs.

The current course at 6,265 yards is not excessively long by modern standards and, at first glance, the absence of trees may indicate an easy test. But that's only part of the story. Fast, firm and undulating greens require sound putting, tidal ditches cross many fairways requiring good course management, and being on the coast, there is usually the wind to consider. It is rare to play in still conditions at Frinton and its open character means that every shot has to be evaluated with both wind strength and direction in mind. Nevertheless, this is a course not to miss while there is also a 2,734-yard, par 58, short course that was established in 1913.

Sec/Manager: Roger Attrill

Professional: Peter Taggart

Directions: 1 mile south of Frinton-on-Sea at the southern end of town. The entrance is at the Esplanade, where it meets Second Avenue.

Date Founded: 1895

Visitors: Welcome: Subject to availability, Contact Club in advance

Societies: Welcome: Contact Club in advance (Unable to play Wednesday, Thursday, Friday)

Facilities: Putting Green, Club Hire, Trolley Hire, Buggy Hire, Bar, Restaurant, Practice Area, Chipping Green

18 Hole Course

Type of Course: Links

No of Holes: 18

Length: 6265 yds (5783 mtrs)

Par: 71

SSS: 70

Green Fees: Weekdays: £26.00; Weekends/ Bank Holidays: negotiable

Short Course

Type of Course: Links

No of Holes: 9

Length: 2734 yds (2523 mtrs)

Par: 29

SSS: 29

Green Fees: Weekdays: £7.50; Weekends/ Bank Holidays: Negotiable

Accommodation, Food and Drink

Reference numbers below refer to detailed information provided in section 2

Accommodation

Maison Talbooth, Dedham, Essex CO7 6HN

Tel: 01206 322367 Fax: 01206 322752

Ten top-notch en-suite bedrooms in a Victorian country house with superb views. Meals are served in the restaurant Le Talbooth, a short walk away. 504

Athelston House, 201 Maldon Road, Colchester, Essex CO3 3BQ

Tel: 01206 548652 e-mail: mackman@mcmail.com

Excellent B&B with friendly and helpful owners. There are 3 bedrooms furnished to a high standard of comfort. The dining room is spacious and there is a pretty garden. No smoking.

The Blackwater Hotel and Restaurant, 20-22 Church Road, West Mersea, Colchester, Essex CO5 8QH

Tel: 01206 383338 Fax: 01206 384288

A fine hotel with 8 guest rooms all decorated and furnished to a high standard. A superb menu is available in the elegant dining room with an excellent choice of wines to accompany your meal. The lounge, bar and courtyard is open to residents and non residents.

Mill House, High Street, Thorpe-le-Soken, Clacton-on-Sea, Essex CO16 0DY

Tel: 01255 861334

A gracious and impressive Tudor house with Georgian frontage, handsome inside and out. Superb, well appointed B&B accommodation, with first class furnishings, is offered here. No smoking.

The Captain Fryatt, Garland Road, Parkeston, Harwich, Essex CO12 4PA

Tel: 01255 503535

Taking its name from a First World War hero, the pub offers a varied list of traditional favourites on its menu as well as a good range of beers, wines and spirits. There are 12 superior guest bedrooms available for visitors wishing to stay in the area.

Food and Drink

Maison Talbooth, Dedham, Essex CO7 6HN

Tel: 01206 322367 Fax: 01206 322752

Ten top-notch en-suite bedrooms in a Victorian country house with superb views. Meals are served in the restaurant Le Talbooth, a short walk away. 504

The Red Lion, 9 South Street, Tolleshunt D'Arcy, Essex CM9 8TR

Tel: 01621 860238 Fax: 01621 858253

This large and impressive building has a convivial atmosphere. A good range of traditional home-cooked food is on offer, including the "Golfers Breakfast" served at 6a.m. every Saturday

The Blackwater Hotel and Restaurant, 20-22 Church Road, West Mersea, Colchester, Essex CO5 8QH

Tel: 01206 383338 Fax: 01206 384288

A fine hotel with 8 guest rooms all decorated and furnished to a high standard. A superb menu is available in the elegant dining room with an excellent choice of wines to accompany your meal. The lounge, bar and courtyard is open to residents and non residents.

Priory Restaurant, 4 Clacton Road, St Osyth, Essex

Tel: 01255 820259

Housed in a magnificent 14th century building, this is a colourful and warm restaurant, tea room and delicatessen. The restaurant specialises in mediterranean cooking , expertly prepared. Check for opening times and booking.

The Captain Fryatt, Garland Road, Parkeston, Harwich, Essex CO12 4PA

Tel: 01255 503535

Taking its name from a First World War hero, the pub offers a varied list of traditional favourites on its menu as well as a good range of beers, wines and spirits. There are 12 superior guest bedrooms available for visitors wishing to stay in the area.

Gosfield Lake

The Manor House, Gosfield, Halstead, Essex CO9 1SE

Tel: 01787 474747 Fax: 01787 476044

Sir Henry Cotton designed many courses in his later years and Gosfield Lake, between Halstead and Braintree, is believed to be his final handiwork in this country. In association with golf architect Howard Swan, he masterminded the 6,756-yard **Lakes** Course (6,615 yards from the white tees) and the less demanding nine-hole **Meadows** Course.

The courses, which were laid out in 1987, shortly before Cotton died in December of that year, are a lasting legacy to one of Britain's greatest golfers and the winner of three Open Championships. Cotton said of the Lakes Course: "It has the potential of becoming the finest inland test of golf in England." But remembering the Maestro's ways, he would say that about his own creation, wouldn't he? Nevertheless, there is no doubting that he had an eye for design and that Gosfield Lake is both a delight to play and a test of golfing skills.

The club is the brainchild of golf enthusiast Ralph Rowe, a businessman who spends most of his time abroad. On the 230 acres of rolling Essex parkland to the north of Gosfield Lake, where Queen Elizabeth I is believed to have taken the air, golfers now enjoy peace and tranquillity away from the bustle of modern life. In this idyllic setting the course winds around and over the lakes, through woods and across streams in some of the most beautiful countryside in England. All of the holes are named and those that border Gosfield Lake itself bear watery titles such as **Boat House**, **Lake Look-out**, and **Lake Wood**. Lake Look-out, which is the par-4 third, is one of the signature holes. You drive along a flat fairway to the top of an incline from where the land sweeps slightly left down to a smaller lake beyond which is a thin green. If your drive finishes on level ground you have every chance of reaching the putting surface in two. But if you are faced with a downhill lie there is every chance of finishing in a watery grave although there is a bale-out area to the right. The other key hole is the 14th, a 448-yard par-4, which was Sir Henry's favourite, which he named **Cotton's Choice**. It is slightly downhill but with out of bounds left, a ditch to the left before the green and another small lake close to the putting surface it has the potential of ruining a good card. The short Meadows Course was Cotton's idea for a beginners' layout but this has been extended over the years and now has eight par-3s and 10 par-4s.

Other facilities include a practice ground, chipping and putting green, while the clubhouse offers a full range of bar and catering services.

Sec/Manager: Tony O'Shea

Professional: Richard Wheeler

Directions: 4 miles north of Braintree. From the eastern outskirts take the A131 towards Sudbury. After 3 miles turn left onto the A1017 towards Sible Hedingham and in Gosfield turn left into Hall Drive.

Date Founded: 1988

Visitors: Welcome: Contact Club in advance. Unable to play at certain times on weekends.

Societies: Welcome: Contact Club in advance, by telephone.

Facilities: Putting Green, Club Hire, Trolley Hire, Buggy Hire, Bar, Restaurant, Practice Area, Practice Ground

Lakes

Type of Course: Parkland

No of Holes: 18

Length: 6756 yds (6236 mtrs)

Par: 72

SSS: 71

Green Fees: Weekdays: £25.00; Weekends/ Bank Holidays: £30.00

Meadows

Type of Course: Parkland

No of Holes: 9 x 2

Length: 4180 yds (3858 mtrs)

Par: 64

SSS: 61

Green Fees: Weekdays: £12.00; Weekends/ Bank Holidays: £12.00

Accommodation, Food and Drink

Reference numbers below refer to detailed information provided in section 2

Accommodation

Stoke by Nayland Club Hotel, Leavenheath, Colchester, Essex CO6 4PZ

Tel: 01206 262836 Fax: 01206 263356

A spacious modern country hotel in 300 acres of rolling countryside. 30 fine bedrooms, restaurant, golf courses, health & fitness centre. 508

The Five Bells, 7 Mill Lane, Colne Engaine, Colchester, Essex CO6 2HY

Tel: 01787 224166

A 500 year old inn in a quiet and secluded location, boasting an extremely handsome interior yet retaining its old world charm. An extensive menu of freshly prepared food is on offer as are 3 comfortable guest bedrooms. A spot perfect for exploring the area.

Brook Farm, Wethersfield, Braintree, Essex CM7 4BX

Tel/Fax: 01371 850284

Amid undulating countryside and set on a working farm, this beautiful listed farmhouse offers accommodation in 3 spacious and tastefully furnished guest bedrooms. Delicious breakfasts are prepared by the host. Evening meals can be easily obtained nearby.

The Bell Inn, Great Dunmow Road, Great Bardfield, Essex CM7 4SA

Tel: 01371 811097

A traditional coaching inn dating back to the 16th century with exposed beams and priests hole, enjoyed by locals and visitors alike. A variety of classic English dishes are served and a choice of comfortable guest rooms are available to anyone wishing to stay.

Food and Drink

The Sugar Loaves, 175 Swan Street, Sible Hedingham, Nr Halstead, Essex CO9 3PX

Tel: 01787 462720

A long-hours pub with two bars and a separate eating area, where pizzas and dishes with chips are favourites - served till 7pm daily.

The Pheasant, Audley End, Gestingthorpe, Nr Halstead, Essex CO9 3AX

Tel: 01787 461196

A small, cosy village pub, off the beaten track but well worth seeking out for some of the best food in the area. 509

Stoke by Nayland Club Hotel, Leavenheath, Colchester, Essex CO6 4PZ

Tel: 01206 262836 Fax: 01206 263356

A spacious modern country hotel in 300 acres of rolling countryside. 30 fine bedrooms, restaurant, golf courses, health & fitness centre. 508

The Five Bells, 7 Mill Lane, Colne Engaine, Colchester, Essex CO6 2HY

Tel: 01787 224166

A 500 year old inn in a quiet and secluded location, boasting an extremely handsome interior yet retaining its old world charm. An extensive menu of freshly prepared food is on offer as are 3 comfortable guest bedrooms. A spot perfect for exploring the area.

The Bell Inn, Great Dunmow Road, Great Bardfield, Essex CM7 4SA

Tel: 01371 811097

A traditional coaching inn dating back to the 16th century with exposed beams and priests hole, enjoyed by locals and visitors alike. A variety of classic English dishes are served and a choice of comfortable guest rooms are available to anyone wishing to stay.

Hartswood

King George's Playing Fields, Ingraves Road, Brentwood, Essex CM14 5AE

Tel/Fax: 01277 214830

Sec/Manager:	Dave Mancy
Professional:	Steve Cole
Directions:	1½ miles south of Brentwood. From Brentwood centre take the A128 (Ingrave Herongate). The entrance is on the right hand side.
Date Founded:	1960
Type of Course:	Parkland
No of Holes:	18
Length:	6192 yds (5715 mtrs)
Par:	70
SSS:	69
Green Fees:	Weekdays: £10.00; Weekends/ Bank Holidays: £15.00
Visitors:	Welcome: Contact Club in advance. Tee times bookable.
Societies:	Welcome: Contact Club in advance by telephone.
Facilities:	Putting Green, Chipping Green, Buggy Hire, Bar, Restaurant

Accommodation, Food and Drink

Reference numbers below refer to detailed information provided in section 2

Food and Drink

The Duke of York, Southend Road (A129), South Green, Billericay, Essex CM11 2PR

Tel: 01277 651403

Grand old pub with a restaurant serving freshly prepared food including an exceptional vegetarian choice. Sunday roast, bar snacks, real ales.

The Alma Arms, Horsemanside, Navestock, Brentwood, Essex CM14 5ST

Tel: 01277 372629 Fax: 01277 375440

Delicious food and outstanding real ales and wines in an 18th century pub of character by Navestock Common.

Prince Albert, Blackmore, Brentwood, Essex CM4 0RJ

Tel: 01277 821705

Delightful village pub with a very popular food operation - booking advisable, especially at the weekend. 505

The Plough, 169 Roman Road, Mountnessing, Brentwood, Essex CM15 0UG

Tel: 01277 352026

A large welcoming pub on the B1002 with brasses and memorabilia adorning the walls inside. The excellent menu changes seasonally and there is a garden equipped for childrens enjoyment.

The Thatchers Arms, Warley Road, Great Warley, Brentwood, Essex CM13 3HU

Tel: 01277 233535
email: JimSarah@supernet.co.uk

A large and handsome pub adjacent to the Warley Place Nature Reserve, makes it an ideal spot for walkers. The panelled interior offers snacks and main meals in the dining room or on the adjoining patio.

The Green Man Pub and Restaurant, Navestock Side, Brentwood, Essex CM14 5SD

Tel: 01277 372231

Previously a hunting lodge, this pristine building has been a pub since 1620. Its menu now offers an exceptional choice of traditional favourites as well as a good selection of ales.

Langdon Hills

Lower Dunton Road, Bulphan,
Essex RM14 3TY

Tel: 01268 548444/544300 Fax: 01268 490084

Sec/Manager: Colin Phillips

Professional: Terry Moncur

Directions: 4 miles south west of Basildon. From Basildon centre take the B1007 (Lainford and Stanford - le-Hope) for 3 miles and turn right into Lower Dunton Road on sharp bend. The entrance is on the left hand side after ½ mile.

Date Founded: 1990

Type of Course: Parkland

Visitors: Welcome: Contact Club in advance.

Societies: Welcome: Contact Club in advance.

Facilities: Putting Green, Chipping Green, Driving Range, Club Hire, Trolley Hire, Buggy Hire, Bar, Restaurant, Private Rooms, Hotel

Langdon

Type of Course: Parkland

No of Holes: 9

Length: 3132 yds (2891 mtrs)

Par: 35

SSS: 35

Green Fees: Weekdays: £9.85; Weekends/ Bank Holidays: £11.95

Bulphan

Type of Course: Parkland

No of Holes: 9

Length: 3372 yds (3112 mtrs)

Par: 37

SSS: 37

Green Fees: Weekdays: £9.85; Weekends/ Bank Holidays: £11.95

Horndon

Type of Course: Parkland

No of Holes: 9

Length: 3054 yds (2819 mtrs)

Par: 36

SSS: 36

Green Fees: Weekdays: £9.85; Weekends/ Bank Holidays: £11.95

Accommodation, Food and Drink

Reference numbers below refer to detailed information provided in section 2

Food and Drink

The Duke of York, Southend Road (A129), South Green, Billericay, Essex CM11 2PR

Tel: 01277 651403

Grand old pub with a restaurant serving freshly prepared food including an exceptional vegetarian choice. Sunday roast, bar snacks, real ales.

The Plough, 169 Roman Road, Mountnessing, Brentwood, Essex CM15 0UG

Tel: 01277 352026

A large welcoming pub on the B1002 with brasses and memorabilia adorning the walls inside. The excellent menu changes seasonally and there is a garden equipped for childrens enjoyment.

The Thatchers Arms, Warley Road, Great Warley, Brentwood, Essex CM13 3HU

Tel: 01277 233535

email: JimSarah@supernet.co.uk

A large and handsome pub adjacent to the Warley Place Nature Reserve. The panelled interior offers snacks and main meals in the dining room or on the adjoining patio.

The Theobald Arms, Kings Walk, Grays, Essex RM17 6HR

Tel: 01375 372253

A very friendly and popular pub by the dockside in Grays. A variety of home-cooked food is available at lunchtimes accompanied by a wide range of real ales. A beer festival is held each summer.

The Park Tavern, Romford Road, Aveley, South Ockenden, Essex RM15 4PH

Tel: 01708 863798

A family run pub, sporting an interesting collection of celebrity photos. Good food is prepared from the freshest ingredients and served daily 2-5. There's live entertainment on Fridays and Saturdays.

The Ship, Princess Margaret Road, East Tilbury Village, Essex, RM18 8PB

Tel: 01375 843041

Renowned for its excellent ales and food, this comfortable pub is open all day every day. Lunchtime and evening menus are available and the beer garden is safe for children.

Lexden Wood

Bakers Lane, Colchester , Essex CO3 4AU

Tel: 01206 843333 Fax: 01206 854775

Sec/Manager:	Phillip Grice
Professional:	Phillip Grice
Directions:	2 miles north west of Colchester. From the north west outskirts take the A135 Cymbeline Way (A12). At the roundabout take the third exit Spring Lane. The entrance is at the start of Barkers Lane.
Date Founded:	1998
Type of Course:	Parkland
No of Holes:	18
Length:	5500 yds (5076 mtrs)
Par:	67

SSS:	65
Green Fees:	Weekdays: £16.00; Weekends/ Bank Holidays: £18.00
Visitors:	Welcome: Contact Club in advance.
Societies:	Welcome: Contact Club in advance by telephone. Unable to play on Saturday mornings.
Facilities:	Putting Green, Chipping Green, Driving range, Trolley Hire, Club Hire, Buggy Hire,Bar, Restaurant, Private Rooms

Accommodation, Food and Drink

Reference numbers below refer to detailed information provided in section 2

Accommodation

Stoke by Nayland Club Hotel, Leavenheath, Colchester, Essex CO6 4PZ

Tel: 01206 262836 Fax: 01206 263356

A spacious modern country hotel in 300 acres of rolling countryside. 30 fine bedrooms, restaurant, golf courses, health & fitness centre. 508

Maison Talbooth, Dedham, Essex CO7 6HN

Tel: 01206 322367 Fax: 01206 322752

Ten top-notch en-suite bedrooms in a Victorian country house with superb views. Meals are served in the restaurant Le Talbooth, a short walk away. 504

Athelston House, 201 Maldon Road, Colchester, Essex CO3 3BQ

Tel: 01206 548652 e-mail: mackman@mcmail.com

Excellent B&B with friendly and helpful owners. There are 3 bedrooms furnished to a high standard of comfort. The dining room is spacious and there is a pretty garden. No smoking.

The Five Bells, 7 Mill Lane, Colne Engaine, Colchester, Essex CO6 2HY

Tel: 01787 224166

A 500 year old inn in a quiet and secluded location, boasting an extremely handsome interior yet retaining its old world charm. An extensive menu of freshly prepared food is on offer as are 3 comfortable guest bedrooms. A spot perfect for exploring the area.

Food and Drink

Stoke by Nayland Club Hotel, Leavenheath, Colchester, Essex CO6 4PZ

Tel: 01206 262836 Fax: 01206 263356

A spacious modern country hotel in 300 acres of rolling countryside. 30 fine bedrooms, restaurant, golf courses, health & fitness centre. 508

Maison Talbooth, Dedham, Essex CO7 6HN

Tel: 01206 322367 Fax: 01206 322752

Ten top-notch en-suite bedrooms in a Victorian country house with superb views. Meals are served in the restaurant Le Talbooth, a short walk away. 504

The Three Horseshoes, Church Road, Fordham, Colchester, Essex CO6 3NJ

Tel: 01206 240195

A beautiful whitewashed 16th century inn retaining many original features. It has gained a high regard for its delicious, home-cooked dishes, its great choice of drinks including real ales and for its homely atmosphere.

The Five Bells, 7 Mill Lane, Colne Engaine, Colchester, Essex CO6 2HY

Tel: 01787 224166

A 500 year old inn in a quiet and secluded location, boasting an extremely handsome interior yet retaining its old world charm. An extensive menu of freshly prepared food is on offer as are 3 comfortable guest bedrooms. A spot perfect for exploring the area.

Nazeing

Middle Street, Nazeing, Essex EN9 2LW

Tel: 01992 893798/893915 Fax: 01922 893882

Sec/Manager: James Speller

Professional: Robert Green

Directions: 3½ miles north of Waltham Abbey. From Waltham Abbey (M25 Junction 26) take the B194 to Lower Nazeing. Turn right onto Middle Street on the sharp bend of the B194. The entrance is one mile on the left hand side

Date Founded: 1992

Type of Course: Parkland

No of Holes: 18

Length: 6600 yds (6092mtrs)

Par: 72

SSS: 72

Green Fees: Weekdays: £20.00; Weekends/ Bank Holidays: £28.00

Visitors: Welcome: Contact Club in advance. Unable to play certain times at weekends.

Societies: Welcome: Contact Club in advance by telephone. Unable to play at weekends.

Facilities: Putting Green, Chipping Green, Driving range, Trolley Hire, Buggy Hire,Bar, Restaurant, Private Rooms

Accommodation, Food and Drink

Reference numbers below refer to detailed information provided in section 2

Food and Drink

King Harolds Head, Bumbles Green, Nazeing Common, Waltham Abbey, Essex EN9 2RY

Tel: 01992 893110 Fax: 01992 893412

A charming old free house on the Waltham Abbey-Harlow road. Friendly ambience, good company, exceptional food. 503

The Horseshoes, Horseshoe Hill, Upshire, Waltham Abbey, Essex EN9 3SN

Tel/Fax: 01992 712745

A grown-ups pub in the countryside just outside Waltham Abbey. Real ales, lunches, darts, quizzes, karaoke.

The New Inn, Waltham Abbey, Essex EN9 1EJ

Tel: 01992 712939

Sociable town centre pub with a good line in food (excellent meat dishes) and 10 letting bedrooms. Live music at the weekend. 510

The Queens Head, Old Harlow, Essex CM17 0JT

Tel: 01279 427266 Fax: 01279 421272

Good eating and drinking in a popular pub next to the church. Two bars and outside areas. 511

The New Inn, Roydon, Essex CM19 5EE

Tel: 01279 792225 Fax: 01279 793641

Village centre pub with period charm and lovely gardens. Bar snacks and evening meals. 513

Sixteen String Jack, Coppice Row, Theydon Bois, Essex CM16 7DS

Tel: 01992 813182

Taking its name from the highwayman Jack Rann, hanged in 1774, the pub which dates from that period, now boasts a comfortable interior serving a good range of food and ales.

The Carpenters Arms, The High Road, Thornwood Common, Epping, Essex CM16 6LS

Tel: 01992 574208

Formerly cottages dating from the late 17th century and standing within the boundaries of Epping Forest, this pub has an extensive choice of ales and food available at lunchtimes.

North Weald

Rayley Lane, North Weald, Epping, Essex CM16 6AR

Tel: 01992 522118 Fax: 01992 522881

Sec/Manager: Peter Newson

Professional: David Rawlings

Directions: 3½ miles south east of Harlow. From Harlow or M11 junction 7, take the A414 (Ongar). At the first roundabout turn right (Rayley Lane) and the entrance is 50 yds on the left hand side.

Date Founded: 1996

Type of Course: Parkland

No of Holes: 18

Length: 6311 yds (5825 mtrs)

Par: 71

SSS: 70

Green Fees: Weekdays: £20.00; Weekends/ Bank Holidays: £27.50

Visitors: Welcome: Contact Club in advance. Unable to play certain times at weekends.

Societies: Welcome: Contact Club in advance by telephone. Unable to play at weekends.

Facilities: Putting Green, Chipping Green, Driving Range, Trolley Hire, Buggy Hire,Bar, Restaurant, Club Hire

Accommodation, Food and Drink

Reference numbers below refer to detailed information provided in section 2

Food and Drink

King Harolds Head, Bumbles Green, Nazeing Common, Waltham Abbey, Essex EN9 2RY

Tel: 01992 893110 Fax: 01992 893412

A charming old free house on the Waltham Abbey-Harlow road. Friendly ambience, good company, exceptional food. 503

The Horseshoes, Horseshoe Hill, Upshire, Waltham Abbey, Essex EN9 3SN

Tel/Fax: 01992 712745

A grown-ups pub in the countryside just outside Waltham Abbey. Real ales, lunches, darts, quizzes, karaoke.

The New Inn, Waltham Abbey, Essex EN9 1EJ

Tel: 01992 712939

Sociable town centre pub with a good line in food (excellent meat dishes) and 10 letting bedrooms. Live music at the weekend. 510

The Queens Head, Old Harlow, Essex CM17 0JT

Tel: 01279 427266 Fax: 01279 421272

Good eating and drinking in a popular pub next to the church. Two bars and outside areas. 511

The New Inn, Roydon, Essex CM19 5EE

Tel: 01279 792225 Fax: 01279 793641

Village centre pub with period charm and lovely gardens. Bar snacks and evening meals. 513

Sixteen String Jack, Coppice Row, Theydon Bois, Essex CM16 7DS

Tel: 01992 813182

Taking its name from the highwayman Jack Rann, hanged in 1774, the pub which dates from that period, now boasts a comfortable interior serving a good range of food and ales.

The Carpenters Arms, The High Road, Thornwood Common, Epping, Essex CM16 6LS

Tel: 01992 574208

Formerly cottages dating from the late 17th century and standing within the boundaries of Epping Forest, this pub has an extensive choice of ales and food available at lunchtimes.

Orsett

Brentwood Road, Orsett, Essex RM16 3DS

Tel: 01375 891352 Fax: 01375 892471

When James Braid laid out the present Orsett course in 1929 he was paid the princely sum of 21 guineas for his handiwork. His accounts show an entry for half that amount before work commenced but not the other half when it was completed. Either he forgot to record it or the club benefited by what was a considerable amount in those days. Nevertheless, much of Braid's design can still be seen on this majestic and testing heathland layout.

The club celebrated its centenary in 1999, having been established with just four holes 100 year earlier, which then became nine. Extra land provided by a generous benefactor, Colonel Sir Francis Whitmore, who brought Braid to what was the curiously sounding Mucking Heath in what is now the Borough of Thurrock. There he created what many regard is now one of the finest circuits in Essex if not the south of England. This is why it features on the list of courses used for regional qualifying for the Open Championship.

Situated above the northern banks of the Thames, Orsett is frequently prone to winds, which is why a playing handicap here can be regarded as true in every regard. To see Orsett at its best you should visit in winter when it is rarely closed. Its sandy subsoil means you can return to the clubhouse with your shoes barely muddy even in the wettest weather. However, fairway watering installed in recent years means it no longer suffers in hot, dry summers. The front nine of 37 is built on the old heath with three par fives that are genuine three-shotters for all but the big-hitters. The short par four 6th occupies a depressed valley, once the site of an old sand and gravel pit from which in the old days the sand for the many bunkers was extracted. The par-35 back nine has perhaps the prettiest hole, the short 12th, which lies in a hollow, while the course possesses a testing finish of three par fours, all over 400 yards, the 17th and 18th invariably played into the prevailing wind. In recent times, the indigenous trees and shrubs have tended to get overgrown so a programme of regeneration has been implemented. Many large bramble bushes together with cherry and fir trees have been removed while more gorse and broom have been planted to restore the heathland image when Braid undertook his original contract. At the same time, some greens and most bunkers have been rebuilt during over recent winters, which will eventually provide the course's earlier cutting edge. Nevertheless, is always a difficult circuit especially if there is a wind about.

Sir Michael Bonallack, the immediate past secretary of the R&A, was a country member while completing his National Service at the adjoining army camp and had a hole-in-one at the eighth. During that time the club's professional was Fred Baisden, who served for 53 years from 1910. He was one of only five pros to serve Orsett in over 100 years.

Sec/Manager:	Trevor Collingwood
Professional:	Paul Joiner
Directions:	7 miles south west of Basildon.From Basildon take the A13 (London) to the A128 (Brentwood) exit. Take Cladwell St Mary Road and the entrance is on the left hand side 400 yds from the roundabout.
Date Founded:	1899
Type of Course:	Heathland
No of Holes:	18
Length:	6603 yds (6095 mtrs)
Par:	72
SSS:	72
Green Fees:	Weekdays: £25.00
Visitors:	Welcome: Contact Club in advance. Unable to play at weekends.
Societies:	Welcome: Contact Club in advance by telephone. Unable to play at weekends.
Facilities:	Putting Green, Chipping Green, Practice Area, Trolley Hire, Buggy Hire,Bar, Restaurant, Club Hire, Private Rooms

Accommodation, Food and Drink

Reference numbers below refer to detailed information provided in section 2

Food and Drink

The Duke of York, Southend Road (A129), South Green, Billericay, Essex CM11 2PR

Tel: 01277 651403

Grand old pub with a restaurant serving freshly prepared food including an exceptional vegetarian choice. Sunday roast, bar snacks, real ales.

The Thatchers Arms, Warley Road, Great Warley, Brentwood, Essex CM13 3HU

Tel: 01277 233535

email: JimSarah@supernet.co.uk

A large and handsome pub adjacent to the Warley Place Nature Reserve, makes it an ideal spot for walkers. The panelled interior offers snacks and main meals in the dining room or on the adjoining patio.

The Theobald Arms, Kings Walk, Grays, Essex RM17 6HR

Tel: 01375 372253

A very friendly and popular pub by the dockside in Grays. A variety of home-cooked food is available at lunchtimes accompanied by a wide range of real ales. A beer festival is held each summer.

The Park Tavern, Romford Road, Aveley, South Ockenden, Essex RM15 4PH

Tel: 01708 863798

A family run pub, sporting an interesting collection of celebrity photos. Good food is prepared from the freshest ingredients and served daily 2-5. There's live entertainment on Fridays and Saturdays.

The Ship, Princess Margaret Road, East Tilbury Village, Essex, RM18 8PB

Tel: 01375 843041

Renowned for its excellent ales and food, this comfortable pub is open all day every day. Lunchtime and evening menus are available and the beer garden is safe for children.

Rochford Hundred

Rochford Hall, Hall Road, Rochford, Essex SS4 1NW

Tel: 01702 544302 Fax: 01702 541343

Rochford is one of 13 Essex clubs to have celebrated their centenaries, its earliest recorded date being 1893. But if it hadn't been for a decision by Southend Borough Council three years later

the Rochford club might not exist. In 1896 the Southend Golf Club had been in existence for three years, playing happily on nine holes at Southchurch Hall Estate until the Council decided to run a sewer through the links, dig a lake and build a pumping station. The club's future was in doubt but James Tabor gave it a lifeline. He offered to lease the club 70 acres a few miles away at Rochford Hall for three years at £10 per annum. It was an offer they couldn't refuse, 18 holes were laid out at Rochford Meadows and the name changed to Rochford Hundred. As the entire membership moved en bloc, it was universally accepted that the establishment of the club be backdated to the formation of the Southend club, so Rochford celebrated its 100th birthday in 1993. James Tabor became club President in 1896 and the title has remained within the Tabor family, Charles being the current incumbent, while his son is also a member.

Rochford is somewhat unique in that it has a church, St Andrews, within its boundaries, being bordered by the first, 17th and 18th holes, while its southern boundary borders Southend Airport. The two are firmly linked in that two First World War pilots are buried in the cemetery, their aircraft having collided after taking off from what was then Rochford Aerodrome. The present clubhouse is a part of the original Rochford Hall, now a Grade One listed building. In the First World War the dining room was occupied by the military, while Adolf Hitler did his best to demolish it in the last war when it was occupied by the RAF and the Army. When they departed a sack of primed Mills Bombs was discovered.

The original course remained virtually intact until 1925 when James Braid carried out a redesign after more land was acquired. However, a farmer had grazing rights for sheep on the course until 1969, which provided an additional hazard. In the Sixties the club was alarmed by Southend Council's threat to extend the airport, while Rochford Parish Council submitted planning permission for additional burial ground for the church. Fortunately, neither plan got very far, much to the delight of the members.

Today's course is very much as Braid laid it down. Like many others, it is deceptively difficult but nonetheless enjoyable. As the airport borders it, aircraft noise can be distracting but not off-putting, while there are a number of water hazards in the form of ponds and drainage ditches, some being deceptively hidden. With a par of 72 for its 6,302 yards off the back tees, it is no pushover.

Sec/Manager:	Alan Bandfield
Professional:	Graham Hill
Directions:	3 miles north west of Southend-on-Sea. From the northern outskirts or the A127, take the B1013 (Hawkwell). At the T junction, after 1¼ miles, turn right into Hall Road (Rochford) and the entrance is on the right hand side.
Date Founded:	1893
Type of Course:	Parkland
No of Holes:	18
Length:	6302 yds (5817 mtrs)
Par:	72
SSS:	70
Green Fees:	Weekdays: £30.00; Weekends/ Bank Holidays: £35.00
Visitors:	Welcome: Contact Club in advance. Unable to play on Sundays.
Societies:	Welcome: Contact Club by telephone in advance. Unable to play at Weekends and Tuesdays.
Facilities:	Putting Green, Chipping Green, Club Hire, Trolley Hire, Buggy Hire,Bar, Restaurant

Accommodation, Food and Drink

Reference numbers below refer to detailed information provided in section 2

Accommodation

Hotel Renouf, Bradley Way, Rochford, Essex SS4 1BU

Tel: 01702 549563 Fax: 07102 549563

Modern Town Hotel, offering 23 en-suite rooms. A la Carte restaurant specialising in French cuisine.

Beaches, 192 Eastern Esplanade, Southend -On-Sea, Essex SS1 3AA

Tel: 01702 586124 Fax: 01702 588377

Edwardian house, sea front location. 8 en-suite rooms close to all local facilities.

Ifracombe House Hotel, 9-13 Wilson Road, Southend-on-Sea, Essex SS1 1HG

Tel: 01702 351000

Licensed hotel, 20 en-suite rooms, private parking, evening meals by prior arrangement. Self contained flat available.

The Chichester Hotel, Old London Road, Raweth, Wickford, Essex SS11 8UE

Tel: 01268 560555 Fax: 01268 560580

Quiet location, 33 en-suite rooms, and private parking. Superb food in a la carte restaurant, mid-week special menus available. Residents and diners bar.

The Lodge Country Inn, Rettendon Lodge, Hayes Chase Battlesbridge, Wickford, Essex SS11 7QT

Tel: 01245 320060 Fax: 01245 322622

On the outskirts of Wickford, licensed 8 en-suite room hotel, a la carte restaurant. Bar and bar snacks available.

Food and Drink

The Duke of York, Southend Road (A129), South Green, Billericay, Essex CM11 2PR

Tel: 01277 651403

Grand old pub with a restaurant serving freshly prepared food including an exceptional vegetarian choice. Sunday roast, bar snacks, real ales.

The Beehive Tearoom, 12 South Street, Rochford, Essex SS4 1BQ

Tel: 01702 547644

Tiny tearoom in the village centre, serving coffee, tea, hot and cold snacks, fry-ups and roasts - a speciality.

The Last Post, Southend-on-Sea, Essex SS1 1SA

Tel: 01702 431682

A large all-day pub in premises that were once the central Post Office - hence the name. 512

The Theobald Arms, Kings Walk, Grays, Essex RM17 6HR

Tel: 01375 372253

A very friendly and popular pub by the dockside in Grays. A variety of home-cooked food is available at lunchtimes accompanied by a wide range of real ales. A beer festival is held each summer.

The Ship, Princess Margaret Road, East Tilbury Village, Essex, RM18 8PB

Tel: 01375 843041

Renowned for its excellent ales and food, this comfortable pub is open all day every day.

Lunchtime and evening menus are available and the beer garden is safe for children.

Hotel Renouf, Bradley Way, Rochford, Essex SS4 1BU

Tel: 01702 549563 Fax: 07102 549563

Modern Town Hotel, offering 23 en-suite rooms. A la Carte restaurant specialising in French cuisine.

Beaches, 192 Eastern Esplanade, Southend -On-Sea, Essex SS1 3AA

Tel: 01702 586124 Fax: 01702 588377

Edwardian house, sea front location. 8 en-suite rooms close to all local facilities.

Ifracombe House Hotel, 9-13 Wilson Road, Southend-on-Sea, Essex SS1 1HG

Tel: 01702 351000

Licensed hotel, 20 en-suite rooms, private parking, evening meals by prior arrangement. Self contained flat available.

The Chichester Hotel, Old London Road, Raweth, Wickford, Essex SS11 8UE

Tel: 01268 560555 Fax: 01268 560580

Quiet location, 33 en-suite rooms, and private parking. Superb food in a la carte restaurant, mid-week special menus available. Residents and diners bar.

The Lodge Country Inn, Rettendon Lodge, Hayes Chase Battlesbridge, Wickford, Essex SS11 7QT

Tel: 01245 320060 Fax: 01245 322622

On the outskirts of Wickford, licensed 8 en-suite room hotel, a la carte restaurant. Bar and bar snacks available.

Saffron Walden

Windmill Hill, Saffron Walden, Essex CB10 1BX

Tel/Fax: 01799 522786

There are certain clubs up and down the land that have that country feeling about them as soon as you step on to the course. Saffron Walden is one and there is no better place to swing a golf club than at this delightful part of north Essex.

The views over the course are typically English with Audley End House visible from many points. The club's history is firmly linked with the stately home although there is evidence of at least two nine-holes courses in the area before the present club was established in September 1919. The 7th Lord Braybrooke agreed for nine holes to be laid out in Audley Park and this course opened 20 days later. The ladies section was formed in May 1922 and three years later their membership was one more than the men's, 51 to 50.

Although Lord Braybrooke offered the club part of the stables, now the centre of the clubhouse, progress wasn't easy and in 1924 the club dispensed with its first professional in order to reduce expenses. In 1929 the club moved to its present site and Harry Vardon assisted club pro Reg Cox to design a nine-hole layout that would include the existing and new areas. However, the Lord was vehemently against big changes so there were no bunkers, tees were level areas with small greens just mown parts of the fairways.

The new course opened in 1930 when Vardon played an exhibition match with Cox. During World War II an Ack-Ack Gun was installed on the course, near the present 4th hole, and the commanding officer of the time presented a trophy aptly named the Ack-Ack Cup which is still played for today. The war was particularly hard on the Braybrooke family. Lord Braybrooke died in 1941 while two of his sons were killed in action. The estate was inherited by Seymour, the 9th Lord who projected a much more liberal attitude. Major construction was necessary and he had no objection to bunkers and new greens and tees being installed but this didn't happen until after 1950.

In the war period the club struggled financially until the arrival of the American Air Force bases near Saffron Walden brought their personnel to play the course and the green fees changed the club's finances. An added bonus came by way of an overzealous American pilot who regularly buzzed the clubhouse. However, he forgot he was flying a fixed undercarriage plane and cut two furrows in the thatched roof. A few days later an open cheque was received.

At the end of the war the Americans asked the club to stage an exhibition match for their servicemen to watch involving four of the day's top American players. One turned out to be Horton Smith, the winner of the inaugural US Masters in 1934 and again in 1936.

The changes in the early Fifties transformed the course, then in 1975 it was extended to the present 18 holes. Measuring 6,606 yards, par 72, it presents a good test. The 2nd and 18th tees provide excellent views over the ancient market town, while from the 5th tee the view stretches for miles. Many fine trees remain of those planted by Capability Brown and the elegant buildings in the gardens are the work of Robert Adam. Although the Saffron Walden club lies within Essex, it is affiliated to the Cambridgeshire Area Golf Union.

Sec/Manager:	D H Smith
Professional:	P Davis
Directions:	1 mile west of Saffron Walden. From Saffron Walden centre take Bridge Street (B184 towards Great Chesterford)and after ¼ mile turn left into New Pond Lane. The entrance is on the right hand side after 200 yds.
Date Founded:	1919
Type of Course:	Parkland
No of Holes:	18
Length:	6364 yds (5874 mtrs)
Par:	72
SSS:	72
Green Fees:	Weekdays: £35.00
Visitors:	Welcome: Contact Club in advance. Unable to play at weekends.
Societies:	Welcome: Contact Club in advance by telephone. Unable to play at weekends, Tuesday and Friday.
Facilities:	Putting Green, Driving Range, Bar, Restaurant

Accommodation, Food and Drink

Reference numbers below refer to detailed information provided in section 2

Accommodation

Riverside Guest House, Melbourn, Royston, Cambridgeshire SG8 6DX

Tel: 01763 226062 Fax: 01763 226063

A renovated 100-year-old property in a delightful riverside setting on the edge of a pretty village. Five en-suite rooms for B&B. 625

Newdegate House, Howlett End, Wimbish, Saffron Walden, Essex CB10 2XW

Tel: 01799 599748

A high standard of service awaits at this B&B, which is set in large grounds. Excellent breakfasts and snacks are available. 10 miles from Stanstead.

Redgates Farmhouse, Redgates Lane, Sewards End, Saffron Walden, Essex CB10 2LP

Tel: 01799 516166

Set in 10 acres of peaceful relaxing countryside, this B&B dates in parts to the 16th century. Excellent breakfasts, evening meals by arrangements in homely surroundings.

White Hart, High Street, Debden, Essex CB11 3LE

Tel: 01799 541109

A completely refurbished establishment dating back to the 17th century, at the centre of the village. Good range of English and Continental cuisine and real ales, Accommodation also available.

The Plough Inn, Sampford Road, Radwinter, Saffron Walden, Essex CB10 2TL

Tel: 01799 599222 Fax: 01799 599161

An old, beamed, country pub standing on the crossroads of the B1053 and B1054. A choice of delicious meals can be enjoyed inside, on the lawn or on the clematis covered patio at lunchtime or in the evening. Three self contained en-suite rooms are available.

Food and Drink

The Hoops, Bassingbourn, Cambridgeshire SG8 5LF

Tel: 01763 242130

300-year-old thatched country pub serving a good variety of food and well-kept ales. 601

The Chequers at Anstey, Nr Buntingford, Hertfordshire SG9 0BW

Tel: 01763 848205

Generous home cooking, well-kept real ales and a good wine list in a family-run village pub. 603

The Chestnut Tree, West Wratting, Cambridgeshire CB1 5LU

Tel: 01223 290384

A well-kept redbrick village pub on the B1052, serving a fine selection of first-class food, with Sunday lunch a highlight. 620

White Hart, High Street, Debden, Essex CB11 3LE

Tel: 01799 541109

A completely refurbished establishment dating back to the 17th century, at the centre of the village. Good range of English and Continental cuisine and real ales, Accommodation also available.

The Cock Inn, Church End, Henham, Bishops Stortford, Essex CM22 6AL

Tel: 01279 850347 Fax: 01279 816676

A 300 year old pub with exposed beams and inglenook fireplace, offering superior home-cooked meals in the dining area with a selection of cask ales to choose from.

The Plough Inn, Sampford Road, Radwinter, Saffron Walden, Essex CB10 2TL

Tel: 01799 599222 Fax: 01799 599161

An old, beamed, country pub standing on the crossroads of the B1053 and B1054. A choice of delicious meals can be enjoyed inside, on the lawn or on the clematis covered patio at lunchtime or in the evening. Three self contained en-suite rooms are available.

South Essex G&CC

Herongate, Brentwood, Essex CM13 3LW

Tel: 01277 811289 Fax: 01277 811304

Sec/Manager: Mr Stitt

Professional: Jonathon Simpson

Directions: 4½ miles west of Basildon. From the northern outskirts take the A127 (Romford) and turn left at the A128 (Brentwood) junction into Brentwood Road. The entrance is on the left hand side.

Date Founded: 1994

Visitors: Welcome: Contact Club in advance.

Societies: Welcome: Contact Club in advance by telephone. Unable to play certain times at weekends.

Facilities: Putting Green, Driving Range, Bar, Restaurant, Club Hire, Trolley Hire

18 Hole Course

Type of Course: Parkland

No of Holes: 18

Length: 6851yds (6324 mtrs)

Par: 72

SSS: 73

Green Fees: Weekdays: £16.00; Weekends/ Bank Holidays £21.00

9 Hole Course

Type of Course: Parkland

No of Holes: 9

Length: 3102yds (2863 mtrs)

Par: 35

SSS: 35

Green Fees:	Weekdays: £9.00; Weekends/ Bank Holidays £12.00

Accommodation, Food and Drink

Reference numbers below refer to detailed information provided in section 2

Food and Drink

The Alma Arms, Horsemanside, Navestock, Brentwood, Essex CM14 5ST

Tel: 01277 372629 Fax: 01277 375440

Delicious food and outstanding real ales and wines in an 18th century pub of character by Navestock Common.

Prince Albert, Blackmore, Brentwood, Essex CM4 0RJ

Tel: 01277 821705

Delightful village pub with a very popular food operation - booking advisable, especially at the weekend. 505

The Plough, 169 Roman Road, Mountnessing, Brentwood, Essex CM15 0UG

Tel: 01277 352026

A large welcoming pub on the B1002 with brasses and memorabilia adorning the walls inside. The excellent menu changes seasonally and there is a garden equipped for childrens enjoyment.

The Thatchers Arms, Warley Road, Great Warley, Brentwood, Essex CM13 3HU

Tel: 01277 233535
email: JimSarah@supernet.co.uk

A large and handsome pub adjacent to the Warley Place Nature Reserve, makes it an ideal spot for walkers. The panelled interior offers snacks and main meals in the dining room or on the adjoining patio.

The Park Tavern, Romford Road, Aveley, South Ockenden, Essex RM15 4PH

Tel: 01708 863798

A family run pub, sporting an interesting collection of celebrity photos. Good food is prepared from the freshest ingredients and served daily 2-5. There's live entertainment on Fridays and Saturdays.

St Cleres

St Cleres Hall, Stanford-le-Hope, Essex SS17 0LX

Tel/Fax: 01375 673007

Sec/Manager:	David Wood
Professional:	David Wood
Directions:	1 mile south west of Stanford-le-Hope. From the west side of Stanford-Le-hope take the A103 (Thurrock) Stanford Road. The entrance is on the left hand side at edge of town.
Date Founded:	1994
Type of Course:	Links and Parkland
No of Holes:	18
Length:	6474 yds (5976 mtrs)
Par:	72
SSS:	71
Green Fees:	Weekdays: £15.00; Weekends/ Bank Holidays: £20.00
Visitors:	Welcome: Contact Club in advance. Unable to play Monday, Wednesday and Friday.
Societies:	Welcome: Contact Club in advance by telephone.
Facilities:	Putting Green, Chipping Green, Driving Range, Club Hire, Trolley Hire, Buggy Hire, Bar, Restaurant

Accommodation, Food and Drink

Reference numbers below refer to detailed information provided in section 2

Food and Drink

The Beehive Tearoom, 12 South Street, Rochford, Essex SS4 1BQ

Tel: 01702 547644

Tiny tearoom in the village centre, serving coffee, tea, hot and cold snacks, fry-ups and roasts - a speciality.

The Last Post, Southend-on-Sea, Essex SS1 1SA

Tel: 01702 431682

A large all-day pub in premises that were once the central Post Office - hence the name. 512

The Thatchers Arms, Warley Road, Great Warley, Brentwood, Essex CM13 3HU

Tel: 01277 233535

email: JimSarah@supernet.co.uk

A large and handsome pub adjacent to the Warley Place Nature Reserve, makes it an ideal spot for walkers. The panelled interior offers snacks and main meals in the dining room or on the adjoining patio.

The Theobald Arms, Kings Walk, Grays, Essex RM17 6HR

Tel: 01375 372253

A very friendly and popular pub by the dockside in Grays. A variety of home-cooked food is available at lunchtimes accompanied by a wide range of real ales. A beer festival is held each summer.

The Park Tavern, Romford Road, Aveley, South Ockenden, Essex RM15 4PH

Tel: 01708 863798

A family run pub, sporting an interesting collection of celebrity photos. Good food is prepared from the freshest ingredients and served daily 2-5. There's live entertainment on Fridays and Saturdays.

The Ship, Princess Margaret Road, East Tilbury Village, Essex, RM18 8PB

Tel: 01375 843041

Renowned for its excellent ales and food, this comfortable pub is open all day every day. Lunchtime and evening menus are available and the beer garden is safe for children.

Stock Brook Manor

Queen's Park Avenue, Stock, Billericay, Essex CM120SP

Tel: 01277 653616Fax: 01277 633063

The golf course explosion that hit Essex in the early Nineties saw the birth of Stock Brook Manor to the west of the commuter town of Billericay. It has proved to one of the best of the new breed and after a few years of bedding in has matured into a fine test that is a pleasure to play.

Named after the Stock Brook which runs through the lower part of the course and the nearby Manor House, Great Blunts, mentioned in the Doomsday Book, the complex features three nines, **Stock**, **Brook** and **Manor**, but the main championship layout features the first two. As far as the principle 6,728-yard, par 72 course is concerned, as with most modern layouts, water is a major feature with three lakes providing not only an addition to the landscape but also irrigation for the courses, hazards for the golfer and a refuge for hosts of waterfowl.

The design is Martin Gillett's who has enhanced the natural rolling landscape with the water features while at the same time blending many of the mature trees into his handiwork. Two lengthy par fours at the start allows the player to open his shoulders before more deft strokeplay is demanded for the 294-yard third and the short fourth where water stretches from tee to green. The 155-yard seventh brings you back to the same hazard while the outward nine ends with a dog-leg par five where the drive must be threaded between two lakes. The back nine is particularly interesting with the 12th and 13th occupying a spit of land that Gillett has used to its maximum. The 319-yard 12th looks innocuous but can easily destroy a good card. With out of bounds right and the Stock Brook to the left, the drive must be accurate to a landing area only 45 yards wide. A successful outcome is rewarded with a simple pitch to a generously long green but another out of bounds waits behind the putting surface. The

short 13th, back the way you came, measures 189 yards from the back tee with a ridged green guarded by two bunkers. There are two more testing short holes to overcome before the long 18th with its six bunkers and lake to be avoided.

The nine holes of the 2,977-yard, par 35 **Manor** course are situated either side of the approach road and feature water on at least four holes. Since the courses were developed a large, impressive clubhouse has been built with all modern facilities including an upstairs banqueting suite.

Sec/Manager: Kevin Roe

Professional: Kevin Merry

Directions: 1 mile north of Billericay.From the roundabout on the B1007 on the northern outskirts. Take the first exit, Queens Park Avenue. The entrance is on the right hand side.

Date Founded: 1992

Visitors: Welcome: Contact Club in advance. Unable to play on Tuesday and Wednesday.

Societies: Welcome: Contact Club by telephone in advance.

Facilities: Putting Green, Chipping Green, Driving Range, Club Hire, Trolley Hire, Buggy Hire, Bar, Restaurant

18 Hole Course

Type of Course: Parkland

No of Holes: 18

Length: 6592 yds (6084 mtrs)

Par: 72

SSS: 72

Green Fees: Weekdays: £25.00; Weekends/ Bank Holidays: £30.00

Manor Course

Type of Course: Parkland

No of Holes: 9

Length: 2977yds (2748 mtrs)

Par: 35

SSS: 35

Green Fees: Not available at time of going to press

Accommodation, Food and Drink

Reference numbers below refer to detailed information provided in section 2

Accommodation

Hotel Campanile & Restaurant, A127 Southend Arterial Road, Pipps Hill, Basildon, Essex SS14 3AE

Tel: 01268 530810 Fax: 01268 286710

Situated one mile from the town centre, 100 en-suite rooms, full bar facilities with large restaurant serving continental cuisine.

The Quays, New Festival Leisure Park, Cranes Farm Road, Basildon, Essex SS14 3AD

Tel: 01268 290400 Fax: 0870 700 1377

Modern town centre hotel, 64 en-suite rooms, and large restaurant serving traditional English food.

The Chichester Hotel, Old London Road, Raweth, Wickford, Essex SS11 8UE

Tel: 01268 560555 Fax: 01268 560580

Quiet location, 33 en-suite rooms, and private parking. Superb food in a la carte restaurant, mid-week special menus available. Residents and diners bar.

The Lodge Country Inn, Rettendon Lodge, Hayes Chase Battlesbridge, Wickford, Essex SS11 7QT

Tel: 01245 320060 Fax: 01245 322622

On the outskirts of Wickford, licensed 8 en-suite room hotel, a la carte restaurant. Bar and bar snacks available.

Food and Drink

The Rodney, Little Baddow, Essex CH3 4TQ

Tel: 01245 222385

17th century premises for a comfortable village pub with front patio and sloping gardens. Home-prepared food on a traditional menu. 502

The Duke of York, Southend Road (A129), South Green, Billericay, Essex CM11 2PR

Tel: 01277 651403

Grand old pub with a restaurant serving freshly prepared food including an exceptional vegetarian choice. Sunday roast, bar snacks, real ales.

Prince Albert, Blackmore, Brentwood, Essex CM4 0RJ

Tel: 01277 821705

Delightful village pub with a very popular food operation - booking advisable, especially at the weekend. 505

The White Hart, Swan Lane, Margaretting Tye, Ingatestone, Essex CM4 9JX

Tel: 01277 840478 Fax: 01277 841178
email: @thewhitehart.uk.com
website: www.thewhitehart.uk.com

An excellent pub dating in parts to the 1600's, with vaulted ceilings and open fires. The mainly traditional menu also caters for children. An ideal base for walking.

The Plough, 169 Roman Road, Mountnessing, Brentwood, Essex CM15 0UG

Tel: 01277 352026

A large welcoming pub on the B1002 with brasses and memorabilia adorning the walls inside. The excellent menu changes seasonally and there is a garden equipped for childrens enjoyment.

Hotel Campanile & Restaurant, A127 Southend Arterial Road, Pipps Hill, Basildon, Essex SS14 3AE

Tel: 01268 530810 Fax: 01268 286710

Situated one mile from the town centre, 100 en-suite rooms, full bar facilities with large restaurant serving continental cuisine.

The Quays, New Festival Leisure Park, Cranes Farm Road, Basildon, Essex SS14 3AD

Tel: 01268 290400 Fax: 0870 700 1377

Modern town centre hotel, 64 en-suite rooms, and large restaurant serving traditional English food.

The Chichester Hotel, Old London Road, Raweth, Wickford, Essex SS11 8UE

Tel: 01268 560555 Fax: 01268 560580

Quiet location, 33 en-suite rooms, and private parking. Superb food in a la carte restaurant, mid-week special menus available. Residents and diners bar.

The Lodge Country Inn, Rettendon Lodge, Hayes Chase Battlesbridge, Wickford, Essex SS11 7QT

Tel: 01245 320060 Fax: 01245 322622

On the outskirts of Wickford, licensed 8 en-suite room hotel, a la carte restaurant. Bar and bar snacks available.

Thorpe Hall

Thorpe Hall Avenue, Thorpe Bay, Essex SS1 3AT

Tel: 01702 582205 Fax: 01702 584498

Based at Thorpe Bay near Southend, Thorpe Hall is unique among British clubs in that two of its members, Sir Michael Bonallack and Peter Dawson, have become secretary of the Royal and Ancient Club at St Andrews. Bonallack was an active member of the club during the time when he dominated amateur golf, winning the Amateur Championship five times, the English title also five times, played Walker Cup regularly from 1957 to 1973, and the Eisenhower Trophy seven times. All these achievements and many more including 11 Essex Championships are displayed on impressive honours boards inside the homely clubhouse. Dawson didn't quite achieve the successes of his predecessor but was a Thorpe Hall cadet while at school in the area.

The club has always been a power in Essex golf and has produced other champions and internationals down the years, the latest being Richard McEvoy, while they can also claim several Curtis Cup representatives. Being so close to the centre of Southend it isn't surprising that the club acts as an oasis in the midst of the housing in this up-market part of the town. The original site was Thorpe Hall Farm, which was mentioned in the Domesday Book in 1086. The golf club was founded in 1907 by K Costley-White, who leased part of the farm. With the help of Bert Batley, the club's first professional, they turned it into an 18 hole course which was described a few years later as being "on fine old meadow pasture, the turf being excellent. The hazards consist of ditches, ponds, whins and artificial bunkers".

The Southend handbook of 1931 went further saying: "At first glance, this seaside course appears easy, as Harry Vardon thought when he started out in a final some years ago. After taking a seven at the first and a seven at the second, he altered his opinion and wrote an article in Golf Monthly about the false impression Thorpe Hall gives". Many more distinguished players have come to the same conclusion so that Thorpe Hall remains a challenge to every standard of golfer to this day. There are five testing short holes in the 6,319 yards off the back tees with a par of 71, while it is worth making yourself aware of the many out of bounds areas as well as the aforementioned ditches and ponds before tackling each hole.

Sec/Manager:	Mr O Hara
Professional:	Bill McColl
Directions:	2 miles east of Southend-On-Sea centre. Where SouthChurch Boulevard and Eastern Avenue meet go South along Thorpe Hall Avenue. The entrance is on the right hand side.
Date Founded:	1907
Type of Course:	Parkland
No of Holes:	18
Length:	6319 yds (5832 mtrs)

Par: 71

SSS: 71

Green Fees: Weekdays: £32.00

Visitors: Welcome: Contact Club in advance. Unable to play at weekends.

Societies: Welcome: Contact Club by telephone in advance. Unable to play on Fridays.

Facilities: Putting Green, Practice Area, Trolley Hire, Buggy Hire, Bar, Restaurant

Accommodation, Food and Drink

Reference numbers below refer to detailed information provided in section 2

Accommodation

Hotel Renouf, Bradley Way, Rochford, Essex SS4 1BU

Tel: 01702 549563 Fax: 07102 549563

Modern Town Hotel, offering 23 en-suite rooms. A la Carte restaurant specialising in French cuisine.

Beaches, 192 Eastern Esplanade, Southend -On-Sea, Essex SS1 3AA

Tel: 01702 586124 Fax: 01702 588377

Edwardian house, sea front location. 8 en-suite rooms close to all local facilities.

Ifracombe House Hotel, 9-13 Wilson Road, Southend-on-Sea, Essex SS1 1HG

Tel: 01702 351000

Licensed hotel, 20 en-suite rooms, private parking, evening meals by prior arrangement. Self contained flat available.

The Grand Hotel, The Broadway, Leigh-On-Sea, Essex SS9 1PJ

Tel: 01702 710768

Seafront location, public house with adjoining 16 en-suite room hotel. Private parking, good pub food available.

Food and Drink

The Duke of York, Southend Road (A129), South Green, Billericay, Essex CM11 2PR

Tel: 01277 651403

Grand old pub with a restaurant serving freshly prepared food including an exceptional vegetarian choice. Sunday roast, bar snacks, real ales.

The Beehive Tearoom, 12 South Street, Rochford, Essex SS4 1BQ

Tel: 01702 547644

Tiny tearoom in the village centre, serving coffee, tea, hot and cold snacks, fry-ups and roasts - a speciality.

The Last Post, Southend-on-Sea, Essex SS1 1SA

Tel: 01702 431682

A large all-day pub in premises that were once the central Post Office - hence the name. 512

The White Hart, Swan Lane, Margaretting Tye, Ingatestone, Essex CM4 9JX

Tel: 01277 840478 Fax: 01277 841178
email: @thewhitehart.uk.com
website: www.thewhitehart.uk.com

An excellent pub dating in parts to the 1600's, with vaulted ceilings and open fires. The mainly traditional menu also caters for children. An ideal base for walking.

The Ship, Princess Margaret Road, East Tilbury Village, Essex, RM18 8PB

Tel: 01375 843041

Renowned for its excellent ales and food, this comfortable pub is open all day every day. Lunchtime and evening menus are available and the beer garden is safe for children.

Hotel Renouf, Bradley Way, Rochford, Essex SS4 1BU

Tel: 01702 549563 Fax: 07102 549563

Modern Town Hotel, offering 23 en-suite rooms. A la Carte restaurant specialising in French cuisine.

Ifracombe House Hotel, 9-13 Wilson Road, Southend-on-Sea, Essex SS1 1HG

Tel: 01702 351000

Licensed hotel, 20 en-suite rooms, private parking, evening meals by prior arrangement. Self contained flat available.

The Grand Hotel, The Broadway, Leigh-On-Sea, Essex SS9 1PJ

Tel: 01702 710768

Seafront location, public house with adjoining 16 en-suite room hotel. Private parking, good pub food available.

Three Rivers

Stow Road, Purleigh, Cold Norton, Chelmsford, Essex CM3 6RR

Tel: 01621 828631 Fax: 01621 828060

This fine 36-hole layout at Cold Norton, some five miles south of Maldon, fits neatly into the family of Clubhaus-owned complexes. It is ap-

proaching its 30th birthday having been in the vanguard of a bunch of new courses constructed prior to the big push of the last Eighties and early Nineties.

Built on farmland composed of traditional Essex clay, the original course, the **Kings**, suffered a lot in the early years when summer droughts followed by wet winters brought many problems on the fairways. Good husbandry has, happily, meant that it is all history now and the Kings has settled into a fine test. Built in 1972, the Kings, designed by Fred Hawtree, measures 6,449 yards from the back tees to a par of 72. It is situated in mature woodland with a number of intricate dog legs, many bunkers, and some water features. There are just three par fives, two coming back-to-back with the third and fourth. The 515-yard third requires an approach over a lake to a bunkerless, raised green, while the 484-yard double dog-leg fourth has many trees, especially in the driving area, and ditches either side of the fairway at middle distance. There is also a pond splitting the left side of the fairway, while the green sits between two large bunkers with more trees beyond. The toughest hole, according to the stroke index, is the 414-yard sixth where six large bunkers have to be avoided before you reach the safety of the green. In its early days, the course was generally open but the growth of the trees has provided more character as well as protection and none more so than at the dog-leg 11th. This measures just 335 yards but the accuracy of drive is all-important to set up the approach and make your par. The round comes to a fitting finale with the superb 18th. Not long at 386 yards, but it is yet another dog-leg while the green sits in front of the clubhouse and invariably requires an approach over the lake which guards the right side.

The newer par 64 **Jubilee** Course offers a completely different concept to the Kings. Opened by top senior golfer Tommy Horton in 1998, it is more forgiving in length at 4,501 yards with eight par threes and 10 par fours. However, with its undulating greens and large bunkers it is no pushover, while you can't get away from those dog-legs. The country club complex also offers the usual golf related facilities as well as tennis, health and fitness areas, beauty treatments and overnight accommodation

Sec/Manager:	John Martin
Professional:	Scott Clark
Directions:	2½ miles north east of South Woodham Ferrers. From the northern outskirts take the B1012 (Burnham -on Crouch). After 1¾ miles, turn left (Honey Pot Lane) at T junction. Turn right into Stow Road (Cold Norton) and the entrance is on the right hand side.
Date Founded:	1972
Visitors:	Welcome: Contact Club in advance. Unable to play on Kings at certain times on weekends.
Societies:	Welcome: Contact Club in advance, by telephone.
Facilities:	Putting Green, Club Hire, Trolley Hire, Buggy Hire, Bar, Restaurant, Practice Area, Caddy Service

Kings

Type of Course:	Parkland
No of Holes:	18
Length:	6449 yds (5952 mtrs)
Par:	72
SSS:	71
Green Fees:	Weekdays: £15.00; Weekends/ Bank Holidays: £25.00

Jubilee

Type of Course:	Parkland
No of Holes:	18
Length:	4501 yds (4154mtrs)

Par:	64
SSS:	62
Green Fees:	Weekdays: £10.00; Weekends/ Bank Holidays: £12.50

Accommodation, Food and Drink

Reference numbers below refer to detailed information provided in section 2

Accommodation

The Benbridge Hotel, The Square, Heybridge, Maldon, Essex CM9 4LT

Tel: 01621 857666 Fax: 01621 841966

An elegant Georgian hotel with a reputation for quality. There are 14 en-suite rooms and English and Continental cuisine is served in the gracious dining room. An ideal base for outdoor activities.

Anchor Hotel, The Quay, Burnham-On-Crouch, Essex CMO 8AT

Tel: 01621 782117

500-year-old inn, 4 en-suite rooms with small intimate restaurant offering good home cooked food.

Railway Hotel, 12 Station Road, Burnham-On-Crouch, Essex CMO 8BQ

Tel: 01621 786868

Victorian building, good recently refurbished restaurant. Four doubles and 2 single en-suite rooms.

Ye Olde White Harte Hotel, The Quay, Burnham -On -Crouch, Essex. CMO 8AS

Tel: 01621 782106

Quaint hotel, overlooking the quay. Parts of building date to 1700. 19 rooms mostly en-suite, separate bar and restaurant

Food and Drink

The Rodney, Little Baddow, Essex CH3 4TQ

Tel: 01245 222385

17th century premises for a comfortable village pub with front patio and sloping gardens. Home-prepared food on a traditional menu. 502

Maldon Pie & Eel House, 136 High Street, Maldon, Essex CM9 8LS

Tel: 01621 842859

Traditional pie & eel shop selling what was once the favourite food of London's East End: eels stewed or jellied, double pie 'n' mash.

Queen Victoria, The Street, Woodham Walter, Maldon, Essex CM9 6RF

Tel: 01245 222176

A lovely 18th century pub situated in a quiet country lane. Snacks and hot meals can be enjoyed in either the comfortable bars or in the small garden, as can a range of real ales.

The Benbridge Hotel, The Square, Heybridge, Maldon, Essex CM9 4LT

Tel: 01621 857666 Fax: 01621 841966

An elegant Georgian hotel with a reputation for quality. There are 14 en-suite rooms and English and Continental cuisine is served in the gracious dining room. An ideal base for outdoor activities.

The Queen's Head Inn, The Hythe, Maldon, Essex CM9 5HN

Tel: 01621 859154 (restaurant)
Tel: 01621 854112 (pub)

An impressive 500 year old building overlooking the Blackwater Estuary, with a nautical feel. Good range of home-cooked food is served in the restaurant and there is a large riverside patio.

The White Horse Inn, Main Road, Mundon, Maldon, Essex CM9 6PB

Tel: 01621 740276

Set in picturesque surroundings, this 400 year old pub with low ceilings, offers a good selection of food and ales. Sunday lunches are a speciality.

Anchor Hotel, The Quay, Burnham-On-Crouch, Essex CMO 8AT

Tel: 01621 782117

500-year-old inn, 4 en-suite rooms with small intimate restaurant offering good home cooked food.

Railway Hotel, 12 Station Road, Burnham-On-Crouch, Essex CMO 8BQ

Tel: 01621 786868

Victorian building, good recently refurbished restaurant. Four doubles and 2 single en-suite rooms.

Ye Olde White Harte Hotel, The Quay, Burnham -On -Crouch, Essex CMO 8AS

Tel: 01621 782106

Quaint hotel, overlooking the quay. Parts of building date to 1700. 19 rooms mostly en-suite, separate bar and restaurant

Toot Hill

School Road, Toot Hill, Ongar, Essex CM5 9PU

Tel: 01277 365523 Fax: 01277 364509

Sec/Manager:	Martin Gilet
Professional:	Mark Bishop
Directions:	2½ miles west of Ongar. From Ongar take B road West, signed Toot Hill. The entrance is on the left hand side opposite Epping Road.
Date Founded:	1991

Type of Course:	Parkland
No of Holes:	18
Length:	6053 yds (5587 mtrs)
Par:	70
SSS:	69
Green Fees:	Weekdays: £30.00; Weekends/ Bank Holidays: £30.00
Visitors:	Welcome: Contact Club in advance. Unable to play at certain times at weekends.
Societies:	Welcome: Contact Club in advance by telephone.
Facilities:	Putting Green, Chipping Green, Driving Range, Trolley Hire, Buggy Hire, Bar, Restaurant

Accommodation, Food and Drink

Reference numbers below refer to detailed information provided in section 2

Food and Drink

King Harolds Head, Bumbles Green, Nazeing Common, Waltham Abbey, Essex EN9 2RY

Tel: 01992 893110 Fax: 01992 893412

A charming old free house on the Waltham Abbey-Harlow road. Friendly ambience, good company, exceptional food. 503

The Queens Head, Fyfield, Essex CM5 0RY

Tel: 01277 899118

A 500-year-old pub near the church in the centre of the little village of Fyfield. Exceptional food has earned wide acclaim. 507

The Horseshoes, Horseshoe Hill, Upshire, Waltham Abbey, Essex EN9 3SN

Tel/Fax: 01992 712745

A grown-ups pub in the countryside just outside Waltham Abbey. Real ales, lunches, darts, quizzes, karaoke.

The New Inn, Waltham Abbey, Essex EN9 1EJ

Tel: 01992 712939

Sociable town centre pub with a good line in food (excellent meat dishes) and 10 letting bedrooms. Live music at the weekend. 510

The Carpenters Arms, The High Road, Thornwood Common, Epping, Essex CM16 6LS

Tel: 01992 574208

Formerly cottages dating from the late 17th century and standing within the boundaries of Epping Forest, this pub has an extensive choice of ales and food available at lunchtimes.

The Green Man Pub and Restaurant, Navestock Side, Brentwood, Essex CM14 5SD

Tel: 01277 372231

Previously a hunting lodge, this pristine building has been a pub since 1620. Its menu now offers an exceptional choice of traditional favourites as well as a good selection of ales.

Top Meadow

Fen Lane, North Ockendon, Essex RM14 3PR

Tel: 01708 852239 Fax: 01708 852598

Sec/Manager:	Danny Stock
Professional:	Kevin Smith
Directions:	2 miles north east of South Ockendon. Take the B186 (North Ockendon) and after 1½ miles turn right into Fen Lane. The entrance is ½ mile onthe right hand side. It can be accessed from M25 junction 29 via the A127 and the B186 (South).
Date Founded:	1986
Type of Course:	Parkland
No of Holes:	18
Length:	6227 yds (5748 mtrs)

Par:	72
SSS:	72
Green Fees:	Weekdays: £12.00
Visitors:	Welcome: Contact Club in advance.
Societies:	Welcome: Contact Club in advance. Unable to play at weekends.
Facilities:	Putting Green, Chipping Green, Driving Range, Trolley Hire, Buggy Hire, Caddy Service, Bar, Restaurant, Hotel

Accommodation, Food and Drink

Reference numbers below refer to detailed information provided in section 2

Food and Drink

The Duke of York, Southend Road (A129), South Green, Billericay, Essex CM11 2PR

Tel: 01277 651403

Grand old pub with a restaurant serving freshly prepared food including an exceptional vegetarian choice. Sunday roast, bar snacks, real ales.

The Thatchers Arms, Warley Road, Great Warley, Brentwood, Essex CM13 3HU

Tel: 01277 233535

email: JimSarah@supernet.co.uk

A large and handsome pub adjacent to the Warley Place Nature Reserve, makes it an ideal spot for walkers. The panelled interior offers snacks and main meals in the dining room or on the adjoining patio.

The Theobald Arms, Kings Walk, Grays, Essex RM17 6HR

Tel: 01375 372253

A very friendly and popular pub by the dockside in Grays. A variety of home-cooked food is available at lunchtimes accompanied by a wide range of real ales. A beer festival is held each summer.

The Park Tavern, Romford Road, Aveley, South Ockenden, Essex RM15 4PH

Tel: 01708 863798

A family run pub, sporting an interesting collection of celebrity photos. Good food is prepared from the freshest ingredients and served daily 2-5. There's live entertainment on Fridays and Saturdays.

The Ship, Princess Margaret Road, East Tilbury Village, Essex, RM18 8PB

Tel: 01375 843041

Renowned for its excellent ales and food, this comfortable pub is open all day every day. Lunchtime and evening menus are available and the beer garden is safe for children.

Warley Park

Magpie Lane, Little Warley, Brentwood, Essex CM13 3DX

Tel: 01277 224891 Fax: 01277 200679

This friendly club, which was able to celebrate the millennium and its 25th birthday in the same year, is situated in the village of Little Warley and in an ideal location being just five minutes from the M25 Motorway, 10 minutes from the Thames Crossing at Dartford, and just a few minutes from both the A12 and A127 trunk roads.

The club was formed as Brett Essex after the farmer who originally owned the land but was renamed when its ownership passed to Bert Greene, whose working background has been in the golf industry. Club professional Reg Plumbridge was responsible for the 18-hole course which opened in 1975 and he returned two years later to add a further nine making Warley Park the largest private club in Essex at that time. Now, the 27 holes are played as three courses by linking the three nines into different combinations.

The club is also three minutes from the Ford Motor Company's central offices which were built on the site of Warley Barracks, home of the Essex Regiment. Here is a significant link with the club in that the land now occupied by the course was originally the training ground for those famous county battalions. One of these was known as the Pompadours after Madam Pompadour, whose favourite colour of purple was adopted as their colours.

In recognition of this, Warley Park took purple and green from the land as its colours while the club's crest includes the Essex Eagle, taken from Napoleon by the Essex Regiment at the Battle of Salamanca and currently held at the Regimental Museum in Chelmsford. The second nine holes to come into play was officially opened by the late Bobby Locke, who marked the occasion by playing an exhibition match during which he put four balls into the woods on the 437-yard 15th (now the 24th), which was duly named **Locke's Spinney**. The great South African isn't the only big name to visit Warley Park. Former Open champion and Ryder Cup captain Tony Jacklin dropped in by helicopter to tackle the short 18th (now the 27th) as part of the Duke of Edinburgh's Dawn to Dusk competition in which he played one hole on 18 different courses in England, Ireland, Scotland and Wales in a day.

Constructed on rolling countryside, Warley Park is a test of all facets of the game. The clubhouse sits in the middle of the course and overlooks a string of lakes, which come into play on five holes. The par four 7th and short 8th are played across the largest lake and the middle lake threatens the drive on the 415-yard 9th. At Locke's Spinney, it is easy to emulate the four-time Open champion as the encroaching trees present a narrow throat to the green, but the signature hole has to be the aforementioned 27th, which lives up to its title of **High Finish**. Measuring 192 yards from the back tee, the golfer is presented with three water hazards strung across his vision as he plays towards the clubhouse. It makes a fearsome yet thrilling conclusion to a round and can be a real card-buster.

Sec/Manager:	Keith Regan
Professional:	Jason Groat
Directions:	2½ miles South of Brentwood. From Brentwood take the B186 (Great Warley) and on the outskirts of Brentwood turn left into Warley Gap, leading into Magpie Lane. The entrance is on the right hand side. Can also be accessed from M25 junction 29 via the A127 and the B186 (North).
Date Founded:	1974
Length:	6200 yds (5723 mtrs)
Par:	71
SSS:	70
Green Fees:	Weekdays: £30.00
Visitors:	Welcome: Contact Club in advance. Unable to play at weekends.
Societies:	Welcome: Contact Club in advanc. Unable to play at weekends.
Facilities:	Putting Green, Chipping Green, Practice Area, Club Hire, Trolley Hire, Buggy Hire, Bar, Restaurant
Green Fees:	Weekdays: £30.00 - played either courses 1&2, 1&3 or 2&3;

Course 1

Type of Course:	Parkland
No of Holes:	9
Length:	2988 yds (2758 mtrs)
Par:	34
SSS:	34

Course 2

Type of Course:	Parkland
No of Holes:	9
Length:	2979 yds (2750 mtrs)
Par:	35
SSS:	34

Course 3

Type of Course:	Parkland
No of Holes:	9
Length:	3244 yds (2994 mtrs)
Par:	36
SSS:	35

Accommodation, Food and Drink

Reference numbers below refer to detailed information provided in section 2

Food and Drink

The Alma Arms, Horsemanside, Navestock, Brentwood, Essex CM14 5ST

Tel: 01277 372629 Fax: 01277 375440

Delicious food and outstanding real ales and wines in an 18th century pub of character by Navestock Common.

The Plough, 169 Roman Road, Mountnessing, Brentwood, Essex CM15 0UG

Tel: 01277 352026

A large welcoming pub on the B1002 with brasses and memorabilia adorning the walls inside. The excellent menu changes seasonally and there is a garden equipped for childrens enjoyment.

The Thatchers Arms, Warley Road, Great Warley, Brentwood, Essex CM13 3HU

Tel: 01277 233535 email: JimSarah@supernet.co.uk

A large and handsome pub adjacent to the Warley

Place Nature Reserve, makes it an ideal spot for walkers. The panelled interior offers snacks and main meals in the dining room or on the adjoining patio.

The Theobald Arms, Kings Walk, Grays, Essex RM17 6HR

Tel: 01375 372253

A very friendly and popular pub by the dockside in Grays. A variety of home-cooked food is available at lunchtimes accompanied by a wide range of real ales. A beer festival is held each summer.

The Park Tavern, Romford Road, Aveley, South Ockenden, Essex RM15 4PH

Tel: 01708 863798

A family run pub, sporting an interesting collection of celebrity photos. Good food is prepared from the freshest ingredients and served daily 2-5. There's live entertainment on Fridays and Saturdays.

Warren

Woodham Walter, Maldon, Essex CM9 6RW

Tel: 01245 223258/223198 Fax: 01245 223989

Within seconds of progressing through the gates and along the drive leading to The Warren there is a sense of history. Here are visions of earlier days when the land was a deer park and where the Lord of the Manor held sway. These are ancient lands which can be traced back to Roman times with a settlement near to the present clubhouse. An excavated burial site lies close to the ninth fairway, artefacts from which are on display in the clubhouse. The deer park was established in the Middle Ages, while in the 17th and 18th centuries the area was given over to farming and the current clubhouse is the conversion of the original barns.

A nine-hole golf course arrived in 1902 when a Scot, H W Thompson, bought the estate. He was keen to create a reminder of his homeland and planted a number of Scots pine to complement the existing heather and gorse. When he died in 1934, the estate passed to Fred Durham Snr, who with his son Fred Jnr, were fanatical golfers. They enlarged the course, converted the farm buildings into a clubhouse and formed the club.

The club is still owned by the Durham family, John Durham, the Chairman and President, being the great grandson of Fred Snr. They have enlarged and improved the Warren while preserving its secluded and peaceful setting, at the same time developing two further courses, **Bunsay Downs**, a pay-and-play layout, and **Badgers**, a par-3, both adjacent to the Warren.

The course is not long at 6,263 yards, par 70, off the back tees, but it is a challenge as well as a joy to tackle. Each half has a slightly different character. The front nine is quite hilly as it progresses along wooded slopes with the occasional water hazard and is a good test of shotmaking. The homeward half is much flatter with majestic mature trees but still requires accuracy. Overall, the course is well designed and the greens generally excellent and in some cases difficult to read. As mentioned before, the clubhouse is charming with enormous character and arguably unlike any other in Essex if not the country.

There is also a well-stocked pro shop and a teaching academy, while the Head Professional is former European Solheim Cup captain Mickey Walker OBE.

Sec/Manager: Mark Durham

Professional: David Brook

Directions: 5 miles west of Chelmsford. From Chelmsford centre take the A414 (Danbury). In Danbury take Herbage Park Road (Woodham Walters) and the entrance is on the left hand side after one mile.

Date Founded: Warren 1930 Bunsay Down 1982

Visitors: Welcome: Contact Club in advance by telephone.

Societies: Welcome: Contact Club in advance. Unable to play at Weekends and Wednesday mornings.

Facilities: Putting Green, Practice Ground, Club Hire, Trolley Hire, Buggy Hire, Bar, Restaurant

Warren

Type of Course: Woodland

No of Holes: 18

Length: 6263 (yds) 5781 (mtrs)

Par: 70

SSS: 70

Green Fees: Weekdays: £30.00-£35.00; Weekends/Bank Holidays: £40.00-£45.00

Bunsay Down

Type of Course: Parkland

No of Holes: 9

Length: 2932 (yds) 2706 (mtrs)

Par:	35
SSS:	34
Green Fees:	Weekdays: £11.00; Weekends/ Bank Holidays: £13.00

Accommodation, Food and Drink

Reference numbers below refer to detailed information provided in section 2

Accommodation

The Spread Eagle Hotel, Newland Street, Witham, Essex CM8 2BD

Tel: 01376 512131 Fax: 01376 502458

A 13th century former coaching inn, full of character and with a relaxing atmosphere. There are 13 bedrooms, most en-suite and the excellent menu offers a choice of tempting dishes.

The Benbridge Hotel, The Square, Heybridge, Maldon, Essex CM9 4LT

Tel: 01621 857666 Fax: 01621 841966

An elegant Georgian hotel with a reputation for quality. There are 14 en-suite rooms and English and Continental cuisine is served in the gracious dining room. An ideal base for outdoor activities.

Chelmer Hotel, 2-4 Hamlet Road, Chelmsford, Essex CM2 OEU

Tel: 01245 353360 Fax: 01245 609055

Town house hotel, offering nine rooms evening meal by prior arrangement. Off street parking.

Food and Drink

Maldon Pie & Eel House, 136 High Street, Maldon, Essex CM9 8LS

Tel: 01621 842859

Traditional pie & eel shop selling what was once the favourite food of London's East End: eels stewed or jellied, double pie 'n' mash.

The Rodney, Little Baddow, Essex CH3 4TQ

Tel: 01245 222385

17th century premises for a comfortable village pub with front patio and sloping gardens. Home-prepared food on a traditional menu. 502

The Wheatsheaf, Malden Road, Hatfield Peveral, Chelmsford, Essex CM3 2JF

Tel: 01245 380330

An attractive and welcoming establishment with low ceilings and open fire. The large beer garden hosts a variety of birds whilst inside there is a good range of home cooked food on offer.

The Spread Eagle Hotel, Newland Street, Witham, Essex CM8 2BD

Tel: 01376 512131 Fax: 01376 502458

A 13th century former coaching inn, full of character and with a relaxing atmosphere. There are 13 bedrooms, most en-suite and the excellent menu offers a choice of tempting dishes.

The Chequers, 32 The Street, Wickham Bishops, Essex CM8 3NN

Tel: 01621 891320

Thought to be the oldest pub in Wickham Bishops, it still retains the wattle and daub walls inside. A good selection of food is served in the dining area at lunchtime and evenings.

Queen Victoria, The Street, Woodham Walter, Maldon, Essex CM9 6RF

Tel: 01245 222176

A lovely 18th century pub situated in a quiet country lane. Snacks and hot meals can be enjoyed in either the comfortable bars or in the small garden, as can a range of real ales.

The Benbridge Hotel, The Square, Heybridge, Maldon, Essex CM9 4LT

Tel: 01621 857666 Fax: 01621 841966

An elegant Georgian hotel with a reputation for quality. There are 14 en-suite rooms and English and Continental cuisine is served in the gracious dining room. An ideal base for outdoor activities.

CAMBRIDGESHIRE AND SOUTH LINCOLNSHIRE

Many people have an affinity with Cambridgeshire even though they weren't born or raised there. Because Cambridge is a world famous seat of learning, these are the thousands of students from all corners of the globe who have spent time attending the many colleges and who graduated with honours. Cambridge is the focal point of the county and a fascinating place to visit whatever your interests. It began as a settlement on the River Granta, then became the Roman camp of Camboritum before the name through various changes eventually became Cambridge. The university dates from 1284 when the first college, Peterhouse, was established while other colleges such as Pembroke, Clare, Trinity Hall and Corpus Christi were formed down the centuries culminating in the 31 we have today. Because the colleges arrived at different eras so their buildings offer a fascinating array of architecture that adds to the enjoyment of exploring the many aspects of the city. Visiting the colleges is something no visitor should miss. Relax in a punt on the Cam as you float under six bridges such as the Bridge of Sighs and the extraordinary Mathematical Bridge, built on mathematical principles so that no nails were used. But any visit to Cambridge must include the famous Kings College Chapel, perhaps the centrepiece of the university. It is where the 12 Lessons and Carols are televised every Christmas and contains breathtaking vaulting and stained glass windows as well as Rubens' Adoration of the Magi. The Pepys Library is housed in Magdalene College while there are many museums covering such diverse subjects as archaeology and polar research.

Bridge of Sighs, Cambridge

Emphasising Cambridge's scientific aspect; there is the Cavendish Laboratory where Rutherford split the atom. Just a stroll around the various seats of academia and the visitor can't but be impressed by the many famous names that have been educated here including 62 Nobel prizewinners – 29 from Trinity alone - 13 prime ministers and nine archbishops of Canterbury. Add to that such famous men as Byron, Pepys, Milton, Tennyson and Wordsworth; Marlowe and Bacon; Charles Darwin; Bertrand Russell; athletes Lord Burghley and Harold Abrahams, whose triumphs were depicted in the film Chariots of Fire; infamous spies Burgess and Maclean, Philby and Blunt; along with present day actors such as Sir Ian McKellen and Sir Derek Jacobi and you begin to realise why Cambridge is such an important place. Science and medical research plays a major role in

Ely Cathedral

Burghley House, Stamford

the modern life of Cambridge, it being an early centre for heart transplants. In recent years high tech companies have gained a foothold there, establishing a silicone valley that has brought much prosperity to the area.

But there is more to Cambridgeshire than the city itself. Just a couple of miles outside the city is the village of Grantchester, where the poet Rupert Brooke lived, while at Duxford, in the south of the county alongside the busy M11 motorway, lies the Aviation Museum with its collection of over 150 historic aircraft, from the first biplanes through wartime machines such as the Spitfire, to modern passenger jets. The River Granta, which is the Cam north of the Cambridge, flows into the Great Ouse on its way into the Fens. At the centre of the region is Ely with its magnificent cathedral, recently restored to its original splendour. It dominates the skyline for miles in this flat terrain and is known as the 'ship of the Fens'. The cathedral dates from 1083 but the wonderful octagonal lantern, the cathedral's most outstanding feature, is somewhat younger. It replaced the original tower, which collapsed in 1322. The city gets its name from Eel Island, a reference to the Saxons' staple diet, and because this was indeed an island until the Fens were drained. Before that, this region was a fairly inhospitable area of marsh and bog, but gradually, down the ages, areas were reclaimed and thanks to the work of Dutch engineer Cornelius Vermuyden, some of the finest agricultural land was created. The Fens stretch over much of Cambridgeshire and would have been familiar to Oliver Cromwell, who spent most of his life in Ely and was elected Member of Parliament for Cambridge in 1640.

A glimpse of what the Fens were like can be seen at Wicken Fen, just nine miles south of Ely. This is England's oldest nature reserve, 600 acres of undrained fenland where naturalists and ramblers can find plants, insects and birdlife in profusion. To the west of the county lie Huntingdon and its neighbour St Ives. Cromwell was born here in 1599 and attended the local grammar school before becoming the town's MP in 1629. He recruited his army from the area and generally ran the country from here until his death in 1659. His school is now the Cromwell Museum. Not far away is Kimbolton Castle, where Catherine of Aragon was imprisoned for the last 18 months of her life, and Grafham Water, created a reservoir in the 1960s and a Mecca

Swaffham Prior Windmill

Ferry Meadows and River Nene

for water sports, fishing and bird-watching. In the north of Cambridgeshire lies Peterborough, its second city with a history dating back to the Bronze Age. Its impressive cathedral housed the remains of both Catherine of Aragon and Mary Queen of Scots until the latter was removed to Westminster Abbey. Just outside the town runs the River Nene, which affords some enjoyable walks and lends its name to the Nene Valley Railway, one of the finest preserved steam railways in the country, which runs 15 miles west to Wansford. Peterborough has seen several changes in its administration over the years. As The Soke (administrative area) of Peterborough, it was once under the control of Northamptonshire, then part of Huntingdonshire until the link up with Cambridgeshire. It is also an important stop off on routes north, being adjacent to the A1 trunk road and the first major stop on the railway's East Coast Main Line to Scotland. The market town March, to the east, was a major railway marshalling centre until recent times, while Wisbech, on the River Nene, with its Georgian architecture, is still a thriving port with trade to various places in Europe.

In golfing terms, Cambridgeshire is a county comprised of relatively modern clubs. Only **St Neots** has celebrated its centenary, having been formed in 1890, while **Gog Magog**, to the south east of Cambridge, reaches its 'ton' in 2001. Apart from a handful of others the rest have been created in the last 40 years and 10 in the past 15 years. Just across the border in south Lincolnshire there are a number of good courses including **Burghley Park**, which has reached its centenary, and **Spalding** and **Sutton Bridge**, established just prior to the First World War. Among the recent additions are **Toft Hotel** and the public layout at **Gedney Hill**. Golfwise, Cambridgeshire is not a powerbase. Its 18-hole courses number around 23 but what it may lack in quantity it more than makes up for in quality. Moves to form a County Union were mooted before the Second World War but it didn't actually happen until 1950 when five clubs, **Links Newmarket**, **Royston**, **St Ives**, **St Neots**, and **Gog Magog** met at the latter. That quintet has now expanded to 28 clubs, while Cambridgeshire is in the Midland Group and plays in the Anglian League. Its most successful golfer is Russell Claydon, English Amateur champion in 1988, a Walker Cup player the following year, and the winner of one title on the European Tour.

Flag Fen

© MAPS IN MINUTES ™ (1998)

Abbotsley

Eynesbury Hardwicke, St Neots, Cambridgeshire PE19 4XN

Tel: 01480 474000 Fax; 01480 471018

Situated just five minutes from the old market town of St Neots, The Abbotsley Golf Hotel and Country Club is a charming 36-hole golfers retreat, nestled on the site of an ancient manor house and amid 250 acres of gently undulating parkland in the old county of Huntingdonshire.

Originally farmland, the complex has been developed over the past 15 years by leading golf tutor and former British Open champion Vivien Saunders OBE, into what today is one of the leading venues in the area of golf, leisure and residential breaks. With faciltiies to suit golfers of all standards as well as a driving range, health club, squash courts and beauty salon, there is something for everyone.

There are two courses at the club, appropriately the **Abbotsley** and the **Cromwell**. The 6,311-yard, par 73 Abbotsley enjoys a reputation as one of the leading courses in the area, with fast, true greens. It can also claim a record unlikely to be beaten in that one of the members achieved possibly the last hole-in-one of the Millennium by holing his tee shot on the 150-yard ninth hole at 1.30pm on 31 December 1999. The Cromwell course, named after one of the area's most famous sons, Oliver Cromwell, measures 6,087 yards with a par of 70 and complements the Abbotsley by offering a less challenging layout yet still providing the golfer with stunning views over the local countryside.

With 42 en-suite bedrooms complementing the old farmhouse buildings, the hotel offers the opportunity to get away from it all with a welcome golfing break. However, watch out for the permanent guest, the ghost of Abbotsley Manor, who is rumoured to wander the grounds at night.

Sec/Manager:	Martin Baines
Professional:	Tim Hudson
Directions:	From St Neots take the B1046. Turn right onto minor road and proceed 1¾ miles. The entrance is on the right.
Date Founded:	1976 Abbotsley 1989 Cromwell
Visitors:	Welcome: Contact Club in advance by telephone.
Societies:	Welcome: Subject to availability.
Facilities:	Putting Green, Chipping Green, Club Hire, Trolley Hire, Buggy Hire, Bar, Restaurant, Driving Range, Bar, Restaurant, Private Rooms, Squash Courts, Driving Bay, Hotel, Health & Fitness Suite

Abbotsley

Type of Course:	Parkland
No of Holes:	18
Length:	6311 yds (5825 mtrs)
Par:	72
SSS:	71
Green Fees:	Weekdays: 1st Nov-31st March £15.00, 1st April-31st October £25.00; Weekends/Bank Holidays: 1st Nov-31st March £25.00, 1st April-31st October £30.00.

Cromwell

Type of Course:	Parkland
No of Holes:	18 holes
Length:	6087 yds (5618 mtrs)
Par:	70
SSS:	69
Green Fees:	Weekdays: 1st Nov-31st March £8.00, 1st April-31st October

£10.00; Weekends/Bank Holidays: 1st Nov-31st March £10.00, 1st April-31st October £17.00.

Accommodation, Food and Drink

Reference numbers below refer to detailed information provided in section 2

Accommodation

Abbotsley Golf Hotel, Eynesbury Hardwicke, St Neots, Cambridgeshire PE19 6XN

Tel: 01480 474000 Fax: 01480 471018

42 attractive modern bedrooms in a purpose-built golf hotel and country club. Golf course, fitness centre, squash, bar, restaurant. 628

The Leeds Arms, Eltisley, Huntingdon, Cambridgeshire PE19 4TG

Tel: 01480 880283

Built in the 18th century as a dwelling and public house, now a free house motel with bars, restaurant and single/twin bedrooms. 613

Halfpenny House, 2 Breach Road, Grafham, Nr Huntingdon, Cambridgeshire PE28 0BA

Tel: 01480 810733

An extended modern house offering pleasant, well-kept Bed & Breakfast accommodation in a peaceful village off the A1/A14.

The Stukeleys Country Hotel, Great Stukeley, Cambridgeshire PE17 5AL

Tel: 01480 456927

Eight en-suite bedrooms and an elegant restaurant in a beautifully preserved 16th-century former coaching inn. 612

Food and Drink

Abbotsley Golf Hotel, Eynesbury Hardwicke, St Neots, Cambridgeshire PE19 6XN

Tel: 01480 474000 Fax: 01480 471018

42 attractive modern bedrooms in a purpose-built golf hotel and country club. Golf course, fitness centre, squash, bar, restaurant. 628

The Waggon & Horses, Eaton Socon, Cambridgeshire PE19 8EF

Tel: 01480 386373

Excellent home-cooked food in a characterful old coaching inn on the Great North Road. Varied menu, with additional lunchtime snacks. 624

The Royal Oak, Hail Weston, St Neots, Cambridgeshire PE19 5JW

Tel: 01480 472527

A beautiful thatched 17th-century pub in a pretty village, with low beams, an inglenook and a lovely garden. Good food served all day. 629

The Leeds Arms, Eltisley, Huntingdon, Cambridgeshire PE19 4TG

Tel: 01480 880283

Built in the 18th century as a dwelling and public house, now a free house motel with bars, restaurant and single/twin bedrooms. 613

Eight Bells, Abbotsley, Cambridgeshire PE19 6UL

Tel: 01767 677305

An 18th-century pub, with creepers and hanging baskets, in a pretty village of thatched cottages. Fine home-cooked food, good ales and wines. 615

The Stukeleys Country Hotel, Great Stukeley, Cambridgeshire PE17 5AL

Tel: 01480 456927

Eight en-suite bedrooms and an elegant restaurant in a beautifully preserved 16th-century former coaching inn. 612

Bourn

Toft Road, Bourn, Cambridge, Cambridgeshire CB3 7TT

Tel: 01954 718057 Fax: 01954 718908

Sec/Manager:	Mr G Boutel
Professional:	Craig Watson
Directions:	From St Neots take the B1046. Turn right onto minor road and proceed approx two miles The entrance is on the left hand side.
Date Founded:	1991
Type of Course:	Parkland
No of Holes:	18
Length:	6498 yds (5998mtrs)
Par:	72
SSS:	71
Green Fees:	Weekdays: £16.00; Weekends/ Bank Holidays: £22.00.
Visitors:	Welcome: Contact Club in advance. Unable to play at weekends.
Societies:	Welcome: Contact Club in advance by telephone.
Facilities:	Putting Green, Chipping Green, Practice Bunker, Club Hire, Trolley Hire, Buggy Hire, Bar, Restaurant

Accommodation, Food and Drink

Reference numbers below refer to detailed information provided in section 2

Accommodation

Orchard Farmhouse, Toft, Cambridgeshire CB3 7RY

Tel: 01223 262309 Fax: 01223 263979

Quiet, comfortable farmhouse B&B accommodation next to Cambridge Meridian Golf Course. e-mail: tebbit.bxb.toft@talk21.com

The Leeds Arms, Eltisley, Huntingdon, Cambridgeshire PE19 4TG

Tel: 01480 880283

Built in the 18th century as a dwelling and public house, now a free house motel with bars, restaurant and single/twin bedrooms. 613

Wallis Farmhouse, 98 Main Street, Hardwick, Cambridgeshire CB3 7QU

Tel: 01954 210347 Fax: 01954 210988

A late Georgian farmhouse on a working farm just off the A428. Eight en-suite B&B rooms. e-mail: wallis@mcmail.com

Food and Drink

The White Horse, 118 High Street, Barton, Cambridgeshire CB3 7BG

Tel/Fax: 01223 262327

16th-century village pub with beams, brasses and open fires. Excellent bar snacks and full à la carte menu. 604

The Blue Lion, Hardwick, Cambridgeshire CB3 7QU

Tel: 01954 210328

17th-century village pub in traditional style, with a deserved reputation for high-quality food served lunchtime and evening. 630

The Pear Tree, North End, Bassingbourn, Nr Royston, Cambridgeshire SG8 5NZ

Tel: 01763 244068

Traditional English food served seven days a week in a welcoming pub with a golfing owner.

The Crown, Church Street, Litlington, Nr Royston, Cambridgeshire SG8 0QB

Tel: 01763 852439

An attractive village inn serving an excellent choice of lunchtime snacks and evening meals. Good wines; real ales.

The Queen Adelaide, Croydon, Cambridgeshire SG8 0DN

Tel: 01223 208278

A peaceful village setting for a friendly family-run pub serving excellent food based on top local produce. Large garden. 626

The Leeds Arms, Eltisley, Huntingdon, Cambridgeshire PE19 4TG

Tel: 01480 880283

Built in the 18th century as a dwelling and public house, now a free house motel with bars, restaurant and single/twin bedrooms. 613

Eight Bells, Abbotsley, Cambridgeshire PE19 6UL

Tel: 01767 677305

An 18th-century pub, with creepers and hanging baskets, in a pretty village of thatched cottages. Fine home-cooked food, good ales and wines. 615

The Hoops, Great Eversden, Cambridgeshire CB3 7HN

Tel/Fax: 01223 264008

A cheerful white-painted pub off the A603, bright and modern behind its period facade. Home-cooked food, real ales, extensive wine list. 709

The Golden Lion, High Street, Bourn, Cambridgeshire CB3 7SQ

Tel: 01954 719305

16th-century pub in a pretty village. Snacks and good home cooking available all day. Darts and pool in the public bar.

Brampton Park

Buckden Road, Brampton, Huntingdon, Cambridgeshire PE28 4NF

Tel: 01480 434700 Fax: 01480 411145

Brampton Park is one of the long list of new courses to come on stream over the last 10 years. Opened in 1991 to a design by Simon Gidman, it is situated in picturesque park and meadowland just threequarters of a mile off the A1 trunk road opposite Brampton RAF Station near Huntingdon.

This 18-hole, par 71 course of 6,403 yards, is dissected by River Lane, with 11 holes to the

North and the other seven to the south, while water comes into play on most holes. Also, the wooded nature of the course is such that it offers a challenge to golfers of all abilities. The lakes and mature woodlands abound with wildlife and great care has been taken to preserve as many of the natural features as possible. In fact, the 16th hole has been named 'Badger Alley' due to the abundance of badger sets lining the fairway. It is here that one of the largest colonies of badgers in Eastern England reside. Muntjac deer inhabit the woodlands, Canada Geese and swans glide the tranquil waters of the lakes, and an abundance of differing species of bird life can be seen around the course. In addition to the natural mature woodland, 3,500 saplings have been planted since 1991.

It is a course that requires every club in the bag. Its signature hole, the short 4th, has a green almost completely surrounded by water and is sure to stick vividly in the mind of any golfer who plays it. Another demanding hole is the 14th which features several water hazards, among which is an old sluice which has been restored. The River Great Ouse forms a natural boundary to part of the course, and Brampton Brook, with its various tributaries, dissects the course adding further interest for the keen golfer. Alongside the 18th fairway and just a few steps from the clubhouse is a practice ground and net, while there is also a chipping and bunker practice facility.

The clubhouse stands on the southern section of the course by the side of the 1st tee overlooking the 18th fairway and putting green. Inside is a Members Bar and a first floor restaurant, which can seat 116 diners and provides panoramic views of the course with a balcony for alfresco dining.

Sec/Manager:	Richard Oakes
Professional:	Alistair Curie
Directions:	3 miles south west of Huntingdon. From the centre take the Brampton road (B1514). At Brampton turn left into Buckden Road and the entrance is on the left hand side after 800 yds.
Date Founded:	1991
Type of Course:	Parkland
No of Holes:	18
Length:	5881 yds (5428mtrs)
Par:	72
SSS:	72
Green Fees:	Weekdays: £20.00; Weekends/ Bank Holidays: £35.00
Visitors:	Welcome: Contact Club in advance. Handicap Certificate preferred.
Societies:	Welcome: Contact Club in writing in advance.
Facilities:	Putting Green, Chipping Green, Practice Range, Club Hire, Trolley Hire, Bar, Restaurant, Private Rooms

Accommodation, Food and Drink

Reference numbers below refer to detailed information provided in section 2

Accommodation

Abbotsley Golf Hotel, Eynesbury Hardwicke, St Neots, Cambridgeshire PE19 6XN

Tel: 01480 474000 Fax: 01480 471018

42 attractive modern bedrooms in a purpose-built golf hotel and country club. Golf course, fitness centre, squash, bar, restaurant. 628

The Talbot Inn, Stilton, Cambridgeshire PE7 3RP

Tel/Fax: 01733 240291

An old coaching inn with a pleasant, cosy atmosphere, a good range of food and drink and five family-size letting bedrooms. 631

Foreman's Bridge Caravan Park, Sutton Road, Sutton St James, Lincolnshire PE12 0HU

Tel/Fax: 01945 440346

web: www.foremans-bridge.co.uk

A pleasant riverside park for touring caravans and tents. Also static caravans for hire (Mar-Nov) and two holiday cottages (all year). B1390.

Halfpenny House, 2 Breach Road, Grafham, Nr Huntingdon, Cambridgeshire PE28 0BA

Tel: 01480 810733

An extended modern house offering pleasant, well-kept Bed & Breakfast accommodation in a peaceful village off the A1/A14.

The Golden Lion Hotel, St Ives, Cambridgeshire PE27 5AL

Tel: 01480 492100

Georgian-fronted former coaching inn offering comfortable accommodation and good eating in the centre of town. Good base for touring the Fens. 609

The Stukeleys Country Hotel, Great Stukeley, Cambridgeshire PE17 5AL

Tel: 01480 456927

Eight en-suite bedrooms and an elegant restaurant in a beautifully preserved 16th-century former coaching inn. 612

The George Hotel, Ramsey, Cambridgeshire PE26 1AA

Historic coaching inn built in 1630 and restored to a high standard in 2000. Eleven en-suite chalet-style rooms. À la carte restaurant. 619

The Black Bull, Godmanchester, Cambridgeshire PE29 2AQ

Tel: 01480 453310

An old coaching inn that now provides comfortable accommodation in four en-suite bedrooms. Attractive bar lounge; excellent value meals. 605

Food and Drink

Abbotsley Golf Hotel, Eynesbury Hardwicke, St Neots, Cambridgeshire PE19 6XN

Tel: 01480 474000 Fax: 01480 471018

42 attractive modern bedrooms in a purpose-built golf hotel and country club. Golf course, fitness centre, squash, bar, restaurant. 628

The Talbot Inn, Stilton, Cambridgeshire PE7 3RP

Tel/Fax: 01733 240291

An old coaching inn with a pleasant, cosy atmosphere, a good range of food and drink and five family-size letting bedrooms. 631

The Waggon & Horses, Eaton Socon, Cambridgeshire PE19 8EF

Tel: 01480 386373

Excellent home-cooked food in a characterful old coaching inn on the Great North Road. Varied menu, with additional lunchtime snacks. 624

The Royal Oak, Hail Weston, St Neots, Cambridgeshire PE19 5JW

Tel: 01480 472527

A beautiful thatched 17th-century pub in a pretty village, with low beams, an inglenook and a lovely garden. Good food served all day. 629

The Golden Lion Hotel, St Ives, Cambridgeshire PE27 5AL

Tel: 01480 492100

Georgian-fronted former coaching inn offering comfortable accommodation and good eating in the centre of town. Good base for touring the Fens. 609

The Angel, High Street, Ramsey, Cambridgeshire PE26 1BS

Tel: 01487 813226

Along the High Street from The George, and in the same ownership. The brick-built Angel is more of a pub pure and simple, with drinks and bar food.

The Stukeleys Country Hotel, Great Stukeley, Cambridgeshire PE17 5AL

Tel: 01480 456927

Eight en-suite bedrooms and an elegant restaurant in a beautifully preserved 16th-century former coaching inn. 612

The George Hotel, Ramsey, Cambridgeshire PE26 1AA

Historic coaching inn built in 1630 and restored to a high standard in 2000. Eleven en-suite chalet-style rooms. À la carte restaurant. 619

The Black Bull, Godmanchester, Cambridgeshire PE29 2AQ

Tel: 01480 453310

An old coaching inn that now provides comfortable accommodation in four en-suite bedrooms. Attractive bar lounge; excellent value meals. 605

St Ives Motel, St Ives, Cambridgeshire PE17 4EX

Tel: 01480 463857

Fifteen spacious en-suite bedrooms in a low building set back from the A1096. Bar snacks and non-smoking restaurant. 602

The White Hart, Alconbury Weston, Huntingdon, Cambridgeshire PE28 4JA

Tel: 01480 890331

A friendly 200-year-old village pub serving real ale and good food. Popular theme nights. Golfing parties welcome. 614

Burghley Park

St Martin's, Stamford, Lincolnshire PE9 3JX

Tel/Fax: 01780 753789

Sec/Manager:	Mr Mulligan
Professional:	Glen Davies
Directions:	2 miles south of Stamford. From Stamford centre take the B1081 (Peterborough) Old Great North Road. The entrance is on the left hand side after one mile.

Date Founded:	1890
Type of Course:	Parkland
No of Holes:	18
Length:	6200 yds (5723 mtrs)
Par:	70
SSS:	70
Green Fees:	Weekdays: £21.00
Visitors:	Welcome: Contact Club in advance unable to play at weekends.
Societies:	Welcome: Contact Club in writing in advance.
Facilities:	Putting Green, Chipping Green, Practice Ground, Trolley Hire, Buggy Hire, Bar, Restaurant, Private Rooms

Accommodation, Food and Drink

Reference numbers below refer to detailed information provided in section 2

Accommodation

The Crown Hotel, Stamford, Lincolnshire PE9 2AG

Tel: 01780 763136 Fax: 01780 756111

An 18-bedroom hotel (all rooms en-suite) built in 1909 and recently extensively renovated to a very high standard. Restaurant. Parking at rear. 702

The Crown Inn, Great Casterton, Stamford, Lincolnshire PE9 4AP

Tel: 01780 763362

A village pub of real charm and character, with abundant hospitality, an excellent menu of home-cooked food and fine wines. One letting bedroom. 701

The George of Stamford, Stamford, Lincolnshire PE9 2LB

Tel: 01780 750750 Fax: 01780 750701

Perhaps England's greatest coaching inn, rich in history and character. Top-quality accommodation in 47 rooms plus superb food and drink. 704

The Paper Mills Inn, Wansford-in-England, Cambridgeshire PE8 6JB

Tel: 01780 782328

Lunchtime snacks and waitress-served restaurant in a 150-year-old pub a minute from the A1. Beer garden. One letting bedroom. 618

The Wishing Well Inn, Dyke, Near Bourne, Lincolnshire PE10 0AF

Tel: 01778 422970 Fax: 01778 394508

Quality en-suite accommodation and superb food in a charming country inn with a beer garden. Hosts a beer festival in August. 705

The Garden House Hotel, St Martin's, Stamford, Lincolnshire PE9 2LP

Tel: 01780 763359 Fax: 01780 763339

A charming 18th-century house transformed into a delightful hotel with single, double and family rooms. B&B or full board available.

Cawthorpe Hall, Cawthorpe, Bourne, Lincolnshire PE10 0AB

Tel: 01778 423830 Fax: 01778 426620

Early 19th-century country house with three large, peaceful en-suite double bedrooms and a single. Lovely gardens full of roses. 707

Food and Drink

The Exeter Arms, Stamford Road, Easton-on-the-Hill, Stamford, Lincolnshire PE9 3NS

Tel: 01780 757503

A French chef produces a tempting range of dishes in a traditionally appointed pub 1 mile west of Stamford. Good wine list. Garden.

The Crown Hotel, Stamford, Lincolnshire PE9 2AG

Tel: 01780 763136 Fax: 01780 756111

An 18-bedroom hotel (all rooms en-suite) built in 1909 and recently extensively renovated to a very high standard. Restaurant. Parking at rear. 702

The Crown Inn, Great Casterton, Stamford, Lincolnshire PE9 4AP

Tel: 01780 763362

A village pub of real charm and character, with abundant hospitality, an excellent menu of home-cooked food and fine wines. One letting bedroom. 701

The George of Stamford, Stamford, Lincolnshire PE9 2LB

Tel: 01780 750750 Fax: 01780 750701

Perhaps England's greatest coaching inn, rich in history and character. Top-quality accommodation in 47 rooms plus superb food and drink. 704

The Paper Mills Inn, Wansford-in-England, Cambridgeshire PE8 6JB

Tel: 01780 782328

Lunchtime snacks and waitress-served restaurant in a 150-year-old pub a minute from the A1. Beer garden. One letting bedroom. 618

The Wishing Well Inn, Dyke, Near Bourne, Lincolnshire PE10 0AF

Tel: 01778 422970 Fax: 01778 394508

Quality en-suite accommodation and superb food in a charming country inn with a beer garden. Hosts a beer festival in August. 705

Cambridge

Station Road, Longstanton, Cambridge, Cambridgeshire CB4 5DR

Tel/Fax: 01954 789388

Sec/Manager:	Ken Green
Professional:	Geoff Hugget
Directions:	7 miles north west of Cambridge. From the city centre take the A1307 (Girton) then join the A14 (Huntingdon). Turn right at Bar Hill onto the B1050 towards Longstanton. The entrance is on the right hand side
Date Founded:	1990
Type of Course:	Parkland
No of Holes:	18
Length:	6256 yds (6217 mtrs)
Par:	72
SSS:	72
Green Fees:	Weekdays: £10.00; Weekends/ Bank Holidays: £13.00
Visitors:	Welcome: Contact Club in advance.
Societies:	Welcome: Contact Club in advance by telephone.
Facilities:	Putting Green, Chipping Green, Driving Range, Club Hire, Trolley Hire, Buggy Hire, Bar, Restaurant

Accommodation, Food and Drink

Reference numbers below refer to detailed information provided in section 2

Accommodation

The Golden Lion Hotel, St Ives, Cambridgeshire PE27 5AL

Tel: 01480 492100

Georgian-fronted former coaching inn offering comfortable accommodation and good eating in the centre of town. Good base for touring the Fens. 609

Clare Farm, 86 Main Street, Witchford, Ely, Cambridgeshire CB6 2HQ

Tel: 01353 664135

Four warm, spacious bedrooms with tv and farmland views. Full English breakfast. Ample parking. No credit cards.

Sycamore House, Ely, Cambridgeshire CB7 4HX

Tel: 01353 662139

A newly renovated, spacious 1920s family house with two double bedrooms and one twin. Good choice for breakfast. Lovely large garden. 606

Greenways, Prickwillow Road, Queen Adelaide, Ely, Cambridgeshire CB7 4TZ

Tel: 01353 666706 Fax: 01954 251629

Comfortable modern ground-floor en-suite bedrooms (single, double, twin, family) in a rural location one mile from Ely.

St Ives Motel, St Ives, Cambridgeshire PE17 4EX

Tel: 01480 463857

Fifteen spacious en-suite bedrooms in a low building set back from the A1096. Bar snacks and non-smoking restaurant. 602

Food and Drink

The Golden Lion Hotel, St Ives, Cambridgeshire PE27 5AL

Tel: 01480 492100

Georgian-fronted former coaching inn offering comfortable accommodation and good eating in the centre of town. Good base for touring the Fens. 609

The Three Kings, Haddenham, Cambridgeshire CB6 3XD

Tel: 01353 749080

17th-century former coaching inn in a pretty village. Good-value food with blackboard specials. Real ales, good selection of wines.

St Ives Motel, St Ives, Cambridgeshire PE17 4EX

Tel: 01480 463857

Fifteen spacious en-suite bedrooms in a low building set back from the A1096. Bar snacks and non-smoking restaurant. 602

The George, High Street, Girton, Cambridgeshire CB3 0QD

A friendly family-run pub serving excellent-value food from bar snacks to full meals. Best to book, especially for Sunday lunch. 607

Cambridge Meridian

Comberton Road, Toft, Cambridge, Cambridgeshire CB3 7RY

Tel: 01223 264702 Fax: 01223 264701

Sec/Manager:	Jill
Professional:	Michael
Directions:	6 miles west of Cambridge.

From M11 Junction 12 take the A603 (Barton). After ¼ mile turn right on the B1046 towards Toft. The entrance is in the middle of the village on the right hand side.

Date Founded: 1994

Type of Course: Links and Parkland

No of Holes: 18

Length: 6700 yds (6184mtrs)

Par: 73

SSS: 72

Green Fees: Weekdays: £14.00; Weekends/ Bank Holidays: £18.00

Visitors: Welcome: Contact Club by telephone in advance.

Societies: Welcome: Contact Club in advance by telephone.

Facilities: Putting Green, Practice Ground, Club Hire, Trolley Hire, Buggy Hire, Bar, Restaurant

Accommodation, Food and Drink

Reference numbers below refer to detailed information provided in section 2

Accommodation

The Blue Ball Inn, 57 Broadway, Grantchester, Cambridgeshire CB3 9NQ

Tel: 01223 840679

An award-winning traditional English pub with two letting bedrooms, good food and excellent real ales from Greene King.

Orchard Farmhouse, Toft, Cambridgeshire CB3 7RY

Tel: 01223 262309 Fax: 01223 263979

Quiet, comfortable farmhouse B&B accommodation next to Cambridge Meridian Golf Course. e-mail: tebbit.bxb.toft@talk21.com

The Leeds Arms, Eltisley, Huntingdon, Cambridgeshire PE19 4TG

Tel: 01480 880283

Built in the 18th century as a dwelling and public house, now a free house motel with bars, restaurant and single/twin bedrooms. 613

Wallis Farmhouse, 98 Main Street, Hardwick, Cambridgeshire CB3 7QU

Tel: 01954 210347 Fax: 01954 210988

A late Georgian farmhouse on a working farm just off the A428. Eight en-suite B&B rooms.

e-mail: wallis@mcmail.com

Food and Drink

The White Horse, 118 High Street, Barton, Cambridgeshire CB3 7BG

Tel/Fax: 01223 262327

16th-century village pub with beams, brasses and open fires. Excellent bar snacks and full à la carte menu. 604

The Blue Ball Inn, 57 Broadway, Grantchester, Cambridgeshire CB3 9NQ

Tel: 01223 840679

An award-winning traditional English pub with two letting bedrooms, good food and excellent real ales from Greene King.

The Old English Gentlemen, High Street, Harston, Cambridgeshire CB2 5QD

Tel: 01223 870287

19th-century pub on the A10, serving excellent bar snacks and full meals. Book ahead for the speciality steaks. Pool, darts.

The Blue Lion, Hardwick, Cambridgeshire CB3 7QU

Tel: 01954 210328

17th-century village pub in traditional style, with a deserved reputation for high-quality food served lunchtime and evening. 630

The Queen Adelaide, Croydon, Cambridgeshire SG8 0DN

Tel: 01223 208278

A peaceful village setting for a friendly family-run pub serving excellent food based on top local produce. Large garden. 626

The Pink Geranium, Melbourn, Cambridgeshire SG8 6DX

Tel: 01763 260215 Fax: 01763 262110

One of the prettiest restaurants in East Anglia, and certainly one of the best, with outstanding food and an excellent wine cellar. 608

The Leeds Arms, Eltisley, Huntingdon, Cambridgeshire PE19 4TG

Tel: 01480 880283

Built in the 18th century as a dwelling and public house, now a free house motel with bars, restaurant and single/twin bedrooms. 613

The Hoops, Great Eversden, Cambridgeshire CB3 7HN

Tel/Fax: 01223 264008

A cheerful white-painted pub off the A603, bright and modern behind its period facade. Home-cooked food, real ales, extensive wine list. 709

The Golden Lion, High Street, Bourn, Cambridgeshire CB3 7SQ

Tel: 01954 719305

16th-century pub in a pretty village. Snacks and good home cooking available all day. Darts and pool in the public bar.

Cambridgeshire Moat House

Bar Hill, Cambridge, Cambridgeshire CB4 5DR

Tel: 01954 789388

Just a short drive, five miles to be precise, north west of historic Cambridge, alongside the A14 trunk road at Bar Hill, you'll find Cambridge Moat House. Set in 134 acres of mature parkland, it possesses a demanding 6,734-yard, par 72, championship course that has not only stood the test of time but also of some of the finest professional golfers that Europe has produced. Opened in 1974, the course has hosted the PGA Senior Championship on three occasions, while the likes of Open champions Tom Watson, Nick Faldo and Seve Ballesteros have all pitted their skills against this well-designed layout.

The opening stretch takes you alongside the A14 until the fourth turns right towards the south. The first short hole, the 146-yard fifth, is arguably the most memorable on the front nine where two ditches have to be negotiated, one in front of a green that slopes from back to front, and one to the left as well as out of bounds. The back nine is more undulating and perhaps more demanding and it contains the stroke index one hole, the 436-yard 12th. This is a right-to-left tree-lined dog-leg with a selection of bunkers and another green that slopes from the back. The only significant water on the course is the lake to the right of the first and 18th fairways.

Cambridge is one of 43 Moat House Hotels across the United Kingdom and as with many of the chain has additional facilities such as a Health and Fitness Club including indoor swimming pool, spa and steam rooms. Situated as it is so close to Cambridge, it is an ideal location from which to explore the city with its many colleges and museums.

Sec/Manager:	Linda Green
Professional:	Adrian Englenan
Directions:	6 miles north west of Cambridge. From Cambridge City centre take the A1307 (Girton) then join the A14. Turn left into Bar Hill and at the roundabout turn into Crafts Way. The entrance is on the left hand side after 150 yds.
Date Founded:	1994
Type of Course:	Parkland
No of Holes:	18
Length:	6736 yds (6217 mtrs)
Par:	72
SSS:	74
Green Fees:	Weekdays: £10.00; Weekends/ Bank Holidays: £13.00
Visitors:	Welcome: Contact Club in advance.
Societies:	Welcome: Contact Club in advance.
Facilities:	Putting Green, Chipping Green, Driving Range, Club Hire, Trolley Hire, Buggy Hire, Bar, Restaurant

Accommodation, Food and Drink

Reference numbers below refer to detailed information provided in section 2

Accommodation

The Leeds Arms, Eltisley, Huntingdon, Cambridgeshire PE19 4TG

Tel: 01480 880283

Built in the 18th century as a dwelling and public house, now a free house motel with bars, restaurant and single/twin bedrooms. 613

The Golden Lion Hotel, St Ives, Cambridgeshire PE27 5AL

Tel: 01480 492100

Georgian-fronted former coaching inn offering comfortable accommodation and good eating in the centre of town. Good base for touring the Fens. 609

St Ives Motel, St Ives, Cambridgeshire PE17 4EX

Tel: 01480 463857

Fifteen spacious en-suite bedrooms in a low building set back from the A1096. Bar snacks and non-smoking restaurant. 602

Wallis Farmhouse, 98 Main Street, Hardwick, Cambridgeshire CB3 7QU

Tel: 01954 210347 Fax: 01954 210988

A late Georgian farmhouse on a working farm just off the A428. Eight en-suite B&B rooms.
e-mail: wallis@mcmail.com

Food and Drink

The Blue Lion, Hardwick, Cambridgeshire CB3 7QU

Tel: 01954 210328

17th-century village pub in traditional style, with a deserved reputation for high-quality food served lunchtime and evening. 630

The Leeds Arms, Eltisley, Huntingdon, Cambridgeshire PE19 4TG

Tel: 01480 880283

Built in the 18th century as a dwelling and public house, now a free house motel with bars, restaurant and single/twin bedrooms. 613

The Golden Lion Hotel, St Ives, Cambridgeshire PE27 5AL

Tel: 01480 492100

Georgian-fronted former coaching inn offering comfortable accommodation and good eating in the centre of town. Good base for touring the Fens. 609

St Ives Motel, St Ives, Cambridgeshire PE17 4EX

Tel: 01480 463857

Fifteen spacious en-suite bedrooms in a low building set back from the A1096. Bar snacks and non-smoking restaurant. 602

The George, High Street, Girton, Cambridgeshire CB3 0QD

A friendly family-run pub serving excellent-value food from bar snacks to full meals. Best to book, especially for Sunday lunch. 607

The Golden Lion, High Street, Bourn, Cambridgeshire CB3 7SQ

Tel: 01954 719305

16th-century pub in a pretty village. Snacks and good home cooking available all day. Darts and pool in the public bar.

Elton Furze

Bullock Road, Haddon, Peterborough, Cambridgeshire PE7 3TT

Tel: 01832 280189 Fax: 01832 280299

Sec/Manager:	Helen Barrow
Professional:	Frank Kiddie
Directions:	4 miles south of Peterborough. From Peterborough centre take the A605 towards Elton. Cross the A1 and turn 1st left into Bullock Road. The entrance is after approx 500 yds.
Date Founded:	1992
Type of Course:	Parkland
No of Holes:	18
Length:	6315 yds (5829 mtrs)
Par:	70
SSS:	69
Green Fees:	Weekdays: £22.00; Weekends/ Bank Holidays: £32.00
Visitors:	Welcome: Contact Club in advance by telephone.
Societies:	Welcome: Contact Club in advance. Unable to play at Weekends, Monday and Friday's.
Facilities:	Putting Green, Chipping Green, Driving Range, Trolley Hire, Buggy Hire, Bar, Restaurant

Accommodation, Food and Drink

Reference numbers below refer to detailed information provided in section 2

Accommodation

The Paper Mills Inn, Wansford-in-England, Cambridgeshire PE8 6JB

Tel: 01780 782328

Lunchtime snacks and waitress-served restaurant in a 150-year-old pub a minute from the A1. Beer garden. One letting bedroom. 618

Longueville Guest House, 411 Oundle Road, Orton Longueville, Peterborough, Cambridgeshire PE2 7DA

Tel/Fax: 01733 233442

Pleasant house with a big garden and five well-decorated en-suite bedrooms, one of family size. Good breakfasts. No smoking.

The Talbot Inn, Stilton, Cambridgeshire PE7 3RP

Tel/Fax: 01733 240291

An old coaching inn with a pleasant, cosy atmosphere, a good range of food and drink and five family-size letting bedrooms. 631

The Old Smithy, 47 Peterborough Road, Castor, Cambridgeshire PE5 7AX

Tel/Fax: 01733 380186

Four en-suite bedrooms in a 300-year-old thatched cottage. Aga-cooked breakfast, dinner by arrangement. 3 miles from Peterborough.

Orton Hall Hotel, Orton Longueville, Peterborough, Cambridgeshire PE2 7DN

Tel: 01733 39111 Fax: 01733 371793

e-mail: martingoodliffe@ortonhall.co.uk

17th century manor house in 20 acres of parkland, with modern facilities in spacious, well-appointed bedrooms. Restaurant, traditional inn.

Food and Drink

The Paper Mills Inn, Wansford-in-England, Cambridgeshire PE8 6JB

Tel: 01780 782328

Lunchtime snacks and waitress-served restaurant in a 150-year-old pub a minute from the A1. Beer garden. One letting bedroom. 618

The Windmill Tavern, Orton Waterville, Peterborough, Cambridgeshire

Tel: 01733 231554

18th-century pub in traditional style, with a garden and children's play area. Good food and wine; real ale. 617

The Cherry Tree, 9 Oundle Road, Woodston, Peterborough, Cambridgeshire PE2 9PB

Tel: 01733 703495

18th-century pub with a traditional ambience. Five real ales, extensive menus from snacks to full meals; live music Thursday-Saturday.

The Talbot Inn, Stilton, Cambridgeshire PE7 3RP

Tel/Fax: 01733 240291

An old coaching inn with a pleasant, cosy atmosphere, a good range of food and drink and five family-size letting bedrooms. 631

Orton Hall Hotel, Orton Longueville, Peterborough, Cambridgeshire PE2 7DN

Tel: 01733 39111 Fax: 01733 371793

e-mail: martingoodliffe@ortonhall.co.uk

17th century manor house in 20 acres of parkland, with modern facilities in spacious, well-appointed bedrooms. Restaurant, traditional inn.

Ely City

107 Cambridge Road, Ely, Cambridgeshire CB7 4HX

Tel: 01353 662751 Fax: 01353 669636

You may be forgiven for thinking that not much goes on in this seemingly quiet part of East Anglia but that wasn't the case back in July 1973 when Lee Trevino, the then Open champion, turned up with the Old Claret Jug. The occasion marked the opening of the 18 hole course and Supermex was there to play an exhibition match against South African Hugh Baiocchi, the club's long established touring professional. In front of a delighted gallery, Baiocchi went round in 67 but Trevino carded 66, which stood as the course record until last year when the club's current professional, Andrew George trimmed it by a stroke.

The new course that Trevino and Baiocchi enjoyed that day was the work of Henry Cotton. But the origins of the Ely club go back to the late 1950s when five local businessmen purchased 36

acres off the Cambridge Road with the idea of constructing a much-needed amenity – a nine-hole golf course. With much volunteer help and machinery, the 'home-made nine' was opened for play on 14 April 1962. By the late 1960s a wooden clubhouse had been erected and in 1971 it was agreed to approach the Church Commissioners for extra land to provide a practice area. The ensuing negotiations ended in the purchase of a further 62 acres to extend the course to 18 holes. This was when Cotton arrived on the scene and the completion of his work by Golf Landscapes of Brentwood led to the opening in the summer of '73 and the exhibition match. The rebuilding of the clubhouse was also completed while it is interesting to note that the original nine holes were constructed largely on what was the site of a Second World War Prisoner of War camp and the original clubhouse was the Officers' Mess.

Since those days Ely has improved every year as the trees have matured until today when it is a joy to play. At 6,627 yards off the back tees (6,348 from the yellows), par 72, the course is as Cotton described it almost 30 years ago: "Golfers go miles to play a good course and at Ely there are many good holes." The maestro's favourites were arguably the key holes you'd pick today. The short 2nd at 160 yards from the back over a pond is perhaps the prettiest hole on the course, while the 387-yard 14th is uphill to a tricky green. This is stroke index two, indicating that it needs some thought and where the second shot must be from the right of the fairway. Add to this a clubhouse that was extended seven years ago, good practice areas, a fine pro shop and good food and it is easy to see why Ely is a favourite destination.

Sec/Manager: Michael Hoare

Professional: Andrew George

Directions: At south west edge of Ely. From Ely City centre by the Lamb Hotel take Cambridge Road. The entrance is on the left hand side after 700 yds.

Date Founded: 1963

Type of Course: Parkland

No of Holes: 18

Length: 6627 yds (6117 mtrs)

Par: 72

SSS: 72

Green Fees: Weekdays: £28.00; Weekends/Bank Holidays: £34.00

Visitors: Welcome: Contact Club in advance. Unable to play Saturday and Monday mornings.

Societies: Welcome: Contact Club in advance by telephone.

Facilities: Putting Green, Chipping Green, Practice Ground, Club Hire, Trolley Hire, Bar, Restaurant

Accommodation, Food and Drink

Reference numbers below refer to detailed information provided in section 2

Accommodation

Crosskeys Riverside Hotel, Hilgay, Downham Market, Norfolk PE38 0LD

Tel/Fax: 01366 387777

A small country hotel in a 17th-century building in grounds beside the River Wissey. Four en-suite bedrooms. Breakfast, cream teas. 348

Rose & Crown, Hilgay, Downham Market, Norfolk PE38 0LJ

Tel: 01366 385414

A traditional village pub offering real ales, snacks and meals, entertainments and a choice of accommodation. 339

The Nyton Hotel, Ely, Cambridgeshire CB7 4HZ

Tel: 01353 662459

Ten-bedroom family hotel with a conservatory lounge and elegant restaurant. Close to Cathedral and a short walk from the City Golf Club. 622

Clare Farm, 86 Main Street, Witchford, Ely, Cambridgeshire CB6 2HQ

Tel: 01353 664135

Four warm, spacious bedrooms with tv and farmland views. Full English breakfast. Ample parking. No credit cards.

Sycamore House, Ely, Cambridgeshire CB7 4HX

Tel: 01353 662139

A newly renovated, spacious 1920s family house

with two double bedrooms and one twin. Good choice for breakfast. Lovely large garden. 606

Greenways, Prickwillow Road, Queen Adelaide, Ely, Cambridgeshire CB7 4TZ

Tel: 01353 666706 Fax: 01954 251629

Comfortable modern ground-floor en-suite bedrooms (single, double, twin, family) in a rural location one mile from Ely.

The Willows Motel, Elm Road, March, Cambridgeshire PE15 8PS

Tel: 01354 661292

Six spacious en-suite bedrooms in a B&B motel on the A141 five minutes north of March. No credit cards.

Food and Drink

Rose & Crown, Hilgay, Downham Market, Norfolk PE38 0LJ

Tel: 01366 385414

A traditional village pub offering real ales, snacks and meals, entertainments and a choice of accommodation. 339

The Bell Inn, Bury Road, Kennett, Nr Newmarket, Suffolk CB8 7PP

Tel: 01638 750286

Exposed beams and cheerful open fires in an atmospheric old coaching inn at the village crossroads. 60-cover restaurant.

The Nyton Hotel, Ely, Cambridgeshire CB7 4HZ

Tel: 01353 662459

Ten-bedroom family hotel with a conservatory lounge and elegant restaurant. Close to Cathedral and a short walk from the City Golf Club. 622

The Three Kings, Haddenham, Cambridgeshire CB6 3XD

Tel: 01353 749080

17th-century former coaching inn in a pretty village. Good-value food with blackboard specials. Real ales, good selection of wines.

The Kings Head, Wilburton, Cambridgeshire CB6 3RA

Tel: 01353 741029

A handsome pub built with local bricks, with a pleasant garden at the back. Bar and restaurant menus, real ales, good wines. 610

Gedney Hill

West Drove, Gedney End Hill, Lincolnshire PE12 0NT

Tel: 01406 330922 Fax: 01406 330323

Sec/Manager: David Hutton

Professional: David Hutton

Directions: 13 miles north east of Peterborough. From Peterborough take the A47 to Guyhirn and turn left onto the B1187, Parson Drive. Follow this to the B1166 Gedney Hill and turn right into West Drove (by thewindmill). The entrance is on the left hand side.

Date Founded: 1989

Type of Course: Fenland and Links

No of Holes: 18

Length: 5285 yds (4878 mtrs)

Par: 70

SSS: 66

Green Fees: Weekdays: £6.50; Weekends/ Bank Holidays: £11.00

Visitors: Welcome: At all times.

Societies: Welcome: Contact Club by telephone in advance.

Facilities: Putting Green, Driving Range, Club Hire, Trolley Hire, Buggy Hire, Caddy Service, Bar, Restaurant, Private Rooms, Bowling Green

Accommodation, Food and Drink

Reference numbers below refer to detailed information provided in section 2

Accommodation

The Wheel Inn, Wisbech St Mary, Cambridgeshire PE14 4RH

Tel: 01945 410504

A beautifully kept 18th century pub with white-painted facade, cosy beamed bars and a lovely garden. Comfortable accommodation; good home cooking. 621

Common Right Barns, Wisbech St Mary, Cambridgeshire PE13 4SP

Tel/Fax: 01945 410424

Self-catering accommodation and a twin B&B room in renovated farm buildings situated in rural Fenland. Wheelchair friendly. Meals available by arrangement. 616

The White House, 318 Oundle Road, Peterborough, Cambridgeshire PE2 9QP

Tel: 01733 566650

Five recently decorated rooms, one en-suite, in a large white house set back from the A605 2 miles from the town centre.

Foreman's Bridge Caravan Park, Sutton Road, Sutton St James, Lincolnshire PE12 0HU

Tel/Fax: 01945 440346
web: www.foremans-bridge.co.uk
A pleasant riverside park for touring caravans and tents. Also static caravans for hire (Mar-Nov) and two holiday cottages (all year). B1390.

Food and Drink

The Drayman's Arms, 44 Little London, Spalding, Lincolnshire PE11 2UE

Tel: 01775 724320
A welcoming little roadside pub southwest of town, with a cosy lounge bar, real ales and generous helpings of home cooking.

The Old Ship Inn, Long Sutton, Lincolnshire PE12 9EE

Tel: 01406 362930
A traditional country inn with low beams, a cosy atmosphere and good home-cooked food. Excellent choice of real ales. 706

The Chequers at Gedney Dyke, Spalding, Lincolnshire PE12 0AJ

Tel/Fax: 01406 362666
A family-run village pub open every day for excellent food and drink. Bar snacks and full à la carte with lots of daily specials. 708

The Wheel Inn, Wisbech St Mary, Cambridgeshire PE14 4RH

Tel: 01945 410504
A beautifully kept 18th century pub with white-painted facade, cosy beamed bars and a lovely garden. Comfortable accommodation; good home cooking. 621

Ye Old Bridge Inn, Crowland, Peterborough, Lincolnshire PE6 0HJ

Tel: 01733 210567
A renovated 150-year-old ale house by the River Welland north of Crowland. Real ales and a good choice of food in the restaurant. 627

The Wheatsheaf, Fengate, Moulton Chapel, Lincolnshire PE12 0XL

Tel: 01406 380525
A delightful 200-year-old pub on the B1357 east of Spalding. Snug bar and 30-cover restaurant serving excellent-value meals. 703

Girton

Dodford Lane, Girton,
Cambridgeshire CB3 0QE

Tel: 01223 276169 Fax: 01223 277150

Sec/Manager: Miss Webb
Professional: Mr Thomson

Directions: 3½ miles north west of Cambridge. From Cambridge City centre take the A1307 (Girton) and after 2 miles turn right into Girton Road. Follow into Cambridge Road, turn right into High Street and then left into Dodford Lane. The entrance is on the right hand side after 150 yds.

Date Founded: 1936
Type of Course: Parkland
No of Holes: 18
Length: 6012 yds (5829 mtrs)
Par: 69
SSS: 69
Green Fees: Weekdays: £20.00
Visitors: Welcome: Contact Club in advance by telephone. Unable to play at Weekends and Bank Holidays.
Societies: Welcome: Contact Club in advance. Unable to play on Monday's.
Facilities: Putting Green, Chipping Green, Practice Area, Trolley Hire, Buggy Hire, Bar, Restaurant

Accommodation, Food and Drink

Reference numbers below refer to detailed information provided in section 2

Accommodation

The Blue Ball Inn, 57 Broadway, Grantchester, Cambridgeshire CB3 9NQ

Tel: 01223 840679

An award-winning traditional English pub with two letting bedrooms, good food and excellent real ales from Greene King.

The Golden Lion Hotel, St Ives, Cambridgeshire PE27 5AL

Tel: 01480 492100

Georgian-fronted former coaching inn offering comfortable accommodation and good eating in the centre of town. Good base for touring the Fens. 609

St Ives Motel, St Ives, Cambridgeshire PE17 4EX

Tel: 01480 463857

Fifteen spacious en-suite bedrooms in a low building set back from the A1096. Bar snacks and non-smoking restaurant. 602

The White Hart, Fulbourn, Cambridgeshire CB1 5BZ

Tel: 01223 880264

A mid-Victorian pub of character, with garden and patio. Seven bedrooms, all en-suite; fully licensed restaurant, carvery Friday evening and Sunday lunch. 611

Wallis Farmhouse, 98 Main Street, Hardwick, Cambridgeshire CB3 7QU

Tel: 01954 210347 Fax: 01954 210988

A late Georgian farmhouse on a working farm just off the A428. Eight en-suite B&B rooms. e-mail: wallis@mcmail.com

Food and Drink

The Blue Ball Inn, 57 Broadway, Grantchester, Cambridgeshire CB3 9NQ

Tel: 01223 840679

An award-winning traditional English pub with two letting bedrooms, good food and excellent real ales from Greene King.

The Blue Lion, Hardwick, Cambridgeshire CB3 7QU

Tel: 01954 210328

17th-century village pub in traditional style, with a deserved reputation for high-quality food served lunchtime and evening. 630

The Golden Lion Hotel, St Ives, Cambridgeshire PE27 5AL

Tel: 01480 492100

Georgian-fronted former coaching inn offering comfortable accommodation and good eating in the centre of town. Good base for touring the Fens. 609

St Ives Motel, St Ives, Cambridgeshire PE17 4EX

Tel: 01480 463857

Fifteen spacious en-suite bedrooms in a low building set back from the A1096. Bar snacks and non-smoking restaurant. 602

The George, High Street, Girton, Cambridgeshire CB3 0QD

A friendly family-run pub serving excellent-value food from bar snacks to full meals. Best to book, especially for Sunday lunch. 607

The Kings Head, Wilburton, Cambridgeshire CB6 3RA

Tel: 01353 741029

A handsome pub built with local bricks, with a pleasant garden at the back. Bar and restaurant menus, real ales, good wines. 610

The White Hart, Fulbourn, Cambridgeshire CB1 5BZ

Tel: 01223 880264

A mid-Victorian pub of character, with garden and patio. Seven bedrooms, all en-suite; fully licensed restaurant, carvery Friday evening and Sunday lunch. 611

The Rose & Crown, Teversham, Cambridgeshire CB1 5AF

Tel: 01223 292245

A handsome 100-year-old pub in a pretty village just off the A1303. Excellent-value home-cooked food, from bar snacks to full meals. 623

Gog Magog

Shelford Bottom, Cambridge, Cambridgeshire CB2 4AB

Tel: 01223 247626 Fax: 01223 414990

In 1896, Gonville and Caius College bought Heath Farm on the Gog Magog Hills outside Cambridge, which had been a disastrous experiment in turning heathland into agricultural land and was in danger of being taken out of cultivation. The intention was to turn it into a golf course for the use of senior members of Cambridge University. After the area was grassed, the college paid W Duncan, the resident professional at Coldhams Common (a mudheap of a course on which the University Club played) one pound to mark out 18 holes. The college provided 36 'slated with

numbered boards, 18 printed red and 18 white, one for each green and one for each tee', and Duncan did the rest. Nine holes were laid out in 1899 and a second nine in 1901.

The college then recognised that it needed to pass the day-to-day responsibilities over to a club, and it oversaw the establishment of Gog Magog in October of that year, which means it celebrates its centenary in 2001. Over the following 33 years the course was gradually developed, with a little help from Willie Park Jnr, J F Abercrombie, and James Braid, from being 'one huge undulating field', as Bernard Darwin described it, into the varied and interesting golfing experience that the **Old Course** is today.

Nine more holes were added in 1971, but they lacked the distinction of the Old Course; and in 1999, after several false starts, a second 18-hole course was completed – the **Wandlebury** – that preserved only a small, and much altered, part of the 1971 nine holes. This is now a test of golf comparable in difficulty and interest to the Old Course, planted with thousands of trees and seeded in the rough with heathland flowers that had flourished before the farm was created. Both courses start and finish neat the clubhouse. There are panoramic views from both courses, on the Old mainly to the north and west, and on the Wandlebury to the east. There is also an abundance of wild life that does not seem to take much notice of passing golfers. The Old Course is somewhat hilly with a lot of large bunkers, so it is worth practising these shots before teeing off. But it is fun and with no water hazards you will probably get round without losing a ball.

Sec/Manager: Barry Galder
Professional: Ian Bamborough
Directions: 4 miles south east of Cambridge. From Cambridge City centre take the A1307 (Haverhill). After leaving city turn left at roundabout onto Cherry Hinton Road. The entrance is on the right hand side
Date Founded: 1901
Visitors: Welcome: Contact Club in advance. Unable to play at weekends and Wednesdays.
Societies: Welcome: Contact Club in advance by telephone. Unable to play Monday, Wednesday, Friday, Saturday and Sunday.
Facilities: Putting Green, Chipping Green, Bar, Restaurant, Driving Range

Old Course

Type of Course: Undulating Parkland
No of Holes: 18
Length: 6398 yds (5905 mtrs)
Par: 70
SSS: 72
Green Fees: Weekdays: £35.00; Weekends/ Bank Holidays: £35.00

Wandlebury

Type of Course: Undulating Parkland
No of Holes: 18
Length: 6754 yds (6234 mtrs)
Par: 72
SSS: 72
Green Fees: Weekdays: £35.00; Weekends/ Bank Holidays: 335.00

Accommodation, Food and Drink

Reference numbers below refer to detailed information provided in section 2

Accommodation

The Blue Ball Inn, 57 Broadway, Grantchester, Cambridgeshire CB3 9NQ
Tel: 01223 840679

An award-winning traditional English pub with two letting bedrooms, good food and excellent real ales from Greene King.

Riverside Guest House, Melbourn, Royston, Cambridgeshire SG8 6DX

Tel: 01763 226062 Fax: 01763 226063

A renovated 100-year-old property in a delightful riverside setting on the edge of a pretty village. Five en-suite rooms for B&B. 625

Juniper Bed & Breakfast, Church Lane, Cheveley, Suffolk CB8 9DJ

Tel: 01638 731244

Next to the church in rural Cheveley, Juniper is a new house offering top-notch Bed & Breakfast accommodation in three beautifully appointed bedrooms.

The Rutland Arms Hotel, Newmarket, Suffolk CB8 8NB

Tel: 01638 664251 Fax: 01638 666298

Forty-six well-equipped modern bedrooms in a handsome hotel built round a cobbled courtyard. Bar meals and full restaurant menu. 405

The White Hart, Fulbourn, Cambridgeshire CB1 5BZ

Tel: 01223 880264

A mid-Victorian pub of character, with garden and patio. Seven bedrooms, all en-suite; fully licensed restaurant, carvery Friday evening and Sunday lunch. 611

Food and Drink

The White Horse, 118 High Street, Barton, Cambridgeshire CB3 7BG

Tel/Fax: 01223 262327

16th-century village pub with beams, brasses and open fires. Excellent bar snacks and full à la carte menu. 604

The Blue Ball Inn, 57 Broadway, Grantchester, Cambridgeshire CB3 9NQ

Tel: 01223 840679

An award-winning traditional English pub with two letting bedrooms, good food and excellent real ales from Greene King.

The Old English Gentlemen, High Street, Harston, Cambridgeshire CB2 5QD

Tel: 01223 870287

19th-century pub on the A10, serving excellent bar snacks and full meals. Book ahead for the speciality steaks. Pool, darts.

The Rutland Arms Hotel, Newmarket, Suffolk CB8 8NB

Tel: 01638 664251 Fax: 01638 666298

Forty-six well-equipped modern bedrooms in a handsome hotel built round a cobbled courtyard. Bar meals and full restaurant menu. 405

The White Hart, Fulbourn, Cambridgeshire CB1 5BZ

Tel: 01223 880264

A mid-Victorian pub of character, with garden and patio. Seven bedrooms, all en-suite; fully licensed restaurant, carvery Friday evening and Sunday lunch. 611

The Rose & Crown, Teversham, Cambridgeshire CB1 5AF

Tel: 01223 292245

A handsome 100-year-old pub in a pretty village just off the A1303. Excellent-value home-cooked food, from bar snacks to full meals. 623

The Chestnut Tree, West Wratting, Cambridgeshire CB1 5LU

Tel: 01223 290384

A well-kept redbrick village pub on the B1052, serving a fine selection of first-class food, with Sunday lunch a highlight. 620

The Hoops, Great Eversden, Cambridgeshire CB3 7HN

Tel/Fax: 01223 264008

A cheerful white-painted pub off the A603, bright and modern behind its period facade. Home-cooked food, real ales, extensive wine list. 709

Heydon Grange

Heydon, Royston, Cambridgeshire SG8 7NS

Tel: 01763 208988 Fax: 01763 208926

Sec/Manager:	Mr Akhtor
Professional:	Stuart Smith
Directions:	4 miles west of Royston. From Royston centre take the A10 (Cambridge). After one mile turn right onto the A505 (Writtlesford). Pass Flint Cross and Fina Service Station and, after 1 mile, turn right on Fowlmere Road (Heydon). The entrance is on the right hand side.
Date Founded:	1993

Type of Course:	Parkland
No of Holes:	27 (3 x 9 hole courses)
Length:	6193-6503 yds (5716-6002 mtrs)
Par:	71-72
SSS:	71-72
Green Fees:	Weekdays: £15.00,;Weekends/ Bank Holidays: £17.00
Visitors:	Welcome: Contact Club in advance
Societies:	Welcome: Contact Club in advance
Facilities:	Putting Green, Chipping Green, Driving Range, Club Hire, Trolley Hire, Buggy Hire, Bar, Restaurant, Private Rooms

Accommodation, Food and Drink

Reference numbers below refer to detailed information provided in section 2

Accommodation

The Blue Ball Inn, 57 Broadway, Grantchester, Cambridgeshire CB3 9NQ

Tel: 01223 840679

An award-winning traditional English pub with two letting bedrooms, good food and excellent real ales from Greene King.

Orchard Farmhouse, Toft, Cambridgeshire CB3 7RY

Tel: 01223 262309 Fax: 01223 263979

Quiet, comfortable farmhouse B&B accommodation next to Cambridge Meridian Golf Course. e-mail: tebbit.bxb.toft@talk21.com

Riverside Guest House, Melbourn, Royston, Cambridgeshire SG8 6DX

Tel: 01763 226062 Fax: 01763 226063

A renovated 100-year-old property in a delightful riverside setting on the edge of a pretty village. Five en-suite rooms for B&B. 625

The White Hart, Fulbourn, Cambridgeshire CB1 5BZ

Tel: 01223 880264

A mid-Victorian pub of character, with garden and patio. Seven bedrooms, all en-suite; fully licensed restaurant, carvery Friday evening and Sunday lunch. 611

Food and Drink

The Blue Ball Inn, 57 Broadway, Grantchester, Cambridgeshire CB3 9NQ

Tel: 01223 840679

An award-winning traditional English pub with two letting bedrooms, good food and excellent real ales from Greene King.

The Hoops, Bassingbourn, Cambridgeshire SG8 5LF

Tel: 01763 242130

300-year-old thatched country pub serving a good variety of food and well-kept ales. 601

The Pear Tree, North End, Bassingbourn, Nr Royston, Cambridgeshire SG8 5NZ

Tel: 01763 244068

Traditional English food served seven days a week in a welcoming pub with a golfing owner.

The Crown, Church Street, Litlington, Nr Royston, Cambridgeshire SG8 0QB

Tel: 01763 852439

An attractive village inn serving an excellent choice of lunchtime snacks and evening meals. Good wines; real ales.

The Chequers at Anstey, Nr Buntingford, Hertfordshire SG9 0BW

Tel: 01763 848205

Generous home cooking, well-kept real ales and a good wine list in a family-run village pub. 603

The Pink Geranium, Melbourn, Cambridgeshire SG8 6DX

Tel: 01763 260215 Fax: 01763 262110

One of the prettiest restaurants in East Anglia, and certainly one of the best, with outstanding food and an excellent wine cellar. 608

The White Hart, Fulbourn, Cambridgeshire CB1 5BZ

Tel: 01223 880264

A mid-Victorian pub of character, with garden and patio. Seven bedrooms, all en-suite; fully licensed restaurant, carvery Friday evening and Sunday lunch. 611

Lakeside Lodge

Fen Road, Pidley, Huntingdon, Cambridgeshire PE28 3DF

Tel: 01487 740540 Fax: 01487 740852

Sec/Manager:	Jane Hopkins
Professional:	Alistair Hedley
Directions:	7 miles north east of Huntingdon. From Huntingdon centre take the A141 (Chatters). Turn right on the B1040 and at Pidley turn left into Fen road. the entrance is on the right hand side after 400 yds.
Date Founded:	1992
Visitors:	Welcome: Contact Club in advance.
Societies:	Welcome: Contact Club in advance. Unable to play at certain times at Weekends.
Facilities:	Putting Green, Chipping Green, Club Hire, Trolley Hire, Buggy Hire, Bar, Restaurant, Driving Range, Private Rooms, 10 Pin Bowling, Indoor Golf Simulator

Lodge Course

Type of Course:	Parkland and Links
No of Holes:	18
Length:	6821 yds (6296 mtrs)
Par:	72
SSS:	73
Green Fees:	Weekdays: £11.00; Weekends/ Bank Holidays: £19.00

Manor Course

Type of Course:	Parkland and Links
No of Holes:	9
Length:	2601 yds (2401 mtrs)
Par:	34
SSS:	33
Green Fees:	Weekdays: £6.00; Weekends/ Bank Holidays: £8.00

Accommodation, Food and Drink

Reference numbers below refer to detailed information provided in section 2

Accommodation

The Golden Lion Hotel, St Ives, Cambridgeshire PE27 5AL

Tel: 01480 492100

Georgian-fronted former coaching inn offering comfortable accommodation and good eating in the centre of town. Good base for touring the Fens. 609

The Stukeleys Country Hotel, Great Stukeley, Cambridgeshire PE17 5AL

Tel: 01480 456927

Eight en-suite bedrooms and an elegant restaurant in a beautifully preserved 16th-century former coaching inn. 612

The George Hotel, Ramsey, Cambridgeshire PE26 1AA

Historic coaching inn built in 1630 and restored to a high standard in 2000. Eleven en-suite chalet-style rooms. À la carte restaurant. 619

The Nyton Hotel, Ely, Cambridgeshire CB7 4HZ

Tel: 01353 662459

Ten-bedroom family hotel with a conservatory lounge and elegant restaurant. Close to Cathedral and a short walk from the City Golf Club. 622

Clare Farm, 86 Main Street, Witchford, Ely, Cambridgeshire CB6 2HQ

Tel: 01353 664135

Four warm, spacious bedrooms with tv and farmland views. Full English breakfast. Ample parking. No credit cards.

Sycamore House, Ely, Cambridgeshire CB7 4HX

Tel: 01353 662139

A newly renovated, spacious 1920s family house with two double bedrooms and one twin. Good choice for breakfast. Lovely large garden. 606

Greenways, Prickwillow Road, Queen Adelaide, Ely, Cambridgeshire CB7 4TZ

Tel: 01353 666706 Fax: 01954 251629

Comfortable modern ground-floor en-suite bedrooms (single, double, twin, family) in a rural location one mile from Ely.

The Black Bull, Godmanchester, Cambridgeshire PE29 2AQ

Tel: 01480 453310

An old coaching inn that now provides comfortable accommodation in four en-suite bedrooms. Attractive bar lounge; excellent value meals. 605

St Ives Motel, St Ives, Cambridgeshire PE17 4EX

Tel: 01480 463857

Fifteen spacious en-suite bedrooms in a low building set back from the A1096. Bar snacks and non-smoking restaurant. 602

Food and Drink

The Golden Lion Hotel, St Ives, Cambridgeshire PE27 5AL

Tel: 01480 492100

Georgian-fronted former coaching inn offering comfortable accommodation and good eating in the centre of town. Good base for touring the Fens. 609

The Angel, High Street, Ramsey, Cambridgeshire PE26 1BS

Tel: 01487 813226

Along the High Street from The George, and in the same ownership. The brick-built Angel is more of a pub pure and simple, with drinks and bar food.

The Stukeleys Country Hotel, Great Stukeley, Cambridgeshire PE17 5AL

Tel: 01480 456927

Eight en-suite bedrooms and an elegant restaurant in a beautifully preserved 16th-century former coaching inn. 612

The George Hotel, Ramsey, Cambridgeshire PE26 1AA

Historic coaching inn built in 1630 and restored to a high standard in 2000. Eleven en-suite chalet-style rooms. À la carte restaurant. 619

The Nyton Hotel, Ely, Cambridgeshire CB7 4HZ

Tel: 01353 662459

Ten-bedroom family hotel with a conservatory lounge and elegant restaurant. Close to Cathedral and a short walk from the City Golf Club. 622

The Three Kings, Haddenham, Cambridgeshire CB6 3XD

Tel: 01353 749080

17th-century former coaching inn in a pretty village. Good-value food with blackboard specials. Real ales, good selection of wines.

The Black Bull, Godmanchester, Cambridgeshire PE29 2AQ

Tel: 01480 453310

An old coaching inn that now provides comfortable accommodation in four en-suite bedrooms. Attractive bar lounge; excellent value meals. 605

St Ives Motel, St Ives, Cambridgeshire PE17 4EX

Tel: 01480 463857

Fifteen spacious en-suite bedrooms in a low building set back from the A1096. Bar snacks and non-smoking restaurant. 602

The Kings Head, Wilburton, Cambridgeshire CB6 3RA

Tel: 01353 741029

A handsome pub built with local bricks, with a pleasant garden at the back. Bar and restaurant menus, real ales, good wines. 610

The White Hart, Alconbury Weston, Huntingdon, Cambridgeshire PE28 4JA

Tel: 01480 890331

A friendly 200-year-old village pub serving real ale and good food. Popular theme nights. Golfing parties welcome. 614

Malton

Malton Lane, Meldreth, Royston, Cambridgeshire SG8 6PE

Tel: 01763 262200 Fax: 01763 262209

Sec/Manager: Serena Boyce

Professional: Graham Harvey

Directions: 5 miles north of Royston. From Royston centre take the A1198 (Huntingdon). At Kneesworth turn right towards Meldreth (2 miles), take Fenny Lane, follow into North End and turn left at Malton Lane. The entrance is on the left hand side after one mile.

Date Founded: 1994

Type of Course: Parkland

No of Holes:	18
Length:	6708 yds (6191 mtrs)
Par:	72
SSS:	72
Green Fees:	Weekdays: £10.00; Weekends/ Bank Holidays: £15.00
Visitors:	Welcome: Contact Club in advance by telephone.
Societies:	Welcome: Contact Club in advance. Unable to play at weekends.
Facilities:	Putting Green, Driving Range, Club Hire, Trolley Hire, Buggy Hire, Bar, Restaurant

Accommodation, Food and Drink

Reference numbers below refer to detailed information provided in section 2

Accommodation

The Blue Ball Inn, 57 Broadway, Grantchester, Cambridgeshire CB3 9NQ

Tel: 01223 840679

An award-winning traditional English pub with two letting bedrooms, good food and excellent real ales from Greene King.

Orchard Farmhouse, Toft, Cambridgeshire CB3 7RY

Tel: 01223 262309 Fax: 01223 263979

Quiet, comfortable farmhouse B&B accommodation next to Cambridge Meridian Golf Course. e-mail: tebbit.bxb.toft@talk21.com

Riverside Guest House, Melbourn, Royston, Cambridgeshire SG8 6DX

Tel: 01763 226062 Fax: 01763 226063

A renovated 100-year-old property in a delightful riverside setting on the edge of a pretty village. Five en-suite rooms for B&B. 625

The White Hart, Fulbourn, Cambridgeshire CB1 5BZ

Tel: 01223 880264

A mid-Victorian pub of character, with garden and patio. Seven bedrooms, all en-suite; fully licensed restaurant, carvery Friday evening and Sunday lunch. 611

Wallis Farmhouse, 98 Main Street, Hardwick, Cambridgeshire CB3 7QU

Tel: 01954 210347 Fax: 01954 210988

A late Georgian farmhouse on a working farm just off the A428. Eight en-suite B&B rooms. e-mail: wallis@mcmail.com

Food and Drink

The Blue Ball Inn, 57 Broadway, Grantchester, Cambridgeshire CB3 9NQ

Tel: 01223 840679

An award-winning traditional English pub with two letting bedrooms, good food and excellent real ales from Greene King.

The Old English Gentlemen, High Street, Harston, Cambridgeshire CB2 5QD

Tel: 01223 870287

19th-century pub on the A10, serving excellent bar snacks and full meals. Book ahead for the speciality steaks. Pool, darts.

The Hoops, Bassingbourn, Cambridgeshire SG8 5LF

Tel: 01763 242130

300-year-old thatched country pub serving a good variety of food and well-kept ales. 601

The Pear Tree, North End, Bassingbourn, Nr Royston, Cambridgeshire SG8 5NZ

Tel: 01763 244068

Traditional English food served seven days a week in a welcoming pub with a golfing owner.

The Crown, Church Street, Litlington, Nr Royston, Cambridgeshire SG8 0QB

Tel: 01763 852439

An attractive village inn serving an excellent choice of lunchtime snacks and evening meals. Good wines; real ales.

The Chequers at Anstey, Nr Buntingford, Hertfordshire SG9 0BW

Tel: 01763 848205

Generous home cooking, well-kept real ales and a good wine list in a family-run village pub. 603

The Queen Adelaide, Croydon, Cambridgeshire SG8 0DN

Tel: 01223 208278

A peaceful village setting for a friendly family-run pub serving excellent food based on top local produce. Large garden. 626

The Pink Geranium, Melbourn, Cambridgeshire SG8 6DX

Tel: 01763 260215 Fax: 01763 262110

One of the prettiest restaurants in East Anglia, and certainly one of the best, with outstanding food and an excellent wine cellar. 608

The White Hart, Fulbourn, Cambridgeshire CB1 5BZ

Tel: 01223 880264

A mid-Victorian pub of character, with garden and patio. Seven bedrooms, all en-suite; fully licensed restaurant, carvery Friday evening and Sunday lunch. 611

The Hoops, Great Eversden, Cambridgeshire CB3 7HN

Tel/Fax: 01223 264008

A cheerful white-painted pub off the A603, bright and modern behind its period facade. Home-cooked food, real ales, extensive wine list. 709

Orton Meadows

Ham Lane, Peterborough, Cambridgeshire PE2 5UU

Tel: 01733 237478 Fax: 01733 332774

Sec/Manager:	Susan Ramsey
Professional:	Jason Mitchell
Directions:	2 miles south west of Peterborough. From Peterborough centre take the A605 Oundle Road. Turn right onto Ham Lane at the roundabout and the entrance is adjacent to the Travel Inn.
Date Founded:	1987
Type of Course:	Parkland
No of Holes:	18
Length:	5613 yds (5181 mtrs)
Par:	67
SSS:	67
Green Fees:	Weekdays: £10.70; Weekends/ Bank Holidays: £13.75
Visitors:	Welcome: Contact Club in advance by telephone.
Societies:	Welcome: Contact Club in advance by writing.
Facilities:	Putting Green, Chipping Green, Club Hire, Trolley Hire, Bar, Restaurant

Accommodation, Food and Drink

Reference numbers below refer to detailed information provided in section 2

Accommodation

The Paper Mills Inn, Wansford-in-England, Cambridgeshire PE8 6JB

Tel: 01780 782328

Lunchtime snacks and waitress-served restaurant in a 150-year-old pub a minute from the A1. Beer garden. One letting bedroom. 618

Longueville Guest House, 411 Oundle Road, Orton Longueville, Peterborough, Cambridgeshire PE2 7DA

Tel/Fax: 01733 233442

Pleasant house with a big garden and five well-decorated en-suite bedrooms, one of family size. Good breakfasts. No smoking.

The White House, 318 Oundle Road, Peterborough, Cambridgeshire PE2 9QP

Tel: 01733 566650

Five recently decorated rooms, one en-suite, in a large white house set back from the A605 2 miles from the town centre.

The Talbot Inn, Stilton, Cambridgeshire PE7 3RP

Tel/Fax: 01733 240291

An old coaching inn with a pleasant, cosy atmosphere, a good range of food and drink and five family-size letting bedrooms. 631

The Old Smithy, 47 Peterborough Road, Castor, Cambridgeshire PE5 7AX

Tel/Fax: 01733 380186

Four en-suite bedrooms in a 300-year-old thatched cottage. Aga-cooked breakfast, dinner by arrangement. 3 miles from Peterborough.

Orton Hall Hotel, Orton Longueville, Peterborough, Cambridgeshire PE2 7DN

Tel: 01733 39111 Fax: 01733 371793

e-mail: martingoodliffe@ortonhall.co.uk

17th century manor house in 20 acres of parkland, with modern facilities in spacious, well-appointed bedrooms. Restaurant, traditional inn.

Food and Drink

The Paper Mills Inn, Wansford-in-England, Cambridgeshire PE8 6JB

Tel: 01780 782328

Lunchtime snacks and waitress-served restaurant in a 150-year-old pub a minute from the A1. Beer garden. One letting bedroom. 618

The Windmill Tavern, Orton Waterville, Peterborough, Cambridgeshire

Tel: 01733 231554

18th-century pub in traditional style, with a garden and children's play area. Good food and wine; real ale. 617

The Cherry Tree, 9 Oundle Road, Woodston, Peterborough, Cambridgeshire PE2 9PB

Tel: 01733 703495

18th-century pub with a traditional ambience. Five real ales, extensive menus from snacks to full meals; live music Thursday-Saturday.

The Talbot Inn, Stilton, Cambridgeshire PE7 3RP

Tel/Fax: 01733 240291

An old coaching inn with a pleasant, cosy atmosphere, a good range of food and drink and five family-size letting bedrooms. 631

Orton Hall Hotel, Orton Longueville, Peterborough, Cambridgeshire PE2 7DN

Tel: 01733 39111 Fax: 01733 371793

e-mail: martingoodliffe@ortonhall.co.uk

17th century manor house in 20 acres of parkland, with modern facilities in spacious, well-appointed bedrooms. Restaurant, traditional inn.

Peterborough Milton

Milton Ferry, Peterborough, Cambridgeshire PE6 7AG

Tel: 01733 380204 Fax: 01733 380489

Sec/Manager:	Mr A Izod
Professional:	Mr M Gallagher
Directions:	3½ miles west of Peterborough. From Peterborough centre take the Thorpe Road and join A47 (Corby, Leicester). Take the first exit (1mile), turn left at end of slip road, and turn left after100 yds into Ferry Hill. The entrance is signed.
Date Founded:	1936
Type of Course:	Parkland
No of Holes:	18
Length:	6479 yds (5980 mtrs)
Par:	72
SSS:	72
Green Fees:	Weekdays: £25.00; Weekends/ Bank Holidays: £35.00
Visitors:	Welcome: Contact Club in advance by telephone.
Societies:	Welcome: Contact Club in advance by telephone.
Facilities:	Putting Green, Chipping Green, Driving Range,Trolley Hire, Buggy Hire, Bar, Restaurant, Private Rooms

Accommodation, Food and Drink

Reference numbers below refer to detailed information provided in section 2

Accommodation

The Crown Hotel, Stamford, Lincolnshire PE9 2AG

Tel: 01780 763136 Fax: 01780 756111

An 18-bedroom hotel (all rooms en-suite) built in 1909 and recently extensively renovated to a very high standard. Restaurant. Parking at rear. 702

The Crown Inn, Great Casterton, Stamford, Lincolnshire PE9 4AP

Tel: 01780 763362

A village pub of real charm and character, with abundant hospitality, an excellent menu of home-cooked food and fine wines. One letting bedroom. 701

The George of Stamford, Stamford, Lincolnshire PE9 2LB

Tel: 01780 750750 Fax: 01780 750701

Perhaps England's greatest coaching inn, rich in history and character. Top-quality accommodation in 47 rooms plus superb food and drink. 704

The Paper Mills Inn, Wansford-in-England, Cambridgeshire PE8 6JB

Tel: 01780 782328

Lunchtime snacks and waitress-served restaurant in a 150-year-old pub a minute from the A1. Beer garden. One letting bedroom. 618

The Garden House Hotel, St Martin's, Stamford, Lincolnshire PE9 2LP

Tel: 01780 763359 Fax: 01780 763339

A charming 18th-century house transformed into a delightful hotel with single, double and family rooms. B&B or full board available.

Longueville Guest House, 411 Oundle Road, Orton Longueville, Peterborough, Cambridgeshire PE2 7DA

Tel/Fax: 01733 233442

Pleasant house with a big garden and five well-decorated en-suite bedrooms, one of family size. Good breakfasts. No smoking.

The White House, 318 Oundle Road, Peterborough, Cambridgeshire PE2 9QP

Tel: 01733 566650

Five recently decorated rooms, one en-suite, in a large white house set back from the A605 2 miles from the town centre.

The Talbot Inn, Stilton, Cambridgeshire PE7 3RP

Tel/Fax: 01733 240291

An old coaching inn with a pleasant, cosy

atmosphere, a good range of food and drink and five family-size letting bedrooms. 631

The Old Smithy, 47 Peterborough Road, Castor, Cambridgeshire PE5 7AX

Tel/Fax: 01733 380186

Four en-suite bedrooms in a 300-year-old thatched cottage. Aga-cooked breakfast, dinner by arrangement. 3 miles from Peterborough.

Orton Hall Hotel, Orton Longueville, Peterborough, Cambridgeshire PE2 7DN

Tel: 01733 39111 Fax: 01733 371793

e-mail: martingoodliffe@ortonhall.co.uk

17th century manor house in 20 acres of parkland, with modern facilities in spacious, well-appointed bedrooms. Restaurant, traditional inn.

Food and Drink

The Exeter Arms, Stamford Road, Easton-on-the-Hill, Stamford, Lincolnshire PE9 3NS

Tel: 01780 757503

A French chef produces a tempting range of dishes in a traditionally appointed pub 1 mile west of Stamford. Good wine list. Garden.

The Crown Hotel, Stamford, Lincolnshire PE9 2AG

Tel: 01780 763136 Fax: 01780 756111

An 18-bedroom hotel (all rooms en-suite) built in 1909 and recently extensively renovated to a very high standard. Restaurant. Parking at rear. 702

The Crown Inn, Great Casterton, Stamford, Lincolnshire PE9 4AP

Tel: 01780 763362

A village pub of real charm and character, with abundant hospitality, an excellent menu of home-cooked food and fine wines. One letting bedroom. 701

The George of Stamford, Stamford, Lincolnshire PE9 2LB

Tel: 01780 750750 Fax: 01780 750701

Perhaps England's greatest coaching inn, rich in history and character. Top-quality accommodation in 47 rooms plus superb food and drink. 704

The Paper Mills Inn, Wansford-in-England, Cambridgeshire PE8 6JB

Tel: 01780 782328

Lunchtime snacks and waitress-served restaurant in a 150-year-old pub a minute from the A1. Beer garden. One letting bedroom. 618

The Cherry Tree, 9 Oundle Road, Woodston, Peterborough, Cambridgeshire PE2 9PB

Tel: 01733 703495

18th-century pub with a traditional ambience. Five real ales, extensive menus from snacks to full meals; live music Thursday-Saturday.

The Talbot Inn, Stilton, Cambridgeshire PE7 3RP

Tel/Fax: 01733 240291

An old coaching inn with a pleasant, cosy atmosphere, a good range of food and drink and five family-size letting bedrooms. 631

Orton Hall Hotel, Orton Longueville, Peterborough, Cambridgeshire PE2 7DN

Tel: 01733 39111 Fax: 01733 371793

e-mail: martingoodliffe@ortonhall.co.uk

17th century manor house in 20 acres of parkland, with modern facilities in spacious, well-appointed bedrooms. Restaurant, traditional inn.

Ramsey

4 Abbey Terrace, Ramsey, Huntingdon, Cambridgeshire PE26 1DD

Tel: 01487 812600 Fax: 01487 815746

Sec/Manager:	Brian Gazzard
Professional:	Stewart Scott
Directions:	7½ miles north of Huntingdon. From the northern outskirts take the A141 to Warboys (Chatteris). At Warboys turn left onto the B1040 and follow into the High Street, Ramsey. Turn right into Hollow Lane and the entrance is on the right hand side after 20 yds.
Date Founded:	1967
Type of Course:	Parkland
No of Holes:	18
Length:	6163 yds (5688 mtrs)
Par:	71
SSS:	68
Green Fees:	Weekdays: £25.00; Weekends/ Bank Holidays: £30.00
Visitors:	Welcome: Contact Club in advance. Weekend booking essential.

Societies: Welcome: Contact Club in advance by writing.

Facilities: Putting Green, Chipping Green, Trolley Hire, Buggy Hire, Bar, Restaurant, Private Rooms, Snooker Tables, Bowls Club

Accommodation, Food and Drink

Reference numbers below refer to detailed information provided in section 2

Accommodation

The Talbot Inn, Stilton, Cambridgeshire PE7 3RP

Tel/Fax: 01733 240291

An old coaching inn with a pleasant, cosy atmosphere, a good range of food and drink and five family-size letting bedrooms. 631

The Stukeleys Country Hotel, Great Stukeley, Cambridgeshire PE17 5AL

Tel: 01480 456927

Eight en-suite bedrooms and an elegant restaurant in a beautifully preserved 16th-century former coaching inn. 612

The George Hotel, Ramsey, Cambridgeshire PE26 1AA

Historic coaching inn built in 1630 and restored to a high standard in 2000. Eleven en-suite chalet-style rooms. À la carte restaurant. 619

The Nyton Hotel, Ely, Cambridgeshire CB7 4HZ

Tel: 01353 662459

Ten-bedroom family hotel with a conservatory lounge and elegant restaurant. Close to Cathedral and a short walk from the City Golf Club. 622

Sycamore House, Ely, Cambridgeshire CB7 4HX

Tel: 01353 662139

A newly renovated, spacious 1920s family house with two double bedrooms and one twin. Good choice for breakfast. Lovely large garden. 606

The Willows Motel, Elm Road, March, Cambridgeshire PE15 8PS

Tel: 01354 661292

Six spacious en-suite bedrooms in a B&B motel on the A141 five minutes north of March. No credit cards.

Food and Drink

The Talbot Inn, Stilton, Cambridgeshire PE7 3RP

Tel/Fax: 01733 240291

An old coaching inn with a pleasant, cosy atmosphere, a good range of food and drink and five family-size letting bedrooms. 631

The Angel, High Street, Ramsey, Cambridgeshire PE26 1BS

Tel: 01487 813226

Along the High Street from The George, and in the same ownership. The brick-built Angel is more of a pub pure and simple, with drinks and bar food.

The Stukeleys Country Hotel, Great Stukeley, Cambridgeshire PE17 5AL

Tel: 01480 456927

Eight en-suite bedrooms and an elegant restaurant in a beautifully preserved 16th-century former coaching inn. 612

The George Hotel, Ramsey, Cambridgeshire PE26 1AA

Historic coaching inn built in 1630 and restored to a high standard in 2000. Eleven en-suite chalet-style rooms. À la carte restaurant. 619

The Nyton Hotel, Ely, Cambridgeshire CB7 4HZ

Tel: 01353 662459

Ten-bedroom family hotel with a conservatory lounge and elegant restaurant. Close to Cathedral and a short walk from the City Golf Club. 622

The White Hart, Alconbury Weston, Huntingdon, Cambridgeshire PE28 4JA

Tel: 01480 890331

A friendly 200-year-old village pub serving real ale and good food. Popular theme nights. Golfing parties welcome. 614

St Ives

St Ives, Huntingdon, Cambridgeshire, Cambridgeshire PE27 6DH

Tel/Fax: 01480 468392

Sec/Manager: Brian Dunn

Professional: Darren Glasby

Directions: 1 mile west of St Ives. From St

	Ives centre take the A1123 (Huntingdon) and turn left into High Ley (¼ mile past Shell Service Station). The entrance is past the school on the left hand side after 400 yds.
Date Founded:	1923
Type of Course:	Parkland
No of Holes:	18
Length:	6200 yds (5723 mtrs)
Par:	70
SSS:	70
Green Fees:	Weekdays: £20.00
Visitors:	Welcome: Contact Club in advance. Unable to play at weekends.
Societies:	Welcome: Contact Club in advance by telephone. Unable to play Moday, Tuesday, Thursday and weekends.
Facilities:	Putting Green, Chipping Green, Trolley Hire, Club Hire, Bar, Restaurant

Accommodation, Food and Drink

Reference numbers below refer to detailed information provided in section 2

Accommodation

The Golden Lion Hotel, St Ives, Cambridgeshire PE27 5AL

Tel: 01480 492100

Georgian-fronted former coaching inn offering comfortable accommodation and good eating in the centre of town. Good base for touring the Fens. 609

The Stukeleys Country Hotel, Great Stukeley, Cambridgeshire PE17 5AL

Tel: 01480 456927

Eight en-suite bedrooms and an elegant restaurant in a beautifully preserved 16th-century former coaching inn. 612

The Black Bull, Godmanchester, Cambridgeshire PE29 2AQ

Tel: 01480 453310

An old coaching inn that now provides comfortable accommodation in four en-suite bedrooms. Attractive bar lounge; excellent value meals. 605

St Ives Motel, St Ives, Cambridgeshire PE17 4EX

Tel: 01480 463857

Fifteen spacious en-suite bedrooms in a low building set back from the A1096. Bar snacks and non-smoking restaurant. 602

Food and Drink

The Golden Lion Hotel, St Ives, Cambridgeshire PE27 5AL

Tel: 01480 492100

Georgian-fronted former coaching inn offering comfortable accommodation and good eating in the centre of town. Good base for touring the Fens. 609

The Stukeleys Country Hotel, Great Stukeley, Cambridgeshire PE17 5AL

Tel: 01480 456927

Eight en-suite bedrooms and an elegant restaurant in a beautifully preserved 16th-century former coaching inn. 612

The Black Bull, Godmanchester, Cambridgeshire PE29 2AQ

Tel: 01480 453310

An old coaching inn that now provides comfortable accommodation in four en-suite bedrooms. Attractive bar lounge; excellent value meals. 605

St Ives Motel, St Ives, Cambridgeshire PE17 4EX

Tel: 01480 463857

Fifteen spacious en-suite bedrooms in a low building set back from the A1096. Bar snacks and non-smoking restaurant. 602

The White Hart, Alconbury Weston, Huntingdon, Cambridgeshire PE28 4JA

Tel: 01480 890331

A friendly 200-year-old village pub serving real ale and good food. Popular theme nights. Golfing parties welcome. 614

St Neot's

Crosshall Road, St Neot's, Cambridgeshire PE19 7GE

Tel/Fax: 01480 472363

This is the oldest club in Cambridgeshire, having been established in 1890. Initially members were only allowed to play on Tuesdays and Thursdays from August to March on the local common. A press report of the day says: "Judging from the numbers enrolled as members the club will prove to be highly successful." How right they were. St Neots is happy to remain a members' club and the current membership is very grateful to the far-sighted committee who purchased the land in the 1940s. After a short stay elsewhere, the club moved to its present site in 1912 when Harry Vardon laid out a new nine-hole course. More land to the north of the River Kym was acquired in the 1960s and the course extended to 18 holes by 1970. This means that the river, which offers many challenging hazards, divides the course.

The current layout is an excellent example of the parkland style and combines two par five's, five par three's and eleven par four holes. It could be argued that it is a little short by current standards at 6,027 yards, par 69, but it is still a challenge to all golfers regardless of their ability. Tee shots must be accurate and thoughtless use of the driver can result in considerable difficulty for the second shot. Water features strongly on the front nine but only wild play will find a water grave coming home. Perhaps the 7th is the signature hole, which requires an accurate tee shot across the river. In 1986, the club completed a new clubhouse with modern changing rooms, a large bar area and a 90-seater upstairs restaurant providing excellent views over the course.

Over the years the club has produced a host of county representatives but none have gone on to higher levels. More recently the junior section has produced quality golfers who have progressed to be successful professionals at other clubs. St Neots Golf Club can be found close to the A1 trunk road, on the B1048 and only a minute's drive from the town centre.

Sec/Manager:	Peter Farrow
Professional:	Graham Bithrey
Directions:	North west of St Neots. From St Neots centre take the B1048 (Staughton Highway) Cross Hall Road. The entrance is on the right hand side 400 yds after Milton Avenue.
Date Founded:	1890
Type of Course:	Parkland
No of Holes:	18
Length:	6033 yds (5568 mtrs)
Par:	69
SSS:	69
Green Fees:	Weekdays: £25.00
Visitors:	Welcome: Contact Club in advance. Unable to play at weekends.
Societies:	Welcome: Contact Club in advance by telephone.
Facilities:	Putting Green, Trolley Hire, Bar, Restaurant, Practice Ground

Accommodation, Food and Drink

Reference numbers below refer to detailed information provided in section 2

Accommodation

Abbotsley Golf Hotel, Eynesbury Hardwicke, St Neots, Cambridgeshire PE19 6XN

Tel: 01480 474000 Fax: 01480 471018

42 attractive modern bedrooms in a purpose-built golf hotel and country club. Golf course, fitness centre, squash, bar, restaurant. 628

The Leeds Arms, Eltisley, Huntingdon, Cambridgeshire PE19 4TG

Tel: 01480 880283

Built in the 18th century as a dwelling and public house, now a free house motel with bars, restaurant and single/twin bedrooms. 613

Halfpenny House, 2 Breach Road, Grafham, Nr Huntingdon, Cambridgeshire PE28 0BA

Tel: 01480 810733

An extended modern house offering pleasant, well-kept Bed & Breakfast accommodation in a peaceful village off the A1/A14.

The Stukeleys Country Hotel, Great Stukeley, Cambridgeshire PE17 5AL

Tel: 01480 456927

Eight en-suite bedrooms and an elegant restaurant in a beautifully preserved 16th-century former coaching inn. 612

The Black Bull, Godmanchester, Cambridgeshire PE29 2AQ

Tel: 01480 453310

An old coaching inn that now provides comfortable accommodation in four en-suite bedrooms. Attractive bar lounge; excellent value meals. 605

Food and Drink

Abbotsley Golf Hotel, Eynesbury Hardwicke, St Neots, Cambridgeshire PE19 6XN

Tel: 01480 474000 Fax: 01480 471018

42 attractive modern bedrooms in a purpose-built golf hotel and country club. Golf course, fitness centre, squash, bar, restaurant. 628

The Waggon & Horses, Eaton Socon, Cambridgeshire PE19 8EF

Tel: 01480 386373

Excellent home-cooked food in a characterful old coaching inn on the Great North Road. Varied menu, with additional lunchtime snacks. 624

The Royal Oak, Hail Weston, St Neots, Cambridgeshire PE19 5JW

Tel: 01480 472527

A beautiful thatched 17th-century pub in a pretty village, with low beams, an inglenook and a lovely garden. Good food served all day. 629

The Leeds Arms, Eltisley, Huntingdon, Cambridgeshire PE19 4TG

Tel: 01480 880283

Built in the 18th century as a dwelling and public house, now a free house motel with bars, restaurant and single/twin bedrooms. 613

Eight Bells, Abbotsley, Cambridgeshire PE19 6UL

Tel: 01767 677305

An 18th-century pub, with creepers and hanging baskets, in a pretty village of thatched cottages. Fine home-cooked food, good ales and wines. 615

The Stukeleys Country Hotel, Great Stukeley, Cambridgeshire PE17 5AL

Tel: 01480 456927

Eight en-suite bedrooms and an elegant restaurant in a beautifully preserved 16th-century former coaching inn. 612

The Black Bull, Godmanchester, Cambridgeshire PE29 2AQ

Tel: 01480 453310

An old coaching inn that now provides comfortable accommodation in four en-suite bedrooms. Attractive bar lounge; excellent value meals. 605

Spalding

Surfleet, Spalding, Lincolnshire PE11 4EA

Tel/Fax: 01775 680988

Sec/Manager:	Barrie Wayler
Professional:	John Spencer
Directions:	3½ miles north east of Spalding. From Spalding outskirts take the A16 (Boston). The entrance is on the right hand side after 2 miles, opposite the second turning into Surfleet.
Date Founded:	1907
Type of Course:	Parkland
No of Holes:	18
Length:	6492 yds (5992mtrs)
Par:	72
SSS:	71
Green Fees:	Weekdays: £20.00; Weekends/ Bank Holidays: £30.00
Visitors:	Welcome: Contact Club in advance
Societies:	Welcome: Contact Club in advance
Facilities:	Putting Green, Chipping Green, Trolley Hire, Bar, Restaurant, Driving Range, Practice Area

Accommodation, Food and Drink

Reference numbers below refer to detailed information provided in section 2

Accommodation

The Wishing Well Inn, Dyke, Near Bourne, Lincolnshire PE10 0AF

Tel: 01778 422970 Fax: 01778 394508

Quality en-suite accommodation and superb food in a charming country inn with a beer garden. Hosts a beer festival in August. 705

Cawthorpe Hall, Cawthorpe, Bourne, Lincolnshire PE10 0AB

Tel: 01778 423830 Fax: 01778 426620

Early 19th-century country house with three large, peaceful en-suite double bedrooms and a single. Lovely gardens full of roses. 707

Foreman's Bridge Caravan Park, Sutton Road, Sutton St James, Lincolnshire PE12 0HU

Tel/Fax: 01945 440346
web: www.foremans-bridge.co.uk

A pleasant riverside park for touring caravans and tents. Also static caravans for hire (Mar-Nov) and two holiday cottages (all year). B1390.

Food and Drink

The Wishing Well Inn, Dyke, Near Bourne, Lincolnshire PE10 0AF

Tel: 01778 422970 Fax: 01778 394508

Quality en-suite accommodation and superb food in a charming country inn with a beer garden. Hosts a beer festival in August. 705

The Drayman's Arms, 44 Little London, Spalding, Lincolnshire PE11 2UE

Tel: 01775 724320

A welcoming little roadside pub southwest of town, with a cosy lounge bar, real ales and generous helpings of home cooking.

The Old Ship Inn, Long Sutton, Lincolnshire PE12 9EE

Tel: 01406 362930

A traditional country inn with low beams, a cosy atmosphere and good home-cooked food. Excellent choice of real ales. 706

The Chequers at Gedney Dyke, Spalding, Lincolnshire PE12 0AJ

Tel/Fax: 01406 362666

A family-run village pub open every day for excellent food and drink. Bar snacks and full à la carte with lots of daily specials. 708

Ye Old Bridge Inn, Crowland, Peterborough, Lincolnshire PE6 0HJ

Tel: 01733 210567

A renovated 150-year-old ale house by the River Welland north of Crowland. Real ales and a good choice of food in the restaurant. 627

The Wheatsheaf, Fengate, Moulton Chapel, Lincolnshire PE12 0XL

Tel: 01406 380525

A delightful 200-year-old pub on the B1357 east of Spalding. Snug bar and 30-cover restaurant serving excellent-value meals. 703

Sutton Bridge

New Road, Sutton Bridge, Spalding, Lincolnshire PE12 9RQ

Tel: 01406 350323

Sec/Manager:	Norman Davis
Professional:	Peter Fields
Directions:	9 miles west of King's Lynn. From King's Lynn take the A17 (Spalding) to Sutton bridge. Turn right into Bridge Road, and after a quarter mile turn right into New Road. The entrance is on the right hand side.
Date Founded:	1914
Type of Course:	Parkland
No of Holes:	9
Length:	5822 yds (5374mtrs)
Par:	70
SSS:	69
Green Fees:	Weekdays: £18.00; Weekends/ Bank Holidays: not available
Visitors:	Welcome: Contact Club in advance, weekends not available.
Societies:	Welcome: Contact Club in advance by writing.
Facilities:	Putting Green, Chipping Green, Trolley Hire, Bar, Restaurant

Accommodation, Food and Drink

Reference numbers below refer to detailed information provided in section 2

Accommodation

Knights Hill Hotel, South Wootton, King's Lynn, Norfolk PE30 3HQ

Tel: 01553 675566 Fax: 01553 675568

A complex of 61 spacious, well-equipped bedrooms and apartments, restaurant, pub, health and leisure club, conference centre and 11 acres of grounds. 338

The Wheel Inn, Wisbech St Mary, Cambridgeshire PE14 4RH

Tel: 01945 410504

A beautifully kept 18th century pub with white-painted facade, cosy beamed bars and a lovely garden. Comfortable accommodation; good home cooking. 621

Common Right Barns, Wisbech St Mary, Cambridgeshire PE13 4SP

Tel/Fax: 01945 410424

Self-catering accommodation and a twin B&B room in renovated farm buildings situated in rural Fenland. Wheelchair friendly. Meals available by arrangement. 616

Foreman's Bridge Caravan Park, Sutton Road, Sutton St James, Lincolnshire PE12 0HU

Tel/Fax: 01945 440346
web: www.foremans-bridge.co.uk

A pleasant riverside park for touring caravans and tents. Also static caravans for hire (Mar-Nov) and two holiday cottages (all year).

Food and Drink

The Drayman's Arms, 44 Little London, Spalding, Lincolnshire PE11 2UE

Tel: 01775 724320

A welcoming little roadside pub southwest of town, with a cosy lounge bar, real ales and generous helpings of home cooking.

The Old Ship Inn, Long Sutton, Lincolnshire PE12 9EE

Tel: 01406 362930

A traditional country inn with low beams, a cosy atmosphere and good home-cooked food. Excellent choice of real ales. 706

The Chequers at Gedney Dyke, Spalding, Lincolnshire PE12 0AJ

Tel/Fax: 01406 362666

A family-run village pub open every day for excellent food and drink. Bar snacks and full à la carte with lots of daily specials. 708

Knights Hill Hotel, South Wootton, King's Lynn, Norfolk PE30 3HQ

Tel: 01553 675566 Fax: 01553 675568

A complex of 61 spacious, well-equipped bedrooms and apartments, restaurant, pub, health and leisure club, conference centre and 11 acres of grounds. 338

The Wheel Inn, Wisbech St Mary, Cambridgeshire PE14 4RH

Tel: 01945 410504

A beautifully kept 18th century pub with white-painted facade, cosy beamed bars and a lovely garden. Comfortable accommodation; good home cooking. 621

The Wheatsheaf, Fengate, Moulton Chapel, Lincolnshire PE12 0XL

Tel: 01406 380525

A delightful 200-year-old pub on the B1357 east of Spalding. Snug bar and 30-cover restaurant serving excellent-value meals. 703

Thorney Golf Centre

English Drove, Thorney, Peterborough, Cambridgeshire PE6 0TJ

Tel: 01733 270570 Fax: 01730 270842

Sec/Manager:	Jane Hind
Professional:	Mark Templeton
Directions:	7 miles north east of Peterborough. From the northern outskirts take the A47 to Thorney (Wisbech). At Thorney turn left on the B1040 (Crawland) and after ½ mile turn right into English Drove. The entrance is on the left hand side.
Date Founded:	1995
Visitors:	Welcome: Contact Club in advance. Unable to play certain times at weekends.
Societies:	Welcome: Contact Club in advance, by telephone.

Facilities:	Putting Green, Club Hire, Trolley Hire, Buggy Hire, Bar, Restaurant, Practice Area, Gym

Fen

Type of Course:	Parkland
No of Holes:	18
Length:	6400 yds (5907 mtrs)
Par:	70
SSS:	70
Green Fees:	Weekdays: £7.00; Weekends/ Bank Holidays: £9.00

Lakes

Type of Course:	Links
No of Holes:	9
Length:	6400 yds (5907 mtrs)
Par:	71
SSS:	71
Green Fees:	Weekdays: £11.50; Weekends/ Bank Holidays: £18.50

Accommodation, Food and Drink

Reference numbers below refer to detailed information provided in section 2

Accommodation

The Wheel Inn, Wisbech St Mary, Cambridgeshire PE14 4RH

Tel: 01945 410504

A beautifully kept 18th century pub with white-painted facade, cosy beamed bars and a lovely garden. Comfortable accommodation; good home cooking. 621

Common Right Barns, Wisbech St Mary, Cambridgeshire PE13 4SP

Tel/Fax: 01945 410424

Self-catering accommodation and a twin B&B room in renovated farm buildings situated in rural Fenland. Wheelchair friendly. Meals available by arrangement. 616

The White House, 318 Oundle Road, Peterborough, Cambridgeshire PE2 9QP

Tel: 01733 566650

Five recently decorated rooms, one en-suite, in a large white house set back from the A605 2 miles from the town centre.

Orton Hall Hotel, Orton Longueville, Peterborough, Cambridgeshire PE2 7DN

Tel: 01733 39111 Fax: 01733 371793

e-mail: martingoodliffe@ortonhall.co.uk

17th century manor house in 20 acres of parkland, with modern facilities in spacious, well-appointed bedrooms. Restaurant, traditional inn.

The Willows Motel, Elm Road, March, Cambridgeshire PE15 8PS

Tel: 01354 661292

Six spacious en-suite bedrooms in a B&B motel on the A141 five minutes north of March. No credit cards.

Food and Drink

The Wheel Inn, Wisbech St Mary, Cambridgeshire PE14 4RH

Tel: 01945 410504

A beautifully kept 18th century pub with white-painted facade, cosy beamed bars and a lovely garden. Comfortable accommodation; good home cooking. 621

The Windmill Tavern, Orton Waterville, Peterborough, Cambridgeshire

Tel: 01733 231554

18th-century pub in traditional style, with a garden and children's play area. Good food and wine; real ale. 617

The Cherry Tree, 9 Oundle Road, Woodston, Peterborough, Cambridgeshire PE2 9PB

Tel: 01733 703495

18th-century pub with a traditional ambience. Five real ales, extensive menus from snacks to full meals; live music Thursday-Saturday.

Ye Old Bridge Inn, Crowland, Peterborough, Lincolnshire PE6 0HJ

Tel: 01733 210567

A renovated 150-year-old ale house by the River Welland north of Crowland. Real ales and a good choice of food in the restaurant. 627

Orton Hall Hotel, Orton Longueville, Peterborough, Cambridgeshire PE2 7DN

Tel: 01733 39111 Fax: 01733 371793

e-mail: martingoodliffe@ortonhall.co.uk

17th century manor house in 20 acres of parkland, with modern facilities in spacious, well-appointed bedrooms. Restaurant, traditional inn.

Thorpe Wood

Nene Parkway, Peterborough, Cambridgeshire PE3 6SE

Tel: 01733 267701 Fax: 01733 332774

Sec/Manager:	Ray Palmer
Professional:	Roger Fittam
Directions:	2 miles west of Peterborough. From Peterborough centre take the A1179 to Longthorpe. At the roundabout joining the A1260 (Nene Parkway) go straight on into Thorpe Wood. The entrance is on the left hand side.
Date Founded:	1975
Type of Course:	Parkland
No of Holes:	18
Length:	7086 yds (6540 mtrs)
Par:	73
SSS:	74
Green Fees:	Weekdays: £10.70; Weekends/ Bank Holidays: £13.75
Visitors:	Welcome: Contact Club in advance by telephone.
Societies:	Welcome: Contact Club in advance by writing.

Facilities: Putting Green, Chipping Green, Club Hire, Trolley Hire, Bar, Restaurant

Accommodation, Food and Drink

Reference numbers below refer to detailed information provided in section 2

Accommodation

The Paper Mills Inn, Wansford-in-England, Cambridgeshire PE8 6JB

Tel: 01780 782328

Lunchtime snacks and waitress-served restaurant in a 150-year-old pub a minute from the A1. Beer garden. One letting bedroom. 618

Longueville Guest House, 411 Oundle Road, Orton Longueville, Peterborough, Cambridgeshire PE2 7DA

Tel/Fax: 01733 233442

Pleasant house with a big garden and five well-decorated en-suite bedrooms, one of family size. Good breakfasts. No smoking.

The White House, 318 Oundle Road, Peterborough, Cambridgeshire PE2 9QP

Tel: 01733 566650

Five recently decorated rooms, one en-suite, in a large white house set back from the A605 2 miles from the town centre.

The Old Smithy, 47 Peterborough Road, Castor, Cambridgeshire PE5 7AX

Tel/Fax: 01733 380186

Four en-suite bedrooms in a 300-year-old thatched cottage. Aga-cooked breakfast, dinner by arrangement. 3 miles from Peterborough.

Orton Hall Hotel, Orton Longueville, Peterborough, Cambridgeshire PE2 7DN

Tel: 01733 39111 Fax: 01733 371793

e-mail: martingoodliffe@ortonhall.co.uk

17th century manor house in 20 acres of parkland, with modern facilities in spacious, well-appointed bedrooms. Restaurant, traditional inn.

Food and Drink

The Paper Mills Inn, Wansford-in-England, Cambridgeshire PE8 6JB

Tel: 01780 782328

Lunchtime snacks and waitress-served restaurant in a 150-year-old pub a minute from the A1. Beer garden. One letting bedroom. 618

The Windmill Tavern, Orton Waterville, Peterborough, Cambridgeshire

Tel: 01733 231554

18th-century pub in traditional style, with a garden and children's play area. Good food and wine; real ale. 617

The Cherry Tree, 9 Oundle Road, Woodston, Peterborough, Cambridgeshire PE2 9PB

Tel: 01733 703495

18th-century pub with a traditional ambience. Five real ales, extensive menus from snacks to full meals; live music Thursday-Saturday.

Ye Old Bridge Inn, Crowland, Peterborough, Lincolnshire PE6 0HJ

Tel: 01733 210567

A renovated 150-year-old ale house by the River Welland north of Crowland. Real ales and a good choice of food in the restaurant. 627

Orton Hall Hotel, Orton Longueville, Peterborough, Cambridgeshire PE2 7DN

Tel: 01733 39111 Fax: 01733 371793

e-mail: martingoodliffe@ortonhall.co.uk

17th century manor house in 20 acres of parkland, with modern facilities in spacious, well-appointed bedrooms. Restaurant, traditional inn.

Toft Hotel

Toft, nr Bourne, Lincolnshire PE10 0XX

Tel: 01778 590616

Sec/Manager: Nick Frame

Professional: Mark Jackson

Directions: 2½ miles south of Bourne. From Bourne centre take the A6121 (Stamford). After 2 miles towards Toft the entrance is on the left hand side.

Date Founded: 1988

Type of Course: Parkland

No of Holes: 18

Length: 6486 yds (5987mtrs)

Par: 72

SSS: 71

Green Fees: Weekdays: £20.00 per round, £25.00 per day; Weekends/ Bank Holidays: £25.00 per round, £30.00 per day

Visitors: Welcome: Contact Club by telephone in advance.

Societies: Welcome: Contact Club by telephone in advance

Facilities: Putting Green, Chipping Green, Practice Ground, Club Hire, Trolley Hire, Buggy Hire, Bar, Restaurant

Accommodation, Food and Drink

Reference numbers below refer to detailed information provided in section 2

Accommodation

The Crown Hotel, Stamford, Lincolnshire PE9 2AG

Tel: 01780 763136 Fax: 01780 756111

An 18-bedroom hotel (all rooms en-suite) built in 1909 and recently extensively renovated to a very high standard. Restaurant. Parking at rear. 702

The Crown Inn, Great Casterton, Stamford, Lincolnshire PE9 4AP

Tel: 01780 763362

A village pub of real charm and character, with abundant hospitality, an excellent menu of home-cooked food and fine wines. One letting bedroom. 701

The George of Stamford, Stamford, Lincolnshire PE9 2LB

Tel: 01780 750750 Fax: 01780 750701

Perhaps England's greatest coaching inn, rich in history and character. Top-quality accommodation in 47 rooms plus superb food and drink. 704

The Wishing Well Inn, Dyke, Near Bourne, Lincolnshire PE10 0AF

Tel: 01778 422970 Fax: 01778 394508

Quality en-suite accommodation and superb food in a charming country inn with a beer garden. Hosts a beer festival in August. 705

The Garden House Hotel, St Martin's, Stamford, Lincolnshire PE9 2LP

Tel: 01780 763359 Fax: 01780 763339

A charming 18th-century house transformed into a delightful hotel with single, double and family rooms. B&B or full board available.

Cawthorpe Hall, Cawthorpe, Bourne Lincolnshire PE10 0AB

Tel: 01778 423830 Fax: 01778 426620

Early 19th-century country house with three large, peaceful en-suite double bedrooms and a single. Lovely gardens full of roses. 707

Food and Drink

The Exeter Arms, Stamford Road, Easton-on-the-Hill, Stamford, Lincolnshire PE9 3NS

Tel: 01780 757503

A French chef produces a tempting range of dishes in a traditionally appointed pub 1 mile west of Stamford. Good wine list. Garden.

The Crown Hotel, Stamford, Lincolnshire PE9 2AG

Tel: 01780 763136 Fax: 01780 756111

An 18-bedroom hotel (all rooms en-suite) built in 1909 and recently extensively renovated to a very high standard. Restaurant. Parking at rear. 702

The Crown Inn, Great Casterton, Stamford, Lincolnshire PE9 4AP

Tel: 01780 763362

A village pub of real charm and character, with abundant hospitality, an excellent menu of home-cooked food and fine wines. One letting bedroom. 701

The George of Stamford, Stamford, Lincolnshire PE9 2LB

Tel: 01780 750750 Fax: 01780 750701

Perhaps England's greatest coaching inn, rich in history and character. Top-quality accommodation in 47 rooms plus superb food and drink. 704

The Wishing Well Inn, Dyke, Near Bourne, Lincolnshire PE10 0AF

Tel: 01778 422970 Fax: 01778 394508

Quality en-suite accommodation and superb food in a charming country inn with a beer garden. Hosts a beer festival in August. 705

The Drayman's Arms, 44 Little London, Spalding, Lincolnshire PE11 2UE

Tel: 01775 724320

A welcoming little roadside pub southwest of town, with a cosy lounge bar, real ales and generous helpings of home cooking.

Ye Old Bridge Inn, Crowland, Peterborough, Lincolnshire PE6 0HJ

Tel: 01733 210567

A renovated 150-year-old ale house by the River Welland north of Crowland. Real ales and a good choice of food in the restaurant. 627

Tydd St Giles

Kirkgate, Tydd St Giles, Wisbech, Cambridgeshire PE13 5NZ

Tel: 01945 871007 Fax: 01945 870566

Sec/Manager: Mandy Hurst

Professional: Martin Perkins

Directions:	4½ miles north west of Wisbech. From Wisbech centre take the A1101 (Long Sutton). Turn left after Four Gates into Swallow Lane (Tydd St Giles). Follow into Sandy Lane, turn left into Kirgate and the entrance is on the right hand side.
Date Founded:	1994
Type of Course:	Parkland
No of Holes:	18
Length:	6226 yds (5747 mtrs)
Par:	70
SSS:	Not available at time of going to press
Green Fees:	Weekdays: £8.50; Weekends/ Bank Holidays: £9.50
Visitors:	Welcome: Contact Club in advance by telephone.
Societies:	Welcome: Contact Club in advance by writing.
Facilities:	Putting Green, Chipping

Accommodation, Food and Drink

Reference numbers below refer to detailed information provided in section 2

Accommodation

Crosskeys Riverside Hotel, Hilgay, Downham Market, Norfolk PE38 0LD

Tel/Fax: 01366 387777

A small country hotel in a 17th-century building in grounds beside the River Wissey. Four en-suite bedrooms. Breakfast, cream teas. 348

Rose & Crown, Hilgay, Downham Market, Norfolk PE38 0LJ

Tel: 01366 385414

A traditional village pub offering real ales, snacks and meals, entertainments and a choice of accommodation. 339

The Wheel Inn, Wisbech St Mary, Cambridgeshire PE14 4RH

Tel: 01945 410504

A beautifully kept 18th century pub with white-painted facade, cosy beamed bars and a lovely garden. Comfortable accommodation; good home cooking. 621

Common Right Barns, Wisbech St Mary, Cambridgeshire PE13 4SP

Tel/Fax: 01945 410424

Self-catering accommodation and a twin B&B room in renovated farm buildings situated in rural Fenland. Wheelchair friendly. Meals available by arrangement. 616

King Harolds Head, Bumbles Green, Nazeing Common, Waltham Abbey, Essex EN9 2RY

Tel: 01992 893110 Fax: 01992 893412

A charming old free house on the Waltham Abbey-Harlow road. Friendly ambience, good company, exceptional food. 503

Foreman's Bridge Caravan Park, Sutton Road, Sutton St James, Lincolnshire PE12 0HU

Tel/Fax: 01945 440346

web: www.foremans-bridge.co.uk

A pleasant riverside park for touring caravans and tents. Also static caravans for hire (Mar-Nov) and two holiday cottages (all year). B1390.

Food and Drink

The Old Ship Inn, Long Sutton, Lincolnshire PE12 9EE

Tel: 01406 362930

A traditional country inn with low beams, a cosy atmosphere and good home-cooked food. Excellent choice of real ales. 706

Rose & Crown, Hilgay, Downham Market, Norfolk PE38 0LJ

Tel: 01366 385414

A traditional village pub offering real ales, snacks and meals, entertainments and a choice of accommodation. 339

The Wheel Inn, Wisbech St Mary, Cambridgeshire PE14 4RH

Tel: 01945 410504

A beautifully kept 18th century pub with white-painted facade, cosy beamed bars and a lovely garden. Comfortable accommodation; good home cooking. 621

King Harolds Head, Bumbles Green, Nazeing Common, Waltham Abbey, Essex EN9 2RY

Tel: 01992 893110 Fax: 01992 893412

A charming old free house on the Waltham Abbey-Harlow road. Friendly ambience, good company, exceptional food. 503

The Wheatsheaf, Fengate, Moulton Chapel, Lincolnshire PE12 0XL

Tel: 01406 380525

A delightful 200-year-old pub on the B1357 east of Spalding. Snug bar and 30-cover restaurant serving excellent-value meals. 703

Accommodation, Food and Drink

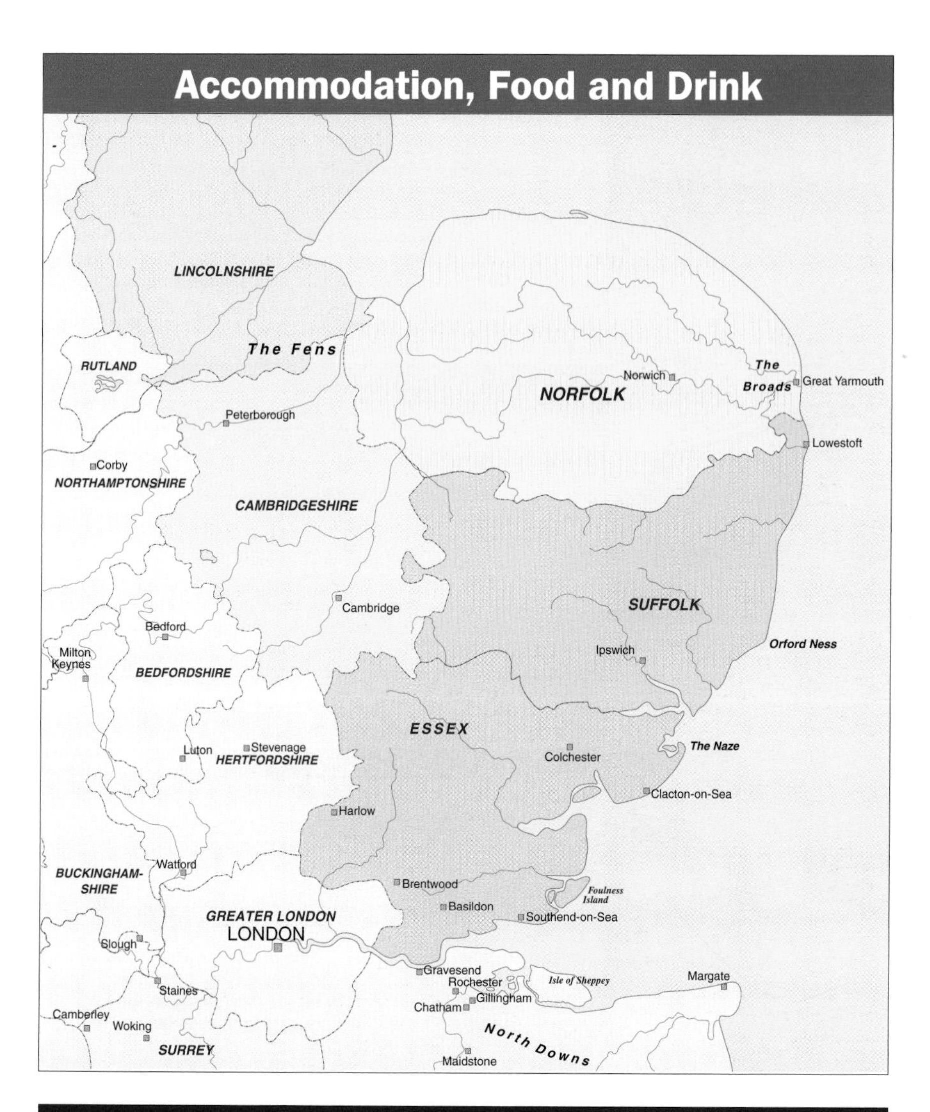

Contents - East Anglia

BARNHAM BROOM HOTEL COUNTRY CLUB 301

Hotel, Golf & Leisure Centre

52 en suite bedrooms, restaurant, golf courses, pool, squash, tennis, gym, Peter Ballinghall golf school
Credit Cards: All the major cards

Barnham Broom, Norwich, Norfolk NR9 4DD Tel: 01603 759393
Fax: 01603 758224 e-mail: enquiry@barnhambroomhotel.co.uk
website: www.barnham-broom.co.uk

In a peaceful valley of the River Yare, Barnham Broom is an outstanding combination of country hotel, golf club, leisure centre and conference centre. The 52 en suite bedrooms, comfortably and comprehensively equipped standard, superior, premier, four-poster and suites. A choice of dining options are available in either Flints restaurant or the Sports Bar & Café is a popular place to unwind. The hotel's 250 acres include two golf courses and a leisure centre with swimming pool, tennis, squash and gym. Signposted from the A47 and all trunk routes. The Peter Ballinghall golf school is on site.

Local Golf Courses: Barnham Broom, Norfolk G&CC, Bawburgh

THE PICKWICK 302

Pub and Restaurant

Pub and Restaurant; snack and à la carte menus
Credit Cards: Access, Amex, Mastercard, Visa

41 Earlham Road, Norwich, Norfolk NR2 3AD
Tel: 01603 628155

A Georgian building just a short drive from the city centre, with plenty of parking space and a cheerful welcome from owners Richie and Corrina Rzepka-O'Connor. It operates both as a public house, with the usual range of drinks in the bar, and as a restaurant (the Dingley Dell) whose wide-ranging menu is supplemented by daily specials and the roasts of the day. Andy Johnson's repertoire includes classics such as paté, lasagne, burgers, fish & chips and steak & kidney pie made with the week's guest ale. For smaller appetites the snack menu proposes sandwiches, filled French sticks and jacket potatoes. Self-catering accommodation is available nearby.

Local Golf Courses: Royal Norwich, Costessey Park, Wensum Valley

GOLDEN BEACH HOLIDAY CENTRE 303

Holiday Centre

Static caravans for rental & space for touring vans

Credit Cards: None

Beach Road, Sea Palling, Norfolk NR12 0AL
Tel: 01692 598269

Nestling beneath a bank of dunes back from the beach, the Golden Beach Holiday Centre is the perfect spot for a family holiday. Ten six-berth static caravan homes are available for rental, and part of the site has been reserved for visitors touring with their own caravans. Shower rooms, toilets and mains electricity are laid on and all the main site's amenities are on hand, from a well-stocked shop and a launderette to a children's play area and a licensed Family Club Lounge. The beach and the sea are right on the doorstep, and it's an easy drive to Great Yarmouth, Cromer, Norwich and the Norfolk Broads.

Local Golf Courses: Royal Cromer, Great Yarmouth, Sprowston Park

THE WOOLPACK INN 304

Pub, Food & Accommodation

City-centre pub with six B&B rooms; home cooking
Credit Cards: Access, Amex, Mastercard, Visa

Muspole Street, Norwich, Norfolk NR1 3JD
Tel: 01603 611139 Fax: 01603 616993
website: www.norfolk-uk.com/woolpack

The Woolpack is a traditional 18th century inn close to Norwich city centre. Landlord Graham Stamp and his staff always have a hearty welcome and a generous supply of hospitality at the ready. The beers are well kept, and the food, all prepared and cooked on the premises, caters for appetites small and large: chips and dips or a baguette sandwich for a quick snack, shepherd's pie, curry or a full English breakfast for something substantial. Bed & Breakfast accommodation comprises six rooms, some suitable for family occupation. Private parking - a boon in this busy city.

Local Golf Courses: Eaton, Bawburgh, Costessey Park

Hotel with Bar and Restaurant

9 en suite bedrooms, tv and phone; bar and restaurant menus
Credit Cards: Access, Amex, Mastercard, Visa

LYDNEY HOUSE HOTEL 305

Norwich Road, Swaffham, Norfolk PE37 7QS
Tel: 01760 723355 Fax: 01760 721410
website: www.lydney-house.demon.co.uk

David and Sarah Impey have spent all their working lives in the hotel business and for the past five years have owned and run Lydney House Hotel. A redbrick Georgian house in a quiet setting just east of the centre of Swaffham, it offers comfortably appointed accommodation in 9 en suite bedrooms, all with tv and telephone. Two rooms have four-poster beds. The bar and restaurant, both open to non-residents, propose a wide range of snacks and full meals. Guests can arrange to be picked up from Downham Market station on the main line from Liverpool Street to King's Lynn.

Local Golf Courses: Swaffham, Middleton Hall, Richmond Park

Pub with Food

Village inn with superb restaurant

Credit Cards: Access, Mastercard, Visa

THE COCK 306

Watton Road, Barford, Norwich, Norfolk NR9 4AS
Tel: 01603 757646

A 200-year-old country inn on the B1108 west of Norwich is gaining a new circle of admirers as an acclaimed restaurant. Owner Peter Turner and his chef Mark, winner of several national awards before coming here, have put together an outstanding menu that makes superb use of the very best and freshest local produce. Such is the success of the enterprise that an extension to the restaurant is planned for 2001. Booking is recommended, especially for the waitress-served evening session. The food is not the only attraction: Peter chooses the wines on trips to France, and the pub has its own brewery on site - the Blue Moon.

Local Golf Courses: Barnham Broom, Bawburgh, Costessey Park

Hotel, Golf & Country Club

39 en suite bedrooms, restaurant, golf courses, leisure club, fishing

Credit Cards: All the major cards

WENSUM VALLEY HOTEL, GOLF & COUNTRY CLUB 307

Beech Avenue, Taverham, Norwich, Norfolk NR8 6HP
Tel: 01603 261012 Fax: 01603 261664
e-mail: enqs@wensumvalley.co.uk
website: www.wensumvalley.co.uk

This family run hotel and leisure complex prides itself on good food and friendly service. Situated in 240 acres of beautiful Norfolk countryside near the River Wensum and only 5 miles north of Norwich, the hotel has 39 superbly equipped en suite bedrooms, many with exceptional views overlooking the Wensum Valley. The hotel serves excellent food in its a la carte restaurant, together with bar snacks and daily specials. Leisure facilities include two golf courses, swimming pool, gym and fishing on the River Wensum

Local Golf Courses: Wensum Valley, Costessey Park, Royal Norwich

Guest House with bar

Seven en suite bedrooms with tv; breakfast; bar; garden

Credit Cards: None

THE BAY LEAF GUEST HOUSE 308

10 Saint Peters Road, Sheringham, Norfolk NR26 8QY
Tel: 01263 823779 Fax: 01263 820041

The Bay Leaf is a charming Victorian licensed guest house close to all the amenities and five minutes from Sheringham Golf Club. There are seven letting bedrooms, two on the ground floor, all en suite, with tv. The bar is well stocked with wines, and an excellent English or Continental breakfast can be enjoyed in an attractive dining room overlooking the sheltered patio and garden. Golfers are welcome and are offered a discount at Cromer Golf Club. Discount also available at many local restaurants and inns. There's plenty to do and see in Sheringham, including the North Norfolk Steam Railway.

Local Golf Courses: Sheringham, Royal Cromer, Royal West Norfolk

Norfolk

Pub, Food & Accommodation

Country pub with 5 bedrooms (tv; phone); home-cooked food
Credit Cards: Access, Diners, Mastercard, Visa

THE VICTORIA INN 309

Church Road, Deopham, Wymondham, Norfolk NR18 9DX
Tel: 01953 850783 Fax: 01953 851733
website: www.the-victoria-inn.co.uk

John and Jean Heeson have put their stamp firmly on this friendly country inn, making it one of the best and most popular hostelries for miles around. The white-painted free house enjoys a peaceful country setting three miles west of Wymondham, and the bars have a cosy, traditional look. John, a keen golfer, designed and built the accommodation, which comprises five attractive en suite rooms. Jean looks after the cooking, preparing a good selection of dishes using fresh local produce. Booking is advisable, especially at the weekend. Real ales, beer garden.

Local Golf Courses: Barnham Broom, Richmond Park, Norfolk G&CC

Hotel with Restaurant

27 en suite bedrooms; à la carte restaurant

Credit Cards: All the major cards

THE GEORGIAN HOUSE HOTEL 310

32-34 Unthank Road, Norwich, Norfolk NR2 2RB
Tel: 01603 615655 Fax: 01603 765689
website: www.georgian-hotel.co.uk

Equally well placed for business or leisure visitors, the Goodwins family hotel stands opposite the Roman Catholic cathedral a short walk from the city centre. Two turn of the century merchant houses were linked to form a hotel with space for 27 comfortable bedrooms - all comprehensively equipped, a restaurant, a lounge and a bar. The non-smoking bedrooms are comprehensively equipped, with en suite bath/shower room, tv, telephone, radio-alarm and hairdryer. Goodwins Restaurant offers a choice of à la carte or table d'hote menus and the bar includes an impressive selection of imported bottled beers. Large car park.

Local Golf Courses: Royal Norwich, Eaton, De Vere Dunston Hall

Pub with Food

Town pub serving good-value food

Credit Cards: None

ROSE VALLEY TAVERN 311

111 Unthank Road, Norwich, Norfolk NR2 2PE
Tel: 01603 626068

Landlord Mike Healey and his zany bar staff create a permanent party atmosphere at this most welcoming of pubs, which stands only five minutes from the city centre and all its amenities. Beyond the door and the wide front windows young and young-at-heart locals gather to enjoy a drink and a chat or to settle down to a snack or a full meal. Value for money is paramount on a menu that includes most of the pub classics, from sandwiches, jacket potatoes and deep-fried mushrooms to lasagne (meat or vegetarian), omelettes, scampi, steaks and a mighty mixed grill. Garden.

Local Golf Courses: Costessey Park, Bawburgh, De Vere Dunston Hall

Hotel with Restaurant

36 en suite rooms; restaurant and bar menus; leisure and sports facilities
Credit Cards: All the major cards

WENSUM COUNTRY HOTEL 312

Fakenham Road, Great Witchingham, Norwich, Norfolk NR9 5QP
Tel: 01603 872288 Fax: 01603 872355
website: www.wensum-country-hotel.co.uk

Comfort, service, fine food and good leisure facilities in a handsome hotel in mock-Tudor style, set in 18 acres of gardens and woodland on the A1067 Norwich-Fakenham road. The 36 well-equipped en suite bedrooms include family rooms and a four-poster room. In the restaurant and Garden Room a good range of dishes both traditional and continental caters for all tastes, and a less formal choice of bar meals is also available. The hotel has several conference and function rooms, a fishing lake, heated pool, tennis courts, squash courts and gymnasium.

Local Golf Courses: Weston Park, Wensum Valley, Royal Norwich

Inn with Accommodation

14 en suite rooms; bar and restaurant menus
Credit Cards: Access, Mastercard, Visa

THE LIFEBOAT INN 313

Ship Lane, Thornham, Nr Hunstanton, Norfolk PE36 6LT
Tel: 01485 512236 Fax: 01485 512323
e-mail: reception@lifeboatinn.co.uk

On the A149 between Hunstanton and Brancaster, The Lifeboat Inn has been a welcome sight for weary travellers for centuries. The original character of this 16th century ale house has been sympathetically restored and modernized. All 14 bedrooms are en suite and most have sea views. The Restaurant, awarded an AA Rosette offers a splendid compromise of innovative and traditional dishes using local produce. Alternatively choose from the extensive bar menu and sit by a roaring fire in the 'Smugglers Bar'. Local attractions - other than golf courses - include several bird and nature reserves, Sandringham House and Holkham Hall.

Local Golf Courses: Hunstanton, Royal West Norfolk, King's Lynn

Country House Hotel

En suite bedrooms; B&B or half-board

Credit Cards: All the major cards

THE NORFOLK MEAD HOTEL 314

Coltishall, Norfolk NR12 7DN
Tel: 01603 737531 e-mail: info@norfolkmead.co.uk
Fax: 01603 737521 website: www.norfolkmead.co.uk

A family run elegant Georgian country house, set in 12 tranquil riverside acres, six miles north of Norwich.Accomodation is offered in one of 9 delightfully individual en-suite rooms.Dinner, with local produce being prepared by the excellent chefs, can be complimented by the selection of fine wines.

Log fires, beauty treatments and attentive, friendly staff will make your stay an enjoyable one.

Johansen's recommended. AA Red Rosette. Two Star Silver Award

Local Golf Courses: Royal Cromer, Royal Norwich, Sprowston Park

Guest House

Eight bedrooms, most en suite, with tv and beverage tray

Credit Cards: None

HIGHFIELDS GUESTHOUSE - AA 4 DIAMONDS 315

5 Montague Road, Sheringham, Norfolk NR26 8LN
Tel: 01263 825524

Gill Caldwell runs the best B&B guesthouse in Sheringham, peacefully located in a quiet road within sight of Sheringham Golf Course. Her non-smoking house has eight comfortable, well-furnished bedrooms, most en suite, with tv, fresh flowers and toiletries. There's a comfortable lounge and dining area, where a choice of excellent breakfasts starts the day.

Golfers can enjoy special rates out of season (October-May). The house is within easy reach of the sea, the shops and all the main amenities of Sheringham, which is itself an ideal base from which to tour this lovely part of the world.

Local Golf Courses: Sheringham, Royal Cromer, Royal West Norfolk

Hotel with Restaurant

14 en suite rooms with tv and telephone; restaurant; riverside setting
Credit Cards: All the major cards

BUXTON MILL HOTEL 316

Mill Street, Buxton, Norfolk NR10 5JF
Tel: 01603 278194 Fax: 01603 279332

In the heart of the Norfolk Broads yet only 15 minutes from the centre of Norwich, family-run Buxton Mill is an ideal holiday base. The 250-year-old mill has been converted into a very stylish and comfortable hotel whose 14 bedrooms all have en suite bath and shower, tv, telephone and a great view. The candlelit restaurant is open for lunch, afternoon tea and dinner, and its main menu features fish caught off the Norfolk coast and game from neighbouring estates. In the bar, guests can relax over a pint of real ale or choose something from the extensive wine list.

Local Golf Courses: Royal Norwich, Sprowston Park, Wensum Valley

THE NAGS HEAD 317

Market Street, East Harling, Norfolk NR16 2AD
Tel: 01953 718140

In a pretty village on the B1111 (leave the A11 south of Attleborough), the Nags Head is a long, low and very attractive building dating back to the 18th century. The traditional look of the frontage is maintained by beams and log fires in the bar, where a genuinely friendly welcome awaits visitors. The food served here is among the very best for miles around, whether it's a simple bar snack or a dish of seasonal game. Glynis does the cooking, and her son Jim helps run the bar. The landlord, James Clark, is a keen golfer and the pub has its own golfing society that meets monthly. James plans to add Bed & Breakfast accommodation in 2002.

Local Golf Courses: Thetford, Diss, Richmond Park

Pub with Food

Village pub serving superior snacks and full meals
Credit Cards: Access, Mastercard, Visa

THE ANDEL LODGE HOTEL & RESTAURANT 318

48 Lynn Road, Tottenhill, King's Lynn, Norfolk PE33 0RH
Tel: 01553 810256 Fax: 01553 811429
e-mail:reception@andellodge.co.uk website: www.andellodge.co.ik

The Andel Lodge, built as a vicarage 300 years ago, became a hotel in the 1950s, and now, after extensive refurbishment, combines modern amenities with old-world charm. Derek and Anne Hurrell, here since 1997, offer comfortable accommodation in nine tastefully decorated non-smoking bedrooms with en suite facilities, tv, telephone and hairdryer. Three ground-floor rooms in the annexe are wheelchair accessible, as are the lounge-bar and the dining room, where an extensive menu is available lunchtime and evening, with an additional 'lite bite' at lunchtime.

Local Golf Courses: King's Lynn, Middleton Hall, Swaffham

Hotel and Restaurant

Nine en suite rooms with tv, telephone; lounge-bar and restaurant
Credit Cards: All the major cards

THE JOHN H. STRACEY 319

West End, Briston, Melton Constable, Norfolk NR24 2JA
Tel: 01263 860891 e-mail: thejohnhstracey@btinternet.uk
website: www.thejohnhstracey

Dating back to the 1500s, Hilary and Ray Fox's grand old freehouse and restaurant brings regular customers from many miles around to enjoy the fine food, the real ales and the great atmosphere. On the edge of the village on the B1354, the pub, winner of many Les Routiers awards, serves a superb range of food, from light snacks to all-time favourites like steaks, steak and ale pie, lasagne and fresh cod, not forgetting the super Sunday roast. Overnight accommodation is available in three bedrooms, one en suite, with more nearby B&B in the village.

Local Golf Courses: Sheringham, Royal Cromer, Royal West Norfolk

Pub, Food & Accommodation

Freehouse with bar snack and full restaurant menus; three B&B rooms
Credit Cards: All the major cards

THE OLD RECTORY HOTEL 320

North Walsham Road, Crostwick, Norwich, Norfolk NR12 7BG
Tel: 01603 738513 e-mail: info@therectoryhotel.fsnet.co.uk
Fax: 01603 738712 website: www.oldrectorycrostwick.com

Old-world charm and modern amenities blend happily at this charming hotel on the B1150 four miles north of Norwich. The original rectory dates back to the mid-18th century, but Dianne and Colin Solomon have added 13 en suite bedrooms with tv, telephone, minibar, hairdryer and trouser press. One room is a luxurious four-poster honeymoon suite. Breakfast and evening meals are served in the conservatory or non-smoking dining room, and guests can take coffee in the cosy lounge. The large gardens include a heated outdoor pool and a play area for children.

Local Golf Courses: Royal Norwich, Sprowston Park, Wensum Valley

Country Hotel and Restaurant

13 luxuriously appointed bedrooms; two restaurants

Credit Cards: All the major cards

Bed & Breakfast

39 en suite rooms with tv; free use of nearby swimming pool

Credit Cards: All the major cards

MARINE LODGE 321

19-20 Euston Road, Great Yarmouth, Norfolk NR30 1DY
Tel: 01493 331120 Fax: 01493 332040
website: www.marinelodge@burlington-hotel.co.uk

A 100-year-old building just 50 yards from the seafront provides bright, up-to-date Bed & Breakfast accommodation in 39 well-appointed bedrooms. All the rooms are en suite, with tv. An excellent breakfast is served in the dining room from 8 till 11, and the hotel has a relaxing bar-lounge. There's ample parking on site, and guests have free use of the swimming pool at the nearby sister hotel the Palm Court. A 20% discount is offered on evening meals at the Burlington, also in the same family ownership.

Local Golf Courses: Great Yarmouth, Gorleston, Rookery Park

Country House Hotel

17 en suite bedrooms with tv and telephone; à la carte restaurant
Credit Cards: Access, Mastercard, Visa

THE DALES COUNTRY HOUSE HOTEL 322

Lodge Hill, Upper Sheringham, Norfolk NR26 8TJ
Tel: 01263 824555 Fax: 01263 822647

Set in splendid parkland and woodland designed by Humphrey Repton, the Grade ll listed Dales Country House Hotel stands on the edge of the village off the A149, equidistant from Cromer and Holt. The house is as magnificent as the surroundings, and recent refurbishment has retained and enhanced many original features, including a marvellous oak staircase. All 17 bedrooms are en suite, with tv and telephone, and are furnished with solid oak handcrafted pieces. One of the deluxe four-poster rooms has a whirlpool bath and private balcony. Upchers Restaurant offers imaginative menus based mainly on prime local produce.

Local Golf Courses: Sheringham, Royal Cromer, Wensum Valley

Pub with Food

Village Pub with food and excellent real ales
Credit Cards: Access, Mastercard, Visa, Debit cards

THE WHITE HORSE 323

5 Norwich Road, Chedgrave, Nr Norwich, Norfolk NR14 6ND
Tel/Fax: 01508 520250
website: thewhitehorsepub.co.uk

Gordon and Lesley Ford, with 20 years experience in the licensed trade, have recently taken over the running of the White Horse, a 19th century pub in a village off the A146 southeast of Norwich. Wooden floorboards, panelled walls and open fires give a traditional look to the bar, where food and drink are both taken very seriously. Steaks are a speciality on the menu of home-cooked dishes, and the selection of well-kept ales has earned the pub a Cask Marque Award for the year 2000. The beer festival which the pub holds every August is always a popular event.

Local Golf Courses: Bungay, Caldecott Hall, De Vere

Hotel with Restaurant

23 en suite bedrooms with tv and phone; restaurant
Credit Cards: Access, Mastercard, Visa

VIRGINIA COURT HOTEL 324

Cliff Avenue, Cromer, Norfolk NR27 0AN
Tel: 01263 512398 Fax: 01263 515529
website: www.virginiacourthotel.com.uk

Built in 1899 as a summer residence for the soon-to-be King Edward Vll, this is now a friendly, relaxing hotel with 23 delightful, spacious en suite bedrooms. Two of the rooms are of family size, and all have tv and telephone. The hotel has a bar, a large, comfortable lounge and a restaurant whose dinner menu is typified by garlic mussels, lamb's liver with onion gravy and fresh Cromer crab salad. The location, in a quiet tree-lined avenue, is two minutes from the town centre and the sea. Special autumn/winter breaks for golfers.

Local Golf Courses: Sheringham, Royal Cromer, Weston Park

THE BLUE BOAR 325

Pub, Restaurant & Rooms

Five en suite bedrooms with tv and phone; long menu
Credit Cards: Access, Mastercard, Visa

259 Wroxham Road, Sprowston, Norwich, Norfolk NR7 8RL
Tel: 01603 426802

Superb overnight accommodation has recently been added to great-value food at David and Claudine Turnbull's welcoming pub-restaurant on the Wroxham road north on Norwich. The accommodation comprises five splendid, spacious, no-smoking bedrooms - two doubles and three twins - all en suite, with tv, telephone and minibar. Good-quality food is prepared to order and served by friendly staff in the restaurant, where the menu runs from Stilton mushrooms and devilled whitebait to salads, burgers, steaks and chicken dishes, with Sunday roast. Locals play pool in the convivial bar.

Local Golf Courses: Sprowston Park, Royal Norwich, Costessey Park

THE SHANNOCKS HOTEL & RESTAURANT 326

Hotel with Restaurant

12 en suite rooms; à la carte restaurant
Credit Cards: Access, Mastercard, Visa

The Sea Front, Sheringham, Norfolk NR26 8JP
Tel: 01263 820368 e-mail: info@shannocks-hotel.co.uk
website: www.shannocks-hotel.co.uk

Sheringham is often described as 'The Jewel of the Norfolk Coast', so with its ideal seafront location The Shannocks Hotel & Restaurant could be called a jewel within a jewel. Owned and run by Pedro and Yvonne Morgan, the Victorian landmark has been carefully modernised, and the bedroom tally of six (all en suite) will become 12 shortly before we publish. All the rooms have tv and most enjoy sea views. In the restaurant, an à la carte menu offers a wide variety of dishes, with pasta, chargrills and fish among the specialities. Carvery, too.

Local Golf Courses: Sheringham, Royal Cromer, Weston Park

PEBBLES COUNTRY INN 327

Pub with food

Village pub serving good food and real ales; accommodation soon
Credit Cards: None

Whimpwell, Happisburgh, Norfolk NR12 0QD
Tel: 01622 651183

Avril Smith and her son Gregory, with many years' experience in top hotels and restaurants, have bought a delightful brick-built village pub and introduced a refreshing new possibility for eating out in this part of the world. Standing on the B1159 coast road south of Happisburgh (call it 'Hazeborough'), the pub does an excellent line in traditional English fare, tempting locals and visitors alike with classic dishes such as liver & bacon, steak & kidney pie and the popular Sunday roast. To accompany the food there's an excellent wine list and a good selection of ales. From spring 2001 two rooms will be available for Bed & Breakfast accommodation.

Local Golf Courses: Royal Cromer, Great Yarmouth, Sprowston Park

KINGSLEY HOUSE HOTEL 328

Town House Hotel

Seven en suite bedrooms with tv; B&B or B&B and dinner

Credit Cards: None

68 King Street, Great Yarmouth, Norfolk NR30 2PP
Tel/Fax: 01493 850948

Resident proprietors Alison and Brian Savoury offer comfort, hospitality and courtesy in their private house hotel, which lies next to the old town wall near the town centre and is only 300 yards from the seafront. Seven en suite bedrooms, from singles to family rooms, provide a restful overnight stay, and days get off to the best of starts with a good choice for breakfast. The hotel lounge overlooks a colourful garden. Guests have the option of either Bed & Breakfast or a tariff that includes a three-course evening meal served at 5.30 in the dining room. Unrestricted free street parking.

Local Golf Courses: Gorleston, Great Yarmouth & Caister, Rookery Park

Country Pub

Country Pub with all-day menu

Credit Cards: Access, Mastercard, Visa

THE RED LION INN 329

77 Church Street, Coltishall, Norfolk NR12 7DW
Tel: 01603 737402 e-mail: lamby-redlion@supanet.com
website: www.redlioncoltishall.com

Standing in the B1354 road to Wroxham Broad, the Red Lion Inn is the oldest pub in Coltishall, dating back some 300 years. Melanie Bird and her staff create a friendly, relaxed atmosphere, and the beamed bars are very snug and cosy. In warm weather the beer garden comes into its own. Rain or shine, seven days a week, visitors can be sure of a warm welcome and something good to eat and drink. One of the real ales is brewed specially for the pub and goes down particularly well with a good choice of home-cooked fare, from sandwiches to steaks and fish fresh from Lowestoft.

Local Golf Courses: Great Yarmouth, Royal Cromer, Sprowston Park

Pub, Food & Accommodation

Village pub with restaurant and 3 bedrooms
Credit Cards: Access, Mastercard, Visa

THE LONGHAM WHITE HORSE 330

Wendling Road, Longham, Dereham, Norfolk NR19 2RD
Tel: 01362 687464

A short drive northwest from Dereham brings the motorist to the Longham White Horse, which stands by the lovely village green in Longham. The garden affords pleasant views over the fields, while inside all is warm and cosy. In the pretty 40-cover restaurant the menu, supplemented by daily specials, provides a good choice and excellent value for money. Local brews are among the real ales on offer, and there are good house wines and a collection of malts. The scope of the pub has recently been widened to include overnight accommodation in three comfortable bedrooms on the first floor.

Local Golf Courses: Swaffham, Norfolk G&CC, Richmond Park

Hotel

Eight en suite bedrooms with tv; B&B and evening meal
Credit Cards: Access, Mastercard, Visa

THE SHIP HOTEL 331

71 Avondale Road, Gorleston-on-Sea, Norfolk NR31 6DJ
Tel/Fax: 01493 662746 e-mail: shipgraham@aol.com
website: www.shiphotelnorfolk.co.uk

Resident proprietors Hugh and Bunty Graham run a relaxing hotel in a fine period house almost on the seafront. Recently refurbished, the hotel has eight letting bedrooms, all en suite, with tv and tea-coffee trays; several rooms enjoy sea views, and two have four-poster beds. The bar is a perfect spot to unwind, and in the adjoining dining room hearty breakfasts and delicious three-course dinners are served. No smoking in the bedrooms or dining room. Golfers are very welcome (Hugh is a keen player) and spring/autumn breaks are available.

Local Golf Courses: Gorleston, Great Yarmouth & Caister, Rookery Park

Inn with Restaurant

Inn with snack and full menus; garden
Credit Cards: Access, Mastercard, Visa

THE BLACK HORSE 332

50 Earlham Road, Norwich, Norfolk NR2 3DE
Tel: 01603 624682 Fax: 01603 617893

Lisa and Kevin Breslin and their staff welcome visitors to the Black Horse, an 18th century brick-built hostelry a short drive from the city centre. Home-cooked food is a major attraction, and the menus offer plenty of variety, from classics like ham, eggs and chips or deep-fried scampi to oriental-style swordfish steak or liver and bacon dumplings with lentils. Sunday brings a choice of roasts and an excellent steak & kidney pie, and on Saturday a morning fry-up starts the day. Pop quiz first Sunday of every month. The inn has a secluded garden and ample car park.

Local Golf Courses: Royal Norwich, Costessey Park, Eaton, Bawburgh

Pub with Food

Village pub serving food lunchtime and evening

Credit Cards: None

THE VICTORIA INN 333

Hockering, Nr Norwich, Norfolk NR20 3HL
Tel: 01603 880507

Graham and Brandie Carter's handsome pub stands in a pretty village on the A47. Built in 1930, it is very well situated for golfers, with two courses within five minutes' drive. Home-cooked food is served lunchtime and evening in the cosy 24-cover eating area of the bar, grills and pub classics such as gammon and egg are always popular orders, but there's plenty of other choice, including Indian dishes and seasonal specials. Excellent beers and a good selection of wines complement the food. Tables and chairs are set out in the beer garden at the back.

Local Golf Courses: Barnham Broom, Weston Park, Wensum Valley

Bed & Breakfast

Six en suite bedrooms; tv lounge

Credit Cards: None

THE WHITE HOUSE 334

44 Hunstanton Road, Dersingham, King's Lynn, Norfolk PE31 6HQ
Tel: 01485 541895 Fax: 01485 544880

Six miles north of King's Lynn, this is a handsome detached house with ample parking. The owner is Valerie Brundle, and the motor racing memorabilia reveal the family connection with the famous Martin (Valerie is his stepmother). Bed & Breakfast accommodation comprises six en suite bedrooms with tea-makers; guests have the use of a tv lounge. Small golf parties are welcome by arrangement, with an evening meal option, and the house has battery-charging facilities for electric golf buggies. The chef prepares first-rate breakfasts to start the day. No smoking.

Local Golf Courses: Hunstanton, King's Lynn, Royal West Norfolk

Hotel with Restaurant

Six rooms, five en suite, with tv; bar and restaurant

Credit Cards: Access, Amex, Visa

THE CROWN HOTEL 335

25 High Street, Watton, Norfolk IP25 6AB
Tel: 01953 882375 Fax: 01953 884120

A handsome old coaching inn on the main street of Watton, which lies on the A1075 between Thetford and Dereham. Recently refurbished by the Edwards family, who have been here six years, it serves as a popular local, with pleasant, spacious bars, as a restaurant and as a centrally-placed base for tourists or visitors enjoying a golfing break. Overnight accommodation comprises six rooms, five of them with en suite facilities, all with tv and tea-making kit. More rooms are planned. This is good walking and cycling country, and places of interest in the neighbourhood include the National Trust's Oxburgh Hall, a fine moated manor house.

Local Golf Courses: Richmond Park, Swaffham, Norfolk G&CC

Free House & Inn

Eight en suite bedrooms with tv and phone; snacks and full meals

Credit Cards: All the major cards

THE MARSHAM ARMS FREE HOUSE & INN 336

Holt Road, Hevingham, Norwich, Norfolk NR10 5NP
Tel: 01603 754268 Fax: 01603 754839
e-mail: m.arms@paston.co.uk website: www.marshamarms.co.uk

Standing in countryside seven miles from Norwich, the Marsham Arms is an early 19th century hostelry with many original features. Run by Nigel and Anne Bradley, it has earned a great reputation for food and drink, and also offers excellent accommodation in eight self-contained en suite bedrooms. Each room is named after a Norfolk bird, and all have tv, radio and phone. Home-cooked English fare ranges from light bites to full meals and a popular help-yourself salad bar, and there's a wide choice of beers and wines. No smoking in the restaurant.

Local Golf Courses: Royal Norwich, Weston Park, Wensum Valley

Country House Hotel

17 elegantly appointed en suite bedrooms; superb restaurant

Credit Cards: All the major cards

CONGHAM HALL 337

Grimston, King's Lynn, Norfolk PE32 1AH Tel: 01485 600250
Fax: 01485 601191 e-mail: reception@conghamhallhotel.co.uk
Website: www.conghamhallhotel.co.uk

A fine Georgian manor has been transformed into one of the finest country house hotels in the land. The setting, in 30 acres of parkland, lawns and gardens, is both beautiful and serene, and guests enjoy the highest standards of comfort and service. Fine antiques are enhanced by exquisite soft furnishings in the day rooms and the 17 non-smoking bedrooms, all with private bathroom, tv, radio and lovely fresh flowers. Smart dress is requested for dinner in the superb Orangery Restaurant. Guests have free use of the tennis courts and outdoor swimming pool.

Local Golf Courses: Swaffham, King's Lynn, Middleton Hall

Hotel with Restaurant

61 en suite rooms with tv and phone; restaurant, pub, leisure and conference centres
Credit Cards: All the major cards

KNIGHTS HILL HOTEL 338

South Wootton, King's Lynn, Norfolk PE30 3HQ
Tel: 01553 675566 Fax: 01553 675568
e-mail: reception@knightshill.co.uk web: www.knightshill.co.uk

The site, one of the highest in West Norfolk, has developed from a hunting lodge via working farm to the present unique complex of hotel, health club and conference centre. The 61 spacious bedrooms, including four-poster rooms and courtyard apartments, all have en suite bathroom, satellite tv, radio, phone, trouser press and hairdryer. Fine food is served in the Garden Restaurant and the Farmers Arms Inn, a traditional pub with real ale. Leisure facilities include an indoor pool and all-weather tennis court. Golfing parties welcome.

Local Golf Courses: King's Lynn, Middleton Hall, Sutton Bridge

Pub with Food and B&B

Pub with snack and full menus; B&B + self-catering accommodation
Credit Cards: None

ROSE & CROWN 339

Bridge Street, Hilgay, Downham Market, Norfolk PE38 0LJ
Tel: 01366 385414

Bob Coia, keen golfer and former amateur boxer, has been in the licensed trade for 35 years. He has spent 5 years at the Rose & Crown which is just off the A10 south of Downham Market. It has its own car park, making it an ideal spot to pause for a drink, a snack or a full meal - or indeed an overnight stop. The pub has a very extensive menu that will appeal to all tastes and, in addition, nine bedrooms offering a choice of Bed & Breakfast or self-catering accommodation.

Local Golf Courses: Middleton Hall, Ely City, Tydd St Giles

Country Hotel & Restaurant

Four en suite bedrooms; bar and restaurant menus
Credit Cards: Access, Mastercard, Visa

THE FEATHERS HOTEL 340

Manor Road, Dersingham, Norfolk PE31 6LN
Tel/Fax: 01485 540207

Tony and Maxine Martin and their family assure visitors to their hotel a relaxing, comfortable stay with good food and good service. Standing on a bend on the B1440 a little way north of Sandringham, the fine carrstone building was originally a coaching inn, and the rooms retain a traditional look. Accommodation comprises four bedrooms with shower en suite and tv. Good-value bar snacks are served lunchtime and evening, and the evening restaurant menu tempts with such dishes as salmon en croute, chicken Roquefort and pork chop on a bed of spaghetti. The landscaped gardens include a children's play area.

Local Golf Courses: Hunstanton, King's Lynn, Middleton Hall

Pub with food

Village pub with garden; food served every day
Credit Cards: Access, Mastercard, Visa

THE KINGS HEAD 341

30 Old Norwich Road, Hethersett, Norfolk NR9 3DD
Tel: 01603 810206

In a pretty village four miles south of Norwich, the Kings Head is a 16th-century pub with log fires to keep winter at bay and a lovely garden for enjoying the summer sun. The proprietors are Trevor and Cathy Seaman, both keen golfers and he sometime Team Lotus mechanic. Together with chef Jonathan Wickham, they offer a very varied menu seven days a week, with sandwiches, salads and hot dishes at lunchtime. Evening main courses include tempting specials like pan-fried lamb with root vegetables and a port and redcurrant sauce. Real ales, fine wines. Golf societies are very welcome, with snacks or meals by arrangement.

Local Golf Courses: Barnham Broom, Bawburgh, Eaton

Hotel with Full Bar Menu

Eight bedrooms, some en suite; all with tv. Bar meals

Credit Cards: None

MARINE HOTEL 342

St Edmunds Terrace, Hunstanton, Norfolk PE36 5EH
Tel: 01485 533310

Resident proprietor Mrs Brown runs this friendly hotel in the town centre. Handy for the shops and only five minutes from the local golf course, the Marine offers comfortable, inexpensive accommodation in eight bedrooms, all with tv, some of them en suite and the majority enjoying sea views. Food is served all day in the Marine Bar, whose menu includes sandwiches, omelettes and familiar favourites such as steak pie, fisherman's pie and meat or vegetarian lasagne. Thursday night is quiz night, with a 9.30 start. Car park. Pets welcome. Holiday flat and cottage also available.

Local Golf Courses: Hunstanton, King's Lynn, Royal West Norfolk

Pub with Food

Pub serving food Wed-Fri eves, all day Sat, Sun lunch. Function room.
Credit Cards: None

THE BRANFORD ARMS 343

Branford Road, Sprowston, Norwich, Norfolk NR3 4QD
Tel/Fax: 01603 427488 e-mail: reservation@branfordarms.com
website: www.branfordarms.com or .co.uk

Take the A1151 road north from Norwich to find the Branford Arms, where the Simpson family have set high standards of hospitality, service and quality. Built around 1900, the pub has great character, with lofty ceilings and an interesting collection of advertising posters on the walls. Home-cooked food is served Wednesday to Friday evenings, all day Saturday (including breakfast) and Sunday lunchtime. The choice includes filled baguettes, stuffed peppers, omelettes and burgers as well as main meals and wicked puds (Spotted Dick with custard, Alabama fudge cake).

Local Golf Courses: Sprowston, De Vere Dunston Hall, Royal Norwich

Hotel with Restaurant

36 en suite rooms with tv. Restaurant, also hotel pub with meals

Credit Cards: All the major cards

LE STRANGE ARMS HOTEL 344

Golf Course Road, Old Hunstanton, Norfolk PE36 6JJ
Tel: 01485 534411 Fax: 01485 534724
e-mail: lestrangearms@netmatters.co.uk

One of the top hotels in the area, with grounds running down to a lovely sandy beach. The hotel offers a variety of first-class accommodation in 36 en suite bedrooms - singles, doubles, twins, four-poster rooms and suites, many with sea views, all with central heating and tv. The restaurant has both table d'hote and à la carte menus, and the lounge bar is a most agreeable spot for a pre-prandial drink. The hotel pub serves traditional ales along with snacks and full meals. A Best Western hotel.

Local Golf Courses: Hunstanton, King's Lynn, Royal West Norfolk

Pub with Food

Family-run pub with snacks (all-day) & main menus; large garden
Credit Cards: Access, Mastercard, Visa

THE JOLLY SAILORS 345

Main Road, Brancaster Staithe, Norfolk PE31 8BJ
Tel: 01485 210314

A sturdy 18th-century free house in the fishing village of Brancaster Staithe, eight miles east of Hunstanton on the North Norfolk coast. George Humphrey and his family are delightful hosts, and George, whose golf handicap was once in single figures, has a particularly warm welcome for fellow players. A varied snack menu is available from 10am to 8pm, including a hearty breakfast that will set anyone up for a round of golf or an invigorating walk along the coastal path. There's also plenty of choice on the main menu, with local seafood always a popular order. Large garden with children's play area.

Local Golf Courses: Royal West Norfolk, Hunstanton, Sheringham

Hotel with Restaurant

Ten bedrooms with tv; six en suite, one four-poster. Bars and restaurant
Credit Cards: All the major cards

THE WASH AND TOPE HOTEL 346

10-12 Le Strange Terrace, Hunstanton, Norfolk PE36 5AJ
Tel: 01485 532250 e-mail: www.washandtope@a.o.l.com
web: www.hunstanton.net/washandtope.com

A 100-year-old building facing the sea has been turned into a friendly, welcoming little hotel run for the past 15 years by Ian Wallace and his family. It has ten guest bedrooms, six with en suite facilities, all with tv and one boasting a four-poster bed. Accommodation is adaptable, and one room can sleep five. The hotel has two bars and an à la carte restaurant with an extensive, well-priced menu for lunch and dinner. Car parking is available at the rear of the hotel. Local attractions include Sandringham House and Titchwell RSPB reserve.

Local Golf Courses: Hunstanton, King's Lynn, Royal West Norfolk

Country Pub with Food

Pub with full menu lunchtime and evening. Garden

Credit Cards: None

THE GATE INN 347

Hill Road, Fair Green, Middleton, King's Lynn, Norfolk PE32 1RW
Tel: 01553 840518

Bob and June Bywater welcome visitors to their traditional country pub, which stands off the A47 two miles east of King's Lynn. Home-cooked food, from quick snacks to full meals, is served lunchtime and evening (not Monday evening) in either the bar or the non-smoking restaurant. An excellent local butcher provides the meat for popular classics such as steak & kidney pie or the mixed grill with steak, pork chop, lamb chop, liver, sausages and bacon. Freshly battered cod is a favourite on Friday and Saturday, and booking is advised for the Sunday roast. Wine by glass or bottle. Golfing parties welcome. Garden.

Local Golf Courses: Middleton Hall, King's Lynn, Swaffham

Hotel

Four bedrooms with tv, all en suite, three with four-posters. Bar.
Credit Cards: Access, Visa

CROSSKEYS RIVERSIDE HOTEL 348

Bridge Street, Hilgay, Near Downham Market, Norfolk PE38 0LD
Tel/Fax: 01366 387777
website: www.crosskeys-hotel.fsbusiness.co.uk

Mary Flint and her family run this delightful little hotel by the River Wissey. Formerly a coaching inn and farm complex, it retains much period appeal, with oak beams and an inglenook in the non-smoking dining room, a rustic residents' bar and a separate non-smoking lounge. Light snacks are served, or there's a pub within 200 yds. The four spacious bedrooms (two on the ground floor) have en suite bathrooms and tv; three have four-poster beds. There's a large riverside garden, from which fishing and boating are available. The 9 hole Ryston Park golf course is within ¼ mile.

Local Golf Courses: Ely City, Tydd St Giles, Middleton Hall

Inn, Food & Accommodation

Country Inn with 8 en suite bedrooms; restaurant

Credit Cards: All the major cards

THE PLOUGH INN — 401

Brockley Green, Hundon, Sudbury, Suffolk CO10 8DT
Tel: 01440 786789 Fax: 01440 786710

Standing in rural calm on a hilltop, with fine views over the Stour Valley, the 180-year-old Plough Inn is an ideal base for a golfing break or a few days holiday spent exploring the delights of East Anglia. The bar, with its redbrick walls, oak beams and cheery log fire, is a great place to unwind, and Simms Restaurant serves a fine selection of English cuisine. The eight well-appointed bedrooms are all en suite, with all the expected amenities and the bonus of splendid views. This fine old inn is owned and run by David Rawlinson, whose family has been here for 40 years, his wife Marion and their excellent staff.

Local Golf Courses: Haverhill, Newton Green, Bury St Edmunds

Hotel with Restaurant

39 en suite rooms with tv and telephone; restaurant

Credit Cards: All the major cards

THE PRIORY HOTEL — 402

Tollgate, Bury St Edmunds, Suffolk IP32 6EH
Tel: 01284 766181 website: www.prioryhotel.co.uk
Fax: 01284 767604 e-mail: reservations@prioryhotel.co.uk

On the A1101 half a mile north of the town centre, the Priory is a very comfortable 39-bedroom hotel set in lovely gardens at the end of a tree-lined drive. Behind the Grade ll listed facade, charm and elegance combine with modern amenities. The en suite bedrooms, including 12 new rooms in an extension, are individually decorated; all have tv, telephone, trouser press and hairdryer, and many enjoy views of the gardens and grounds. Fine traditional British and Modern European food is served in the restaurant, and refreshments are always available in the bar.

Local Golf Courses: Bury St Edmunds, Suffolk G&CC, Thetford

Pub with Food

Old-world pub serving super food

Credit Cards: Access, Mastercard, Visa

KINGS HEAD INN — 403

Market Hill, Woodbridge, Suffolk IP12 4LX
Tel: 01394 387750

In the market square, with shops and antique galleries for neighbours, the Kings Head Inn has gained a well-deserved reputation for the excellence of its food (accolades include Best Pub Food in Suffolk 1999). Barry Warnes, a Suffolk man who has lived in Woodbridge for 25 years, is the tenant here and also the chef, and his superb food, from lunchtime snacks to hearty casseroles, tastes even better in the company of Adnams Ale brewed along the coast at Southwold. 'Barry's House and Home' is the oldest building in Woodbridge; it's a notably warm, friendly place with beams, inglenook fireplaces, nooks and crannies, and a great atmosphere.

Local Golf Courses: Woodbridge, Ufford Park Waldringfield Heath

Restaurant

Top-notch restaurant open for breakfast, lunch and dinner
Credit Cards: Access, Mastercard, Visa

THE LIGHTHOUSE — 404

77 High Street, Aldeburgh, Suffolk IP15 5AU
Tel: 01728 453377

Sara Fox and Peter Hill opened The Lighthouse in 1995, since when it has won constant acclaim from the top restaurant critics. The tightly packed tables on its two floors (one non-smoking) are in great demand, so booking ahead is vital. The reward is a meal of non-stop delights that makes the finest use of the best that the sea and land can offer. Fish and seafood from Aldeburgh is always a good bet, and other Lighthouse classics include roasted red pepper with toasted goat's cheese, duck confit and wicked bread & butter pudding with a slug of scotch. Great wine list, too. Open all sessions, also for breakfast Tuesday-Saturday.

Local Golf Courses: Aldeburgh, Thorpeness, Ufford Park

Hotel with Restaurant

46 comprehensively equipped bedrooms; bar and restaurant

Credit Cards: All the major cards

THE RUTLAND ARMS HOTEL 405

High Street, Newmarket, Suffolk CB8 8NB
Tel: 01638 664251 Fax: 01638 666298

This handsome redbrick hotel stands at the eastern end of the main street of the headquarters of British horseracing. The earliest parts are said to date from the time of Charles ll, and the ground floor, built round a cobbled courtyard, has great character. Charles was a frequent visitor to the town, often with Nell Gwynn in tow. The 46 modern bedrooms are designed for comfort and convenience, with private bathroom, tv, telephone, hairdryer, trouser press and tea-making facilities. The bar is a relaxing spot for a drink or a light meal, and a full menu is served in the excellent restaurant.

Local Golf Courses: Newmarket Links, Bury St Edmunds, Suffolk G&CC

Pub with Food

Pub near town centre; food available all day
Credit Cards: Access, Amex, Mastercard, Visa

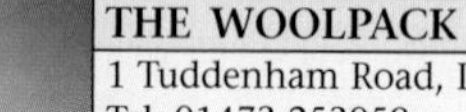

THE WOOLPACK 406

1 Tuddenham Road, Ipswich, Suffolk IP4 2SH
Tel: 01473 253059

Scott Doughty, 25 years in the licensed trade, welcomes all comers to the Woolpack, which stands less than half a mile from Ipswich town centre. The setting may be suburban, but the brick-built Woolpack, which dates from the 16th century, has the feel of a country pub, and there's a warm, traditional atmosphere in the bars, where log fires keep winter at bay. Hearty home-cooked fare is served lunchtime and evening, with basket meals available all day. Typical main courses on the à la carte menu include pan-fried liver, bacon & onions, true Suffolk hotpot and cauliflower & broccoli cheese bake.

Local Golf Courses: Ipswich (Purdis Heath), Rushmere, Fynn Valley

Pub, Food & Accommodation

Pub serving food all day; six bedrooms

Credit Cards: All the major cards

THE GOLF HOTEL 407

Foxhall Road, Ipswich, Suffolk IP4 5TR
Tel: 01473 727450

Built by Tolly Cobbold in tall-chimneyed Tudor style 100 years ago, this large, handsome pub is now owned by Scottish & Newcastle. Run in friendly, welcoming style by long-serving landlady Elizabeth Hart, the Golf offers an extensive menu to suit all appetites, with options running from sandwiches and salads to spicey lamb kebabs to beer-battered fish & chips and steak & Guinness suet pudding. Pool and darts are played in the bar, where there is a separate children's area. Golf parties are very welcome, and the landlady and staff will happily assign a special area and arrange a special menu. New for 2001 are six letting bedrooms.

Local Golf Courses: Fynn Valley, Rushmere, Purdis Heath

Hotel with Restaurant

38 bedrooms, mostly en suite, with tv and phone; restaurant, bar, terrace
Credit Cards: All the major cards

WENTWORTH HOTEL 408

Wentworth Road, Aldeburgh, Suffolk IP15 5BD
Tel: 01728 452312 Fax: 01728 454343
website: www.wentworth-aldeburgh.com

Privately owned and run by the Pritt family since 1920, the Wentworth offers comfort, style and elegance in a seafront setting at the north end of town. All the rooms have tv, radio and telephone, and most look out beyond the beach and the fishermen's huts to the sea. In the restaurant, an imaginative daily changing menu makes good use of local produce from land and sea, and light lunches are served on the garden terrace - weather permitting. Day rooms also include lounges and a convivial bar. The hotel can arrange river cruises on the Alde.

Local Golf Courses: Aldeburgh, Thorpeness, Ufford Park

Suffolk

Inn, Food & Accommodation

Three bedrooms; home-cooked food

Credit Cards: All major cards

THE FERRY BOAT INN 409

Felixstowe Ferry, Felixstowe, Suffolk IP11 9RZ Tel: 01394 284203
e-mail: fbinn@globalnet.co.uk website: www.ferryboatinn.com

The Ferry Boat Inn is a fine old hostelry dating from around 1450, standing at the water's edge and adjacent to the 4th tee of Felixstowe Golf Course. Its previous roles have included fish house, ferry house and customs office. Rob and Jacquie Ward now offer three centrally heated letting bedrooms, each with its own character. All have recently been redecorated and refurbished; they share a bathroom and kitchen. A selection of home-cooked food is always available. Interior features include highly polished stone floors and a massive wood-burning stove; outside are a large garden and car park.

Local Golf Courses: Felixstowe Ferry, Ipswich (Purdis Hth), Rushmere

Bed & Breakfast

Four en suite bedrooms; good breakfasts

Credit Cards: None

RED HOUSE FARM 410

Station Road, Haughley, Stowmarket, Suffolk IP14 3QP
Tel: 01449 673323 Fax: 01449 675413
e-mail: mary@noy1.fsnet.co.uk

Farmers Mary and Eric Noy provide delightful Bed & Breakfast facilities in quiet surroundings on a farm near the A14. Their handsome house is pink on the outside - and inside all is spick and span, comfortable and inviting. Two of the four bedrooms are small singles, but the space is well used and central heating adds to the cosiness. The main day room is a guest sitting room with tv, a piano and lots of books. A good breakfast is served in the dining room, which has a wood-burning stove in a large open hearth.

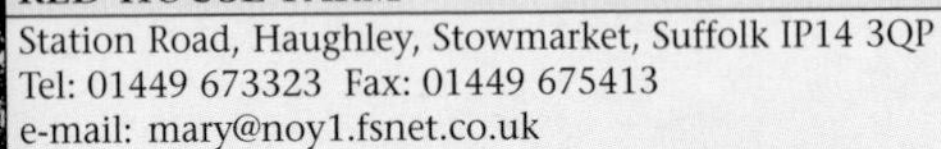

Local Golf Courses: Stowmarket, Bury St Edmunds, Diss

Pub, Food & Accommodation

Pub serving lunches and dinners; three en suite bedrooms
Credit Cards: Access, Mastercard, Visa

THE KINGS HEAD INN 411

Front Street, Orford, Suffolk IP12 2LW
Tel: 01394 450271

The charm of yesteryear lives on in the pretty village of Orford, and nowhere is that charm more apparent than in this 13th century inn. There's atmosphere aplenty in the bar, with its beams and woodburning stove, and in the floor-boarded restaurant, where food is served every session (except Sunday evenings during winter). The choice could be anything from a sandwich to a full à la carte meal, with locally caught fish amongst the specialities. For overnight guests there are three en suite bedrooms. Local attractions include the nearby smokehouse, the 12th century castle and the RSPB sanctuary at Havergate Island.

Local Golf Courses: Aldeburgh, Woodbridge, Thorpeness

Pub with Food

Country pub serving food seven days a week
Credit Cards: Access, Mastercard, Visa

THE WHITE LION 412

Lower Street, Lower Ufford, Woodbridge, Suffolk IP13 6DW
Tel: 01394 460770

A fine old pub located off the A12 one mile north of Woodbridge. Tanya and Neil Howard, here for five years, have extensive experience in the business, and there's a warm, welcoming ambience in the bar with its beams and log fires. Food is served lunchtime and evening seven days a week, and the dishes are notable for generous portions and great value for money. Home-cooked pies, casseroles and steaks typify the hearty fare, as well as Beouf Bourguignon and Salmon & King Prawn parcels. The pub stands in large paddocks and a garden where barbecues are a popular summer attraction. Tanya is happy to arrange private golf party suppers.

Local Golf Courses: Woodbridge, Ufford Park Waldringfield Heath

Pub, Food & Accommodation

Three bedrooms with tv; snacks and meals

Credit Cards: None

THE RAILWAY INN 413

Leiston Road, Aldeburgh, Suffolk IP15 5PP
Tel: 01728 453864

The railway stopped serving the town in the 1960s, but the long-established Railway Inn continues to do sterling service. Located on a roundabout at the top end of the town, it is no more than a gentle stroll from the beach, with the lovely parish church en route. It's a very sociable pub, serving the local community rather than the tourists who flock here in the summer, and in the convivial bar darts and big-screen tv provide the entertainment. Chef Gary Davis produces an excellent selection of food, with fish and steaks among the most popular items. For guests staying overnight there are three letting bedrooms with tv.

Local Golf Courses: Aldeburgh, Thorpeness, Ufford Park

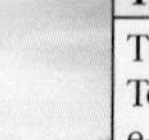

Hotel with Restaurant

30 en suite bedrooms; restaurant and Golf Club

Credit Cards: All the Major Cards

THORPENESS HOTEL & GOLF CLUB 414

Thorpeness, Suffolk IP16 4NH
Tel: 01728 452176 Fax: 01728 453868
e-mail: info@thorpeness.co.uk website: www.thorpeness.co.uk

Thorpeness is a unique holiday village designed at the end of the 19th century 'to provide healthy family fun free from piers and promenades'. The Country Club and Golf Club followed in the 1920s, and today's visitors can enjoy traditional hospitality throughout the year in the splendidly appointed Thorpeness Hotel. The facilities include 30 en suite bedrooms, a snooker room, a relaxing clubhouse, a bar serving light lunches, a fine restaurant overlooking the third tee of the demanding Thorpeness course. Guests can also use the bar and the tennis courts at the Country Club.

Local Golf Courses: Thorpeness, Aldeburgh, Ufford Park

Riverside Pub, Food and Rooms

Three bedrooms; lunches and dinners; riverside location
Credit Cards: Access, Mastercard, Visa

THE RAMSHOLT ARMS 415

Dock Road, Woodbridge, Suffolk IP12 3AB
Tel: 01394 411229 Fax: 01394 411818

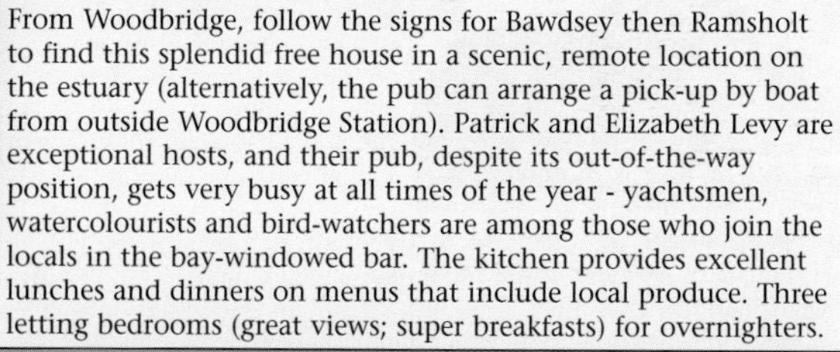

From Woodbridge, follow the signs for Bawdsey then Ramsholt to find this splendid free house in a scenic, remote location on the estuary (alternatively, the pub can arrange a pick-up by boat from outside Woodbridge Station). Patrick and Elizabeth Levy are exceptional hosts, and their pub, despite its out-of-the-way position, gets very busy at all times of the year - yachtsmen, watercolourists and bird-watchers are among those who join the locals in the bay-windowed bar. The kitchen provides excellent lunches and dinners on menus that include local produce. Three letting bedrooms (great views; super breakfasts) for overnighters.

Local Golf Courses: Woodbridge, Waldringfield Heath, Ufford Park

Inn, Food & Accommodation

Country inn serving lunch and dinner; ten en suite bedrooms
Credit Cards: Access, Mastercard, Visa

THE THREE TUNS COACHING INN 416

Main Road, Pettistree, Nr Woodbridge, Suffolk IP13 0HW
Tel: 01728 747979 e-mail: jon@threetuns-coachinginn.co.uk
Fax: 01728 746244 website: www.threetuns-coachinginn.co.uk

Built some 150 years ago, the Three Tuns stands just off the A12 north of Woodbridge. Owners John and Brenda Pallett generate a warm, friendly atmosphere, and guests find relaxation easy in the bar, in the lounge or out on the conservatory sun terrace. An extension houses ten comfortable, well-appointed en suite bedrooms, all at ground floor level. In the Victorian conservatory restaurant a pleasing choice of fine home cooking is on offer lunchtime and evening: favourite dishes include steak & kidney pie and bread & butter pudding, and there are wines to suit all tastes.

Local Golf Courses: Ufford Park Hotel, Woodbridge, Cretingham

Hotel with Restaurant

47 top-class en suite bedrooms, many with sea views; restaurant and bar
Credit Cards: All the major cards

THE BRUDENELL HOTEL 417

The Parade, Aldeburgh, Suffolk IP15 5BU
Tel: 01728 452071 Fax: 01728 454082
e-mail: info@brudenellhotel.co.uk website: www.brudenellhotel.co.uk

For many years a landmark on the Aldeburgh seafront, the Brudenell Hotel enjoys a stunning location right on the beach at the south end of the promenade. The whole place is kept in apple-pie order, and the 47 spacious bedrooms, all en suite, have everything needed for a comfortable stay. Some look out to sea, others to the river and marshes. Many are suitable for family occupation. The hotel has a stylish bar that's perfect for sipping a cocktail before moving on to the restaurant, where local produce features strongly on the constantly changing menus.

Local Golf Courses: Thorpeness, Aldeburgh, Ufford Park

Inn, Accommodation & Food

18 en suite bedrooms; superb à la carte restaurant
Credit Cards: Access, Mastercard, Visa

THE CROWN AND CASTLE 418

Orford, Nr Woodbridge, Suffolk IP12 2LJ Tel: 01394 450205
Fax: 01394 450176 e-mail: info@crownandcastlehotel.co.uk
website: www.crownandcastlehotel.co.uk

David and Ruth Watson are in the process of transforming this delightful old inn opposite the imposing 12th century castle. Behind the inn's black-and-white facade many improvements have been made, notably to the accommodation, which includes five new light, stylish rooms among the total of 18, all with en suite facilities. Ruth is a well-known cookery and food writer, and the menu in the superb Trinity restaurant runs from local oysters or pork and prune terrine to griddled scallops or rump of lamb with lentil and rosemary ragout and parsnip crisps.

Local Golf Courses: Aldeburgh, Woodbridge, Waldringfield Heath

Country Inn with Food

Thatched country inn specialising in fish dishes

Credit Cards: None

THE BELL INN 419

Main Road, Marlesford, Nr Woodbridge, Suffolk IP13 0AY
Tel: 01728 746242

Directly on the A12, The Bell Inn is a thatched 16th Century Coaching Inn with low beams and log fires and includes an old barn full of past time interest. It offers a selection of fish dishes, from local catch to the Mediterranean, including Shark Steaks, Barracuda, Kingfish Mahi, Mahi and many, many more. If fish is not your fancy there's plenty more besides, including lasagne, home-made pies and vegetarian dishes as well as fine cask ales.

Local Golf Courses: Aldeburgh, Thorpness, Cretingham

Pub with Food

Village pub serving breakfast and full menu

Credit Cards: None

THE CRICKETERS 501

7 West Street, Coggeshall, Essex CO6 1NL
Tel: 01376 561533

Close to the River Blackwater in the Heritage Town of Coggeshall, The Cricketers is a favourite with both locals and the considerable number of motorists visiting the many nearby places of interest. Warmth and conviviality is extended to all in the splendid old-world atmosphere generated in the bar by exposed beams, a double-sided brick fireplace, old sepia photographs and converted oil lamps. Food is taken seriously here, with breakfast adding to a full menu of classic dishes such as steak and ale pie, and a regularly changing list of real ales includes guest beers. Ample off-road car parking.

Local Golf Courses: Braintree, Colne Valley, Essex G&CC

Pub with Food

Village pub with full menu

Credit Cards: Access, Mastercard, Visa

THE RODNEY 502

North Hill, Little Baddow, Essex CM3 4TQ
Tel: 01245 222385 e-mail: rodney@barstewards.com

Built about 1650 as a farmhouse, the Rodney has been a hostelry for most of its life. Peter and Lynne Smeeton took over the tenancy in 1989 and purchased the freehold in 1992. They have created a very comfortable village pub atmosphere at the Rodney, whose wooden-floored bars are filled with memorabilia associated with various *HMS Rodneys*. The pub, which has a front patio and sloping gardens, has earned a fine reputation for its food - even the chips are home-made - and the traditional menu is available every lunchtime and evening and all day Sundays and Bank Holidays. Good choice of real ales (CAMRA member).

Local Golf Courses: Channels, Chelmsford, Warren

Village Pub with Food

Free House with seasonal menu and daily specials
Credit Cards: Access, Mastercard, Visa

KING HAROLDS HEAD 503

Bumbles Green, Nazeing Common, Waltham Abbey, Essex EN9 2RY Tel: 01992 893110 Fax: 01992 893412
website: www.kingharoldshead.co.uk

Hosts Jim and Linda Sharp and their staff offer the warmest of welcomes at their quaint old pub on the Waltham Abbey-Harlow road. Said to date back to the 11th century, its bars are full of character, with exposed beams, open fires, old pictures of the village and framed trophies won by Jim in his running days. The food here is exceptional, and in the restaurant (well behaved children welcome) a seasonal à la carte menu is supplemented by daily specials such as spaghetti carbonara, chargrilled pork chop with mushrooms or roast baby chicken with cranberry and orange stuffing. Great puds, too, and a well-chosen wine list. Booking advised.

Local Golf Courses: Canons Brook, Nazeing, North Weald

Hotel with Restaurant

10 superb, spacious bedrooms; nearby riverside restaurant

Credit Cards: All the major cards

MAISON TALBOOTH 504

Dedham, Nr Colchester, Essex CO7 6HN
Tel: 01206 322367 Fax: 01206 322752
e-mail: mtreception@talbooth.co.uk website: www.talbooth.com

The Milsom family are the hands-on proprietors of this peaceful, elegant Victorian house in the heart of lovely Constable country. There are fine views down Dedham Vale from the sunny lounge, and the ten spacious bedrooms are models of good taste, with beautifully co-odinated furnishings and a host of thoughtful extras, along with superb bathrooms, some with jacuzzi or sunken bathtub. The hotel's renowned restaurant, Le Talbooth, is a short walk away in a Tudor building on the River Stour. Maison Talbooth is one of the top establishments of its kind in the country.

Local Golf Courses: Ipswich (Purdis Heath), Colchester, Hintlesham

Essex

Pub with Food

Village pub serving good food

Credit Cards: Access, Mastercard, Visa

PRINCE ALBERT 505

1 The Green, Blackmore, Brentwood, Essex CM4 0RJ
Tel: 01277 821705

Follow the signs for Blackmore from the A414 Chipping Ongar-Chelmsford road to find this attractive pub near the village green - watch out for the 'Ducks Crossing' sign. Wood-burning fires keep things cosy in the bars, where plates and brasses hang on the walls and wagon wheels serve as chandeliers. There are flowers everywhere. This a very popular pub for food, and advance booking is recommended, especially at the weekend. The Prince Albert has no garden, but children are very welcome with their parents, and the pub is a favourite place for walkers and cyclists to take a refreshment break.

Local Golf Courses: Bentley, Chelmsford, Hartswood

Pub with Food

Pub with all-day menu

Credit Cards: None

THE OAK 506

Oak Road, Tiptree, Nr Colchester, Essex CO5 0NF
Tel: 01621 815579

John and Victoria Murrell run this most convivial of pubs, which stands on the outskirts of Tiptree off the B1022 Colchester-Maldon road. It's a very sporty pub, with teams for darts, pool and football, and the go-ahead owners organise events and outings throughout the year. In the flagstoned bar a wide range of food is served, including an all-day breakfast, sandwiches, pizza and steak & kidney pie. For visitors in a hurry to get to the golf course a takeaway service is available. Barbecue evenings take place on an enormous flagstoned patio surrounded by barrels of flowers.

Local Golf Courses: Benton Hall, Five Lakes, Forrester Park

Pub with Food

Village pub with food and real ales; garden
Credit Cards: Access, Mastercard, Visa

THE QUEENS HEAD 507

Queens Street, Fyfield, Essex CM5 0RY
Tel: 01277 899118 Fax: 01277 899231

Ivan Streeter's 500-year-old pub is located near the church in the tiny village of Fyfield, on the B184 a short drive north from Chipping Ongar. Here for only a few months, Ivan is consolidating the high reputation the pub has earned for the quality of the cooking, which brings the customers from many miles around. The fine food is complemented by a good range of local and East Anglian beers, with four guest ales in the summer. The large bar has a wooden floor, high-backed chairs and pew seating at scrubbed wooden tables, a wood-burning stove and old sepia photographs. There's a beer garden at the rear.

Local Golf Courses: Canons Brook, Chelmsford, Toot Hill

Hotel and Country Club

30 en suite bedrooms, restaurant, golf courses, health & fitness centre
Credit Cards: All the major cards

STOKE BY NAYLAND CLUB HOTEL 508

Keepers Lane, Leavenheath, Colchester, Essex CO6 4PZ
Tel: 01206 262836 Fax: 01206 263356 e-mail: info@golf-club.co.uk
website: www.stokebynaylandclub.co.uk

A spacious, luxurious modern hotel that can truly be called a golfer's paradise. It is set in 300 acres of rolling countryside on the edge of Dedham Vale, and the grounds include two golf courses, a 20-bay covered driving range and a health & fitness centre. The 30 beautifully appointed bedrooms include honeymoon suites and family rooms; all have superb en suite bathrooms, satellite tv, telephone, ISDN terminal and hairdryer. There's a good choice of eating, from the fine dining restaurant to the bistro in the fitness centre and casual dining in the bar or conservatory.

Local Golf Courses: Stoke by Nayland, Brett Vale, Newton Green

Pub with Food

Village pub serving fine food and ales; book
Credit Cards: Access, Mastercard, Visa

THE PHEASANT 509

Audley End, Gestingthorpe, Nr Halstead, Essex CO9 3AX
Tel: 01787 461196

A gem of a pub - nice people, good beer, great food - run by Janet and Ron Sullivan. Small, cosy and intimate, and looking more like a cottage than a pub, it offers some of the very best pub food in the region and is well worth seeking out in its out-of-the-way setting off the A1017 or B1058. All the food is freshly prepared each day, and the blackboard menus in the 38-cover restaurant are constantly changing, with special curry nights among the regular features. Booking is recommended at all times (no food Sunday evening or Monday). The Colne Valley Railway runs near this delightful place.

Local Golf Courses: Newton Green, Gosfield Lake, Haverhill

Pub with Food

Town centre pub with good food and live weekend music
Credit Cards: Access, Mastercard, Visa

THE NEW INN 510

Sun Lane, Waltham Abbey, Essex EN9 1EJ
Tel: 01992 712939

Michael and Myra Coyle run this very sociable pub, which occupies a corner site in the middle of the ancient town made famous by King Harold. The interior is open-plan in modern style, with open fires, pine tables and sofas to relax in. A jukebox plays in the bar, giving way at the weekend to live music performances. Myra does the cooking, using a very good local butcher for the steaks (up to 32oz!), the gammon and the Barnsley chops that the hungry young customers tuck into with relish; other choices include fish and vegetarian dishes, a kiddies' menu and a Sunday carvery. The inn has ten letting bedrooms.

Local Golf Courses: Nazeing, North Weald, Abridge, Toot Hill

Pub with Food

Pub serving food lunch and evening; good wines
Credit Cards: Access, Mastercard, Visa

THE QUEENS HEAD 511

26 Churchgate Street, Old Harlow, Essex CM17 0JT
Tel: 01279 427266 Fax: 01279 421272

Leave the M11 at Junction 7 and follow the signs on the A414 to Old Harlow, where Bob Webster's popular public house stands next to the church. One of the bars is tiny and very cosy, the other much larger, with exposed beams, masses of brasses and old framed bills. The ancient windows are a most unusual feature. Food is served lunchtime and evening, with Sunday lunch a real crowd-puller, and the hearty food is complemented by a particularly good and varied selection of wines - not surprising, as Bob has his own wine business. Alternatively, there are always four well-kept cask-conditioned ales. Large car park and outside seating area.

Local Golf Courses: Canons Brook, North Weald, Nazeing

Pub with Food

Centrally located pub open all day

Credit Cards: None

THE LAST POST 512

Weston Road, Southend-on-Sea, Essex SS1 1SA
Tel: 01702 431682

The former Sorting Office and Central Post Office - hence the name - has been turned into a vast, cavernous pub in the Wetherspoons Group. Run by Geordie Frank Bell and his wife, it stands in the middle of town right opposite Southend Central railway station. Some of the original wrought ironwork has been retained, and the high angled roof gives an almost cathedral-like appearance to the open-plan bars. The Last Post is open all day long serving a wide variety of refreshments both liquid and solid. Carpeted throughout, and with some open fires to dispel the seaside chill, it has designated smoking areas.

Local Golf Courses: Belfairs, Rochford Hundred, Thorpe Hall

Inn with Food

Village inn serving food lunchtime and evening
Credit Cards: Access, Mastercard, Visa

THE NEW INN 513

90 High Street, Roydon, Essex CM19 5EE
Tel: 01279 792225 Fax: 01279 793641

On the B181 three miles west of Harlow, Mary Snell's village centre inn has changed little down the years. Open fires warm the bars, where pictures of the village in days gone by hang on the walls and old milk churns do duty as bar stools. Food is served lunchtime and evening, with bar snacks at lunchtime (a traditional lunch on Sunday) and an à la carte menu in the evening. At the weekend a separate 35-cover restaurant is used. Popular with business people at lunchtime, local residents in the evening, golfers in the summer, when the beautiful gardens are an additional attraction.

Local Golf Courses: North Weald, Canons Brook, Nazeing

Pub with Food

Country pub with good home cooking
Credit Cards: Access, Mastercard, Visa

THE HOOPS 601

High Street, Bassingbourn, Cambridgeshire SG8 5LF
Tel: 01763 242130

In a pleasant village just off the A1198 north of Royston, Keith Hammond's pub has a history stretching back some 300 years. Partly thatched, with weatherboarded skirting, it is attractive both outside and in the bars, where home-cooked food is a popular feature. Good value is provided on a menu that runs from pizzas and burgers to weekly specials such as curry, tagliatelle, gammon steak or liver & bacon, and there's always something for vegetarians. Off-road parking. Golfers should find time between rounds to visit the nearby National Trust 18th century Wimpole Hall, the biggest house in Cambridgeshire, and its farm.

Local Golf Courses: Malton, Heydon Grange, Saffron Walden

Motel and Restaurant

15 en suite bedrooms; restaurant and bar snack menu
Credit Cards: Access, Mastercard, Visa

ST IVES MOTEL 602

London Road, St Ives, Cambridgeshire PE17 4EX
Tel: 01480 463857 Fax: 01480 492027
website: www.stivesmotel.co.uk

Set back from the A1096 and just five minutes from the A14, this is a practical, pleasant spot to stop for a drink and a meal, or to use as a base for a touring or golfing holiday. Motel-style accommodation consists of 15 spacious en suite bedrooms, recently redecorated and in excellent order. In the non-smoking restaurant the menu caters for all appetites, offering anything from potato wedges with a chilli mayonnaise dip and goujons of sole to steaks, chicken curry, lasagne and poached salmon on a bed of samphire. Easy parking; lovely gardens; tv lounge.

Local Golf Courses: Brampton Park, Cambridge, St Ives

Pub with Food

Village pub serving food; darts and pool
Credit Cards: Access, Mastercard, Visa

THE CHEQUERS AT ANSTEY 603

Anstey, Nr Buntingford, Hertfordshire SG9 0BW
Tel: 01763 848205

The Chequers is a family-run pub in the village of Anstey, which can be reached along a country road off the B1368. Meals, served lunchtime and evening in the bar and dining room, offer generous helpings of good home cooking: the grills are excellent, the steaks are big and juicy, and there's always a choice for vegetarians. A good selection of wines accompanies the meal, and beer-drinkers will appreciate the well-kept real ales. Golf parties are very welcome, and meal times can be arranged to fit in with tee-off times. Darts and pool are played in the bar.

Local Golf Courses: Malton, Heydon Grange, Saffron Walden

Pub with Food

Pub serving all-day snacks, evening carte, Sunday carvery
Credit Cards: Access, Amex, Mastercard, Visa

THE WHITE HORSE 604

118 High Street, Barton, Cambridgeshire CB3 7BG
Tel/Fax: 01223 262327
web: www.whitehorse-barton.co.uk

On the main street of the village, just half a mile from the M11, this traditional pub offers charm, hospitality and good food and drink in abundance. Among the beams, brasses and inglenooks visitors enjoy excellent bar snacks - anything from a filled baguette to an all-day breakfast - or a full meal from the evening carte: favourites include mixed grill and chef's beef stroganoff. The Sunday carvery, with a choice of three roasts, is a popular feature. Pool, darts, pétanque; patio garden. Richard and Lynn Ellis and their family run this most delightful place.

Local Golf Courses: Bourn, Cambridge Meridian, Gog Magog

Cambridgeshire

Pub with Accommodation

Pub with four en suite rooms; restaurant menu
Credit Cards: Access, Mastercard, Visa

THE BLACK BULL 605

Post Street, Godmanchester, Huntingdon,
Cambridgeshire PE29 2AQ Tel: 01480 453310

Peter Howe's fine old coaching inn is an excellent base for a golfing holiday, with its attractive rooms and good-value eating. Accommodation comprises four en suite bedrooms, and weekend breaks should be booked well ahead. Daily specials add to the choice for diners, and there are private dining rooms for parties. Four real ales are on tap in the bar-lounge and there's a good choice of wines to accompany the food. Godmanchester, which is linked to Huntingdon by an ancient bridge across the Ouse, was a Roman settlement and Port Holme Meadow is a major site of Roman remains.

Local Golf Courses: Brampton Park, Lakeside Lodge, St Ives

Bed & Breakfast

B&B family house; adjoins golf course

Credit Cards: None

SYCAMORE HOUSE 606

91 Cambridge Road, Ely, Cambridgeshire CB7 4HX
Tel: 01353 662139

The Webster family's spacious, newly renovated 1920s home stands in an acre of mature gardens adjoining the City of Ely golf course (a private gate leads to a public footpath) and just a short walk from the Cathedral and the Riverside. Guest Bed & Breakfast accommodation comprises two double bedrooms and a twin, all with en suite facilities and tv. There's an excellent choice for breakfast, and guests have the use of a comfortable drawing room to swap tales of birdies and eagles. Ample private car parking. Sycamore House is a non-smoking establishment.

Local Golf Courses: Ely City, Lakeside Lodge, Ramsey

Pub with Restaurant

Village pub with restaurant and bar meals; garden
Credit Cards: Access, Mastercard, Visa

THE GEORGE INN 607

71 High Street, Girton, Cambridgeshire CB3 0QD
Tel: 01223 276197

A cheerful, welcoming sight on the main street of the village where the first Cambridge College for women relocated from Hitchin in 1873. The facade of the Culpeck family's pub is adorned with hanging baskets, window boxes and white-painted shutters; there are seats outside at the front, and more in the garden at the back overlooking fields. There's plenty of room in the comfortable main bar where you can enjoy excellent-value home-cooked food. Booking is advisable, particularly for Sunday lunch.

Local Golf Courses: Girton, Cambridge, Cambridge Moat House

Restaurant

Top-quality Modern British cuisine

Credit Cards: All the major cards

THE PINK GERANIUM 608

25 Station Road, Melbourn, Cambridgeshire SG8 6DX
Tel: 01763 260215 Fax: 01763 262110
website: www.pinkgeranium.co.uk

A 16th century thatched cottage just off the A10 north of Royston is the charming setting for one of the very best restaurants in the whole region. The colour and the flower both feature strongly in the pretty decor, along with original oak beams and inglenook fireplaces, and the food is every bit as appealing as the surroundings. Modern British cooking by innovative chef Mark Jordan earns high praise from the top critics, and the fine food is complemented by an excellent wine list that offers outstanding value for money.

Local Golf Courses: Cambridge Meridian, Malton, Heydon Grange

Hotel with Restaurant

20 en suite rooms with tv and phone. Restaurant and bar food
Credit Cards: Access, Amex, Mastercard, Visa

THE GOLDEN LION HOTEL 609

Market Hill, St Ives, Cambridgeshire PE27 5AL
Tel: 01480 492100 Fax: 01480 497109

St Ives, named after the Persian Saint Ivo, is famed for its market, and in the centre of the market place, dominated by the statue of Oliver Cromwell, stands the Golden Lion Hotel. In the same family ownership for more than 30 years, it was once a coaching inn, and behind its Georgian frontage low beams give a traditional look. Comfortable overnight accommodation is provided in 20 en suite bedrooms, all with tv and telephone; they range from singles to family rooms. The 60-cover restaurant is open for dinner Monday to Saturday, and bar meals are served at lunchtime.

Local Golf Courses: Lakeside Lodge, Brampton Park, Cambridge

Pub with Restaurant

Roadside country pub with bar and restaurant meals
Credit Cards: Access, Mastercard, Visa, Switch

THE KINGS HEAD PUB AND RESTAURANT 610

45 High Street, Wilburton, Nr Ely, Cambridgeshire CB6 3RA
Tel: 01353 741029 e-mail: chrispaddock@lineone.net

Five miles south from the Ely golf club and just off the A10 on the A1123 stands this freehouse, which accurately describes itself as "much more than meets the eye and simply a nice place for nice people". The warm airy interior is complimented by log fires and agreeable background music. Well presented home-made foods from baguettes and bar meals to an interesting a la carte menu are served in two spacious dining rooms (one non-smoking). An excellent wine list compliments quality real ales. Bookings are advisable. Ample parking to the rear. Meals are served from 12.00-14.00 and 19.00-21.30.

Local Golf Courses: Ely City, Lakeside Lodge, Girton

Pub, Food & Accommodation

Seven en suite bedrooms; lunch, dinner menu and all-day snacks

Credit Cards: All the major cards

THE WHITE HART 611

1 Balsham Road, Fulbourn, Cambridgeshire CB1 5BZ
Tel: 01223 880264 website: www.whitehartfulbourn.co.uk

Adrian and Bernadette Browne's Greene King pub is a hostelry of great character, first licensed in 1867 and set in a delightful village four miles east of Cambridge. The restaurant/bar is roomy and comfortable, with beams and a log fire, and a full menu is served lunchtime and evening, with snacks available all day. The Friday night and Sunday lunchtime carvery is particularly popular. An interesting wine list provides abundant choice, and beer-drinkers will also find plenty to please them. Overnight accommodation comprises three singles and four doubles, all en suite. A nature reserve is located behind the pub.

Local Golf Courses: Gog Magog, Girton, Links (Newmarket)

Country Hotel & Restaurant

Eight en suite bedrooms. Bar meals and restaurant
Credit Cards: Access, Amex, Mastercard, Visa

THE STUKELEYS COUNTRY HOTEL 612

Great Stukeley, Huntingdon, Cambridgeshire PE17 5AL
Tel: 01480 456927 Fax: 01480 450260
e-mail: janmick@stukeleys.fsnet.co.uk

On the B1043 just five minutes from the A1/A14 junction stands a distinguished 16th-century country hostelry where the Denny family have taken great care to preserve the period look and feel while providing the visitor with up-to-date comforts. Accommodation comprises eight en suite bedrooms with tv, telephone and antique-style furniture. The lounge and bar, where a snack menu is available at all times, have a warm, traditional feel, and the restaurant is an elegant setting for excellent dining from a menu that mixes English and French classics with more exotic choices.

Local Golf Courses: Brampton Park, Ramsey, St Neots, Abbotsley

Cambridgeshire

Pub, Motel, Bars & Restaurant

Three twin rooms (baths) and six singles (showers); bar and restaurant menus
Credit Cards: All the major cards

THE LEEDS ARMS 613

The Green, Eltisley, Huntingdon, Cambridgeshire PE19 4TG
Tel: 01480 880283 Fax: 01480 880379
website: theleedsarms@tinyworldco.uk

George and Lesley Cottrell, here for 20 years, are the popular hosts at a free house motel that started life in the 18th century as a dwelling and public house. Used as a coaching stop in the early days, it now welcomes visitors for a drink or a meal in the beamed bars and cosy restaurant, or to stay overnight in the motel-style rooms in an adjoining building. Accommodation comprises three twin rooms with bath and six singles with shower; all have tv and telephone. The pretty village lies just off the A428.

Local Golf Courses: Abbotsley, Cambridge Moat House, Bourn

Village Pub

Pub serving snacks and full meals

Credit Cards: Access, Mastercard, Visa

THE WHITE HART 614

2 Vinegar Hill, Alconbury Weston, Huntingdon, Cambridgeshire PE28 4JA
Tel: 01480 890331 website: www.downourlocal.com/whitehart

Kim Sewell puts out the welcome mat at this friendly 200-year-old family-run pub in a village on the old Great North Road (A1). Home-cooked food using local produce provides excellent value for money, with main courses running from pizzas and grills to Cumberland sausage, liver with bacon and onions and chicken, leek and mushroom pie. Sunday lunch offers a choice of two roasts, and the regular special food theme nights are always very popular. Three real ales plus guest ales and good house wines. Golf parties are particularly welcome, and the local B&B is just next door.

Local Golf Courses: Brampton Park, Lakeside Lodge, St Ives

Pub with Restaurant

Village pub serving excellent food

Credit Cards: Access, Mastercard, Visa

EIGHT BELLS 615

Main Street, Abbotsley, St Neots, Cambridgeshire PE19 6UL
Tel: 01767 677305

Peter and Gill Gunn run a really super pub in a pretty village of thatched cottages. The pub dates from the 18th century, and behind its cheerful white-painted frontage adorned with hanging baskets there's masses of character, with cosy bars and a separate dining room where the home-cooked food is a great attraction. The choice runs from lunchtime snacks of sandwiches and jacket potatoes to grills, curries, vegetarian dishes and tempting puddings. Well-kept real ales and a good wine cellar are further pluses at this splendid place, where Peter, a keen golfer, is pleased to welcome golfing parties.

Local Golf Courses: Abbotsley, Bourn, St Neots

Self-catering and B&B

Farm buildings for 4 and 2 guests; self-catering, but meals also available
Credit Cards: None

COMMON RIGHT BARNS 616

Plash Drove, Tholomas Drove, Wisbech St Mary, Cambridgeshire PE13 4SP Tel/Fax: 01945 410424
e-mail: teresa@commonrightbarns.co.uk
website: www.commonrightbarns.co.uk

Signposted at Guyhirn on the A47, Common Right Farm, a working arable farm, is located in rural Fenland in the hamlet of Tholomas Drove and offers ETC 4 Star self-catering accommodation in renovated farm buildings and is wheelchair-friendly. The Barn is for up to four guests, with a bedroom on ground and first floors, while the Stable is for two, with one bedroom. Breakfast, cream tea and dinner are available by arrangement, or there's a pub-restaurant a short walk away. Also available a twin B&B room.

Local Golf Courses: Tydd St Giles, Thorney, Gedney Hill

Cambridgeshire

Public House with Restaurant

Pub with garden; good choice for eating and drinking
Credit Cards: Access, Mastercard, Visa

THE WINDMILL TAVERN & RESTAURANT 617

29 Cherry Orton Road, Orton Waterville, Peterborough, Cambridgeshire PE2 5EQ
Tel: 01733 231554

Mick and Colette Benstead run a handsome 18th-century tavern in a pretty village three miles from the centre of Peterborough. Thirsty visitors will find good real ales (resident and guest beers), and there's an excellent wine list to accompany the fine food on offer, which ranges from filled baguettes (meals in themselves!) to grills, burgers, salads, steaks and daily chef's specials. Waitress service is fast and efficient, and group bookings are welcome - golf societies can use the restaurant for private functions. The tavern has a pleasant garden with a children's play area.

Local Golf Courses: Orton Meadows, Thorpe Wood, Elton Furze

Pub,Restaurant and Rooms

Pub with snack and à la carte menus. One letting bedroom
Credit Cards: Access, Mastercard, Visa

THE PAPER MILLS INN 618

London Road, Wansford-in-England, near Peterborough, Cambridgeshire PE8 6JB Tel: 01780 782328

One minute from the A1 and five minutes from Peterborough stands this handsome 150-year-old inn run in fine style by keen golfers Peter and Virginia Robinson. Snacks such as baguettes and ploughman's platters are served at lunchtime, while two excellent chefs offer a long and imaginative menu to tempt serious eaters in the 60-cover non-smoking restaurant. Blackboard specials widen the choice still further, and there's always a particularly good choice for vegetarians. The pub has a patio area and lovely gardens, and for guests staying overnight there's a double bedroom with adjacent bathroom.

Local Golf Courses: Burghley Park, Peterborough Milton, Elton Furze

Hotel with Restaurant

Town-centre hotel with 11 en suite rooms; separate restaurant
Credit Cards: Access, Mastercard, Visa

THE GEORGE HOTEL 619

High Street, Ramsey, Cambridgeshire PE26 1AA
Tel: 01487 815264

The oldest building in Ramsey, dating from 1630 and sympathetically renovated by the Russell family for the new millennium. It was originally a coaching inn, and the entrance to the bar and car park is through the old archway under which the coaches passed. Knights Restaurant, with a separate entrance, offers a nicely varied menu that could include such temptations as lobster thermidor, grilled skate wing, Stilton chicken and carpetbagger steak. The 11 en suite bedrooms are in a chalet-style building at the rear. Guests enjoy a 50% reduction in green fees on weekdays at Ramsey Golf Club.

Local Golf Courses: Ramsey, Lakeside Lodge, Brampton Park

Village Pub

Pub with bar snacks and full menu (no food Sunday & Tuesday Evenings)
Credit Cards: All the major cards

THE CHESTNUT TREE 620

High Street, West Wratting, Cambridgeshire CB1 5LU
Tel: 01223 290384

The best of local produce and fish are the basis of the first-class dishes served in this immaculate redbrick pub on the B1052. Vicki and Phil Cole have recently taken over the reins, and Vicki's imaginative menus are proving to be a great draw. Snacks run from duck and port paté to ham, egg and chips and traditional bangers and mash, while evening meals include grilled trout, steak with stilton and daily specials. To finish, perhaps apple pie or traditional Spotted Dick. Sunday roasts are served from 12.30 - 15.00. Pool and darts are available in the public bar with tables and beer garden outside.

Local Golf Courses: Saffron Walden, Haverhill, Newmarket Links

Inn, Food & Accommodation

Village inn with snack and full menus; 5 letting bedrooms

Credit Cards: None

THE WHEEL INN 621

High Road, Wisbech St Mary, Cambridgeshire PE14 4RH
Tel: 01945 410504

With a history going back over 300 years, Brian and Carolle Scarisbrick's convivial village pub is located off the B1169 or A47 west of Wisbech. The Wheel Inn retains many original features behind its immaculate white-painted facade; open fires enhance the traditional feel, and the walls are hung with old photographs of the village. The beer garden is a popular spot in summer. Brian uses prime, fresh local produce to prepare a selection of splendid snacks and meals - the day's roast joint is a surefire winner, and the local Elgoods Brewery provides excellent ales. Comfortable accommodation comprises five bedrooms including a family room.

Local Golf Courses: Tydd St Giles, Thorney, Gedney Hill

Hotel with Restaurant

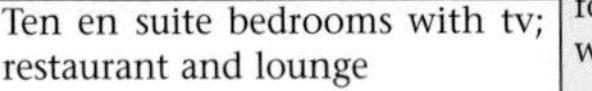

Ten en suite bedrooms with tv; restaurant and lounge

Credit Cards: All the major cards

THE NYTON HOTEL 622

7 Barton Road, Ely, Cambridgeshire CB7 4HZ
Tel: 01353 662459 Fax: 01353 666217
e-mail: nytonhotel@yahoo.co.uk

A family-run hotel and restaurant in a well-kept 100-year-old building next to the City Golf Course. There are ten letting bedrooms, all with en suite facilities and tv, some of them with views of the Fenland countryside or the historic Cathedral. The conservatory lounge has an interesting period fireplace, and in the elegant oak-panelled restaurant à la carte and table d'hote menus offer a choice for diners. Guests enjoy a discount at the neighbouring Golf Club, with 10% off B&B at the hotel for golf societies.

Local Golf Courses: Ely City, Lakeside Lodge, Ramsey

Village Pub

Pub with Food and bar games

Credit Cards: None

THE ROSE & CROWN 623

High Street, Teversham, Cambridgeshire CB1 5AF
Tel: 01223 292245

Excellent-value home-cooked food is a major attraction at Terry Rayner's handsome public house, which stands in a pretty village just off the A1303, close to Cambridge Airport. Lunchtime snacks, bar meals and a full menu provide plenty of choice, and there's a good selection of real ales and wines. Golf societies are always welcome, with special menus available by arrangement. This is also very much a locals' pub, where real coal fires create a cosy atmosphere and pool, darts and tv provide alternatives to a good chat. A convivial spot that's very popular with younger golfers.

Local Golf Courses: Gog Magog, Girton, Newmarket Links

Pub with Restaurant

Roadside pub with Restaurant menu and lunchtime snacks
Credit Cards: Access, Mastercard, Visa

THE WAGGON & HORSES 624

184 Great North Road, Eaton Socon, St Neots, Cambridgeshire PE19 8EF Tel: 01480 386373

A 400-year-old coaching inn of real charm and character, easy to find on the A1 Great North Road. Behind the cheerful white-painted front the interior is everything it should be, with flagstone floor and inglenook fireplace. In the restaurant, which has a non-smoking section, grills and the fish of the day are among the popular orders, and other home-cooked choices range from paté and crispy fried whitebait to chargrilled Caribbean chicken, lasagne, Thai-style stir-fried pork and always main courses for vegetarians. Additional snacks - sandwiches, jacket potatoes, omelettes - at lunchtime. Closed Sunday evening. Landlord Gerry Smith is a keen golfer.

Local Golf Courses: Abbotsley, Brampton Park, St Neots

Guest House

5 en suite rooms with tv; riverside setting
Credit Cards: Access, Mastercard, Visa

RIVERSIDE GUEST HOUSE 625

Station Road, Melbourn, Royston, Cambridgeshire SG8 6DX
Tel: 01763 226062 Fax: 01763 226063
e-mail: bookings@riverside.uk.com website:www.riverside.uk.com

Pat and Barbara Harding and their daughter Paula are the proprietors and hosts at their family home on the banks of the River Mel. Recently renovated and tastefully redecorated, the 100-year-old house overlooks farmland, providing a peaceful, attractive setting for a break from the bustle of the city. The house has five letting bedrooms, all with en suite facilities, tv, radio-alarm and tea/coffee-making kit. This is a Bed & Breakfast establishment, but there are good pubs in the village as well as the outstanding Pink Geranium restaurant.

Local Golf Courses: Malton, Heydon Grange, Gog Magog

Pub with Food

Country pub serving food daily

Credit Cards: Access, Mastercard, Visa, Amex

THE QUEEN ADELAIDE 626

High Street, Croydon Village, South Cambridgeshire SG8 0DN
Tel: 01223 208278 website: queen-adelaide.co.uk

Set in 2½ acres of meadowland in the peaceful village of Croydon, the Queen Adelaide is a lovely spot to pause for a drink and something to eat. Michelle, Raymond and staff are on hand to provide a friendly welcome. The pub is a great place for families. Traditional English fayre is served lunchtime and evenings. Booking is recommended, especially at weekends. The pub is wheelchair friendly and has plenty of parking space. Michelle and Raymond have plans to add accommodation.

Local Golf Courses: Bourn, Cambridge Meridian, Malton

Free House and Restaurant

Country inn serving bar snacks and restaurant menu
Credit Cards: Access, Mastercard, Visa

YE OLD BRIDGE INN 627

The Common, Crowland, Near Peterborough,
Lincolnshire PE6 0HJ Tel: 01733 210567 Fax: 01733 210452
e-mail: yeolde-bridgeinn@yahoo.co.uk

A renovated 150-year-old ale house with lots of beams and brasses. Run by Lynne and Ian Cook, and Ann Cooper with staff to look after visitors, it stands by the River Welland on the B1166 Crowland-Market Deeping road just north of Crowland. In the 48-seat restaurant (booking advised at the weekend), hotel-trained chef Adam produces a tempting range of dishes to suit all tastes and appetites, from snacks like filled baguettes and jacket potatoes to steaks, pies, scampi, curries, Lincolnshire lamb and sausages, and a set roast dinner menu. Children welcome. Patio garden.

Local Golf Courses: Thorney, Spalding, Gedney Hill

Sporting Hotel

42 en suite bedrooms, restaurant, bar. Golf, fitness and leisure facilities
Credit Cards: All the major cards

ABBOTSLEY GOLF HOTEL & COUNTRY CLUB 628

Eynesbury Hardwicke, St Neots, Cambridgeshire PE19 6XN
Tel: 01480 474000 Fax: 01480 471018

In a rural location off the B1046 south-east of St Neots, this purpose-built modern complex is an ideal retreat for golfers, with two courses, a short par 3 course and a driving range. Forty-two attractive en suite bedrooms provide peaceful, comfortable accommodation, and besides the golf the facilities include a fitness centre and four squash courts. All this sporting activity is great for building up a thirst and an appetite, and a good range of drinks and meals awaits in the cosy bar and restaurant. The hotel is owned by American Golf (UK) Ltd, whose portfolio also includes St Mellion.

Local Golf Courses: Abbotsley, Brampton Park, St Neots

Village Pub with Restaurant

Thatched pub with beamed bar-lounge; restaurant
Credit Cards: Access, Mastercard, Visa

THE ROYAL OAK 629

High Street, Hail Weston, St Neots, Cambridgeshire PE19 5JW
Tel: 01480 472527
website: www.theroyal-oak.co.uk

A really delightful thatched 17th-century pub in a pretty village west of St Neots, half a mile off the A1. Christine and Eric Bresitz, who took over the pub in early 2000, have created a lovely atmosphere, and the bar-lounge, with its low beams and inglenook, is the perfect spot to relax with a glass of real ale. In the restaurant (booking advisable), a blackboard lists the day's dishes, which use fresh local produce and meat from Smithfield - pork schnitzel is a speciality. No food Monday night. Darts in the bar; petanque in the garden.

Local Golf Courses: Abbotsley, Brampton Park, St Neots

Pub with Food

17th-century village pub with à la carte restaurant
Credit Cards: Access, Mastercard, Visa

THE BLUE LION 630

Main Street, Hardwick, Cambridgeshire CB3 7QU
Tel: 01954 210328 Fax: 01954 212945
e-mail: powellbluelionhardwick@supernet.com

Off the A428 three miles west of Cambridge, and close to the A14/M11, the Blue Lion is one of the top pubs in the area for food. Dating back to the 17th century, its facade is adorned with plants and hanging baskets, and in the attractive no-smoking conservatory restaurant a fine range of cooked-to-order dishes can be enjoyed every lunchtime and evening. Daily specials supplement the printed menu, which might include such delights as filo-wrapped prawns with a barbecue sauce, or crisp-baked magret of duck with cherries.

Local Golf Courses: Bourn, Cambridge Meridian, Bar Hill, Girton

Inn with Accommodation

Inn with full menu and 5 letting bedrooms

Credit Cards: None

THE TALBOT INN 631

5 North Street, Stilton, Peterborough, Cambridgeshire PE7 3RP
Tel/Fax: 01733 240291

Chris Holloway, a 7-handicap golfer, runs this fine old coaching inn, the oldest in Stilton, with his partner Fran, who has built up a fine reputation for excellent home-cooked food. Anything from a quick snack to Sunday roasts or a three-course meal is available lunchtime and evening, with Charles Wells and Adnams ales and a good selection of wines to accompany. Tables are set out in the lounge, while in the front bar there's entertainment in the shape of darts and big-screen TV. For guests staying overnight, five family-size bedrooms provide comfortable accommodation.

Local Golf Courses: Elton Furze, Peterborough Milton, Brampton Park

THE CROWN INN 701

Pub,Restaurant & Rooms

Pub with full restaurant menu and one en suite bedroom
Credit Cards: Access, Mastercard, Visa

Main Street, Great Casterton, Stamford, Lincolnshire PE9 4AP
Tel: 01780 763362

A village pub of great charm and character, owned and run by Joy Dawson ably assisted by her daughter Claire (behind the bar) and Claire's partner Andrew (with Joy in the kitchen). It's a great place to relax over a meal in the non-smoking restaurant, where the table is yours for the evening and there's no pressure to rush. The menu makes excellent use of prime fresh ingredients in dishes such as steaks, chicken breast with a rich wine sauce or dabs filled with crabmeat and scallops. No food Sunday night; pub closed Monday. The Crown has one en suite bedroom for overnight guests.

Local Golf Courses: Burghley Park, Peterborough Milton, Toft

THE CROWN HOTEL 702

Hotel with Restaurant

18 en suite twin bedrooms; restaurant with full menus
Credit Cards: Access, Amex, Mastercard, Visa

All Saints Place, Stamford, Lincolnshire PE9 2AG
Tel: 01780 763136 Fax: 01780 756111
e-mail: the crownhotel@excite.com

Owners Sue Olver and Michael Thurlby are giving a major facelift to The Crown Hotel, which was built in 1909 on the site of an earlier coaching inn. The 18 bedrooms - all twins with en suite facilities - have been smartly redecorated, and other work has included cleaning the stonework and levelling the car park. A full menu is served in the restaurant, and a wide range of wines and beers is available. A town-centre position behind All Saints Church puts The Crown within walking distance of all the main sights of Stamford.

Local Golf Courses: Burghley Park, Peterborough Milton, Toft

THE WHEATSHEAF 703

Pub with Restaurant

Country pub with full restaurant menu

Credit Cards: None

Fengate, Moulton Chapel, Near Spalding, Lincolnshire PE12 0XL
Tel: 01406 380525

Paul and Sharon Hollely's cheerful white-painted pub on the B1357 is a great place to pause for a drink in the cosy bar or a meal in the restaurant. Paul, a keen golfer, does all the cooking, and his excellent-value menus offer something to please everyone. Some dishes are familiar favourites - prawn cocktail, battered cod, steak and kidney pie - while others have a more exotic ring, typified by lamb samosas, Cajun-style chicken breast or vegetarian Thai schnitzel. Desserts such as apricot crumble or 'crazy about coconut' are hard to resist, and to finish off there's even a choice of medium or dark roast coffee. Friday barbecue.

Local Golf Courses: Spalding, Sutton Bridge, Tydd St Giles

THE GEORGE OF STAMFORD 704

Hotel with Restaurant

Historic hotel with 47 en suite bedrooms and both formal and informal eating
Credit Cards: All the major cards

St Martins, Stamford, Lincolnshire PE9 2LB Tel: 01780 750750
Fax: 01780 750701 web: www.georgehotelofstamford.com/
e-mail: reservations@georgehotelofstamford.com

The gallows sign straddling the road welcomes visitors to what is probably England's greatest coaching inn, which combines the charm and character of its long history with all the modern comforts. The 47 en suite bedrooms are individually designed using the finest materials, and the day rooms include the oak-panelled York Bar and the plant-filled Garden Lounge. The restaurant, where gentlemen should wear a jacket and tie, is among the finest in the area, and a less formal menu is available in the Garden Lounge or in the ivy-clad courtyard in summer.

Local Golf Courses: Peterborough Milton, Burghley Park, Toft

Inn, Restaurant and Rooms

Country inn with bar and restaurant menus and 14 en suite bedrooms
Credit Cards: All the major cards

THE WISHING WELL INN — 705

Dyke, Near Bourne, Lincolnshire PE10 0AF
Tel: 01778 422970 Fax: 01778 394508
web: www.brannigans.co.uk

Half a mile off the A15 just north of Bourne stands a truly outstanding inn run by resident owners Barrie and Wendy Creaser. Each of the 14 en suite bedrooms has a charm and character of its own, and the period appeal of the place is enhanced by old oak beams, inglenooks and stone walls. A real wishing well occupies pride of place in one of the two restaurants, where fine food is available both lunchtime and evening, seven days a week. An extensive lighter menu is served in the lounge bar. The inn hosts a beer festival each August.

Local Golf Courses: Spalding, Burghley Park, Toft

Pub with Food

Traditional country pub with real ales and home-cooked food.
Credit Cards: Access, Mastercard, Visa

THE OLDE SHIP INN — 706

London Road, Long Sutton, Lincolnshire PE12 9EE
Tel: 01406 362930 e-mail: ianship@fsmail.net
website: www.theoldeshipinn.co.uk

A traditional country pub, some 300 years old, with a cosy atmosphere and a warm welcome from Ian and Joy Day. Under the low beams in the bar visitors can enjoy an excellent glass of real ale, or settle down to some good home-cooked food. The menu offers first-rate value for money, with daily specials adding to the choice. There's plenty to see in the vicinity, notably the lead-spired St Mary's Church and the fascinating Butterfly and Falconry Centre, whose attractions include an animal centre, honey farm, ant room and reptile land.

Local Golf Courses: Sutton Bridge, Tydd St Giles, Spalding

Country House for B&B

Three en suite doubles and a single. Superb rose garden

Credit Cards: None

CAWTHORPE HALL — 707

Cawthorpe, Bourne, Lincolnshire PE10 0AB
Tel: 01778 423830 Fax: 01778 426620

In a tiny hamlet off the A15 Peterborough-Lincoln road, Cawthorpe Hall is a sturdy early 19th-century building with an ashlar stone frontage and a slate roof. It makes a marvellous country retreat, with three large, comfortable en suite double bedrooms and a single. Guests can take breakfast in the splendid farmhouse kitchen and have the use of a studio with a wood-burning stove and tv. A marvellous feature of John and Chantal Armstrong's lovely home is the large garden, with three acres of roses from which the owners produce rose water and rose oil. A perfect base for a quiet break or a golfing holiday.

Local Golf Courses: Spalding, Burghley Park, Toft

Country Pub,Bar & Restaurant

Village pub with a choice of snack and restaurant menus

Credit Cards: All the major cards

THE CHEQUERS AT GEDNEY DYKE — 708

Gedney Dyke, Near Spalding, Lincolnshire PE12 0AJ
Tel/Fax: 01406 362666
web: www.chequerspub.co.uk

A real gem in a fenland village off the A17. Linda and Simon Rattray attract visitors to their homely white-painted pub restaurant from miles around as well as keeping a loyal local clientele happy with a wide range of excellent home cooking. The bar menu offers simple, satisfying snacks, but the main draw is the restaurant menu, which makes fine use of the best local produce, including frequent deliveries of fresh fish from Grimsby. Daily specials widen the choice still further, and the super food is complemented by real ales and choice wines. Eat inside or in the garden.

Local Golf Courses: Gedney Hill, Spalding, Sutton Bridge

Pub with Restaurant

Village pub with full restaurant menu
Credit Cards: Access, Mastercard, Visa

THE HOOPS 709

2 High Street, Great Eversden, Cambridgeshire CB3 7HN
Tel/Fax: 01223 264008

The Gale family run this really delightful pub, which stands off the A603 south-west of Cambridge. Behind its cheerful white-painted period facade, all is bright and modern, with cream walls and pine tables. Home cooking is the major attraction, and the menus offer something for everyone: at lunchtime, perhaps a generously filled baguette or a hot favourite such as steak & ale pie or Mediterranean salmon; in the evening, hot & spicy prawns could precede lamb goulash or cherry duck, with a mouthwatering dessert to finish. Local attractions include the National Trust's majestic Wimpole Hall.

Local Golf Courses: Bourn, Gog Magog, Cambridge Meridian, Malton

Alphabetic List of Golf Courses

N

O

P

R

S

T

U

W